# Palgrave Studies in Islamic Banking, Finance, and Economics

The aim of this series is to explore the various disciplines and sub-disciplines of Islamic banking, finance and economics through the lens of theoretical, practical, and empirical research. Monographs and edited collections in this series will focus on key developmentsin the Islamic financial industry as well as relevant contributions made tomoral economy, innovations in instruments, regulatory and supervisory issues, risk management, insurance, and asset management. The scope of these books will set this series apart from the competition by offering in-depth critical analyses of conceptual, institutional, operational, and instrumental aspects of this emerging field. This series is expected to attract focused theoretical studies, in-depth surveys of current practices, trends, and standards, and cutting-edge empirical research.

More information about this series at
http://www.springer.com/series/14618

Muhammad Al Bashir Muhammad Al Amine

# Islamic Finance and Africa's Economic Resurgence

## Promoting Diverse and Localized Investment

palgrave
macmillan

Muhammad Al Bashir Muhammad Al Amine
Bank Alkhair
Busaiteen-Muharraq, Bahrain

Palgrave Studies in Islamic Banking, Finance, and Economics
ISBN 978-3-319-28834-5 ISBN 978-3-319-28835-2 (eBook)
DOI 10.1007/978-3-319-28835-2

Library of Congress Control Number: 2016940808



Printed on acid-free paper

This Palgrave Macmillan imprint is published by Springer Nature
The registered company is Nature America Inc. New York

# Glossary of Arabic Terms

| | |
|---|---|
| Bay 'Bithaman Ajil or *bay' mu'ajjal* | Sale on credit (I.e., a sale in which goods are delivered immediately but payment is deferred |
| bay' al-dayn | Sale of debt. According to a large majority of Muslim scholars, debt cannot be sold for money except at its face value, but it can be sold for goods and services |
| Fatawā | Plural of *fatwa*. Religious verdicts by a Muslim Scholar or a resolution by a number of scholars or organization. |
| Gharar | Literally, it means deception, danger, risk and uncertainty. Technically it means exposing oneself to excessive risk and danger in a business transaction as a result of uncertainty about the price, the quality and the quantity of the counter-value, the date of delivery, the ability of either the buyer or the seller to fulfil his commitment, or ambiguity in the terms of the deal, thus exposing either of the two parties to unnecessary risks. |
| *Hadith* | Sayings, deeds and endorsements of the Prophet Muhammad (peace be upon him) narrated by his Companions |
| *Haram* | Things or activities prohibited by the Shariah |
| Ijārah | Leasing. The sale of usufruct of an asset. The lessor retains the ownership of the asset with all the rights and the responsibilities that go with ownership. |

| | |
|---|---|
| Istisna | A contract whereby a manufacturer (contractor) agrees to produce (build) and deliver a well-described good at a given price on a given date in the future payment of the consideration can be at the beginning of the transaction, by installment or at the end. |
| Maysir | Technically, gambling or any game of chance. |
| Mudarabah | A contract between two parties, capital owner(s) or financiers (called *rabb al-mal*) and an investment manager (called *mudarib*). Profit is distributed between the two parties in accordance with the ratio agreed upon at the time of the contract. Financial loss is borne only by the financier(s). The entrepreneur's loss lies in not getting any reward for his services. |
| *Murābaḥah* | Sale at a specified profit margin. The term, however, is now used to refer to a sale agreement whereby the seller purchases the goods desired by the buyer and sells them at an agreed marked-up price, the payment being settled within an agreed time frame, either in installments or in a lump sum. The seller bears the risk for the goods until they have been delivered to the buyer. |
| *Mushārakah* | Partnership. A musharakah contract is similar to a mudarabah contract, the difference being that in the former both partners participate in the management and the provision of capital, and share in the profit and loss. Profits are distributed between the partners in accordance with the ratios initially set, whereas loss is distributed in proportion to each one' share in the capital. |
| *Ribā* | Literally, it means increase or addition or growth. Technically it generally refers to the 'premium' that must be paid by the borrower to the lender along with the principal amount as a condition for the loan or an extension in its maturity. This is also called riba al-nasia. Interest as commonly known today is a form of riba. Another form of riba is riba al-fadl pertaining to trade contracts. It refers to exchange of different quantities (but different qualities) of the same commodity. Such exchange is prohibited in particular commodities defined in the Shariah |
| Salam | A sale in which payment is made in advance by the buyer and the delivery of the goods is deferred by the seller |

| | |
|---|---|
| Sharī'ah | Refers to the corpus of Islamic law based on Divine guidance as given by the Quran and the Sunnah and embodies all aspects of Islamic faith. |
| Sukūk | Certificates of equal value representing undivided shares in ownership of tangible assets, usufructs and services (in the ownership of) the assets of particular projects or special investment activity |
| Takāful | It is the Islamic alternative to insurance. It is based on the commitment of the participants to make donations for the sake of their own interest. The participants, therefore, protect their group by payment of contributions that constitute the resources of the insurance fund, and assign the management of that fund to a committee of policyholders, or to a joint stock company that possesses the license of practicing insurance business. In the latter case, the company assumes this job on the basis of a remunerated wakala (agency) contract. In addition to managing the insurance operations, the committee of policyholders or the company also assumes the responsibility of investing the assets of the fund through mudaraba or investment agency |
| Wakalah | Agency contract whereby one person appoints another to perform a specific task on his behalf, usually against a fixed fee. The agent is liable as a result of negligence and misconduct. |
| Waqf | Appropriation or tying up a property in perpetuity for specific purposes. No property rights can be exercised over the corpus. Only the usufruct is applied towards the objectives (usually charitable) of the waqf |
| Zakah | Literally means blessing, purification, increase and cultivation of good deeds. It is one of the pillars of Islam. Technically it is an obligation in respect of funds paid for a specified type of purpose and for specified categories. It is an individual duty if the criteria for making it obligatory are satisfied. The government has the authority and responsibility to collect it and distribute it to the prescribed categories of people. The government may also authorize shareholders to pay it personally if it is satisfied that they will do so. |

# ACKNOWLEDGEMENTS

All praise to Allah (s.w.t) the most Gracious and most Merciful, by whose grace and blessing this work has been completed. I would like to take this opportunity while relying on the instruction of the Prophet to the effect that "whoever does not thank people does not thank Allah" to express my thanks and gratitude to those who have contributed in one way or another through their advice, criticism, and support in strengthening the quality of this work. Special thanks and appreciation are due to Sister Isabel Mary Zahra Rehman for her valuable help and assistance in editing an early draft of this book and to her husband Brother Aziz Rehman Sheikh. Similar thanks and gratitude are due to Brother Dr Zamir Iqbal, Brother Dr Abdul Kabir Hassan, Brother Shafiq Flynn, Brother Dr Mohammed Burhan Arbouna, Brother Dr Ahmad Arrifai, Brother Kamal Abdelkarim Hassan, Brother Mohamed Ikram Thowfeek, Brother Naeem Thowfeek, Brother Imad Ali, Brother Akram Traboulsi, and Sister Kifah Rashid. May Allah rewards them all for their help and assistance. However, any shortcoming or mistake remains the author's own responsibility.

Finally, I express my sincere indebtedness and gratitude to my family for their support, patience, perseverance, and encouragement, particularly my wife and children.

# Contents

# Abbreviations

| | |
|---|---|
| AAOIFI | Accounting & Auditing Islamic Financial Institutions |
| AfDB | African Development Bank |
| AMAF | Africa Microfinance Action Forum |
| AMU | Arab Maghreb Union |
| AMU | Arab Magreb Union |
| ARCIFI | Arbitration and Reconciliation Centre for Islamic Financial Institutions |
| ASFIM | Association des Sociétés de Gestion et Fonds d'Investissement Marocains |
| BCEAO | Central bank of West African States |
| BESA | Bond Exchange of South Africa |
| BMS | Bank Al Muamelat Aooahiha |
| BPM | Banque Populaire de Mauritanie |
| BRIC | Brazil, Russia, India and China |
| BRVM | Bourse Regionale des Valeurs Mobilieres |
| CBL | Central Bank of Libya |
| CBN | Central Bank of Nigeria |
| CBOS | Central Bank of Sudan |
| CBSS | Central Bank of South Sudan |
| CDB | China Development Bank |
| CDC | British Colonial Development Corporation |
| CEMAC | Central African Economic and Monetary Union |
| CFC | Casablanca Finance City |
| CGAP | Consultative Group to Assist the Poor |
| COMESA | Common Market for Eastern and Southern Africa |
| COSUMAF | Commission for Market Surveillance of the Central African Financial Market |

| | |
|---|---|
| COSUMAF | Commission for Market Surveillance of the Central African Financial Market |
| DBSA | Development Bank of Southern Africa |
| DMO | Debt Management Office |
| DSX | Douala Stock Exchange |
| EAC | East African Community |
| ECOWAS | Economic Community of West African States |
| EFSA | Egyptian Financial Supervision Authority |
| EMPEA | Emerging Markets Private Equity Association |
| ETF | Exchange Traded Fund |
| FAO | Food and Agriculture Organization |
| FDI | Foreign Direct Investment |
| FEWACCI | Federation of West African Chambers of Commerce and Industry |
| FIBE | Faisal Islamic Bank of Egypt |
| FSC | Financial Services Commission |
| GCC | Gulf Cooperation Council |
| GDP | Gross domestic products |
| GEF | Global Environmental Fund |
| GSE | Ghana Stock Exchange |
| HPA | Hire Purchase Act |
| HSBC | Hong Kong and Shanghai Banking Corporation |
| IADI | India Africa Diamond Institute |
| IAIEPA | India-Africa Institute of Education, Planning and Administration |
| IAIFT | India Africa Institute of Foreign Trade |
| IAIIT | India-Africa Institute of Information Technology |
| ICBC | Industrial and Commercial Bank of China |
| ICD | Islamic Corporation for the Development of the Private Sector |
| IFAAS | Islamic Finance Advisory & Assurance Services |
| IFAD | International Fund for Agricultural Development |
| IFC | International Finance Corporation |
| IFSB | Islamic Financial Services Board |
| IIFM | International Islamic Financial Market |
| IILM | International Islamic Liquidity Management Corporation |
| IIRA | International Islamic Rating Agency |
| IMF | International Monetary Fund |
| IRTI | Islamic Research & Training Institute |
| IsDB | Islamic Development Bank |
| ISFD | Islamic Solidarity Fund for Development |
| KSE | Khartoum Stock Exchange |
| LDCs | Less developed countries |
| MDG | Millennium Development Goals |

| | |
|---|---|
| MENA | Middle East and North Africa |
| MIGA | Multilateral Investment Guarantee Agency |
| NBE | National Bank of Ethiopia |
| NDIC | Nigeria Deposit Insurance Scheme |
| NIBoU | National Islamic Bank of Uganda |
| ODA | Official Development Assistance |
| OIC | Organization of Islamic Cooperation |
| PIDA | Program for Infrastructure in Africa |
| PROPARCO | Investment and Promotions Company for Economic Cooperation |
| SADC | Southern African Development Community |
| Sesric | Statistical, Economic and Social Research and Training Centre for Islamic Countries |
| SGA | Sale of Goods Act |
| SPDA | Special Programme for the Development of Africa |
| TICAD | Tokyo International Conference on African Development |
| TIKA | Turkish International Cooperation and Development Agency |
| UBS | Union Bank of Switzerland |
| UEMOA | West African Economic and Monetary Union |
| UNDP | United Nations Development Programme |
| UN-OSAA | United Nations Office of the Special Advisor on Africa |
| W FEWACCI | West African Chambers of Commerce and Industry |
| WWB | Women's World Banking |

CHAPTER 1

# Introduction

Until recently, African Muslims and non-Muslims alike have had limited access to Islamic banking and finance services. With the exception of Sudan and some limited and modest experiences in a number of other countries, the overall Shari'ah compliant financial system in Africa is a recent phenomenon. While some Islamic financial institutions, such as the Dallah Albaraka Group or Dar Al-Mal Al-Islami, have been operating in some African countries for a number of years, the vast majority of Islamic finance presence in the continent is recent.[1] What is interesting is that the first Islamic bank, the first Islamic insurance or *Takāful* company, and the first Shari'ah -compliant exchange traded fund (ETF) are all of African origin.

Africa is the most diverse continent on the planet, with an area of more than 30 million sq. km, 54 countries, and a population of approximately one billion. Countries in Africa are geographically diverse—ranging from the Seychelles with a size close to that of Singapore, to Sudan, which, until recently, had an area equivalent to a quarter of the size of the USA. Every country has its own unique characteristics. African countries are linked by political, economic, and cultural connections and interests. It is based on this vision that the continent is often researched as one body. As was rightly emphasised by one observer, "Although the fifty-three[2] countries of Africa rarely present a united position on controversial issues, there is often an African consensus."[3]



M. Al Bashir M. Al Amine, *Islamic Finance and Africa's Economic Resurgence*, DOI 10.1007/978-3-319-28835-2_1

Taken together, the continent has a larger land mass than China, the USA, India, Europe, Argentina, and New Zealand combined. With an estimated 1500 languages spoken by multiple ethnic and religious groups, the continent is indeed a large mosaic of cultures. The most populous country is Nigeria with approximately 170 million, while the smallest is Seychelles with a meagre 100,000 inhabitants.[4] In many cases, national boundaries have been carved arbitrarily by accidents of history or as a result of colonial legacy. Thus, religious and urban groupings frequently cut across borders.[5] Differences among the 54 African countries exist at the level of development, economic structure, and political and social environments. Per capita incomes, for instance, range from US$200 to US$20,000—as is the case with Burundi and Equatorial Guinea, respectively.[6]

Although it is too early to consider the African economy as one entity or a whole, it can be useful to consider the continent as an evolving organism, with lessons learnt in one country providing useful information for evaluation and doing business in another. Learning from the lessons of others and adapting new strategies to new markets could be useful strengths for financial institutions entering the African market or expanding their operations into other African countries.[7]

Some might divide the continent into North and South; or into North, South, and Middle; or a North subordinated to the Middle East and the Sub-Saharan. However, we adopt the most widely used division by international institutions by taking the continent as one entity while keeping in mind the regional economic grouping, and avoiding any classification based on race, colour, or political affiliation. As pointed out by Siemens' CEO in Africa, "Some companies divide Africa into North and South or have a separate Middle East and North Africa division, but we decided the continent is a strong framework."[8] In fact, there is a sense of one Africa among the business community, as articulated by KPMG in one of its reports.[9] A similar position has been pointed out by the head of the Casablanca Finance City (CFC), Saïd Ibrahimi, rejecting the expression "Sub-Saharan Africa" and arguing that "Africa begins in Tangier." He further added that "Morocco is Africa. We feel we are much more African than we are Middle Eastern."[10]

The present study divides the continent (with regard to Islamic finance) into five different regions, based on the regional division of the continent influenced by the existing economic blocks. The five economic groupings are the Arab Maghreb Union (AMU), the Economic Community of West African States (ECOWAS), the Central African Economic and Monetary

Union (CEMAC), the Common Market for Eastern and Southern Africa (COMESA), and the Southern African Development Community (SADC). Although every African country is a possible market for Islamic finance, in this research, not all its 54 countries are examined with the same degree of depth. Instead, the focus has been on those countries with some signs of Islamic finance penetration or those who have clearly expressed official backing to the industry. Thus, the Northern African countries covered in this study include Egypt, Morocco, Algeria, Tunisia, Libya, and Mauritania. The second group includes countries in the Eastern region of Africa, such as Sudan, Kenya, Mauritius, Tanzania, Uganda, Djibouti, Rwanda, and Ethiopia. The West African region is represented by Nigeria, Senegal, Gambia, Ghana, Burkina Faso with references to Mali, Guinea, Benin, and Niger. For the Southern African region, we have selected South Africa and Zambia. In the central African region, despite the fact that recent developments show a strong appetite for Islamic finance from the private sector in Chad, Cameroon, and an early public initiative from Gabon, countries in this region seem generally indifferent to Islamic finance despite its great potential.

The study briefly outlines the different investment opportunities for Islamic finance in Africa, its financial system, and economic development. These opportunities include unprecedented economic growth in the continent whereby some countries are registering some of the highest growth globally. As the World Bank notes, "Africa could be on the brink of an economic take-off, much like China was 30 years ago, and India 20 years ago."[11] Indeed, Africa has seen what can be termed according to the World Bank's *Africa's Competitiveness Report 2011* as an "economic resurgence" over the past decade. Similarly, PricewaterhouseCoopers noted that, "Sub-Saharan Africa is experiencing an economic resurgence."[12] Between 2001 and 2010, gross domestic product growth on the continent averaged 5.2 % annually, and with the exclusion of South Africa, GDP growth in Sub-Saharan Africa remained robust. Despite a weaker than expected global economy, with a number of major countries showing mixed performances, growth prospects for Africa remained positive through 2013–14 and the region's GDP growth is projected to increase to 5.2 % in 2015–16 and 5.3 % in 2017. After slowing to 3.4 % in 2015, economic growth is expected according to World Bank to pick up to 4.2 % in 2016 and to 4.7 % in 2017–18.[13] Africa's regional growth is supported by strong public investment in infrastructure, increased agricultural production, and a buoyant services sector. Overall, Sub-Saharan Africa is forecast to remain one of the fastest growing regions.[14] Similarly, the International Monetary Fund (IMF)'s latest *Regional Economic Outlook for Sub-Saharan Africa* projects regional GDP growth to pick up from approximately 5 % in 2013–14 to 5¾ % in 2015.[15]

Africa's spectacular and steady economic growth in the last decade and its positive outlook in the short, medium, and long term are widely acknowledged by multilateral institutions such as the World Bank,[16] the IMF,[17] the United Nations,[18] the World Trade Organisation,[19] and the African Development Bank.[20] It is also recognised by international financial conglomerates such as Citigroup Bank,[21] Credit Suisse,[22] Goldman Sachs,[23] Merrill Lynch,[24] Société Générale,[25] Crédit Agricole,[26] European Investment Bank (EIB),[27] Standard Bank,[28] Renaissance Capital,[29] Deutsche Bank,[30] or by rating agencies such as Standard and Poor's,[31] and Moody's.[32] It has also been advocated by leading advisory and consultancy firms such as McKinsey,[33] Ernst & Young,[34] KPMG,[35] PricewaterhouseCoopers,[36] Accenture,[37] Deloitte,[38] the Boston Consultancy Group,[39] and Roland Berger[40]—to mention a few. In addition, Africa's growth has also been well reported and documented by leading economic and financial media giants such as *The Economist*,[41] *The Banker*,[42] *Newsweek Magazine*,[43] *The Financial Times*,[44] *The Wall Street Journal*,[45] *The Economist Intelligence Unit*,[46] *Bloomberg*[47] and others.

Another pillar for the success of Islamic finance in Africa is the fact that almost half of the African population is Muslim, with more than half a billion people making it a huge market for Islamic finance. In fact, "Africa was the second continent that Islam spread into and currently almost one-third of the world Muslim population resides in this continent."[48] Connecting the above demographic figures with the potential growth of Islamic banking and finance in Africa, the *International Business Times* pointed out that Islamic finance is set to expand in Africa over the coming decades as the number of Muslims on the continent grows from 240 million to an estimated 400 million.[49]

Furthermore, the current size of the Islamic financial market in Africa is far below its real potential. Some observers pointed out that Africa is highly expected to be the next area of growth, with Sub-Saharan Africa having the largest "room to grow" in Islamic finance.[50] It is this large room for growth that has led some to consider the continent as *the Sleeping Giant*[51] in terms of Islamic finance. Therefore, any new investment will be well received as it will be a real boost to the financial sector in general and contribute towards economic growth and development. The market potential for Islamic finance in Africa has been emphasised by institutions such as Moody's noting that the market is potentially worth close to US$235 billion.[52]

Although there is no exact figure for the number of Islamic financial institutions operating in Africa, estimates posit that the continent currently hosts over 250 Islamic financial institutions that offer Islamic financial services, including Islamic banks, Takaful companies, Islamic funds, Mudārabah companies, and Islamic microfinance.[53]

Moreover, many on the continent have no banking account. Only an estimated 20 % of African families have a bank account.[54] One of the many reasons behind this boycott of the conventional banking system is the fact that Muslims in these countries try to avoid *ribā* (interest-based transactions) and the only possible way to preserve their religious belief is to remain unbanked. As was rightly stressed in one of the IMF's Working Papers, pious Muslims are reluctant to put their money into interest-based financial systems. The immediate result is that this under-banking of an important segment of the population meant that savings were not used efficiently.[55]

Similar facts have been emphasised by other institutions such as Ernst & Young in one of their report,[56] or the Islamic Research & Training Institute of the Islamic Development Bank and Islamic Financial Services Board in their Master Plan regarding the Islamic finance industry. The two institutions emphasised that the compliance of financial services with Shari'ah is a primary concern for the users of these services within a large segment of Muslim societies, and therefore, according to the report, successful financial sector development in such communities requires the promotion of Islamic financial services. This will allow a much larger proportion of the population to participate actively and effectively in the process of economic development.[57]

The broad introduction of Islamic financial services throughout Africa will encourage many of the unbanked to subscribe to formal banking services, thereby increasing the market. The direct consequences of the lack of Islamic finance in some African countries have thus far resulted in the loss of significant formal trade. A very significant volume of trade, in many regions with a Muslim majority, is conducted through informal means. A large amount of money is outside the banking system. Moreover, this lack of Islamic finance has contributed to the inaccessibility to capital for trade and consumer ownership, for a large part of the population. The absence of Islamic financial products has limited the growth or emergence of other vital sectors such as capital markets due to the limited participation of Muslims in securities. This has resulted in limited alternatives for the funding of infrastructure and other developmental projects.[58] This is exactly what has been emphasised by Nigeria's former Central Bank Governor, Sanusi Lamido, who pointed out that the introduction of Islamic finance will bring into the financial system a large group of people who, for religious reasons, have remained unbanked, and open the door for new products.[59]A similar conclusion was reached by the former CEO of Gulf Africa Bank, Asad Ahmed, who highlighted that a large segment of their customer base consisted of people who were opening an account for the first time. Although some of these people were not bankable, the vast majority were people who were not banking due to the non-availability of an Islamic alternative.[60]

Return on investment in Africa is higher than in any other developing region, as recognised by a number of international institutions, such as the IMF, Mckinsey Global Institute, the United Nations, Ernst & Young, or Boston Consulting Group, to name a few.[61] Different observers maintain that global executives and investors, including Islamic finance investors, must take heed of this unprecedented opportunity. As has been pointed out by *The Banker*, the attractive proposition for investment in Sub-Saharan Africa is based on a number of factors—such as an underdeveloped banking industry, favourable macroeconomic conditions, and a very high return on equity %.[62] Stressing this preferential position with regard to return on capital, *The Banker* connects this fact to Bob Diamond, the former Barclays chief's plan to build the leading financial institution in Sub-Saharan Africa. *The Banker* stressed that returns in Africa are the highest in the world. Average return on capital in Africa is heading towards 25 % while it is around 20 % in the Asia-Pacific region, just over 15 % for North America and Central and Eastern Europe, and a paltry sub-5 % for Western Europe.[63]

With regard to the banking sector, *The Banker* ranked African banks as having generated the highest returns to shareholders in 2013. In its 2014 Top 1000 Bank rankings, *The Banker* reported that "in terms of profit generation, African banks make the highest returns on capital of 24 %—double the average return for the rest of the globe. … This is despite African banks holding less than 1 % of global capital."[64]

Pointing out to some of the reasons behind the better returns in Africa compared to other regions, the head of the International Finance Corporation (IFC) referred to the lower level of competition and the fact that IFC is breaking new ground in Africa.[65] Stressing the above position, the Standard Chartered Africa CEO pointed out that "it is this risk-reward equation that makes African investment so compelling—the returns remain among the highest in the world, while risks are diminishing and can be effectively managed."[66]

It is pertinent to point out that Islamic banking and finance in Africa complements the existing conventional banking system and is by no means presenting itself as a substitute.[67] This is a market reality evidenced by the experience of more than 100 countries operating an Islamic banking and financial system. Therefore, there is no threat to the existing conventional banking system in African countries. On the contrary, Islamic finance will strengthen the existing financial system by broadening its reach and creating a new atmosphere of competition—as it has done elsewhere.

The success of Islamic finance in Africa is also backed by the growing openness and acceptability of the system by many regulators and politicians across the continent. At times, the strongest support does not come from Muslim officials, but from non-Muslim leaders driven by wise and objective decisions that give priority to national interests, the wider benefits to the country's population, and avoiding getting caught up in narrow sectarian or religious divide. A few years back, Moody's noticed that "Sub-Saharan regulators have been more flexible in granting banking licenses to onshore, deposit-taking, fully fledged Shari'ah -compliant banks than their North African counterparts.[68]" This flexibility by Sub-Saharan regulators in countries such as South Africa, Kenya, Uganda, Tanzania, Mauritius, and Nigeria is driven by national interests and the independence of regulators in designing and implementing the right policies. Yet, even the non-flexibility of North African regulators noted earlier has drastically changed with Islamic finance now high on the agenda of many political leaders in the region.

Trade and investment between African countries and other Muslim countries—whether in the Middle East or Asia—is growing rapidly and Islamic finance can be a catalyst in strengthening these ties as it has already done in the case of the Middle East and Asia, where strong trade relationships have been forged. The Governor of Bank Negara (the Central Bank of Malaysia) underlined that the internationalisation of Islamic finance has strengthened trade and investment ties between Asia and the Middle East. It has revitalised economic ties between the two regions and reinforced growth prospects.[69] The Governor added that Islamic finance is contributing towards global financial stability, supporting global economic growth, forging greater connectivity among emerging economies, and facilitating resource allocation across borders. These combined efforts will contribute to the stability of the international financial system and global economic prosperity.[70]

A similar position has been expressed by Lim Hng Kiang, Minister for Trade and Industry and Deputy Chairman of the Monetary Authority of Singapore, who maintained that "Asia's share of total trade with the GCC grew from just 10 % in 1980 to 36 % in 2009." The minister stressed that "among other areas Islamic finance can potentially play a part in facilitating more trade between Asia and the Middle East with the involvement of more global and Islamic banks from both regions."[71]

The above reasoning is applicable to the role of Islamic finance in reinforcing and consolidating the growing trade relations between Africa and other Muslim countries. This has been clearly articulated by the Governor of the Bank of Zambia, who maintained that the increased trade between the Sub-Saharan region and Islamic nations in the Middle East only reinforces our view that partnerships among the corporate players between the two regions will foster more developments in the area of Islamic finance.[72]

Another reason for the possible success of Islamic finance in Africa is the abundance of natural resources in the continent, backed by rising global demands for Africa's natural riches. This presents an important opportunity for those engaged in Islamic finance to develop new forms of local partnerships. Also among the indicators is the remarkable increase in foreign direct investment, the rise of urbanism, rocketing consumer spending, and an expanding young labour force, as will be detailed later. In short, as rightly pointed out by Ernst & Young in one of its reports, "Africa is a significant growth market that no consumer products business can afford to ignore".[73]

There are tremendous opportunities in the agribusiness for Islamic financial institutions whereby Africa has 60 % of the world's uncultivated arable land, and has two of the world's largest rivers. Some have gone further to suggest that food—and the means to produce it—is being viewed as the "new oil" of the twenty-first century, and therefore, Africa's immense, and largely dormant, agricultural potential will be gaining a lot of attention.[74] Despite this potential, Africa depends on food imports, with a food trade deficit amounting to US$ 20 billion. A massive increase in the production and productivity of the continent's agriculture is needed to transform Africa from a net food importer into a food exporter. Thus, it is believed that with its vast amounts of cultivable land and the significant scope to increase productivity, the continent is endowed with the resources to both service its own demands and to take advantage of rising global market potential.[75]

Another growth area is the telecommunication sector, where the continent is recognised as a leader in terms of growth and innovation, especially with mobile banking. The huge demand for infrastructure projects represents another huge investment potential. These opportunities are already being reflected in a steady GDP growth, which started at the turn of the century, backed by improved macroeconomic stability that is well acknowledged by international institutions.

The financial sector, in particular, holds very promising investment opportunities. There is potential in the banking system, insurance sector, capital markets, and microfinance. Africa's financial services sector is responding rapidly to the continent's altering economic reality. Rising incomes, technological enhancements, and rapid urbanisation are bringing more people within reach of a broader suite of financial services, according to Standard Bank.[76] This, in turn, will provide profound support to economic growth assertions. The strength of the African banking system is not only due to the fact that the banking sector in Africa grew at 15 % in the last decade, but also because it is expected to exhibit the same growth for the next decade. The retail banking sector, in particular, is expected to grow at 18 %, according to a recent study by Bain & Company.[77] Despite the challenges facing the industry, such as legal issues, slow court proceedings, the absence of credit assessment information, and little protection for property rights, the banking system in Africa is reasonably sound and the capital adequacy ratio average of 16 % of risk-weighted assets is widely respected. Moreover, the system is characterised by lower banking penetration, presenting major opportunities for growth. Return on capital (ROC) and return on assets (ROA) are among the highest in the world, supported by the lowest average cost-to-income ratios, according to *The Banker*, as will be detailed later. There are also vast opportunities for mergers and acquisitions. The African financial market is expected to grow and evolve further over the next decade in terms of development, openness, and consolidation. According to the consultancy firm Roland Berger, there is, without question, a huge unmet need for financial services across the region and it is predicted that the sector will grow approximately 15 % annually to reach US$ 390 billion in annual revenues by 2020.[78]

International interest in the banking system in Africa is rapidly growing, whether through expansion of existing businesses, the acquisition of local financial institutions, partnerships, or through the establishment of new ventures. Institutions such as Citigroup, JP Morgan Chase & Co, Morgan Stanley, Standard Chartered, Barclays, and Société Générale are expanding their business in the continent while Chinese banks such as the Industrial and Commercial Bank of China (ICBC), Bank of China, and Export-Import Bank of China are vigorously investing in Africa in order to facilitate the growing partnership between Africa and China. Portuguese banks such as Millennium BCP, Bank Espirrito Santo (BES), and Banco BPI have been very active in recent years, particularly in Portuguese-speaking countries. Many other financial institutions are also taking advantage of the vast opportunities in the continent. These include, among many others, Singapore-based Templeton Asset Management's Emerging Market Group, Russia's Renaissance Asset Managers, and Brazil's Bradesco and state-controlled Banco do Brasil. Even African financial giants such as Standard Bank, Eco Bank, Nepad Bank, and Attijārahwafa Bank are expanding across the continent. Thus, everyone is looking at Africa and Islamic banks and financial institutions should not be latecomers as these windows of opportunities will not remain open for long.

In regards to capital markets, there is a surge of interest in the establishment of stock exchanges in Africa, which have proliferated over the last two decades. Despite the challenges associated with liquidity and infrastructure, African stock markets have performed well, both in terms of absolute returns and on a risk-adjusted basis. The average annual return for these markets over the past 10 years was 25 % with the exception of 2008 and it is reported that the median profit margin was 11 % better than comparable figures for Asia and South America. Some of the Islamic funds which have been wisely invested in these markets, such as (the Saudi-based) Jadwa Africa Equity Freestyle Fund, have recorded exceptional returns. It is time for other Shari'ah -compliant asset managers to look at emerging markets where huge opportunities still await the right investors. Observing Shari'ah principles with regard to stock selection and screening is no longer a mystery. Different international financial institutions have developed Shari'ah -compliant indices that are applied worldwide. Among others, we have the Dow Jones Islamic Index, the FTSE Islamic Index, the S&P Islamic Index, and The MSCI Global Islamic Indices. Cooperating with the existing providers of Islamic indices or developing new ones for the African markets is simply a matter of regulatory and political formality.

Beside the Khartoum stock Exchange, which is based on Shari'ah principles, in 2012, the Nigerian Stock Exchange (NSE) and wealth management firm Lotus Capital set up the NSE Lotus Islamic Index of Shari'ah -compliant companies.[79]

Investing in Africa is less risky than investing in developed equity markets amid current volatility. Risk is better priced in Africa than in developed markets and the underlying market fundamentals are stronger.[80] Moreover, as reported by *The Wall Street Journal*, Africa was the top performing region over the past 10 years in terms of equity investments, with a 31 % return compared with 25 % globally, according to the International Finance Corporation (IFC).[81] It is, therefore, time for Muslim investors to channel their liquidity where the returns are higher and risks are lower rather than dumping it elsewhere.

The bond and *ṣukūk* market is another area that holds enormous prospects. Although the African debt market is still in its infancy, there is growing interest in African credit and a number of sovereign states have already tested the international markets. There is also mounting interest in *ṣukūk*. Countries such as Ivory Coast, Nigeria, Tunisia, Morocco, and Kenya have expressed their desire to issue *ṣukūk* to fund infrastructure projects while Senegal and South Africa have already entered the market in 2014 with highly oversubscribed *ṣukūk* issues. Pointing to the possible contribution by Islamic finance to infrastructure, the *Economist* maintains that "the continent's vast need for infrastructure is matched only by the shortage of investment funds. Shari'ah -compliant investors could help bridge the gap."[82] The *ṣukūk* market is one of the fastest growing segments of international finance. This study will touch on the development of the main structures, and how it is useful to the continent's financial system and economic development, given the fact that these products require clear links to real economic activity and tangible, identifiable assets, and thus, are well-suited for infrastructure projects.[83]

Insurance in the continent is another growth area since the African insurance industry is accelerating.[84] Although the conventional African insurance sector itself is still in its infancy, *Takāful* or Islamic insurance holds great potential and could help in expanding the industry across the continent. The issue was highlighted by the Chief Editor of *The African Reinsurer*, indicating that Islamic insurance (*takāful*) is one of the new developments areas in the insurance industry, and taking into consideration the current turnover, the future of the industry is bright. Thus, some of Africa's insurance giants such as Africa Re have decided to position themselves so as to offer better services to Islamic insurers in Africa and beyond, while hoping that the ethical values and principles of *Takāful* will protect it against the ills and errors of conventional insurance.[85]

Private equity is another area of opportunity in African financial services. A number of private equity funds have been active on the continent for many years and have established strong records of accomplishment in a number of different sectors such as telecommunications and the financial services. They have enjoyed the benefits of a market with few competitors. Islamic private equity can play an important role in this area. It is a very promising asset class that is expected to gain prominence and importance in the coming years, as shown in a recent survey by the *Economist Intelligence Unit*, whereby 40 % of investors expect to use equity funds in the coming 3 years.[86]

The success of microfinance initiatives in the continent and recognition of the importance of Islamic microfinance by institutions operating on the ground, such as the Consultative Group to Assist the Poor (CGAP)[87] or the Africa Microfinance Action Forum,[88] is a testimony to the bright future of Islamic microfinance in the continent. Cooperation with these organisations familiar with the sector could help broaden the industry's reach and constitutes another platform for the potential success of Islamic microfinance in Africa. Referring to some of the practical successful experiences in Islamic microfinance, the International Fund for Agriculture Development (IFAD) refers to the experience of the Agricultural Bank of Sudan (ABS) and its pilot programme, which started in 2010. The programme was supported by three key stakeholders: the IFAD-funded Western Sudan Resources Management Programme, Agricultural Bank of Sudan (ABS), and the Microfinance Unit of the Central Bank of Sudan. The results as per the IFAD report are resounding and it is believed the implementation of such programmes in other African countries would help alleviate poverty and promote greater financial inclusion. The International Fund for Agricultural Development upheld that the risk carried by the financing service is zero and the model has cultivated strong credit discipline among rural populations, with a repayment rate of 100 %. As of April 2014, the programme had reached 27,700 female members, representing 13,400 households, through 1440 female groups. It mobilised savings worth US$ 540,000 with a client base of 25,060 borrowers and a loan portfolio of US$ 3.4 million. Its financing, based on *murābahah* and *mushārakah*, supports small agricultural activities, livestock fattening and rearing, and a range of microenterprises such as petty trading, tea stalls, and brick making.[89]

In short, the future of the financial sector in Africa and its various segments is very promising. As emphasised by South Africa's Standard Bank, "at current growth rates, Africa's financial services sector could make up around 20 % of the continent's collective GDP within the next decade, compared to 10 % today".[90]

These investment opportunities have attracted companies, funds, and asset managers, and more importantly, many emerging economic powers, especially the BRIC countries—namely, Brazil, Russia, India, and China—are interested in the continent. Interest in the continent is also evident in the activities of countries such as Japan, South Korea, Turkey, and some Gulf Cooperation Council countries and companies in these countries. Everyone is interested in the continent and everyone is trying to portray himself as a reliable partner. Trade relations between Africa and its emerging-market partners are developing rapidly. The new partnership has extended beyond trade by embracing foreign direct investment and development aid. This new partnership is an opportunity towards economic development, but it also carries genuine risks that need to be carefully mitigated by African leaders.[91]

Thus, the objective of the present study is to highlight the immense potential of Islamic finance in Africa for investors looking for new investment opportunities after a possible saturation in their traditional markets. It is addressed to those who are keen to promote the principles of Islamic finance globally not only as a business venture, but also as a mission. It is directed to those seeking to save humanity from the economic injustices and the perils of interest-based and non-Shari'ah -compliant transactions. It is aimed at those who are willing to build long-term strategies and who are not distracted by short-term gains and media propaganda. Apart from the moral and religious aspects, investing in Africa through Islamic finance is not a charitable or an aid-based calling. It is about new markets, higher profit margins, risk diversification, and competing with big players who are already making money on the continent. Investment in Africa through Islamic finance is mainly for sophisticated investors capable of innovation and ready to confront the challenges.

Moreover, the study aims at putting before the African economic players and regulators the advantages of the adoption of Islamic finance in Africa. It argues that Islamic finance will be another new investment opportunity that will unlock the real potential of the financial system throughout the continent and provide financial products satisfying the desires and belief of all consumers. The uniqueness of Islamic financial principles makes it a perfect alternative to traditional banking systems that leave a larger proportion of Africans dissatisfied. Standard and Poor's stressed in one of its reports that "the use of Islamic finance could help Africa pay for multibillion dollars' worth of infrastructure projects a year and help fund countries' fiscal deficits." The agency added that "African nations are also looking to diversify their funding sources and gain access to a pool of wealthy investors…who can only invest in Sharia-compliant products."[92]

It is important to highlight here that Islamic modes of financing not only provide better competition, but can coexist with interest-based conventional financing to ensure the African population is properly served. Islamic banking in Africa has a large untapped market.[93] The industry can attract hundreds of millions who will automatically become part of the banking system.[94]

If the developed countries of the West or economic giants of the East are enthusiastic about incorporating Islamic finance in their financial systems by amending legislation and adapting tax regulations, why should African countries not look for every dollar of investment that will help sustain their unprecedented economic growth and work towards poverty eradication? It is also argued that if countries such as the UK, Singapore, Thailand, Japan, Hong Kong, South Africa, and others with Muslim minorities can have Islamic banks and financial institutions, why are many African countries with Muslim majorities or sizable Muslim minorities putting their own citizens at a disadvantage by not facilitating such alternative banking products and services?

Islamic finance is becoming part of the growth strategies of an increasing number of global financial institutions. If global banks such as HSBC, Citigroup, Standard Chartered, Barclays, BNP Paribās, Deutsche Bank, Société Générale, Calyon Bank, Credit Agricole, and other renowned international institutions can have Islamic banking subsidiaries or windows and become very active in Islamic finance, sometimes taking the lead, as in the case of Islamic capital markets, why would not well-established conventional banks on the continent do the same?

Introducing Islamic banking and finance in Africa would not be alien to the broader strategic policies of many African countries maintaining a good relationship with other Muslim countries and cooperating with these countries towards realising the common benefits of Muslims around the globe. It is based on this strategic policy that almost half of the member countries of the Islamic Development Bank (IDB) are African nations. As concluded in a recent Policy Research Paper by the World Bank, a right implementation of Islamic finance can help in reducing poverty and inequality in Muslim countries. Therefore, the paper added that Muslim countries concerned about financial inclusion should utilise Islamic finance to achieve this goal.[95]

Africa adopting Islamic finance is the industry's call to benefit from its robust growth and proven record of accomplishments. From a customer's perspective, Islamic finance is not just a Muslim business; the industry is also very popular with non-Muslim investors in many countries, as shall be discussed later. The growth rate of Islamic financial services has outpaced that of conventional banking over the past decade, making it one of the most dynamic areas in international finance. The number of institutions registered to conduct Shari'ah -compliant activities has risen from 525 in 2007 to 675 in 2011, according to *The Banker*. In 2012, the number of these institutions reached 716.[96] *The Banker* also reported that conventional banking assets nearly tripled between 2003 and 2008 while Islamic banking assets have multiplied sevenfold, albeit starting from a much lower base.[97] This steady growth continued through 2013 and 2014, where the industry continued to rise from US$ 1267 billion in 2013 to US$ 1391 billion in 2014. More importantly, according to *The Banker*, total assets have increased annually from 2014, representing an impressive compound annual growth rate of 15.73 %.[98] Moreover, following the recent financial crisis, the industry stands relatively robust compared to the conventional financial system, as it demonstrated in a number of studies and working papers by institutions such as the IMF, Ernst & Young, Standard & Poor's, and many others.

Economists have proven that the wider the freedom of choice, the higher the level of social welfare. Furthermore, wider choice implies greater respect for human rights. Moreover, the different services to be provided by Islamic finance are compatible with the principle of "social inclusiveness," which is a basic requirement for ensuring just and equitable social progress.[99] Therefore, introducing an alternative financial system in the form of Islamic banking and finance presents the market with new choices, entailing obvious social and economic benefits, including constituting a sound expression of freedom of religion.[100]

The vibrant Islamic banking and finance industry is looking for new markets for growth. Strategically, it is almost impossible for the Islamic finance industry to compete globally and claim to be a real alternative industry while its share is just 1 % of the global financial market. Thus, looking for new markets is necessary. Some of the means of achieving this target is reaching out to untapped markets and consolidating existing platforms.[101]

Africa is well positioned to play an important role in Islamic finance due to its large market in which an estimated 45–50 % of the African population are Muslim. African leaders are under a moral obligation to be part of this vibrant market and work on how to exploit its potential towards realising development objectives. As a faith-based offering, Islamic banking has the potential to appeal to those who are currently unbanked and to those who are underbanked primarily due to an aversion to conventional banking. There are also many affluent Muslim traders who could join the industry, which means that potential Islamic banking customers fall into low, middle, and high income groups. The industry has enormous potential to increase the percentage of Africans joining the formal banking system.[102] As concluded by one observer, "Africa has everything to gain and nothing to lose by growing its Islamic banking sector."[103]

As stressed by Ernst & Young, which set up a specialised office on Islamic finance in South Africa to tap the African market, the increasing levels of awareness and the growing popularity of Shari'ah finance in Africa and globally and the acknowledgment by regulators and legislators of the need to accommodate the requirements of Islamic finance within the regulatory and legislative frameworks, are good signs for the continued growth of this sector in Africa.[104]

However, the development of Islamic finance in Africa is not without challenges. These challenges could be related to the sustainability of the present economic growth, addressing the general challenges facing the Islamic finance industry, or the particular challenges arising from the implementation of Islamic finance in Africa. One of the challenges that needs to be paid particular attention is the issue of perception. This pertains to perceptions of Islamic finance and perceptions of Africa. In both cases, there is an issue of media propaganda and negative reporting. Some of the negative perceptions regarding Islamic finance should not be strange to African politicians, regulators, and businessmen as Africa also is still suffering from negative media reporting and biased coverage or underreporting of positive news. This media attitude is one of the biggest challenges facing the continent. Similarly, maintaining the belief that Islamic finance is about the implementation of Shari'ah on non-Muslims or the allegation that the industry is associated with terrorism and money laundering, based on media propaganda, is akin to believing the same media propaganda that Africa is still associated with famine, conflicts, and diseases despite the positive strides made by the continent in the last decade in terms of GDP growth, democracy, increase in foreign direct investment, urbanism, and a growing consumer class.

However, Africa still has to face up to various challenges that could disrupt its present growth. There is a need to give prime consideration to factors that could strengthen its economic development and neutralise impediments to business. Thus, it is paramount to deal with issues such as corruption, the infrastructure gap and reducing inefficiencies related to poor transport, electricity, railways, and healthcare infrastructures, designing new methods for alternative FDI, managing political risk, and the lack of security through conflict resolution. Moreover, Africa needs to work towards reducing barriers to trade, making good education a priority, given the fact that one of the obstacles facing investors working in the continent is the lack of local skilled talent. Education levels are relatively low and this undermines the skill levels of the labour force.

It is also very important to point out here that although the above challenges represent a real concern, we must be careful not to exaggerate. Despite many investors continuing to view Africa as a challenging place to conduct business in, compared to other emerging markets, this does not deny the fact that in the World Bank's most recent Ease of Doing Business rankings, 14 African countries ranked ahead of Russia, 16 ahead of Brazil, and 17 ahead of India. It is also necessary to point out here that while corruption no doubt remains a big challenge in Africa, the reality is not as gloomy as some perceive. In fact, 14 African countries ranked higher than India and 35 higher than Russia in the Transparency International's Corruption Perceptions Index.[105]

Nevertheless, the spread of Islamic finance throughout Africa will present new challenges that need to be addressed by African regulators and business leaders. Among others, it is vital to ensure that the new financial system is fully integrated with the existing financial system and that an appropriate legal, institutional, and regulatory framework that allows the two systems to efficiently interface is in place. The lack of Shari'ah scholars knowledgeable in conventional economics, law, accounting, banking, and finance is yet another challenge limiting the growth of the industry globally. Islamic finance in Africa also faces the challenge of taxation, lack of Shari'ah -compliant liquidity management instruments, the issue of standardisation and harmonisation, and other concerns facing the Islamic finance industry globally, as will be discussed in Chap. 8.

Attracting investors into Africa requires African countries to strive harder towards achieving better rankings in globally recognised metrics such as the Transparency International Index, the World Economic Forum Competitiveness Index, the World Bank's "Doing Business," the Ibrahim Index of African Governance, and better ratings from credit ratings agencies.

Besides the direct and usual ways of addressing each of the above challenges individually, African leaders as well as those investing in the continent through Islamic finance are advised to work in close cooperation with multilateral financial institutions already assisting the continent towards developing its financial system and are directly involved in the global development of the Islamic finance industry. These multilateral institutions include, among others, the Islamic Development Bank, the World Bank, the IMF, and the African Development Bank. These institutions have a great responsibility in addressing the issue of financial inclusion in the continent. The study touches on the developmental role of these institutions in Africa and their involvement in Islamic finance and how these experiments can benefit the development of Islamic finance in Africa.

The present study is divided into seven chapters, besides this introduction, and a conclusion. Chapter 2 briefly outlines the general principles of Islamic finance and its growth globally. Chapter 3 paints a panorama of the current penetration of Islamic finance in Africa while Chap. 4 is dedicated to the current economic growth in the continent, its main indicators, and investment opportunities. Chapter 5 is dedicated to Africa's banking and microfinance sectors and the role of Islamic finance, while Chap. 6 deals with non-banking financial services in Africa and the role of Islamic finance. Chapter 7 landscapes the rise of international interests in Africa, while the final chapter focuses on the different challenges that will face the implementation of Islamic finance in Africa and suggests ways in which they can be overcome.

## Notes

1. Anouar Hassoune & Adel Satel, *Islamic Finance Explores New Horizons in Africa*, Moody's Global Banking March 2008, www.moodya.com, retrieved May 2010, pp. 1–18.
2. That was before the split of Sudan into separate countries.

3. David H. Shinn, "The Rise of Non-Western Influence in Africa", *Global Studies Review*, vol. 6, no. 3, Fall 2010, www.globality-gmu.net, retrieved January 2012, pp. 14–16.
4. Pieter Becker and Michelle van Zyl, *The Dynamic African Consumer Market: Exploring Growth Opportunities in Sub-Saharan Africa*, Accenture, 2011, www.accenture.com, retrieved January 2012, p. 3.
5. Ernst & Young, *Growing in Africa Capturing the Opportunity for Global Consumer Product Business*, Ernst & Young, 2011, www.ey.com, retrieved January 2012, p. 6.
6. The World Bank, *Africa's Future and the World Bank's Support to It*, March 2011, p. 4
7. JP van der Merwe, "Africa: Local Banks Capturing the Market", www.allafrica.com, September 30, 2010. Retrieved January 2011.
8. Ernst & Young, *Ernst & Young's 2011 Africa Attractiveness Survey, It is Time for Africa*, May 2011, www.ey.com, retrieved December 2011.
9. KPMG, "Africa A continent Whose Time has Come", *New Frontiers*, Issue no. 30, Autumn 2011, p. 2.
10. Paul Wallace, "Casablanca Looks to Dispel African Divide", *The Banker*, April 2012, p. 100.
11. The World Bank, *Africa's Future and the World Bank's Support to It*, March 2011, p. 4.
12. PricewaterhouseCoopers, "Into Africa: Investment Prospects in the Sub-Saharan Banking Sector", 2008, www.pwc.com, retrieved December 2010.
13. World Bank, Global *Economic Prospects- Sub-Saharan Africa* January 2016, p.153, www.worldbank.org, retrieved April 2016
14. World Bank, "Africa's Pulse: Decades of Sustained Growth is Transforming Africa's Economies", www.worldbank.org, October 2014
15. Marco Pani "Strong Growth in Sub-Saharan Africa, but Pockets of Difficulty", IMF African Department, October 20, 2014, www.imf.org
16. The World Bank, *Africa's Future and the World Bank's Support to It*, March 2011; Punam Chuhan-Pole & Manka Angwafo (Editors) *Yes Africa Can: Success Stories from a Dynamic Continent*,The World Bank 2011; Thorsten Beck & others, *Financing Africa Through the Crisis and Beyond*, The African Development Bank, the German Federal Ministry for Economic Cooperation and Development and The World Bank, September 2011, www.afdb.org, retrieved April 2012.
17. IMF, *Regional Economic Outlook Sub-Saharan Africa Recovery and New Risks* 2011, www.imf.org, retrieved January 2012; Shawn Ladd, "Emerging Africa Expected To See Rise in Investment", *IMF Survey Magazine: Countries & Regions*, January 12, 2011, www.imf.org, retrieved June 2011; Andrianaivo and Charles Amo Yartey, *Understanding the Growth of African Financial Markets*, IMF Working Paper International Monetary Fund,

August 2009, www.imf.org retrieved June 2011; Simon Willson "Private Sector Gains Ground in Africa", IMF Survey Magazine, March 4, 2010, www.imf.org, retrieved June 2011; Jeremy Clift, "Africa Faces Twin Challenges After Global Crisis", *IMF Survey Magazine*, March 4, 2010.

18. United Nations Economic Commission for Africa, Economic and Social Conditions in Africa in 2010 and Prospects for 2011", *Economic Report on Africa 2011*, www.uneca.org, retrieved January 2012.
19. World Trade Organization *Trade growth to ease in 2011 but despite 2010 record surge, crisis hangover persist*, Press Releases, April 7, 2011, www.wto.org
20. African Development Bank, *Africa in 50 Years Time: The Road Towards Inclusive Growth*, African Development Bank Group, Tunis, Tunisia, September 2011, www.afdb.org, retrieved December 2011.
21. Willem Buiter & Ebrahim Rahbari, *Global Economics View Global Growth Generators: Moving beyond 'Emerging Markets' and 'BRIC'*, Citigroup Global Market, February 21, 2011, www.cepr.org, p. 4, retrieved May 2012.
22. Robert Ruthann, *Africa's Development Prospects Remain Intact*, Equity Research, Credit Suisse, January 11, 2011, www.credit-suisse.com, retrieved June 2011.
23. Jim O'Neill and Anna Stupnystka, *How Exiting is Africa Potential*, Goldman Sachs Asset Management Strategy Series, October 14, 2010, pp. 1–8.
24. Richard Bernstein, *Africa: The Final Frontier*, Merrill Lynch- Investment Strategy, July 23, 2007.
25. Clement Gillet, *Is Africa About to Take Off*, Société Générale Economic Study Department, May 10, 2011, http://www.societegenerale.com, retrieved January 2012, pp. 1–10.
26. Nanou Keita Sub-Saharan Africa: a Challenging New Frontier, Crédit Agricole, Bimonthly No. 139 January–February 2010, www.etudes-economiques.credit-agricole.com, retrieved May 2011.
27. European Investment Bank (EIB), "Banking in sub-Saharan Africa Challenges and Opportunities", www.eib.org January 2013, retrieved April 2013, pp. 1–112.
28. Simon Freemantle, *Africa Macro Insight, The Five Trends Powering Africa's Enduring Allure, Trend 4 Africa, Africa Dormant Resources Potential*, Standard Bank, October 6, 2011, www.standardbank.com, retrieved January 2012; Simon Freemantle, *Africa Macro Insight, Five Trends Powering Africa's Enduring Allure, Trend 2 Africa Transformational Urban Swell*, Standard Bank, September 21, 2011, www.standardbank.com, retrieved January 2012; Simon Freemantle, *Africa Macro Insight and Strategy African Election Map 2011/2012*, Standard Bank 15 December, 2011, www.standardbank.com, retrieved January 2012; Simon Freemantle & Jeremy Stevens, *Africa Macro Insight and Strategy BRIC Africa The Redback's Rise*

*Opportunities to Africa*, Standard Bank 29 August 2011, www.standard-bank.com, retrieved January 2012; Simon Freemantle, *Africa Macro Insight, The Five Trends Powering Africa's Enduring Allure, Trend 5 Africa Deepening Financial Sector*, Standard Bank, October 10, 2011, www.standardbank.com, retrieved January 2012.

29. Charles Robertson, Yvonne Mhango and Nothando Ndebele, "Africa: The bottom billion becomes the fastest billion," Renaissance Capital, July 2011.
30. Schaffnit-Chatterjee, *Sub-Saharan Africa: A bright spot in spite of key challenges*, Deutsche Bank Research. Current Issues/Emerging Markets., July 2013, www.dbresearchech.com, retrieved December 2014.
31. Christian Esters "Sub-Saharan African Sovereigns Have Withstood External Shocks Well, But Volatile Commodity Prices Remain A Risk", in *Europe, Middle East and Africa Market Outlook 2011*, January 2011, Standards &Poor's, www.standardandpoors.com, retrieved June 2011, pp. 33–37.
32. Anouar Hassoune & Adel Satel, *Islamic Finance Explores New Horizons in Africa*, Moody's Global Banking March 2008, www.moodya.com, retrieved May 2010, pp. 1–18; Oritseweyimi Omamuli, Moody's, "Improving credit dynamics among sovereigns in Sub-Saharan Africa, despite challenges", Global Credit Research, June 8, 2011, www.moodys.com, retrieved June 2012; David Berman "Moody's upbeat on Africa", www.theglobeandmail.com, retrieved June 2012.
33. McKinsey Global Institute, *Lion on the Move: the Progress and Potential of African Economies*, June 2010, www.mckinsey.com, retrieved January 2011.
34. Ernst & Young's 2011 *Africa Attractiveness Survey, It is Time for Africa*, May 2011; Richard Taylor, *Growing in Africa Capturing the Opportunity for Global Consumer Product Business*, Ernst & Young, 2011; Jonathan Kruger "Hidden Opportunities" In *Eye on Africa*, Ernst & Young vol. 3, March 2011.
35. KPMG, "Africa A continent Whose Time has Come", *New Frontiers*, Issue no. 30 Autumn 2011, www.kpmg.com, retrieved March 2012; KPMG, *KPMG Survey of Current Economic and Business Conditions in Africa*, December 2010, www.kpmg.com, retrieved March 2011, pp. 1–20.
36. Nick Page & Others, *Into Africa: Investment Prospects in the Sub-Saharan Banking Sector*, PricewaterhouseCoopers, 2008; *The Africa Business Agenda*, www.pwc.com, retrieved December 2012; PricewaterhouseCoopers, "10 Minutes on Investing in Africa", September 2011, www.pwc.com, pp. 1–5.
37. Accenture *Africa The New Frontier for Growth*, 2010, www.accenture.com, retrieved May 2011; Pieter Becker and Michelle van Zyl, *The Dynamic African Consumer Market: Exploring Growth Opportunities in Sub-Saharan Africa*, Accenture, 2011, www.accenture.com, retrieved January 2012; Noel Gordon & Others, *At the Tipping Point: Financial Services in Africa comes of age How Financial Institutions can Capitalize on the Growth*

*Opportunities in Africa*, Accenture, 2011, www.accenture.com, retrieved December 2012.

38. Lwazi Bam, "Africa Poised for Growth", April 14, 2011, www.deloittesa.wordpress.com, retrieved March 2012.
39. Lionel Are & others, *The African Challengers Global Competitors Emerges from the Overlooked Continent*, The Boston Consulting Group, 2010, www.bcg.com, retrieved June 2011.
40. Chriatian Wessels and others, *Inside Africa*, Think: act study, Roland Berger January 2012, www.rolandberger.com,retrieved January 2013.
41. *The Economist* "Africa's impressive growth", Jan. 6th 2011, www.economist.com, retrieved December, 2011; *The Economist*, "Africa's hopeful economies The sun shines bright", December 3, 2011; *The Economist* "*The Lions Kings*", January 6, 2011; *The Economist*, "The hopeful continent Africa rising", December 3, 2011; *The Economist* "Turning towards Mecca Islamic banks join in the race for Africa", vol. 387, Issue 8579, May 10, 2008.
42. The Banker, "*African Returns Make it the Place to be*", June 2011, p. 6.
43. Jerry Guo, "How Africa is Becoming the New Asia", *Newsweek Magazine*, vol. 155, no. 09, February 18, 2010, www.newsweek.com, retrieved April 2011.
44. William Wallis, Andrew England and Katrina Manson, "Africa: Ripe for Appraisal", *Financial Times,* May 18, 2011, www.ft.com, retrieved August 2011; Fiona Rintoul "Vibrant Africa beckons investors" *Financial Times*, July 18, 2010, www.ft.com; retrieved August 2011; Stefan Wagstyl "Unilever: Mr. Africa, I presume?" *Financial Times* October 4, 2011, www.ft.com; retrieved August 2012; Sid Verma, "Africa's decade-long banking bull run in pictures", *Financial Times*, July 3, 2011, www.ft.com, retrieved December 2011; Ruth Sullivan, "Potentials of Africa growth outlook", *The Financial Times*, November 6, 2011; Simeon Kerr, Emaar founder eyes Africa's commodity riches", *The Financial Times*, May 4, 2011, www.ft.com, retrieved June 2012.
45. Peter Wanacott, "A New Class of Consumers Grows in Africa", *The Wall Street Journal*, May 2, 2011, www.online.wsj.com, retrieved June 2011. Matthew Curtin, "Catching Africa's Investment Bug Is Proving Contagious", *The Wall Street Journal*, October 6, 2010, www.online.wsj.com, retrieved June 2011.
46. James Watson & Others, *Into Africa Institutional investor intentions to 2016*, Invest AD & Economist Intelligence Unit, January 2012, www.investad.com; Ayesha Sabavala and Ali al-Saffar, *GCC Trade and Investment Flows: The Emerging-Market Surge* Economist Intelligence Unit 2011, www.eiu.com, retrieved May 2012, The 2011, The Economist Intelligence Unit, *Banking in Sub Saharah Africa to 2020 Promising Frontiers*, August 2011,

www.eiu.com, retrieved January 2012; Economist Intelligence Unit, *Africa: Open for Business: The Potential, Challenges and Risks*, 2012.

47. *Bloomberg Businessweek*, "Africa: Coke's Last Frontier", October 28, 2010, www.businessweek.com, retrieved June 2011; Bonorchis & Nasreen Seria "The Rise of Middle Africa", *Bloomberg Markets Magazine*, June 2011, vol. 6, no. 6, pp. 107–111.
48. H. Kettani, "World Muslim Population: 1950–2020," *International Journal of Environmental Science and Development* (*IJESD*), vol. 1, no. 2, June 2010.
49. Christopher Harress, "Islamic Banking Revolution: Africa Is Seeing an Explosion In Banks Looking To Cash In On Continent's Growing Muslim Population", *International Business Times*, September 26, 2013, www.ibtimes.com, retrieved January 2015.
50. Greg Rung & Others, *Islamic Finance: Building 150 Financial Institutions by 2020*, Oliver Wyman Financial Services, 2011.
51. Nazneen Halim, "The Sleeping Giant", *Islamic Finance News Supplement -IFN Supplement Africa*, July 29, 2011, www.islamicfinancenews.com, retrieved January 2012.
52. See, Anouar Hassoune & Adel Satel, *Islamic Finance Explores New Horizons in Africa*, p. 2.
53. Mohammed Iqbal Belath, Second Deputy Governor of the Bank of Mauritius, at the opening ceremony of the seminar on the "Role of Islamic finance in the development of Africa", Balaclava, Mauritius, September 6, 2012, BIS central bankers' speeches, www.bis.org, retrieved December 2012, p. 2.
54. Peter Ondiege, "Mobile Banking in Africa: Taking the Bank to the People", *Africa Economic Brief* African Development Bank, vol. 1 Issue 8, December 2010; Alberto Chaia and Others *Half of the World is Unbanked*, Financial Access Initiative, October 2009, www.financialaccesss.org, retrieved May 2011.
55. Patrick Imam and Kangni Kpodar, *Islamic Banking: How Has it Diffused?*, International Monetary Fund, August 2010, www.imf.org, retrieved June 2011, p. 6.
56. Ernst & Young, *Growing in Africa Capturing the Opportunity for Global Consumer Product Business*, p. 10.
57. Islamic Research & Training Institute, Islamic Development Bank and Islamic Financial Services Board, *Islamic Financial Services Industry Development Ten Year Framework and Strategies*, p. 1.
58. Femi Sunmonu & Associates, Barristers & Solicitors, "Islamic Financial Services in Nigeria", *Islamic Finance News Guide 2007*, pp. 90–92.
59. *This is Africa*, "The Future of African Banking", *This is Africa,* www.thisisafricaonline.com, retrieved January 2012.

60. Islamic *Business* & *Finance*, "The Ultimate Alternative", Issue 70, p. 13.
61. Acha Leke & others, "What's driving Africa's growth, *Mckinsey Quarterly*, Mckinsey Global Institute, June 2010, www.mckinsey.com, retrieved January 2011; Charles Roxburgh *Lion on the Move: The progress and Potential of African Economies*, McKinney Global Institute, June 2010, www.mckinsey.com, retrieved January 2011, p. 1; United Nations, *Foreign Direct Investment in Africa: Performance and Potential*, 1999, p. iv; Sarona Asset Management, "Roaring African Lions", *Quarterly Report*, 2011; Ernst & Young's 2011 Africa Attractiveness Survey, *It is Time for Africa*, May 2011, p. 2, 8, 9. Lionel Are and others, *The African Challengers Global Competitors Emerge from the Overlooked Continent*, the Boston Consulting Group, 2010; IMF, *Regional Economic Outlook Sub-Saharan Africa Recovery and New Risks* 2011; Matthew Curtin, "Catching Africa's Investment Bug Is Proving Contagious" *The Wall Street Journal*, October 6, 2010.
62. *The Banker*, "Africa offers huge returns on investment for foreign institutions", June 1, 2011, www.thebanker.com, retrieved June 2012.
63. Brian Caplen, "Top 100 Banks in Africa Ranking: Africa Continues to Outperform", *The Banker*, January 5, 2015, p. 54.
64. Ibid
65. *McKinsey Quarterly*, "Lars, H. Thunell on encouraging private-sector investing in emerging markets", *McKinsey Quarterly*, June 12, 2012, www.mckinseyquarterly.com.
66. Diana Layfield, "Seeking the opportunity, managing the risk "in *Ernst & Young's attractiveness surveys Africa* 2013 *Getting Down to Business*, www.ey.com, retrieved May 2013, 2011, p. 3.
67. Patrick Imam and Kangni Kpodar, *Islamic Banking: How Has it Diffused?*, p. 14.
68. Anouar Hassoune & Adel Satel, *Islamic Finance Explores New Horizons in Africa*, p. 5.
69. Zeti Akhtar Aziz, "Thoughts and Visions on Islamic Finance", Welcoming remarks by the Governor of the Central Bank of Malaysia, at the Malaysia Showcase Dinner, Manama, 3 May 2010. *Bank for International Settlement Review* 60/2010, www.bis.org, p. 1.
70. Ibid.
71. Lim Hng Kiang, Minister for Trade and Industry and Deputy Chairman, Monetary Authority of Singapore Opening Address at the 2nd World Islamic Banking Conference: Asia Summit 2011, June 8, 2011 at Pan Pacific Hotel Singapore, www.mondovisione.com, retrieved January 2012.
72. Michael Gondwe, "Talking Notes at the Launch of the Islamic Finance Guidelines", A Key Note Address by the Governor, Bank of Zambia, December 30, 2014.

73. Richard Taylor, *Growing in Africa Capturing the Opportunity for Global Consumer Product Business*, p. 2.
74. Simon Freemantle, *Africa Macro Insight, The Five Trends Powering Africa's Enduring Allure, Trend 4 Africa, Africa Dormant Resources Potential*, p. 7.
75. Making Finance Work for Africa (MFW4A) Conference, *Zipping Finance and Farming in Africa—Harnessing the Continent's Potential, Kampala Uganda June*, June 29–30, 2011, www.mfw4a.org, retrieved June 2012, p. 4.
76. Simon Freemantle, *Africa Macro Insight, The Five Trends Powering Africa's Enduring Allure, Trend 5 Africa Deepening Financial Sector*, p. 1.
77. Bain & Company, "Financial Services in Africa A Decade of Opportunities", January 2011.
78. Chriatian Wessels and others, *Inside Africa, Think: act study*, p. 36.
79. Neil Ford, "The Rise and Rise of Islamic Finance", *African Banker*, November 12, 2012, www.africanbusinessmagazine.com, retrieved January 2013.
80. Ruth Sullivan, "Potentials of Africa growth outlook", *The Financial Times*, November 6, 2011.
81. Neanda Salvaterra, "Mobile Pioneer Sees Rich Promise in Africa", *The Wall Street Journal*, April 18, 2011, www.online.wsj.com, retrieved January 2012.
82. *The Economist*, "Turning towards Mecca Islamic banks join in the race for Africa".
83. The Economist Intelligence Unit, *Risk and Reward: The Gulf Push into African Infrastructure*, commissioned by Dubai Chamber, 2014.
84. Bakary H. Kamara, "Changing Seasons, Differing Fortunes", *The African Reinsurer*, 22nd Edition, June 2008, p. 4.
85. Ibid.
86. James Watson & Others, *Into Africa Institutional investor intentions to 2016*, p. 15.
87. Karim, Nimrah, Michael Tarazi, and Xavier Reille, "Islamic Microfinance: An Emerging Market Niche." Focus Note 49. Washington, DC: CGAP, August 2008, www.cgap.org, retrieved January 2011, pp. 1–16.
88. See, Africa Microfinance Action Forum, *Diagnostic to Action: Microfinance in Africa* October 2008, www.swwb.org, retrieved June 2011, p. 113.
89. International Fund for Agriculture Development (IFAD), *Islamic microfinance: Unlocking New Potential to Fight Rural Poverty*, November 2014, www.ifad.org, retrieved January 2015.
90. Simon Freemantle, *Africa Macro Insight, The Five Trends Powering Africa's Enduring Allure, Trend 5 Africa Deepening Financial Sector*, p. 1.
91. Monica Ioana Enescu, *Emerging powers: New economic partners for Africa?* Credit Agricole Aperiodic—No. September 14, 2011, www.economic-research.credit-agricole.com, p. 4.

92. Samira Mensah, *After A Mixed 2013, The Global Sukuk Market Looks Promising In 2014*, February 4, 2014 in Standard & Poor's Islamic Finance Outlook 2015.
93. Kevin Mwanza, "Is Islamic Banking a Better Option for Africa? *The African Executive*, www.africanexecutive.com
94. Emilio Pera, "A Review of the Islamic Finance industry" in *Eye on Africa*, Ernst & Young, vol. 3, March 2011, pp. 16–18.
95. Mahmoud Mohieldin, Zamir Iqbal, Ahmed Rostom and Xiaochen Fu, *The Role of Islamic Finance in Enhancing Financial Inclusion in Organization of Islamic Cooperation (OIC) Countries*, Policy Research Working Paper 5920, The World Bank, Islamic Economics and Finance Working Group, December 2011, p. 3.
96. Joseph DiVanna & Melissa Hancock, "Islamic Finance Reaches Critical Mass", *The Banker* Special Supplement, *Top Islamic Financial Institutions*, November, 2012, p. 2.
97. Joseph DiVanna & Melissa Hancock, "Islamic Finance Roars Again", *The Banker* Special Supplement, *Top 500 Islamic Financial Institutions*, November, 2011, p. 2.
98. Joseph DiVanna & James King, "Islamic Finance Unstoppable Rise", *The Banker* Special Supplement, *Top 500 Islamic Financial Institutions*, November, 2014, p. 2.
99. Islamic Research & Training Institute, Islamic Development Bank and Islamic Financial Services Board, Islamic Financial Services Industry Development *Ten Year Framework and Strategies*.
100. Kabir Hassan, Mervyn Lewis (editors), *Handbook on Islamic Banking*, p. 283.
101. Baljeet Kaur Grewal, "Constraints on Growth in Islamic Finance", IFSB 4th Public Lecturer on Financial Policy and Stability Amman Jordan 2011.
102. Nazneen Halim, "The Sleeping Giant" *Islamic Finance News Special Supplement*, pp. 6–7.
103. Ibid, p. 7.
104. Emilio Pera "A Review of the Islamic Finance industry" in Eye on Africa, Ernst & Young, vol. 3, March 2011, pp. 16–18.
105. See Ernst & Young, *Ernst & Young's 2012 Africa attractiveness survey Building Bridges*, www.ey.com, retrieved July 2012, p. 5.

CHAPTER 2

# Islamic Finance: Principles and Global Growth

## Basic Principles of Islamic Finance

There are five major principles that differentiate Islamic finance from conventional finance. These principles are: the prohibition of *ribā* (usury or interest), the prohibition of *gharar* (excessive risk or ambiguity), the prohibition of financing or trading products of illicit sectors in Sharī'ah (such as drugs, alcohol, and pork), the preference of the profit and loss-sharing principle over debt-based products, and the principle that all transactions have to be backed by a real economic transaction that involves a tangible asset.

The above restrictions are balanced by the recognition of Islamic finance of the theory of freedom of contract. Contracting parties can agree on any conditions as long as they do not violate any Sharī'ah ruling. All conditions agreed upon by the parties are upheld except any condition that allows what is prohibited or prohibits what is lawful. This gives a wide scope to create and structure new contracts.

Among the five major principles, the most important distinguishing feature of Islamic finance is the prohibition of *ribā* or interest, which refutes the core principle of conventional finance. Islam is not the first or only religion that opposes usury or *ribā*. At least four of the world's major religions (Judaism, Christianity, Hinduism, and Islam) prohibit interest.[1] Usury is also declared illegal by many ancient nations, such as China, Greece, and Rome. However, one of the momentous changes occurred in


M. Al Bashir M. Al Amine, *Islamic Finance and Africa's Economic Resurgence*, DOI 10.1007/978-3-319-28835-2_2

1545, when "An Act Against Usuries" was promulgated during the reign of King Henry VIII.[2]

The prohibition of *ribā* essentially implies that the fixing in advance of a positive return on a loan as a reward for time is not permitted. It makes no difference whether this amount of interest is big or small, fixed or variable, an absolute amount to be paid in advance or on maturity, or a gift or service to be received as a condition for the loan. It also makes no difference whether the loan was agreed for consumption or business purposes. Thus, in its basic meaning, *ribā* can be defined as anything (big or small) pecuniary or non-pecuniary, in excess of the principal in a loan that must be paid by the borrower to the lender, along with the principal as a condition (stipulated or by custom) of the loan or for an extension in its maturity.[3]

Islam, however, wishes to eliminate not merely the exploitation that is intrinsic in the institution of loan with interest, but also that which is inherent in other forms of dishonest and unjust exchanges in business transactions. Thus, the term *ribā* has a more comprehensive meaning and is not merely restricted to loans. *Ribā* can also arise in sales transactions, which is generally described as *ribā al-buyu*.[4]

Another form of *ribā* arises in the barter exchange of commodities. It refers to the excess taken by one of the trading parties while trading in any of the six commodities mentioned in a well-known authentic *hadith*: "Gold for gold, silver for silver, wheat for wheat, barley for barley, dates for dates and salt for salt, like for like, payment being made hand by hand. If anyone gives more or asks for more, he has dealt in *ribā*."[5]

Connecting the prohibition of *ribā* or interest with its negative social and economic consequences, if there is anyone who should be opposing interest, it should be Africa, given the fact that the continent is one of the regions most badly affected by debt and the payment of interest. A report by the United Nations on Africa's debt profile highlighted that "the continent received some $540 billion in loans and paid back some $550 billion in principal and interest between 1970 and 2002. Yet Africa remained with a debt stock of $295 billion."[6] The report added that Africa's debt burden has been a major obstacle to the region's prospects for increased savings and investment, economic growth, and poverty reduction.[7]

Similarly, Christian Aid, in one of its report ..., noted that since 1996, the world's poorest 66 countries have paid more than US$230 billion between them to service their foreign debt. The amount surpasses the donations and aids they have received from donor countries. Servicing debt rather than spending on healthcare, education and infrastructure has denied many of these countries an opportunity to achieve the millennium development goals as envisaged.[8] In 2000, former Nigerian President Obasonjo spoke about Nigeria's mounting debt to international creditors and the injustice in the payment of interest rates, saying: "If you ask me what the worst thing in the world is, I will say it is compound interest."[9]

However, despite promises of a "sustainable exit from debt crisis," while some countries received significant debt relief under the Heavily Indebted Poor Countries (HIPC) initiative, most countries received little or no debt cancellation, with many facing worse debt problems today, compared to a decade ago, according to Christian Aid.[10] Despite the recognition by many that poor governance in debtor countries is one of several reasons for the debt crisis, the causes behind the debt that is crippling African countries could not be justified under Islamic law or any other religion. Thus, Christian Aid argues that much of the debt accumulated by poor countries is illegitimate because the accumulated debts are odious and based on penalties and exorbitant interest rates.[11] Odious debt, according to Christian Aid, refers to a debt where the original loans were given to corrupt or despotic regimes, where the money was likely to go missing. It is an illegitimate kind of debt because of interest on the arrears and the imposition of financial penalties for late payments.[12]

This ban on interest, agreed upon by all Islamic scholars, is based on the Sharī'ah precept that money has no intrinsic worth. Money can increase in value only if it joins other resources to undertake productive activity. For this reason, money cannot be bought and sold as a commodity, and money not backed by assets cannot increase in value over time. This should not be confused with foreign exchange, which is permissible. Moreover, fund providers must share the business risk. Providers of funds are not considered creditors typically guaranteed a predetermined rate of return, but investors who share the rewards as well as risks associated with their investment.

The Sharī'ah principles also prohibit excessive leverage and speculative financial activities, thus insulating the parties involved from excessive risk exposures. These issues are covered by the prohibition of *gharar* and *maysir* or gambling. The following examples, although not exhaustive, offer a comprehensive idea of what the prohibition of *gharar* implies:

1. Ignorance of the genus: for example, A promising to sell B 1 kg of apples for $5. It involves *gharar* because it is not clear what type of apples are the subject of sale.

2. Ignorance of the species: for example, A promising to sell B a pet for $100.
3. Ignorance of the attributes: for example, A promising to sell B a car for $5000.
4. Ignorance of the quantity of the object: for example, A promising to sell B a box of oranges for $20.
5. Ignorance about price: for example, A promising to sell B a dress for a month's salary.
6. Ignorance of the specific identity of the object: for example, A promising to sell B a flat in a building for $550,000.
7. Ignorance of the time of payment in deferred sales: for example, A promising to buy a house from B for $100,000, to be paid later.
8. Inability to deliver the object: for example, promising to sell a bird sitting in a tree.
9. Contracting on a non-existent object: for example, A promising to sell B the harvest of his farm from the next crop.
10. Not being able to inspect the object: for example, A promising to sell B the contents of a carton for $50.
11. More than one option in a contract unless one is specifically chosen: for example, saying that someone can either take your car for $10,000 or your boat for $15,000. The sale would become valid only after the other person exercised his option and specifically chose which to buy.[13]

As pointed out by Ernst & Young, Sharī'ah restrictions against excessive leverage contributed to the robust performance of Islamic finance during the financial crisis.[14] Similarly, a working paper by the IMF noted that in contrast to most conventional banks, Islamic banks tend to finance their activities out of deposits rather than from wholesale funding, and are thus less subject to the vagaries of the markets. Moreover, Islamic law prohibited Islamic bankers from dealing in second-hand, interest-bearing mortgages—the financial assets at the root of the US subprime property market crisis that precipitated the global crisis.[15]

Islamic finance, however, extends beyond the ban on interest-based and speculative transactions. Additional key financial principles include the principle that Islamic financial transactions must be linked, either directly or indirectly, to real economic activity. This precludes the permissibility of financial speculation, and therefore, activities such as short-selling—as practiced in the conventional system—are considered violations of

Sharī'ah.[16] Emphasising the above principle, the governor of the Central Bank of Malaysia noted that the soundness and viability of Islamic finance are based on the requirement that financial transactions be supported by an underlying productive activity and a close link between financial and productive flows. A transaction must be accompanied by genuine trade or lease-based and business-related transactions. Moreover, providing financing to a venture should be based on a pre-specified profit sharing arrangement. Moreover, Islamic finance also puts explicit restrictions on unethical and speculative financial activities.

Islamic finance encourages risk management and requires explicit disclosure and transparency of the roles and responsibilities defined in the contract. Through its integration with real activities, Islamic finance minimises and manages risk. The real activities, thus, need to generate enough wealth to compensate for such risks. In contrast, according the Governor, conventional instruments generally separate the risks from the underlying assets. As a result, risk management and wealth creation may, at times, move in different—or even opposite—directions. Commoditisation of risks is another problem in the conventional financial system as it will lead towards its proliferation through multiple layers of leveraging and disproportionate distribution that could result in higher systemic risks, increasing the potential for instability and inequitable concentration of wealth.[17]

The next principle in Islamic finance is to avoid financing activities inconsistent with Sharī'ah principles, such as those relating to the consumption of alcohol or pork and those relating to gambling and the development of weapons of mass destruction. In broader terms, Sharī'ah prohibits the financing of any activity that is considered harmful to society as a whole. It is part of Islamic law's broader emphasis on ethics.

Throughout history, societies have drawn on the shared values of their members to limit or curb commercial activities believed to be unethical despite the material profit therein. The belief that business practices should be guided by ethical principles is deeply held in the social norms and legal systems of different countries Thus, the principles of fairness, honesty, responsibility and justice—found throughout the world's ethical systems—apply to financial activities as well as other realms of life. In contrast, the behaviour of financial actors leading up to the crisis represented, in several ways, departures from the ethical principles customarily expected to govern commercial activity.[18]

Under the risk sharing arrangement, the Islamic financial institution will share the profit or loss incurred by the entrepreneur. The real activity is expected to generate sufficient wealth to compensate for the risks. This arrangement, thus, entails appropriate due diligence and the integration of risks associated with the real investment activity with the financial transactions.[19]

Debt-based financing is permitted in Islam, especially for productive assets. Debt for consumption purposes, though permitted through asset-intermediated financing, is discouraged by Islamic economists. Having debts greater than the value of one's assets is considered particularly hazardous. This understanding of the dangers of consumer debt is illustrated by the actions of the Prophet Muhammad (SAW). In a famous incident, the Prophet refused to offer funeral prayers for a member of the community whose debts exceeded his assets, until a person came forward to assume the debts of the deceased. Further, it is reported that the Prophet said, "A believer's soul remains in suspense until all his debts are paid off."[20]He would also say in his prayers, "O God, indeed I seek refuge with you from being overcome with debt."[21] Thus, lending and borrowing—especially for productive economic activity—are important for the functioning of an economy. Debt for consumption, however, should have a limited role, according to the widely held views of Islamic economists.

The Sharī'ah perspective on the securitisation of debt is that the sale of debt that involves interest or *ribā* is impermissible. The discounting of cash flows inherent in the sale of debt (e.g. selling a $100 receivable for $97) is seen as a form of *ribā,* and is therefore prohibited. The implications of the ban on selling debt (*bay' al-dayn*) are sweeping. First, the separation between origination and bearing credit risk is removed, and the originator is forced to assume the credit risk. This will naturally lead to more careful lending. Second, the lack of transfer of the debt would mean that the holders of credit risk would keep track of the actual loans making them better aware of the risks. Rather than relying solely on credit ratings, lenders would have access to information specific to the underlying transactions.[22]

Another fundamental Sharī'ah principle is the ban of any contractual exploitation. Contracts are required to be by mutual agreement and must stipulate exact terms and conditions. Additionally, all involved parties must have precise knowledge of the product or service being bought or sold.[23] It should be clear that Islamic finance is a Sharī'ah-compliant financial system and not a mere profit–loss sharing industry. As emphasised by Umer Chapra, greater reliance on equity does not necessarily mean that debt financing is totally ruled out. .Debt, however, gets created in the Islamic financial system through the sale or lease of real goods and services via the sales-based modes of financing (*murābaḥah*, *ijārah*, *salam*, and *istisnā'*). The predetermined rate of return on sales-based modes of financing may, however, make them look like interest-based products. However, they are not so because of significant differences between the two for a number of reasons.[24]

The suitability of Islamic finance as a viable alternative to conventional finance is not only acknowledged by academicians and practitioners, but also by regulators and central bankers. This emphasises that what sets Islamic finance apart is the degree to which its prohibition on *ribā* requires its adherents to rethink the way they make their money. The sacred principle is that money should not produce money. This commitment is translated in the fact that to every credit extended there should be an underlying asset. Money should be used only to finance the real economy. Adherence to this principle affects the relationship that each nurtures with money, be they an individual or enterprise. An entity cannot borrow more than the total value of its listed shares while a person cannot *de facto* suffer from over-indebtedness. Such principles cannot be harmful to borrowers![25]

Another principle of Islamic finance, very relevant following the global financial crisis, is that uncertainty in contractual terms and conditions is not permissible. All the terms and conditions of a financial transaction need to be clearly understood. This principle has insulated Islamic financial institutions from exposure to toxic assets.[26]

## Islamic Finance: Global Growth and Relevance to Africa

Islamic finance is no longer regarded an infant industry that needs to prove its viability and competitiveness in the global financial environment. The industry has witnessed—particularly after the recent financial and economic crisis—a rapid period of growth, evolution, and expansion. It is increasingly recognised as a viable and competitive form of financial intermediation not only in Muslim countries, but outside the Muslim world, offering a wide range of financial products and services.[27] The industry continues to be an area with great potential.[28] Addressing the issue, the Governor of the Central Bank of Malaysia, in her keynote address at the State Street Islamic Finance Congress, Boston USA 2008, noted that Islamic finance is no longer focusing on retail financing, but is providing a wide range of financial products and services. It is serving not only Muslims but humanity as a whole. The industry has formulated its own accounting, governance, and Sharī'ah standards and has become increasingly internationalised.[29]

From a customer's perspective, Islamic finance is not just a Muslim business; the industry is also very popular with non-Muslim investors. This is witnessed in a number of countries, such as Malaysia, where many of the depositors are non-Muslim. A reported 63 % of HSBC's total Amanah customers in Malaysia, for example, are non-Muslims while in the country as whole, more than 50 % of the industry customers are non-Muslim. In addition, investors buying *ṣukūk or* Islamic bonds, for instance, have overwhelmingly been non-Muslim customers and Islamic financial vehicles are attractive to clients of all faiths.[30] Thus, it has been observed in the case of Hong Kong that although the Islamic community is not large, there is a belief that the development of Islamic finance can take off even in environments in which the domestic Islamic community is relatively small, for the simple fact that "investors nowadays are looking beyond domestic boundaries and traditional finances."[31] Thus, if Islamic finance does not make commercial sense, the participation of non-Muslim individuals or entities would be unlikely. This is a fact recognised by different players in the industry. The Governor of the Central Bank of Mauritius observed that "We must bear in mind that Islamic finance is just finance. It provides an alternative mode of financing that may appeal to all depositors and investors, irrespective of their religious beliefs."[32]

The growth rate of Islamic financial services has outpaced that of conventional banking during the past decade, making it one of the most dynamic areas in international finance. Estimates put the industry growth in the last decade between 20 % and 30 %.[33] According to HSBC, the Islamic finance industry enjoyed a compound annual growth rate for 2006–2009 of 28 %.[34] A much more optimistic recent report held that Islamic finance market has been growing at over 30 % annually since 2000 and is set for continued strong growth.[35] In the Gulf countries, it is estimated that up to 50 % of the consumer population favours Islamic finance.[36]

The number of Islamic banks and financial institutions increased from a single institution in 1974 to several hundred today. According to *The Banker*, "the number of institutions registered to conduct Sharī'ah-compliant activities has risen from 525 in 2007 to 675 in 2011[37] and to 716 institutions in 2012."[38] This rise continued through 2013 and 2014. In recent years, the growth of Islamic banking assets has outstripped that of conventional banking assets. Thus, while conventional banking assets nearly tripled between 2003 and 2008, Islamic banking assets have multiplied sevenfold, albeit starting from a much lower base.[39]

According to *The Banker's* 2014 survey, total assets of Sharī'ah-compliant institutions increased to US$139,166 billion[40] while a much more positive estimate by the international rating agency Standard & Poor's put the assets held by Islamic financial institutions worldwide at about $1.8 trillion, and the industry is likely to sustain double-digit growth over the coming few years, to reach about $3 trillion.[41] Ernst & Young, on the contrary, in its Competiveness Report 2012–2013 stated, "Islamic Banking assets are forecast to grow beyond the millstone of $2 trillion by the end 2014". *The Banker,* in an earlier Special Supplement of the Top 500 Islamic Financial institutions 2011, noted that what is remarkable is that since *The Banker's* Top 500 Islamic Financial institutions survey began in 2007, the growth in the industry assets has maintained a persistent double digit rate, averaging a compound annual growth rate (ACGR) of 18.82 %. Islamic assets rise almost 21.5 % in *The Banker's* survey 2011, surpassing 1000 billion for the first time. By contrast, assets in the Banker's Top 1000 World Banks survey in July 2011 had grown just 6.4 % year on year, and that, after a decline of almost 1 % the year before.[42]

It is also observed by Standard & Poor's that the potential market for Islamic financial services is closer to $4 trillion.[43] This implies that Islamic finance is currently far below its real market share globally, and therefore, has a long way to go to achieve its full potential. Another report by Moody's estimates that the market's potential is worth at least US$5 trillion.[44] The bottom line is that there is great potential growth for the industry, which has already expanded to include private equity, project finance, *ṣukūk*, investment funds, and wealth management activities.

Following the aftermath of the recent financial crisis, the conventional financial system has been crumbling while Islamic finance, although not totally immune, appeared relatively robust. This industry is attracting more and more supporters, some of whom are from unexpected quarters. In an article published in its official newspaper *L'Osservatore Romano* in March 2008, the Vatican argued that banks worldwide should look at adopting the principles of Islamic finance to restore confidence and ease the dangers of excessive credit generation by stating, "The ethical principles on which Islamic finance is based may bring banks closer to their clients and to the true spirit which should mark every financial service."[45]

This hypothesis is supported by a recent empirical study, the results of which show that conventional bank returns were highly volatile during the crisis period, while Islamic banks saw their volatility—initially low—increase during the crisis, though by a much more moderate extent. The results of the study corroborate both the hypothesis that Islamic banks were at least partially immune to the subprime crisis and the underlying hypothesis that Islamic banks are not subject to the same risks as conventional banks due to their links with the real economy, although they did eventually suffer the consequences of the subprime crisis.[46] This is supported by many other studies by different institutions, such as the IMF,[47] Ernst & Young,[48] Standard &Poor's,[49] and many others.

For instance, in order to assess the impact of the crisis, a study by the IMF uses bank-level data covering 2007–2010 for 120 Islamic banks (IBs) and conventional banks (CBs) in eight countries, including Bahrain Jordan, Kuwait, Malaysia, Qatar, Saudi Arabia, Turkey, and the UAE. These countries host more than 80 % of the Islamic banking industry—if we exclude Iran. The key variables used to assess the impact are changes in profitability, bank lending, bank assets, and external bank ratings. The study concluded that in terms of profitability, IBs performed better than CBs in 2008. However, this was reversed in 2009. IBs' growth in credit and assets continued to be higher than that of CBs in all countries, except the UAE. Finally, in terms of risk assessment, as reflected in the rating of banks by various rating agencies, IBs' risk assessment has been better than or similar to that of CBs. Hence, IBs showed stronger resilience, on average, during the global financial crisis.[50]

The phenomenal growth of the Islamic finance industry is clearly reflected in the expansion of the industry in major financial markets outside the Muslim world, particularly in some of the leading industrial economies in the West. In the UK, for example, there are six Sharī'ah-compliant banks and a *Takāful* company. The UK's offering of Islamic financial services encompasses a total of 22 banks. Moreover, professional Islamic finance services are provided by 25 law firms, and all of the Big Four largest professional services firms—PricewaterhouseCoopers, KPMG, Ernst & Young and Deloitte—have each established Islamic finance teams in London.[51] There are 55 institutions offering educational and training products in Islamic finance.[52] At least 16 universities and business schools offered an Islamic-based MBA or similar qualification in 2013, compared to just 9 in 2011.[53] The UK has amended regulations to cater to Islamic banking and finance. Sir Andrew Cahn, former UK Trade & Investment

Chief Executive Officer said, "Despite its origins overseas, Islamic finance has found a natural home in the UK. Though no sector is immune to the global financial crisis, Islamic finance has shown great resilience."[54]

More importantly, Britain has cemented its position as the Western hub for Islamic finance by becoming the first country outside the Islamic world to issue sovereign *Ṣukūk* in 2014 worth £200 million, maturing on July 22, 2019. The issue has been sold to investors based in the UK and in the major hubs for Islamic finance around the world and has seen very strong demand. Total orders were approximately 10 times higher than the amount sold. Allocations have been made to a wide range of investors, including sovereign wealth funds, central banks, and others institutions. The profit rate on the *sukūk* has been set at 2.036 %, in line with the yield on gilts of similar maturity. Based on a lease structure, the *sukūk* will pay out profits based on the rental income from three government-owned properties in lieu of interest.[55] The Chancellor of the Exchequer George Osborne considers the issuance of the first sovereign *Ṣukūk* as part of the government's commitment to become the Western hub of Islamic finance and the undisputed centre of the global financial system in the longer term.[56] The UK's commitment to the industry can be traced back to the 1970s.[57] London's supportive policies are intended to broaden the market. This is clearly reflected in the removal of double tax and extension of tax relief on Islamic mortgages and the reform of arrangements for issues of debt.[58]

Luxembourg is another country taking a positive approach towards Islamic finance. The Governor of the Central Bank of Luxembourg held, "Despite its traditional approach, Islamic finance is a key 'innovation' in the financial area since the seventies."[59] Luxembourg is now the fourth most popular domicile of choice for *Sharī'ah*-compliant funds in the world, with 7 %, after Malaysia (23 %), Saudi Arabia (19 %), and Kuwait (9 %).[60] In terms of tax policies, the tax authorities are looking for solutions in order to have a level playing field and ensure tax neutrality for Islamic transactions, particularly *ṣukūk* and *murābaḥah*. By early 2010, the government of Luxembourg had issued the tax neutrality circular that will ensure *murābaḥah* and *ṣukūk* are treated "like" interest in terms of tax.[61]

Luxembourg strengthened its position in Islamic finance in 2014 by issuing its first €200 million ($254 million) 5-year *Ṣukūk*, with an order book that was more than two times oversubscribed. It becomes the first AAA-rated government to issue euro-denominated ṣukūk. The AAA-rated sovereign priced the *ṣukūk* at a profit rate of 0.436 %, with half of the *ṣukūk* placed with central banks and other official institutions while banks took 40 % of the issue, highlighting the growing appetite for high-rated listed *ṣukūk* that can qualify for use by Islamic banks to help meet their capital adequacy requirements.[62]

Another European country showing strong interest in Islamic finance is France, with nearly two-thirds of French Muslims declaring their willingness to change to an Islamic bank, if available. Most French Muslims keep their savings in current accounts to avoid *ribā* and avoid consumer credit and mortgages.[63] The official position is that it is no longer about introducing the principles of Islamic finance to France, but about implementing the practicalities to make it as convenient as conventional finance. France has already allowed the listing of *ṣukūk* and Islamic mutual funds on the Paris Stock Exchange.[64] The French government has also overhauled its tax laws to facilitate Islamic financial transactions, such as *murābaḥah* and *ṣukūk*.[65] Some French banks, such as BNP Paribās, Société Générale and Calyon, are already offering Islamic products in Middle Eastern countries and could replicate this offering in their local market.[66]

In the Irish Republic, the Department of Finance, the Revenue Commissioners and some of the country's leading accountants are already looking at ways to tap into the Islamic finance industry. There is a vision for the Irish Financial Services Centre (IFSC) to become the European home to Islamic banks and investment funds. The IFSC is already home to a growing number of Sharī'ah funds and the financial regulator has set up a team to specialise in the authorisation of Sharī'ah funds and to foster familiarity between the regulatory system in Ireland and in the Middle Eastern countries.[67]

The USA, which shunned Islamic finance after the September 11 attacks because of misplaced fears over links to terrorist financing, has shown signs of growing interest among investors. According to Maris Strategies, there are 15 institutions with Islamic finance operations in the USA.[68] Investors in the USA have started to invest in *ṣukūk* to gain exposure to the Middle East whilst US companies have also started to use the *ṣukūk* market to raise funds. The *ṣukūk* market reached a milestone in 2009, when General Electric issued a $500 million *ṣukūk*.[69] Recently, Goldman Sachs raised $500 million with its debut sale of *ṣukūk*, becoming the first conventional US bank to issue such certificates. This is another sign that Islamic finance is steadily developing beyond its traditional homes in the Middle East and South-east Asia. The issue drew about $1.5 billion of orders, reflecting heavy demand. The Goldman *ṣukūk* was listed on the Luxembourg Stock Exchange. The *ṣukūk* carries a profit rate of 2.844 %.[70]

In Asia, Hong Kong has strongly embraced Islamic finance. The Chief Executive of the Hong Kong Special Administrative Region, in his Policy Address in 2007, acknowledged that Islamic finance offers huge potential for development and would further consolidate Hong Kong's position as a global financial centre. The Chief Executive maintained that Hong Kong should actively leverage on this new trend by developing an Islamic finance platform. Hong Kong authorities are now focusing their efforts in four areas. First, building Hong Kong's international profile and forging closer ties with market participants in the Middle East. Second, promoting market infrastructure and establishing policies conducive to the development of Islamic finance. Third, disseminating talent and knowledge of Islamic financial principles among market professionals, and fourth, encouraging the development and launch of Islamic finance products in Hong Kong.[71]

An important development in Hong Kong in 2014 was the successful offering of its inaugural US$1 billion *ṣukūk* with a tenure of 5 years, which marks the world's first US$-denominated *ṣukūk* originated by an AAA-rated government. The *ṣukūk* issue saw strong demand, attracting orders exceeding US$4.7 billion, allowing final pricing to tighten by 7 basis points from its initial price guidance. Pricing at a spread of 23 basis points over the corresponding yield of US Treasuries represents the tightest spread ever achieved on a benchmark US$ issuance from an Asian (ex-Japan) government, setting an important new benchmark not only for Hong Kong, but also, for the rest of Asia. The *ṣukuk* was allocated to over 120 global institutional investors, with 36 % of the *ṣukūk* distributed to the Middle East, 47 % to Asia, 6 % to Europe, and 11 % to the USA. By investor type, 11 % was distributed to fund managers, 56 % to banks and private banks, 30 % to sovereign wealth funds, central banks and supranationals, and 3 % to insurance companies.[72] The *ṣukūk* marks the first US$ *ṣukūk* originated by an AAA-rated government in the global Islamic financial market.[73] The *ṣukūk* issuance came after the legislative changes made in Hong Kong in July 2013, which provided a taxation framework for *ṣukūk* issuances comparable to that for issuances of conventional bonds.[74]

Singapore is another prominent financial centre interested in Islamic finance. The Monetary Authority of Singapore has worked to establish a level playing field between Islamic and conventional financing deals. This includes the waiver of additional stamp duties incurred by qualifying Islamic financing arrangements involving immovable property. Other steps taken include providing tax incentives to help offset initial additional set-up costs. In February 2008, a 5 % concessionary tax rate on income derived from qualifying Sharī'ah-compliant financial activities was announced. Singapore has also implemented several measures, including removing the double imposition of stamp duty for Sharī'ah-compliant financing structures, and refining the banking rules to allow banks to offer *murābaḥah* financing and deposits. Singapore-based banks may enter into *murābaḥah* interbank placements and offer *ijārah wa iqtina* financing. Singapore has also taken the initiative to develop a platform to facilitate sovereign-rated *ṣukūk*. Furthermore, the first home-grown Islamic bank in Singapore, the Islamic Bank of Asia (IBA), was set up in Singapore in 2007.[75] Singapore has also issued its first *ṣukūk* in early 2009. This *ṣukūk* is the Sharī'ah-compliant equivalent of Singapore Government Securities (SGS) and is of the highest credit standing. The *ṣukūk* has been given equal regulatory treatment as SGS.[76]

China, the world's most populous nation, has an estimated 80 million Muslims and has recently discovered the opportunities of Islamic finance. It has awarded its first licence for Islamic banking to Bank of Ningxia, which could pave the way for Islamic financing in the vast Chinese retail and wholesale sectors.[77]

Australia is one of the latest countries reviewing its tax laws relating to financial transactions in order to ensure neutrality for the treatment of equivalent Islamic products. The Australian financial services industry has established a working group to review and recommend to the Australian tax authorities how this issue could be mitigated. Discussions on the elimination of double stamp duty on Islamic property and real estate are ongoing in the Australian Parliament. Several Australian financial institutions are already involved in the Islamic finance sector in various capacities. Australia's largest financial group, Macquarie Bank, is providing a $100 million *murābaḥah* facility as part of the capital raising exercise of the Gulf Finance House, the Bahrain-based Islamic investment bank. Similarly, in early 2009, LM Investment Management Ltd., a specialist global Australian income funds manager, launched the first onshore Sharī'ah-compliant real estate fund in the Australian market, investing in a portfolio of real estate assets in different parts of Australia and across a variety of sectors, such as construction, industrial, retail, and residential.[78] A recent study by the Australian Trade Commission (Austrade) pointed to the potential of Islamic finance in Australia and the country's aspirations to be a financial services centre in the region. It is believed that Islamic finance will facilitate further innovation and competition in the wholesale and retail banking sectors and support the Australian Government's commitment towards credit market diversification.[79] This positive approach towards Islamic finance is developing while Australia has a Muslim population of just 365,000. Although the number is small compared to large Muslims communities, it exceeds the combined Muslim population of Hong Kong and Japan and is more than half of that of Singapore. Australia's political stability and geographic position, especially its proximity to the large Muslim populations of the Asia Pacific, present an important base to service this fast-growing sector in the global financial services market.[80]

Japan, another world economic giant, is not indifferent to the growing importance of Islamic finance. The Eastern giant has started taking positive steps towards Islamic finance. Some Japanese financial institutions, such as Nomura, have been involved in Islamic finance in one way or another since the late 1990s, but from outside Japan. In December 2008, the Financial Services Agency of Japan amended the banking regulations to allow banks' subsidiaries to engage in Islamic banking activities. Backed by these changes, two large Japanese banks have established Islamic banking units. Sumitomo Mitsui Banking Corporation launched its Islamic business in London, whilst the Bank of Tokyo-Mitsubishi UFJ Malaysia started an Islamic unit. In the *Takāful* industry, Japan has some experience, especially with Tokio Marine. Recently, there have been some Japanese *ṣukūk* issuers, although from outside Japan.[81] These important developments have taken place in Japan despite the fact that there are only around 10,000 Muslims in a population of 127.3 million.[82] In addition, new Japanese equity indices have been created to meet demand from Islamic investors for access to Japanese investment products that are Sharī'ah-compliant.[83] For example, the S&P Japan 500 Sharī'ah, the S&P/TOPIX 150 (a subset of the S&P Japan 500 Sharī'ah), and The FTSE Sharī'ah Japan 100 Index were introduced. Based on the above and as rightly stressed by Moody's, Islamic investment and financing are flourishing across the board, with the entry of such significant economies as Japan, the UK, and China. This is providing even more credibility to the industry. Africa is no exception to this trend.[84]

Another important sign of the growing globalisation of Islamic finance is the issuance of *ṣukūk* by the International Finance Corporation (IFC). IFC is the private sector arm of the World Bank. The IFC $100 million Hilal *ṣukūk* is an AAA-rated dollar-denominated *ṣukūk*.[85] The multilateral institution issued its second ṣukūk issue in September 2015, with the objective of encouraging growth in developing economies. It is a $100 million issue. It should be noted that IFC carried out its first Islamic finance investment in 1995, supporting a leasing project in Pakistan. So far, IFC has approved about 28 Islamic financing transactions, worth a total of $742 million.[86]

It is clear that Islamic finance as an alternative financial management model continues to flourish. With a predominantly Muslim population of more than half a billion, Islam in Africa has the largest number of practicing followers of any religious group on the African continent, and the demand for Islamic financing should be huge as the continent holds promising growth opportunities. Clearly, Islamic financial services in Africa have a big untapped market and the industry is bound to grow very fast in order to satisfy its clients, both financially and spiritually. Even in countries where Muslims are minorities, there is considerable demand for such services.

Western banks, on the contrary, have long recognised the importance of the emerging Islamic financial markets and are now starting to offer Islamic products through "Islamic windows" or through subsidiaries or full-fledged entities. Islamic windows are not independent financial institutions; rather, they are specialised setups within conventional financial institutions that offer Islamic products provided that they have a segregation of fund, account and have a Sharī'ah Board to supervise their activities. The number of conventional banks offering Islamic windows is growing, and several leading conventional banks such as the Hong Kong and Shanghai Banking Corporation (HSBC) through their brand Amanah, Standard Chartered through Saadiq, or Citicorp Group through their full-fledged subsidiary Barclays ABN Amro, American Express Bank, ANZ Grindlays, BNP Paribas, and Union Bank of Switzerland (UBS) are aggressively pursuing this market with the objective of promoting diverse Islamic products. If global banks such as HSBC, Citigroup, Standard Chartered, PNB Paribās, Deutche Bank Société Générale and other renowned international banks can have Islamic banking subsidiaries or windows, why would well-established conventional banks in the continent not do the same? These institutions are seeking to introduce Islamic financial products to serve their clients, regardless of their religion. They realise that the new industry is already an integral part of the international financial system, constituting an alternative system of financial management. As observed by the IMF, the Islamic finance industry is one of the fastest growing segments of the global financial industry and is too big to be ignored.[87]

It is clear that not being a Muslim country or not having a majority Muslim population is irrelevant. The example of South Africa is a case in point. Although the Muslim population is only 2 %, the level of affluence of this population makes Islamic banking a viable proposition. Thus, the issue is about business and business only and African political leaders and regulatory authorities are obligated to work towards sustaining the current growth and alleviating poverty.

In the midst of the worst financial crisis, the world is desperately looking for a viable solution towards a sustainable financial system; therefore, the Islamic finance industry has an opportunity to become an important stakeholder of the new world financial order to regain trust and build confidence. This is due to its resilience to the global financial crisis and its negative effects.[88] As Ernst & Young rightly pointed out in one of its reports, the case for expansion of the Islamic finance sector is relatively straightforward and the industry is projected to see growing demand from an increasingly wealthy group of Muslim investors.[89]

The direct consequence of the lack of Islamic finance in some African countries is reflected in the perpetuation of informality for a very significant volume of trade, especially in the regions with a Muslim majority. In Nigeria, for instance, it is estimated that money outside the banking system is N250 billion or US$1.95 billion. Moreover, the lack of Islamic finance has contributed to the inaccessibility to capital for trade and home ownership for a large number of the population. Third, its absence has contrib uted to the curtailment of growth or emergence of other vital sectors of the economy, such as the capital market, due to the limited involvement of Muslims in securities markets. This has resulted in limited alternatives for the funding of infrastructure and other developmental projects.[90]

The demand for Islamic finance is not limited to countries where Muslims are majorities. Some of the keenest African customers for Islamic products are people in countries where Muslims are a small minority. The industry could provide these minorities a means of affirming their cultural heritage and being part of the banking and financial system of their countries.[91] Africa is considered a new frontier. With few international Islamic institutions currently active in the market, there are opportunities for growth from a number of areas, including Islamic mortgage products and Islamic personal finance, among others.[92] Government intervention, mainly through legislation and active support, is necessary for the wide-scale establishment and effective development of Islamic banking and finance. In Muslim countries, the authorities actively or passively participate in the establishment of Islamic banks and financial institutions.

Based on the above recognition and attractiveness of Islamic finance at the international level, Islamic finance is no longer a niche market, but an integral part of the global financial system, and, "one of the fastest growing sectors within the global financial services industry."[93] It has a presence in major international financial centres in both the East and the West and has strong support from the regulatory authorities in these centres. As noted by the international advisory PricewaterhouseCooper, "Islamic finance is the fastest growing segment in the world and PricewaterhouseCooper expects this to continue."[94]

The potential for growth of the industry is huge. Of the 1.6 billion Muslims in the world, an estimated 14 % only use banks. By comparison, 92 % of US households use banks, while in the UK, it is 95 %. At the same time, Islamic finance represents about 1 % of the global financial system whilst the Muslim world accounts for 7.6 % of global nominal gross domestic product, according to the Statistical, Economic and Social Research and Training Centre for Islamic Countries (SESRIC). According to SESRIC, growth among the 57 Muslim nations is much higher than the rest of the world. As these emerging Muslim nations grow, more of their citizens will start using banks, and many will want to do so in line with their religion.[95]

Nevertheless, despite enthusiasm for Islamic finance, the industry remains small. More importantly, many Muslims willing to be served by the industry could not get access to such services as they are not available in their respective areas.[96] However, the market has been growing at over 30 % annually since 2000 and is set for continued growth.

According to the October 2009 report compiled by the Financial Access Initiative, nearly all of the 2.5 billion unserved adults live in Africa, Asia, and Latin America. For these regions, the total percentage of unserved adults climbs to 62 % of the adult population. In Sub-Saharan Africa, 80 % of the adult population or 325 million people remain unserved, as compared to only 8 % in high income OECD countries. Billions of people, especially those who live on less than $5 a day, are not using formal financial services. This can inhibit their ability to build wealth, increase their income, and manage uncertainty.[97]

This shortage of financial institutions and lack of access is compounded by the preference of most Muslims for Islamic banks. Many Muslims will only bank with Sharī'ah-compliant institutions. Unfortunately, despite its exceptional growth, the industry seems to be far from satisfying the needs of Islamic products. Given the size of the demand, the most successful entrants will be those that adopt a structured approach to institution-building so that it can be scaled up across segments, sectors, and geographies.[98]

Around 150 additional Islamic financial institutions will be needed globally to satisfy the increasing demand for access to financial services. It is also forecasted by the International management consultancy firm Oliver Wyman that the majority of new Islamic financial institutions—around 135 institutions—are needed in the Muslim world, and the remaining Islamic institutions need to be established in countries with a Muslim population of less than 10 %. Africa is highly expected to be the next area of growth, with Sub-Saharan Africa having the largest room to grow in Islamic finance. The next region will be the Middle East and North Africa, with 25 % of the total Islamic financial services gap. This forecast for the need for Islamic finance shows the great interest that has been generated in Islamic finance on a global scale. Islamic finance has shown great resilience and attracted many. Africa was no exception. On a regional and sub-regional sphere, several countries are struggling to become the hub of Islamic finance in Africa or in their respective sub-region.[99]

Based on the above, it is clear that Islamic finance is now an integrated part of the international financial system. covering all forms of Islamic intermediation such as banking, capital market, money market asset management, private equity, and insurance.

Looking at the different experiences of adoption of Islamic finance around the globe, it can be observed that the introduction to Islamic finance takes different forms. Some countries allow institutions to establish Islamic windows within a conventional system to cater to limited Islamic financial products. Other countries allow fully-fledged Islamic financial institutions to be established to offer a wide range of Islamic financial products. Experience also shows that the development of an Islamic banking system is the initial stage in the development of a complete Islamic financial system. Considering the fact that most countries in Africa are at this initial stage of development of the Islamic financial system, a good start should be through the banking system, whether it is a fully-fledged banking system or an Islamic window. *Takāful* or Islamic insurance is another promising area and could be the following stage that will be followed by capital markets, private equity, asset management, and other sophisticated investment financial products. In short, there are real opportunities for Islamic finance in all segments of the financial system. However, before, looking into the details, let us look at the present penetration of Islamic finance in Africa and the challenges it faces.

## Notes

1. Umer Chapra, "The Case Against Interest: Is It Compelling?" *Thunderbird International Business Review*, vol. 49 (2), March–April 2007, pp. 161–186. Zamir Iqbal & Abbas Mirakhor, *Introduction to Islamic Finance: Theory and Practice*, 2007.
2. Mohammed Iqbal Belath, "Role of Islamic finance in the development of Africa", p. 1.
3. See, Munawar Iqbal and Tariqullah Khan (Editors), *Financial Engineering and Islamic Contracts*, Palgrave, 2005, p. 4.
4. Ibid.
5. Ibid.
6. United Nations, "Economic Development in Africa: Debt Sustainability—Oasis or Mirage?", *South Bulletin*- 90/91, October 30, 2004, p. 21.
7. Ibid, p. 520.
8. Christian Aid, *Enough is enough: The debt Repudiation Option, 2007*, p. 6.
9. Bashir Aliyu Umar, "Islamic Finance in Nigeria: Issues and Challenges", *The Guardian*, January 5, 2011, p. 25.
10. Ibid, p. 3.
11. Ibid, p. 14.
12. Ibid.
13. See, Munawar Iqbal and Tariqullah Khan (Editors), *Financial Engineering and Islamic Contracts*, Palgrave, 2005, p. 4.
14. Edwin Chew and others, "Islamic finance offers capital opportunities", *Capital Agenda Insights*, Ernst & Young February 2011, www.ey.com, retrieved June 2012.
15. Patrick Imam and Kangni Kpodar, *Islamic Banking: How Has it Spread?*, p. 7.
16. Zeti Akhtar Aziz, "Enhancing Interlinkages and Opportunities: The Role of Islamic Finance", *The National Bureau of Asian Research (NBR)*, vol. 18, no. 4, March 2008, p. 9.
17. Zeti Akhtar Aziz Speech by the Governor of the Central Bank of Malaysia, at the Islamic Finance Conference "Islamic Finance in Southeast Asia: Local Practices, Global Impact"; Georgetown University, Washington, DC, October 18, 2007, BIS Review 121/2007, p. 3.
18. Aamir Rehman, "The Relevance of Islamic Finance Principles to the Global Financial Crisis", Panel Discussion on The Evolution of The Global

Financial Crisis from The Current Crisis, Harvard Law School, Islamic Legal Studies Program Islamic Finance Project, March 16, 2009, www.ifp.law.harvard.edu, retrieved June 2011, p. 3.
19. Zeti Akhtar Aziz, "Enhancing Interlinkages and Opportunities: The Role of Islamic Finance", p. 3.
20. Sunan Al Tirmizi, vol. 3, p. 389.
21. See, Sahih Al Bukhari hadith no. 6369; Sunan Abi Dawaood, hadith no. 1555.
22. Aamir Rehman, "The Relevance of Islamic Finance Principles to the Global Financial Crisis", p. 8.
23. Karim, Nimrah, Michael Tarazi, and Xavier Reille, "Islamic Microfinance: An Emerging Market Niche", p. 2.
24. Umer Chapra, "The Case Against Interest: Is It Compelling? "*Thunderbird International Business Review,* vol. 49 (2), March–April 2007, pp. 179–180.
25. Rundheersing Bheenick, Islamic Finance and its Development in Mauritius", Address by the Governor of the Central Bank of Mauritius at the Opening Seminar on Islamic Capital Markets Port Louis, May 19, 2009, BIS Review 62/2009, p. 3, pp. 1–5.
26. Ibid, p. 4.
27. See, Zeti Akhtar Aziz, "Towards Positioning the Islamic finance as an integrated Component of the International Financial System.", Opening speech at the 5th Annual Islamic Finance Summit, London, January 24, 2006, BIS Review 4/2006, pp. 1–4.
28. Josh Martin, "Islamic banking goes global", *The Middle East,* No. 357, June 2005, pp. 50–52.
29. Zeti Akhtar Aziz, "Islamic Finance: A Global Growth Opportunity Amidst a Challenging Environment", Boston, October 6, 2008, Bank of International Settlements Review BIS Review 121/2008, p. 1.
30. David Hodgkinson, "Islamic Finance: Global Perspectives" Speech at the Islamic Finance Intelligence Summit *FT Islamic Finance Forum*, Radisson Edwardian Mayfair Hotel, London, UK, November 7, 2007, pp. 1–3. See also PricewaterhouseCooper *Malaysia Asia Islamic finance* Hub, www.pwc.com, 2008, p. 12, retrieved January 2012.
31. Eddie Yue, Deputy Chief Executive of the Hong Kong Monetary Authority and Executive Board Chairman of the Treasury Markets Association, ": Hong Kong's possible role in Islamic finance at the Hong Kong Showcase on Islamic Finance, Dubai and Amman, May 11–12, 2008, *Bank of International Settlements Review*, (BIS Review) 59/2008, pp. 1–4.
32. Rundheersing Bheenick, "Putting Mauritius on the world's Islamic finance map", Governor of the Bank of Mauritius, at the official launching of

HSBC Amanah Islamic Banking Mauritius, Les Guibies, Pailles, May 5, 2009, BIS Review, p. 2.
33. Jeffrey Woodruff & Raymond Hill, *Demystifying Corporate Ṣukūk*, Fitch Rating, March 5, 2007, www.fitchrating.com, p. 1.
34. Reuters, "HSBC Seeks Big Growth, *Ṣukūk* Pickup in 2010" *Reuters*, http://www.reuters.com, January 15, 2010, retrieved June 2011.
35. Mike Gallgher, "From Niche to Mainstream", *Islamic Banking and Finance*, May 2009. p. 19.
36. See, Josh Martin, "Islamic Banking Goes Global", *The Middle East*, June 2005, Issue 357, pp. 50–52.
37. Joseph DiVanna & Melissa Hancock, "Islamic Finance Roars Again", *The Banker* Special Supplement, *Top 500 Islamic Financial Institutions*, November, 2011, p. 2.
38. Joseph DiVanna & Melissa Hancock, "Islamic Finance Reaches Critical Mass", *The Banker* Special Supplement, *Top Islamic Financial Institutions*, November, 2012, p. 2.
39. Nicolas Hardi and Emanual Volland, Islamic Banking has Reached Critical Mass in the Gulf after Sustained Growth, and Expansion is to continue" in *Islamic Finance Outlook 2010*, Standard & Poor's, Articles publication date December 4, 2009, pp. 20–21.
40. Joseph Divanna& Melissa Hancock, "Islamic Finance Reaches Critical Mass", *The Banker* Special Report November, 2012, p. 2.
41. Standard & Poor, Islamic Finance Outlook 2015, September 2014, www.standardandpoors.com, retrieved on December 2014.
42. Philp Alexender & Guillaume Hingel, "The Big Islamic Finance Opportunities Islamic Banking", *The Banker* Special Supplement, *Top 500 Islamic Financial Institutions*, November, 2011, p. 9.
43. Volland Emmanuael and Mohamed Damak, *Chief Drivers Behind Islamic Finance's Global Expansion Commentary Report* Standard and Poor's, April 2007, pp. 1–2.
44. Anouar Hassoune, *Derivatives in Islamic Finance: Examining the Role of Innovation in the Industry*, Moody's, April 4, 2010.
45. Robin Wigglesworth, "Credit Crunch may test industry beliefs", *Financial Times Special Report*, May 6, 2009, p. 1.
46. Aniss Boumediene & Jérôme Caby, "The stability of Islamic Banks during the Subprime Crisis", *Social Science Research Network*, www.ssrn.com, December 2009, retrieved June 2011, p. 1.
47. May Khamis & others, *Impact of the Global Financial Crisis on the Gulf Cooperation Council Countries and Challenges Ahead*, International Monetary Fund, The Middle East and Central Asia Department Washington, DC, 2010, www.imf.org, retrieved June 2011 p. 66.
48. IFSB-IRTI-IDB, *Islamic Finance and Global Stability Report*, April, 2010, p. 34.

49. Mohamed Damak & Emmanuel Volland, "Islamic Finance is Likely to Advance in 2010 on Firm Growth and Widening Geographic Reach", in *Islamic Finance Outlook 2010* Standard & Poor's, February 1, 2010, p. 10.
50. Maher Hasan and Jemma Dridil, *The Effects of the Global Crisis on Islamic and Conventional Banks: A Comparative Study*, IMF Working Paper, September 2010, p. 6.
51. UK Islamic Finance Secretariat (UKIFS), "UK, the Leading Centre for Islamic Finance", The City UK, October 2013, London.
52. International Financial Services London, *Islamic Finance 2009*, IFSL RESEARCH, WWW.IFSL.ORG.UK, February 2009, p. 1 & *CPI Financial*, "Islamic finance grows in London, rides out worst of crunch", www.CPI.Financial.net
53. UK Islamic Finance Secretariat (UKIFS), "UK, the Leading Centre for Islamic Finance", p. 5.
54. Ibid.
55. Elaine Moore and Thomas Hale, "UK sukuk bond sale attracts £2bn in orders", June 25, 2014, www.ft.com; "Government issues first Islamic bond." www.gov.uk
56. Ibid.
57. For a detailed report on Islamic Finance in the UK, see Ahmed Belouafi, and Abdelkader Chachi, "Islamic Finance in the United Kingdom: Factors Behind its Development and Growth" *Islamic Economic Studies*, vol. 22, no. 1, May, 2014, pp. 37–78.
58. UK Islamic Finance Secretariat (UKIFS), "UK, the Leading Centre for Islamic Finance", p. 5.
59. Yves Mersch, "Islamic finance—partnerships opportunities between Luxembourg and the Arab countries" Speech by Mr. Yves Mersch, Governor of the Central Bank of Luxembourg, at the 5th Economic Forum Belgium-Luxembourg-Arab Countries, Brussels, November 17, 2009, *BIS Review* 149/2009, pp. 1–4.
60. See Ernst & Young's *Islamic Funds* & *Investment Report,* 2009, p. 72.
61. Julia Berris, "Luxembourg guns for LSE's *Ṣukūk* Prestige" *The Lawyer*, www.thelawyer.com, July 27, 2009.
62. Bernardo Vozcaino, "Luxembourg's debut sukuk sees strong demand from government accounts", Reuters, October 1, 2014, www.reuters.com
63. Mathieu Vasseux, *The Next Chapter in Islamic Finance Higher Rewards but Higher Risks* Report by Oliver Wyman, 2009, p. 11. www.oliverwyman.com, retrieved January 2011, p. 10.
64. Isla MacFarlane, "French Fancy" *Islamic Banking and Finance*, March 2009, pp. 36–37.
65. Mushtak Parker, "France Introduces Tax Neutrality laws", *Arab News*, April 6, 2009, www.arabnews.com, retrieved June 2010.
66. Ibid.

67. Thomas Molloy, "Islamic Banking System provides a unique opportunity in tough time", *Irish Independent*, November 5, 2009, www.independent.ie/business/irish, retrieved December 2010.
68. David Oakley, "Dubai Debacles Overshadows Growth", The Future of Islamic Finance *Financial Times* Special *Report*, December 8, 2009, www.ft.com, retrieved March 2010.
69. ALin Van Duyn, "The US hold its Breath on Bonds", *The Future of Islamic Finance*" *Financial Times Special Report*, December 8, 2009, p. 4.
70. Reuters, "Goldman Sachs gets strong demand for landmark sukuk issue" Reuters, September 16, 2014.
71. Eddie Yue, "Islamic finance—its potential to bring new economic growth to Hong Kong", Keynote address by Mr. Eddie Yue, Deputy Chief Executive of the Hong Kong Monetary Authority, for the Hong Kong Islamic Finance Forum, Hong Kong SAR, November 25, 2008, pp. 1–4.
72. Hong Kong Monetary Authority, "HKSAR Government's Inaugural Sukuk Offering", September 11, 2014, www.hkma.gov.hk
73. Ibid.
74. Ibid.
75. Heng Swee Keat, Managing Director of the Monetary Authority of Singapore, at the 5th Annual Islamic Financial Services Board Summit, Amman, Jordan, 13 May 2008, "Monetary Authority of Singapore's initiative to develop Singapore dollar sovereign-rated *Ṣukūk*" *BIS Review*, 63/2008, pp. 1–5.
76. Heng Swee Keat, "Singapore's commitment to the development of Islamic finance" Opening remarks at the Singapore ṣukūk Signing Ceremony, Singapore, January 19, 2009, *BIS Review 9/2009*, pp. 1–2.
77. David Oakley, "Dubai Debacles Overshadows Growth", p. 1.
78. Mushtak Parker, "Australia is opening up to Islamic finance", *Arab News*, December 28, 2009, www.arabnews.com, retrieved June 2011.
79. The Australian Trade Commission (Austrade), *Islamic Finance*, January 2010, www.austrade.gov.au, retrieved March 2011, p. 5.
80. Ibid.
81. Etsuaki Yoshida, "Country Presentation: JAPAN" IFN 2009 Asia Forum, Mandarin Oriental Kuala Lumpur, August 3–5, 2009 & Etsuaki Yoshida "The Development of Islamic Finance in Japan", *Islamic Finance News*, vol. 6, Issue 40, October 9, 2009.
82. Etsuaki Yoshida, "The Development of Islamic Finance in Japan", *Islamic Finance News*, vol. 6, Issue 40, October 9, 2009, p. 13.
83. The Australian Trade Commission (Austrade), *Islamic Finance*, p. 5.
84. Anouar Hassoune & Adel Satel, *Islamic Finance Explores New Horizons in Africa*, p. 5.

85. See, Nasir Saidi, "Islamic Finance is coming of Age: IFC lists ṣukūk in the DIFC", November 7, 2009, www.zawya.com, retrieved June 2011.
86. Riham Mustafa, "IFC Launches $100 million Sukuk to Support Private Sector Development", www.ifc.org, September 10, 2015.
87. Islamic Banks: More Resilient to Crisis?" *IMF Survey Magazine online*, October 2010, www.imf.org, retrieved June 2011.
88. Ekmeleddin Ihsanoglu, Key note Address In Enhancing Economic Cooperation Among Muslim Countries, "The Role of OIC", Ekmeleddin Ihsanoglu Secretary General, Organization of Islamic Conference, *IIUM Journal of Economics and Management*, The International Islamic University Malaysia, no. 1 (2009): 13–30.
89. Edwin Chew and others, "Islamic finance offers capital opportunities, *Capital Agenda Insights*, Ernst & Young, www.e.y.com, February 2011, retrieved June 2012.
90. Femi Sunmonu & Associates, Barristers & Solicitors, "Islamic Financial Services in Nigeria", *Islamic Finance News Guide 2007*, pp. 90–92.
91. *The* Economist, "Turning towards Mecca Islamic banks join in the race for Africa".
92. John Lee & Others *Frontiers in Finance Supplement Islamic Finance: The New Agenda* KPMG, October 2010, www.kpmg.com, retrieved January 2011.
93. KPMG, *Development of an Islamic Bond Market in Hong Kong what are the tax implications?* March 2009, p. 3. www.kpmg.com, retrieved January 2011.
94. PricewaterhouseCooper, *Malaysia Asia Islamic Finance Hub*, 2008, p. 3, www.pwc.com, retrieved January 2011.
95. David Oakley, "Dubai Debacles Overshadows Growth", p. 4.
96. Baljeet Kaur, "Global Overview: Issues, Challenges and Opportunities", *Prospects and Challenges in the Development of Islamic Finance for Bangladesh*, Islamic Financial Services Board, 2014, www.ifsb.org, retrieved December 2014.
97. Alberto Chaia and Others, *Half of the World is Unbanked*, p. 1.
98. Greg Rung & Others, Islamic Finance: Building 150 Financial Institutions by 2020, Oliver Wyman Financial Services, 2011, p. 3. www.oliverwyman.com, retrieved May 2011.
99. Ibid, p. 5.

CHAPTER 3

# Islamic Finance in Africa: Current Penetration

As highlighted in the introduction, there are many reasons for the success of Islamic finance in Africa, among which the fact that half of Africa's one billion population is Muslim and that there is a high percentage of unbanked—especially among those who demand a Sharī'ah-compliant financial system. However, the industry is far from reaching its real potential. Moreover, there is growing support from regulators and political leaders across the continent for greater trade with the Muslim world, for which Islamic finance is increasingly recognised as an important facilitating tool. At the same time, Islamic finance will help attract deposits from new customers and boost the banking industry throughout Africa.[1] Africa is home to one billion people, 41 % of whom are under the age of 15, with 52 cities with at least one million inhabitants, a mobile phone penetration of approximately 50 %, over 300 million people now classified as "middle class" (up 27 % from 2000), and with 60 % of the world's arable land that has yet to be cultivated. It possesses approximately 10 % of the world's oil reserves, 40 % of gold reserves, and 80–90 % of chromium and platinum group metals. Average inflation during the 2000s was 8 %, down from 22 % in the 1990s. According to the International Monetary Fund (IMF), inflation has moderated from 10 % at the end of 2011 to less than 8 % at the end of 2012.[2] Average government debt as a percentage of GDP was 59 % in the 2000s, compared to 81.9 % in the 1990s.[3] Such statistics have encouraged giant financial institutions to explore opportunities in many African countries, based on their belief that "Islamic banking will be good for the African economy."[4]



M. Al Bashir M. Al Amine, *Islamic Finance and Africa's Economic Resurgence*, DOI 10.1007/978-3-319-28835-2_3

Standard Chartered perceives Islamic finance as its fastest growing market segment and aims to double its African income to US$2.5 billion within the next 5 years. The growth will include increasing headcount past its current 7000 and adding another 100 branches across the continent by 2015, from the present 160. It is also looking into exploring the possibility of entering fast-growing markets, such as Senegal, Mozambique, Ethiopia, and South Sudan. Seven of the sixteen African countries in which Standard Chartered operates generated revenues of over US$100 million each in 2011.[5] In a recent report on the banking sector in Africa, Standard Chartered stressed that it is planning to provide Islamic banking services in East and West Africa, an area of growing interest for African financial markets. Moreover, it is projected that by the end of this decade, it is quite possible that Islamic banking could grow to account for up to 10 % of banking assets in countries such as Kenya and Nigeria. Therefore, the bank is using its expertise and contacts to facilitate the development of Islamic banking in the region.[6]

An editorial by *Islamic Finance News* entitled "Africa the Sleeping Giant" stressed that many see Africa as the next Islamic finance haven, considering the growing saturation of the GCC and Asian markets, and the limited enthusiasm from countries in North America and most European countries. Africa is considered to be the sleeping giant which, when awoken, could allow the Islamic finance industry to achieve its full potential.[7]

Although penetration statistics of Islamic finance in Africa are regularly changing, what is certain is that there is a huge untapped potential. This has led KPMG to report Africa as the new frontier, with few international Islamic institutions currently active in the market.[8]

## Islamic Finance in North Africa

The northern part of the continent includes Egypt, Algeria, Morocco, Tunisia, Libya, and Mauritania. Theoretically, the region is expected to lead Islamic finance in Africa, not only because the vast majority of the population is Muslim, but also due to its early exposure to Islamic finance—with Egypt being the birthplace of modern Islamic finance—through the establishment of Mit Ghamr Bank in 1963. Interestingly, this initial experiment was short lived and the region has a relatively underdeveloped Islamic financial industry.

After decades of reluctance and lost opportunities, governments in the region have started to perceive Islamic finance as an opportunity for creating capital and fostering economic development. Despite limited political support so far, there is a sense that this will change due to the tangible benefits of foreign direct investment inflows and the opportunity of "banking the unbanked." Islamic financial institutions should consider having a real interest in the alternative asset classes offered by North African economies as potential investments for new clients and as a mean to recycle the excess liquidity of the Gulf into profitable asset classes compatible with Islamic precepts in a promising and underexploited region.[9] Nevertheless, though the prospect of Islamic finance in the region is promising, the industry is not yet popular due to lack of information and higher taxation on Islamic products. Moreover, progress is retarded by the dominant misconception that Islamic financial institutions are associated with Islamic political parties.

Overall, North Africa's contribution to global Islamic banking assets stood at approximately 1 % as of mid-2013, according to Standard and Poor's. Until recently, this minimal growth has been linked to the low-key presence of Islamic finance in the public debate. Islamic finance was, at best, exotic for regulators and financial sector practitioners. Now, perceptions are changing and public awareness is increasingly supporting the belief that Islamic finance could make significant advances in North Africa over the coming years.[10]

The asset-backing principle embedded in Islamic finance and the significant infrastructure needs in North African countries could work hand-in-hand. Moreover, traditional financiers have been very active in infrastructure financing in North Africa, with total commitments exceeding US$4.9 billion in 2012, according to Standard and Poor's. However, the capacity of these institutions to satisfy the full demand for infrastructure financing is limited. Several projects in renewable energy, transport infrastructure, and communication are ongoing or expected to be launched in the near future. Therefore, North African countries will need to attract additional financing sources. Islamic finance, through its *sukūk* and other products, could be a good fit for infrastructure and project finance, helping to diversify investors' base and tap an additional pool of resources for the long-term funding that these projects require.[11]

### *Islamic Finance in Egypt*

Although only 3–4 % of its banking industry is Islamic, Egypt is likely to remain a country with great opportunities for Islamic finance, not so much because it is its birthplace, but because it is the sixth-biggest Muslim nation, with over 80 million people. There are many factors negatively impeding the growth of Egypt's Islamic finance—not least among which is the issue of tax. There has yet to be any significant effort to address the tax obstacles. Islamic finance is not engaged in mere lending, but real economic transactions such as sale, purchase, or leasing, which incur additional tax on capital gains.[12] The reluctance to support Islamic finance is also enshrined in the tax code, with successive Egyptian government making no effort to address inherent obstacles in the implementation of Islamic financial transactions.

During the last decade, the Central Bank of Egypt has been unable to issue regulations for the Islamic banking industry, thereby preventing the creation of Islamic banks. Investment laws provide no special rules for Islamic asset management and approvals to launch Islamic funds are rare, resulting in a dearth of Islamic private equity. Meanwhile, the absence of a secondary market for short-term investors to sell Islamic products has deterred institutional investors. Moreover, Islamic finance received a setback when Sheikh Mohammed Sayed Tantawi issued a fatwa, stating that simple bank interest was permissible. The fatwa has effectively sidelined the need for Islamic finance by giving conventional banking religious approval. Based on the above reasons and others, to date, Egypt has just three fully-fledged Islamic domestic banks, and an absence of any international bank offering Islamic products. The three Islamic banks are:

- Faisal Islamic Bank of Egypt (FIBE): was founded in 1979 as the first bank in Egypt to operate entirely in accordance with Sharī'ah principles.[13] Despite the bank's recent successes, the CBE's refusal to allow the opening of new branches has prevented it from expanded its network. This has reportedly led to the overcrowding of FIBE's existing branches.[14]
- Al Bakara Bank Egypt: is a subsidiary of the Bahrain-based Al Baraka Banking Group and was previously known as the Egyptian Saudi Finance Bank.[15]
- The National Development Bank of Egypt: restructured into an Islamic bank in 2010 after the Abu Dhabi Islamic Bank, the second-largest Islamic bank in the Emirates, acquired a 51 % stake for US$28 million under the Egyptian government's privatisation drive.[16]

There is no denying that Egypt has impressive growth prospects. According to industry experts, a government-backed Islamic finance market could grow by up to 50 % in 3 years, driven by the possibility of Gulf-based banks importing their cash and expertise. Some predict that within 5–7 years, Islamic finance could control at least 30–40 % of the Egyptian financial sector. Islamic banks in the Gulf are already anticipating the day when their home markets are saturated, and Egypt is at the forefront of plans to develop regional Islamic banking.[17]

For Egyptian individuals, as is the case with many in different Muslim countries, religion is a very important factor in people's daily lives—including their earnings and savings. Most would prefer to deposit into an Islamic bank, even with poor service quality, uncompetitive returns, or limited accessibility.[18] This could explain the high percentage of unbanked in Egypt, which has led some to describe it as a cash-based society, with a small percentage of Egyptians having a bank account.[19]

The prospects of Islamic finance in Egypt are not limited to banking; potential also exists in non-banking Islamic financial services. Even before the revolution, there were tentative moves to expand the market, with the Egyptian Financial Supervision Authority (EFSA) planning to issue its first Islamic debt guidelines in 2011. Islamic mutual funds have the potential to grow, given the right incentives, and this could in turn push companies to modify their financial strategies to be eligible for Islamic portfolios. Islamic private equity is another prospective growth area, which, according to some observers, has a potential value of over US$100 billion in direct investment, especially in the area of infrastructure projects, education, and innovation. Islamic private equity could influence parties to push for the fighting of corruption and the enforcement of laws. Opportunities also exist in the arena of microfinance. In a country where 40 % of the population still lives on less than US$2 per day, microfinance has the potential to make a considerable impact in terms of poverty eradication, financial inclusion, and economic development.[20] However, these opportunities can only be realised within politically conducive and secure environments. As rightly noted by one observer, when democracy is in place, public freedom will lead to a knowledge-driven economy. Corruption will be gradually reduced and law will be enforced. Such a favourable environment will encourage entrepreneurship, reduce costs of new direct investments, and encourage private equity initiatives. It is the ideal environment for the growth of Islamic finance.[21]

Unfortunately, despite high expectations following the fall of Mubarak and the election of Morsi as president and his subsequent removal from office by his defence minister, progress towards the adoption of Islamic finance in the country has been slow and disappointing. There has been no genuine effort to address major obstacles to the industry, such as regulations for the industry, addressing the tax obstacles, or initiating an intellectual and scholarship debate on the issue of *ribā* and the characteristics of the Islamic alternative. The only positive move so far was on the possibility of issuing *ṣukūk*. However, even this initiative has been surrounded by controversies—ranging from political manoeuvres and wrangling due to lack of expertise and confusion over Sharī'ah compliance. There have been polemical debates whether the *ṣukūk* are intended to plug the deficit gap or to finance new projects and whether they should be asset-backed, and therefore, similar to unsecured bonds. These problems are not expected to be resolved soon, given the nature of the Egyptian political scene following the "revolution," the wide difference of opinion among various Sharī'ah scholars regarding Islamic finance, and the role of Al-Azhar in the development of Islamic finance in the country after decades of marginalisation and lack of practical expertise in the new field. It is based on this background that the Egyptian Central Bank has so far refused to issue licences for the establishment of new standalone Islamic banks.[22]

### *Islamic Finance in Morocco*

Morocco is another African country with great potential. Until recently, efforts towards the implementation of Islamic finance in the kingdom were driven by a cautious political will, with Islamic banks being considered by some in the kingdom to be tied to Islamic political parties—consequently, resulting in the refusal of licences.[23] However, in October 2007, Bank al-Maghrib, the country's central bank, permitted the use of *ijārah* and *murābaḥah* and *mushārakah* under the concept of "alternative products" rather than Islamic banking products.[24] This is perhaps a response to popular public demand for interest-free financial transactions. These products are aimed at integrating demand for such products into the official financial system rather that developing a genuine and officially recognised Islamic banking industry. The three approved products are globally recognised and are approved by some major European and US banks. Such international recognition likely contributed to a level of comfort among regulators with the products. The regulatory requirements encompassing these "alternative products" are offered by established commercial banks as traditional financial and banking products, given the absence of a full-fledged Islamic bank in Morocco. Moreover, the central bank leaves it to each bank to choose the manner it deems most appropriate for marketing these products, either through its regular agencies, special windows, or through specialised branches. Moreover, the authorised "alternative products" are concerned solely with financing and not banking deposits.[25] Another obstacle facing these products is that they are treated like any conventional banking service. For example, the *ijārah* product, which may involve property financing, is treated by the tax authority as a product subjected to 20 % value added tax (VAT).[26] Similarly, *murābaḥah* is considered a credit account for tax purposes and is subjected to a 10 % VAT. However, in January 2010, the VAT on alternative banking products such as *murābaḥah* and *ijārah* was reduced to 10 %, as opposed to the previously charged 20 %.[27] Given the fact that the profit margin is subject to VAT, Islamic products will be more expensive than conventional banking products, rendering them less attractive.

The introduction of "alternative products" between 2007 and 2011 was limited and considered a subdued experimentation with Islamic banking products by some Moroccan institutions. Only a small handful of conventional banks and institutions in the country launched *ijāra*, *mushāraka*, and *murābaḥah* products. The experiment failed to gain proper momentum in Morocco due to taxation issues, public perception that the products lacked Islamic authenticity, and regulatory constraints on bank promotion and marketing of alternative financial products. *Murābaḥah* was the dominant product during this period, with all alternative banking products during this period not exceeding MAD one billion (approximately US$120 million).[28]

In May 2010, Dar Assafa, a subsidiary of Attijariwafa Bank, received approval from Bank Al-Maghrib to offer Islamic products based on *murābaḥah* contracts. Since its establishment, Assafaa Litamwil has marketed a range of alternative financial products. All its products are based on *murābaḥah* contracts and target individuals.

The drive for Islamic finance in Morocco accelerated after a moderate Islamist-led government took power through elections in late 2011.[29] In January 2013, the kingdom finalised and adopted a new securitisation law that will allow the state and companies to issue *ṣukūk*. The introduction of *ṣukūk* in Morocco will pass through the reform of the country's securitisation law—enacted in 2002 and amended in 2010—to broaden the range of eligible assets and allow institutions other than banks to use securitisation.

The pace of reform aimed at strengthening Islamic finance in the kingdom has culminated in the parliament's final approval of an Islamic finance bill that will allow the creation of full-fledged Islamic banks in November 2014. The law also contains provisions on *takaful*.[30] Some of the main features of the new law include:

- The new banking law will allow the creation of any alternative financial product that is consistent with Sharī'ah provisions. It will allow the creation of participatory banks (i.e. Islamic banks), which will be licensed by the central bank.
- Conventional banks will also be allowed to offer the same products to their customers. The new law defines some of them—*murābaḥah*, *mudārabah*, *mushārakah*, and *ijāra*—but other products will also be allowed. All products must be approved by the central Sharī'ah board.
- It is also reported that Morocco seeks to unify *fatāwā* for Islamic finance under the Central Shariah Board (which will follow the Maliki School of jurisprudence), with the secretariat based at the central bank.
- Conventional insurance companies will not be allowed to open *takaful* windows; *takaful* operations must be separated and operate out of a different branch.
- Members of the Central Shariah Board for Islamic finance will be appointed from the Supreme Council of Scholars, with the secretariat based at Bank Al-Maghrib.
- According to Bank Al-Maghrib, there will be no restrictions as to who can apply for participatory banking licences. However, joint ventures between local banks and foreign investors might be encouraged.[31]

This law officially permits Islamic banks to operate in Morocco. Conventional banks will also be able to offer Islamic banking windows. For the first time in Morocco, Islamic banking is legally recognised and being put on an equal footing with conventional banking. This includes the taxation of Islamic financial products. The approval of the new law follows the introduction of law number 119-12 in September 2013, which allows sovereign and corporate bodies to issue *ṣukūk*.

Prior to the adoption of the new law, there were already signs that Morocco's biggest banks were preparing to take advantage of the legal changes. For instance, Banque Populaire plans to establish an Islamic subsidiary bank, with the hope of opening 60 big branches over the space of 4–5 years, with a concentration on Islamic products for individuals rather than corporate or small and medium-sized enterprises. Attijariwafa Bank, which is the biggest bank in Morocco and the third largest in Africa, also plans to create an Islamic bank. The Banque Marocaine du Commerce Exterieur (BMCE) and the Banque Centrale Populaire (BCP) have expressed similar interests.[32] From outside Morocco, it is reported that some Gulf banks from Kuwait, Bahrain, and the United Arab Emirates have expressed interest in entering the Moroccan market.[33]

With banking penetration around 40–45 %, a large part of the Moroccan population remains unbanked. Some of those unbanked avoid taking out loans or opening savings accounts for religious reasons, thereby underscoring the potential for Islamic banking. Some analysts further argue that Morocco is keen to attract investment from the Gulf by issuing *ṣukūk* to finance infrastructure projects in the kingdom. A recent research[34] offers evidence of healthy demand for Islamic banking in Morocco, whereby 98 % expressed interest in Islamic finance, 88 % of retail consumers expressed interest in Islamic banking, and 87 % said they would switch to Islamic banking within 2 years.[35]

Despite the optimism, it is observed that among the challenges that still need to be addressed are: poor public knowledge of Islamic finance, the lack of individuals trained in Islamic banking in the country, the fact that converting existing banking talent and training new resources will require time and money, and the need to ensure that *Sharī'ah* principles are not compromised for the sake of elimination of risks, thereby putting the credibility of the industry at risk.[36]

A report entitled *Islamic Finance in Morocco—Sizing the Retail Market* by IFAAS (Islamic Finance Advisory & Assurance Services) pointed to the strong interest from local consumers towards Islamic Finance products and services. Over 80 % of the kingdom's consumers indicated their likelihood to take up a Sharī'ah-compliant financing product if such products are launched. According to the report, the majority of consumers are dissatisfied with interest-based banking, but due to the absence of Islamic alternatives, many are compelled to engage in conventional finance. Thus, it is believed that the introduction of Islamic finance will result in significant growth in the penetration of banking and finance products among consumers in the kingdom.[37]

It is interesting to note that nine out of ten among the institutions surveyed by the Moroccan financial market authority expressed interest in issuing *ṣukūk,* if legally permitted. The issuance of *ṣukūk* can also be supported by Morocco's political stability and investment grade rating with S&P assigning the kingdom a foreign currency rating of BBB-, the second highest in Africa after South Africa's BBB. The country can also count on a vibrant domestic investor community. The volume of assets managed by Moroccan mutual funds amounted to Dh 241bn (US$28bn) in 2012, more than a quarter of the country's GDP, according to the Association des Sociétés de Gestion et Fonds d'Investissement Marocains (ASFIM)—the professional association of Moroccan OPCVM (mutual funds) managers.[38]

## *Islamic Finance in Algeria*

To date, there are three Islamic financial institutions in Algeria. They are two banks and one Takāful company: El Baraka Bank, al-Salam Banque, and Salama Assurance, controlling approximately 5 % of the private market and 1.5 % of the public sector market. Two foreign entities—Abu Dhabi Islamic and Haider Islam—are said to be looking for possibilities to enter the Algerian market. However, among the reported obstacles slowing the development of Islamic finance in Algeria are the partnership rules of 49–51 % and the minimal capital requirement of €100 million.[39] Worth noting is the report that the authorities in Algeria have started reviewing banking laws to better address Islamic finance without announcing deadlines or target dates for its finalisation or introduction. Tax regulations are also being reviewed to avoid double taxation in cases of temporary transfer of ownership.[40] Following the 2010 important legislative development in Algeria, with the adoption of the amended version of the Law of Money and Credit, there is growing optimism about the future of Islamic finance in the country. The law was amended in May 2010 with the objective of making it easier for banks to offer both conventional and Sharī'ah-compliant finance and enable them to establish their own respective Sharī'ah board. Enthusiasm for Islamic finance is further supported through a growing number of conferences to promote its cause.[41]

## *Islamic Finance in Tunisia*

Founded in 1983, Al Baraka Bank Tunisia is the oldest Islamic financial institution in Tunisia. It is an offshore institution known before 2009 as Bank Et-tamweel Al-Tunisi Al-Saudi. Tunisia recently launched its first Islamic bank, Banque Zitouna, with a capital of US$30 million. The bank started with nine branches and anticipates positive future growth.[42]

Its number of branches is reported to have reached 30 by the middle of 2012. Following the revolution, the central bank seized control of the bank assets, with the state now owning 87 % of the bank's capital, with the remaining owned by private shareholders.[43]

It is believed that the new political atmosphere of freedom following the recent revolution will positively influence the development of Islamic finance in Tunisia in the long term. In March 2012, the Tunisian government established the Council of Islamic Finance in coordination with the Ministry of Finance to establish a legislative framework for the development of the industry by looking at existing Islamic financial hub models and attract new market entrants. The council includes representatives from the central bank and stock exchange as well as institutions from the private sector, such as the Bahrain-headquartered Al Baraka banking group. There is also a government plan to provide tax advantages for Islamic financial institutions to create a level playing field with conventional institutions.[44] A market research in Tunisia conducted in May 2010 showed that 72 % of the population thought it is important for banks to offer Islamic products.[45] As noted by a number of observers, there is considerable potential for Islamic finance in Tunisia; however, much will depend on the future growth of the Tunisian economy and the ability of its new government to provide a favourable environment for the development of the industry.[46]

Among recent developments in Islamic finance in Tunisia is the launch of the country's first Islamic mutual fund—Theemar. Capitalised at approximately US$30 million, the fund seeks to finance SMEs and to create enterprise. Shareholders comprise the Islamic Development Bank, Kuwait Project Company, Al Baraka Bank, and the Caisse des Dépôts et Consignations, which is a public fund set up by the Tunisian government to finance big infrastructure projects.[47]

### *Islamic Finance in Mauritania*

In Mauritania, the banking structure regroups four Islamic banks. An estimated 40 % of the money in Mauritania circulates outside banks. Numerous businessmen in Mauritania regard most traditional banking operations as illicit due to their use of interest. There have been several uneventful attempts at opening Islamic banks in Mauritania due to structural or financial reasons.[48]

One of the recent Islamic banks introduced in Mauritania is the Banque Islamique de Mauritanie (BIM), which is one of the four West African banks falling under the Dakar-based Tamweel Africa Group. BIM is a start-up universal bank with a paid-up capital of MRO 6,000,000,000, equivalent to US$ 21,201,401. Tamweel Africa Holding, the main shareholder of BIM (99.99 %) is a joint venture between the ICD (60 %), the private sector arm of the Islamic Development Bank Group, and Bank Asya (40 %), the leading participating bank in the Republic of Turkey. The Banque Populaire de Mauritanie (BPM) is another recent Islamic bank in the country. It is 100 % owned by Groupe Mauritanie Leasing, one of Mauritania's largest financial services groups, and focuses on servicing the specific credit needs of small and medium enterprises (SMEs) as well as private customers.[49]

### *Islamic Finance in Libya*

Libya has a population that is almost entirely Muslim. Unfortunately, until recently, Islamic finance in the country has not developed.[50] This situation was prevailing despite the fact that the Libyan retail consumer attitude towards the potential use of Islamic finance has been very encouraging. A recent study concluded that most of the respondents (85.9 %) are potential users of Islamic finance products and are religiously motivated.[51]

Before the recent Libyan crisis, the government was moving towards the liberalisation of the country's financial system and part of this process foresaw the contribution of Islamic financial institutions, products, and services.[52] An important move was the Islamic Banking Law number 9, issued by the Central Bank of Libya (CBL) in June 2009, allowing commercial banks to open Islamic windows or full-fledged Islamic subsidiaries. CBL regulations also address the issue of the Sharī'ah Board and the basis of accounting to be used by Libyan commercial banks. It has adopted for that purpose the Accounting & Auditing Islamic Financial Institutions (AAOIFI) and the Islamic Financial Services Board (IFSB) standards. Islamic branches and windows have to be independently managed and accounted for in reporting to the CBL. The CBL defined *murābaḥah*, *mushārakah*, *mudārabah*, *al salam*, *ijārah*, and *istisnā'* as the first Islamic products to be introduced.[53] In 2010, the CBL invited bids from foreign banks for joint ventures and to provide a wider range of banking services at more competitive prices to help the Libyan economy. Three European banks—Unicredito SpA, HSBC, and Standard Chartered—were shortlisted, together with three Arab banks—Qatar Islamic Bank, Mashreq Bank, and Emirates NBD (National Bank of Dubai). These institutions prepared licence bids by June 2010 and were evaluated by the CBL. Qatar Islamic Bank is a full Sharī'ah-compliant bank while the two other Arab banks have Islamic banking subsidiaries The second initiative in January 2011 was by Gumhouria Bank, the second largest bank in Libya, with assets worth US$6.46 billion, 5800 employees, and 142 branches. It merged in 2008 with the Al Ummah Bank. Gumhouria Bank was planning to establish a subsidiary that would offer Islamic financial products and convert seven of its branches to exclusively supply these products. Although these developments may have been delayed by the disruption caused by the February 2011 events and its aftermath, momentum had been established.[54] Just before the start of the civil war, several banks had introduced some sort of Islamic offerings through their existing networks, with plans to develop these further. Gumhouria Bank had an Islamic banking window in their 150 branches and one full-fledged Islamic branch. It planned another seven branches by 2011. In 2011, the CBL announced the formation of a committee comprising different banks in the country to prepare a law allowing the sale of Islamic bonds (*ṣukūk*).[55] Several years since the outbreak of the civil war, regulatory and infrastructure problems remain a challenge for Libya's banking sector. The prolonged civil and military unrest means the nation's economic potential might not be realised for a long time to come. Reforms have been slow to emerge and are generally uncoordinated. Some have gone to the extent of suggesting that the environment for banks has worsened, with additional pressures from the precarious security situation and hastily drawn-up revolutionary legislation.[56]

The real shake-up to the Libyan financial system took place in January 6, 2013, when the General National Congress took the drastic and unexpected move of passing a law that not only introduced Islamic banking, but banned interest on financial transactions. Although the law has yet to come into effect, once implemented, banks will no longer be allowed to pay or receive interest from individuals. Companies and state entities will be prohibited from receiving and paying interest from the beginning of 2015. However, considering the continuing unrest in the country up to this moment, it is not expected that such a law will come onto effect anytime soon. The law did not stipulate when the transition would start. It is believed that although the move could be popular, given the fact the Libya's population are generally practicing Muslims, the law could be problematic from a practical perspective. A short period of just 2 years to become fully Sharī'ah-compliant could create confusion. This has led some to suggest that this law was drafted without proper study on how the banking sector is going to be affected.

The law has been criticised by institutions such as the IMF noting that the new legislation could damage the economy and further isolate Libya's economy. It has also warned that the ban could constrain the private sector efforts to invest and create employment, given the fact that the proper foundations for Islamic finance are not yet in place. The IMF also cautioned that the hasty legislation could pose risks to the financial sector and paralyse financial intermediation unless Shariah-compliant instruments and institutions are operational. It could also reduce access to credit for start-ups, entrepreneurs, and SMEs.[57] Meanwhile, although the banking sector appears well-capitalised, it may be vulnerable to asset quality deterioration.[58]

The above panorama of Islamic banking and finance in the North African region clearly identifies several factors retarding the progress of Islamic finance. Among others, the following are some of these obstacles:

1. Until recently, governments in the region have not been strong advocates of Islamic banking and finance, in contrast to some Gulf and Asian countries, where central bank authorities have acted in some instances as the main driving force behind the emergence of such practices in their respective countries. The political and regulatory authorities in North Africa have been relatively reluctant to support the development of Islamic finance as some continue to perceive this mode of financing as politically loaded. In other words, the political choices that have decelerated the emergence of Islamic finance in North African countries have cultural and religious dimensions. And as is rightly pointed out by one observer, "Islamic finance could not develop without political backing."[59]
2. The above political and regulatory constraints have also been backed by religious opinions from politically appointed religious clerics, who are not supportive of Islamic banking and finance. This is clearly expressed in the fatwa pronounced in 2005 by the chairman of Al-Azhar University, who claimed that interest cannot be considered *ribā* per se, but would be viewed unlawful only if it became "excessive" or "usurious." This fatwa has been rejected by the vast majority of scholars. Yet, it still has it supporters, particularly those willing to use it to support their political objection to Islamic finance. Moreover, there is a lack of commitment from scholars to genuinely

denounce the evil of *ribā* and urge governments and individuals to look for Sharī'ah-compliant alternatives.

3. The above factors have influenced customers by reducing demands for Islamic banking products out of fear of being associated with political Islam. *The Banker* stressed that years of suspicions and reservations among the authoritarian governments in the region that Islamic finance will be used to gain prominence has left such countries trailing behind their Gulf and Asian counterparts. Consequently, the lack of knowledge and understanding about the industry in these countries will need to be improved.[60]
4. It is worth stressing that the banking industry in North Africa, whether Islamic or conventional, is relatively underdeveloped, compared to the GCC countries or Malaysia, where retail banking is successful. Commercial banking is dominant in North Africa, with banks serving government-owned enterprises.[61]

However, as noted earlier, North African regulators and practitioners are warming up to Islamic banking and finance. They have started to identify the benefits of Islamic financial intermediation, especially from the perspective of attracting foreign direct investment (FDI).[62] This is further evidenced by Bank Al-Maghrib joining the International Financial Services Board (IFSB).[63] Although these initiatives are positive steps in the right direction, they remain far from capitalising on the immense market opportunities.

### *Claims and Responses*

Commenting on the slow progress of Islamic finance in Africa, particularly in North Africa, Thorsten Beck and others observed that despite the presence of a large Muslim population, the development of Islamic finance in North African countries has not been as rapid as one might have expected for the following reasons.[64]

- North African countries follow a less conservative interpretation of Sharī'ah, relative to Gulf countries. Al-Azhar University's interpretation of *ribā*, according to the authors, is confined to excessive interest and not interest per se.
- North African clients are favouring conventional banks due to their transparency on interest rates and the cost of transactions and their

openness towards the rest of the world, particularly the practices of Western banks.

- The average cost for Islamic banking instruments and services have generally been higher than for conventional instruments counterparts, and therefore, unacceptable to less well-off North African clients.
- The determination to avoid religious tensions and to avoid any perception that the conventional financial system is unlawful because Islamic finance has been authorised.

Although the above analysis may, to some extent, be justified, it nevertheless contains sweeping contentions that require clarification. The lack of development of Islamic finance in North Africa is not based on a less conservative interpretation of Sharī'ah, but based on the lack of support from the political establishment, lack of freedom, and well-entrenched corruption. Similar analyses have led some to characterise Islamic finance in South East Asia as more liberal than that of the GCC countries. However, as has been rightly pointed out by one Malaysian scholar, "There is one *Sharī'ah* and it applies equally to every person on earth." The prohibition of usury is one of the religion's fundamentals and it is strictly observed in GCC or South-East Asia. However, the operationalisation of certain contracts can be the source of differences as the law needs to be interpreted, and therefore, there is room for different conclusions from various scholars.[65] Moreover, Tantawi's definition of *ribā,* as excessive interest and not interest per se, is not that of Al-Azhar University, but a personal opinion that has been rejected by scholars from around the world, including Al-Azhar itself.

To claim that customers in North Africa prefer conventional banks over Islamic ones could only be true if real choices are provided. In cases where there is only one imposed system, the discussion of preference is irrelevant. Regarding the issue of cost, it is true that in countries where Islamic finance lacks political support, the cost of transactions will be high due to unfair tax systems or inadequate legislations on ownership transfer.

Besides the specific and mainly unsubstantiated reasons behind the lack of development of Islamic finance in North Africa, the study has made some general statements regarding the viability and benefit of Islamic finance to Africa. These assertions need to be carefully analysed, as some—if not all—seem to be based on shaky foundations. These claims are summarised below, followed by some clarifications:

1. The study asserts that Islamic finance will certainly pose regulatory challenges as regulators have to become, and remain, familiar with the Sharīʼah compliance of financial products offered in their jurisdictions and with the accounting and auditing standards of Islamic institutions.
2. The equity-like nature of some Islamic finance instruments increases the risk-taking incentives for Islamic banks, which might require more intensive monitoring by supervisors.
3. Islamic finance also poses problems of financial literacy in terms of transparency. In Islamic finance, the interest rate structures of conventional banking are often replaced by fee structures. While, at first glance, this may be easier for clients to understand, it raises the challenge of disclosure.[66]
4. Islamic finance in northern Sudan is rigorous in complying with the no-interest rule, while Islamic finance in Malaysia, a sophisticated financial system, resembles conventional banking.
5. A large-scale expansion of Islamic finance would involve the creation of parallel structures for bond markets, discount windows, and so on. Given the current resource and skill constraints in many African countries, it seems unlikely that this can occur outside the larger markets such as Kenya, Nigeria, or South Africa.
6. Moreover, it is questionable that this should be a priority among policymakers and donors.[67]
7. The ultimate question—the extent to which the provision of Sharīʼah-compliant products can expand the banked population—is still open.
8. Such products might overcome the reluctance of religious households and entrepreneurs to use formal financial services. This population segment, however, is probably small in most African countries.
9. The main barriers of cost and risk are also present in Islamic finance, so Islamic banking is unlikely to help push the frontier outward.
10. Islamic finance seems to offer opportunities to attract additional resources from the oil-exporting countries of the Middle East. However, most African countries face an intermediation constraint, but not a resource constraint.[68]
11. Although the experience of the past few years suggests that the share of Islamic finance in overall intermediation will continue to increase across the continent, it will help deepen and broaden the financial system only at the margin and will not be a game changer.[69]

The outcome of the Thorsten study with regard to Islamic finance seems to stand in sharp contrast with the high importance given by the World Bank to Islamic finance, which has, "formally recognised Islamic finance and have designated it a priority area in its financial sector program."[70] Speaking at the 8th Islamic Financial Services Board Annual Summit in Luxembourg on May 2011, Sri Mulyani Indrawati, the Bank's managing director for the Middle East and North Africa (MENA) region explained that the World Bank's strategy for Islamic finance is based on four pillars that are, first, capacity building and knowledge management; second, influencing policy and market development; third, conducting diagnostic work and analysis in the industry; and finally, providing technical assistance, especially in developing a regulatory framework. "The World Bank," she adds, "has always closely cooperated with the Islamic financial services sector. This demonstrates our commitment to help strengthen the institutional development of the industry. The World Bank will play a positive role in industrial development and economic growth, as such."[71] More importantly, the World Bank is strongly advancing Islamic finance as another means of financial inclusion.[72] Thus, it has been emphasised that one area of innovation that is directly related to financial inclusion is the introduction of Islamic financial products to low-income consumers and microenterprises. Therefore, a lack of Sharī'ah-compliant financial services is a constraint on financial inclusion.[73]

Regarding regulatory challenges, the recent international financial crisis has revealed fragilities in the world's financial system, including in advanced economies. These have brought to the fore key issues regarding financial intermediation, financial innovation, and the regulatory and surveillance framework that need to be put in place to provide the necessary oversight of such activities. Although the Islamic financial services industry was relatively less affected by the crisis, the underlying causes of this crisis bear important lessons for the industry. This is even more important as Islamic finance operates within a global financial system characterised by increasingly large and volatile cross-border capital flows amid an environment of deeper international financial integration.[74]

To better manage the risks associated with the recent global financial crisis, the IFSB-IDB have established a Task Force for Islamic Finance and Global Financial Stability and a report was released in 2010. It identified important building blocks on managing potential risks and vulnerabilities to the Islamic system. These steps include the implementation of prudential standards; the development of a liquidity management infrastructure;

the introduction of strong financial safety nets; the development of an effective crisis management framework; the development and implementation of accounting, auditing, and disclosure standards; the formulation of an effective macro prudential framework; the development of credible credit rating institutions and processes; and finally, to strengthen efforts for capacity building and talent development for the Islamic financial services industry.[75]

The regulatory framework of Islamic financial institutions is undertaken by several institutions—in particular the Islamic Financial Services Board (IFSB), which has a mandate of serving as an international standard-setting body of regulatory and supervisory agencies in ensuring the soundness and stability of the Islamic financial services industry. In advancing this mission, the IFSB promotes the development of a prudent and transparent Islamic financial services industry through introducing new, or adapting existing international standards consistent with Sharī'ah principles, and recommends them for adoption. More importantly, the work of the IFSB complements that of the Basel Committee on Banking Supervision, the International Organisation of Securities Commissions, and the International Association of Insurance Supervisors.[76]

The core objectives of the IFSB are:

1. To promote the development of a prudent and transparent Islamic financial services industry through introducing new, or adapting existing, international standards consistent with Sharī'ah principles, and recommending these for adoption.
2. To provide guidance on the effective supervision and regulation of institutions offering Islamic financial products and to develop for the Islamic financial services industry the criteria for identifying, measuring, managing, and disclosing risks, taking into account international standards for valuation, income and expense calculation, and disclosure.
3. To liaise and cooperate with relevant organisations currently setting standards for the stability and the soundness of the international monetary and financial systems and those of the member countries.
4. To enhance and coordinate initiatives to develop instruments and procedures for efficient operations and risk management.[77]

The IFSB has so far issued 17 Standards, guiding principles, and technical notes for the Islamic financial services industry in areas such as risk management, capital adequacy, corporate governance, transparency and market discipline supervisory review process, governance for collective investment schemes, special issues in capital adequacy, and guiding principles on governance for Islamic insurance. According to the former secretary general of the IFSB, by "developing these standards, the IFSB demonstrates that they are still within Basel II provisions but at the same time cater for the specificities of Islamic finance."[78]

As of December 2014, the 184 members of the IFSB comprise 59 regulatory and supervisory authorities, including a number of African central banks. Some of them have full membership, followed by a second group, which has an associate membership while the third group includes those having an observer membership status. Full members include the Bank of Mauritius, Bank Central de Djibouti, Central Bank of Sudan, Central Bank of Egypt, and Central Bank of Nigeria. The Bank of Zambia, Banque Centrale Des Etats de L'Afrique de l'Ouest, (Central Bank of West African States), Central Bank of Tunisia, and Ministry of Economy and Finances of Senegal are in the associate membership category, while Bank Al-Maghrib (Morocco Central Bank) is an observer member. There are also eight international inter-governmental organisations that include the Islamic Development Bank, the Bank for International Settlements, the World Bank, the International Monetary Fund (IMF), the Asian Development Bank, and 128 market players, professional firms, and industry associations operating in 44 jurisdictions in the IFSB membership. Worthy of note is that the membership of the IFSB also includes several authorities and international institutions from non-Muslim countries, such as the Monetary Authority of Singapore, the Central Bank of the Philippines, Bank of Japan, Bank Central Du Luxemburg, Financial Services Commission & Financial Supervisory Services, Korea, Hong Kong Monetary Authority, and The People's Bank of China.[79] This highlights that the IFSB's membership in Africa is expanding. Of its 184 members (as at April 2014), 34 are from 12 African nations and regional groups and include 13 regulators as well as 21 market players. Thus, there is a strong, diverse, and growing African voice in the IFSB.[80]

The IFSB complements efforts undertaken by the Accounting and Auditing Organisation for Islamic Financial Institutions (AAOIFI), established in 1991, in setting accounting standards that ensure that financial transactions reflect true and fair values and ensure greater accountability and responsibility among financial institutions. Other infrastructure institutions working on developing the industry include the International Islamic Financial Market (IIFM), the Arbitration and Reconciliation Centre for Islamic Financial Institutions (ARCIFI), and the International Islamic Rating Agency (IIRA).

Regarding the claim that the equity-like nature of some Islamic finance instruments increases the risk-taking incentives for Islamic banks, it is necessary to note here that Islamic finance even in its ideal form is not just an equity-based system. Debt-based financial instruments are part and parcel of the system, provided that they are used as a means to solve genuine needs with direct links to the real economy and are not used for speculative purposes. At the same time, Islamic finance works towards raising the share of equity in businesses and of profit-and-loss sharing (PLS) in projects and ventures through the *mudārabah* and *mushārakah* modes of financing. Moreover, although in the ideal form Islamic finance is inclined towards more reliance on PLS, in practice the system is still dominated by debt-based instruments such as *murābaḥah*, *istisnā*, and *ijārah*. Furthermore, greater reliance on equity financing is not peculiar to Islamic finance as it has supporters even in mainstream economics.[81] The proponents of equity-based financing argue that a system based on PLS is more efficient and equitable in the distribution of wealth and income than a debt-based system. Allocation of funds under risk sharing will be based on the viability and expected profitability of the proposed entrepreneurial undertakings rather than on the creditworthiness of competing entrepreneurs. Furthermore, risk sharing offers both entrepreneurs and investors incentives to be truly engaged in productive economic activities, wherein entrepreneurs will be encouraged by the prospect of seeing their ideas transformed into business entities, and financiers will be obliged to assess the risks involved more cautiously and effectively monitor the use of funds by the entrepreneurs. The appropriate implementation of such partnership contracts increases the likelihood of business success, injects more discipline into the financial market by reducing excessive lending, undertaking appropriate due diligence to ensure that the profits are commensurate with the risks assumed, and will ultimately have positive implications for the socio-economic well-being of society.[82]

Moreover, research by the World Bank Group conveys completely contrasting messages from those intended by the authors of the above book. It has been emphasised by one of these studies that the recent financial crisis has not only cast doubts on the functioning of the conventional banking system, but has also focused the attention on Islamic banking products that are attractive for people who demand financial services consistent with their religious beliefs. The study added that if we compare "indicators of business orientation, cost efficiency, asset quality and stability of conventional and Islamic banks, we find little significant differences between the two groups." Moreover, the study pointed out that there are little differences between the performance of Islamic and conventional banks during the crisis, "except that Islamic banks increased their liquidity holdings in the run up to and during the crisis relative to conventional banks. This also explains why Islamic banks' stocks performed better during the crisis compared to conventional banks' stocks."[83]

With regard to the claim that the segment that will benefit from Islamic finance is small, it can be argued that if a population of half a billion is small, then what is the magic member that could be considered big and necessitate the introduction of Islamic finance. Moreover, if countries such as Australia, Japan, and Hong Kong have a combined Muslim population of half a million, but are opening the doors to Islamic finance and amending legislation to accommodate its principles, is it right to claim that the population that will be benefit from Islamic finance in the African context is small while in every African country, we have more than half a million Muslims? Moreover, research by the IMF notes that "Islamic banking is expanding not only in nations with majority Muslim populations, but also in other countries where Muslims are a minority."[84]

Another research by the IMF has argued that the rapidly growing Islamic banking sector may accelerate economic development of the Muslim world. In their working paper, Patrick Imam and Kangni Kpodar noted that Islamic banking with its finance potential can solve the problem of slow growth in the Muslim nations due to the fact that large Muslim populations are underbanked and there is a tremendous need for infrastructure projects.[85] With particular reference to Africa, Standard &Poor's stressed that provided that the continent maintained its current unprecedented growth rate, incremental wealth creation will make it easier for the Islamic financial services sector—including not just Islamic commercial banking but also Sharī'ah-compliant insurance (*Takaful*), investment, and microfinance—to develop.[86]

Emphasising the potential of Islamic finance in Africa, *The Economist* noted that the Gulf states are exploring profitable opportunities among the hundreds of millions of Muslims in Africa. Given the consideration that the continent's economies are growing fast, many people on the continent are unbanked, the banking systems in some of these countries are growing increasingly sophisticated, investors from the Gulf hope that the middle class, particularly in Muslim-majority countries, will turn to Islamic finance and that firms will raise money through *ṣukūk*, given the continent's vast need for infrastructure. It is expected that GCC investors could help bridge the shortage of investment funds gap.[87] The magazine added that "It could be a 21st-century version of 'the scramble for Africa'. But this time the Gulf is moving in alongside China.".[88]

Notwithstanding the forgoing, it could be argued against the assumption by the above study that even if the market for Islamic finance is probably small, it is always the right strategy to include the different segments of society into the financial system. Individuals and households lacking adequate access to a full range of affordably priced, convenient, formal financial services would be severely constrained from fully participating in the economy. As rightly emphasised by the Central Bank of Kenya, failure in this endeavour limits expansion and longevity and retards overall economic development.[89] Prof Njuguna noted that for a financial system to be relevant to society, it needs to safeguard that the eligible target population has the opportunity to access the various sectors of the financial system as "inclusion is an essential pre-condition to enhancing wealth creation and poverty reduction and ultimately broad based economic development."[90] With particular reference to Islamic finance, the Governor stated, "In Africa, Islamic banking is a fast growing financial sector attracting all customers even of different religious orientation. The uptake of Islamic banking is projected to grow exponentially in Sub-Saharan Africa… The future of Islamic finance in Kenya and in the region remains bright."[91]

Similar forward-looking strategy has been expressed by the Bank of Zambia Governor, Michael Gondwe, who pointed out that the limited access to financial services and the limited number of instruments accessible to the different sectors of the economy has hindered the Zambian economy from reaching its full potential. There is a need to ensure that the financial sector is meeting the challenges in order to accelerate sustained investments in key sectors of the economy. The Governor added that this can only be achieved if the financial system improves its allocative efficiencies by providing suitable products and services to all segments of the population, including the Muslim community.[92]

Concerning the Sharī'ah interpretation between Malaysia and Sudan, many of the assumptions on the issue are over-blown and the actual differences are very limited. Over the last decade, only 5 % of the *fatawā* in Islamic finance have differed.[93] Challenges will always exist. However, leadership requires interested parties to rise up and face these challenges. For instance, a number of challenges are facing Kenya's ambition to be a hub of Islamic finance. These include, among others, the shortage of Sharī'ah-compliant investment vehicles, the absence of an enabling legal and regulatory framework, and the lack of awareness by the majority of the populace. However, these challenges have not prevented the Kenyan regulatory authority from pursuing their goals. It is this forward-looking vision that constitutes the basis for the introduction of Islamic finance in the country, with two banks "offering exclusive *Sharī'ah* products, with a growing market footprint."[94] In fact, Islamic finance has become one of the fastest growing financial segments in the international financial system,[95] with total Sharī'ah-compliant assets approaching US$2 trillion,[96] with an annual growth rate of 15–20 %.[97] Therefore, denying the continent the enormous benefits of such an industry would be a great mistake.

## Islamic Finance in the Southern African Region

In contrast to the northern part of Africa, where Muslims form an overwhelming majority, the Muslim communities in the southern part of the continent constitute a minority. However, this has not prevented Islamic finance from entering the region.

### *Islamic Finance in South Africa*

Being the second largest economy in the continent, South Africa is also taking a lead position with regard to Islamic finance. Despite its small percentage of Muslims, Islamic banking and finance have existed for some time in South Africa. The country's only Islamic bank, Albaraka, was set up in 1989. Africa's Absa opened an Islamic banking division in 2006.[98] Conventional banks in South Africa have also started offering products designed to attract those customers willing to remain in compliance with Sharī'ah requirements.[99] Moreover, the success of new entrants such as the Oasis Group, a fast-growing asset management company with over 40 Sharī'ah-compliant funds under its Crescent label, has encouraged customers. The Islamic banking windows of major banking institutions such as Absa, FNB, Standard Bank, and Nedbank form another major factor in the new financial inclusion policy of the National Treasury with respect to Islamic finance. Some observers have alluded that the recent positive move by South Africa towards Islamic finance comes as a reaction to Mauritius' aggressive attempt in promoting itself as an offshore banking centre, including for Islamic capital market products. Interest in Islamic banking and finance has gone beyond serving the domestic Muslim communities, as some South African conventional banking groups have expressed intentions to issue *ṣukūk*. This is part of a broader strategy to diversify funding sources away from the domestic market.[100]

Over the last decade, mainstream banks in South Africa have started to show interest in offering Sharī'ah-compliant products, both domestically and regionally, to Sub-Saharan Africa in countries such as Nigeria and Tanzania. They include First National Bank (FNB); Absa, in which Barclays Bank Plc of the UK has a 55.5 % stake; Nedbank; and Standard Bank. They have thriving Islamic banking windows and have overtaken Albaraka Bank South Africa in terms of book business and branch reach. They are spearheading the Islamic finance foray into the African continent.[101] In July 2011, the Central Bank of Nigeria, for instance, issued a licence to Stanbic IBTC Bank, the Nigerian subsidiary of Standard Bank, to set up an Islamic banking subsidiary, subject to compliance with the approval terms. In Tanzania, Standard Bank has launched a number of Islamic consumer finance products, including Islamic mortgages, leasing, business account facilities, and *Takaful*. The South African National Treasury has introduced tax neutrality measures for *mudārabahh*, *murābaḥah,* and diminishing *mushārakah* products, and has maintained that "the development of Islamic finance in South Africa is critical to the expansion of National Treasury's strategy to position South Africa as a gateway into Africa. The Treasury envisages South Africa being a central hub for Islamic product development and ensuring the rollout of such products into African markets."[102]

Several asset management companies in South Africa are currently offering Sharī'ah-compliant investment schemes or mutual funds as well as discretionary and multi-managed portfolios. These make up a quarter of the total number of asset management companies registered under the country's Financial Services Board (FSB). The largest number of Islamic funds are managed by the Oasis Group. They are managing an estimated 63 Sharī'ah-compliant domestic and offshore funds. The first Islamic fund to be launched in South Africa was Albaraka Equity Fund.[103] Less well-known is that South Africa is also home to Africa's first Sharī'ah-compliant exchange traded fund (ETF), launched in 2009 by New Funds, and which is a joint venture between Absa Capital and Vunani Capital. The Sharī'ah Top 40 Exchange Traded Fund (ETF) includes Sharī'ah-compliant companies selected from the FTSE/JSE Top 40 index listed on the main board of the Johannesburg Stock Exchange, as measured by market capitalisation.[104]

Another important development with regard to Islamic finance in South Africa is the decision by the Financial Services Board to introduce several exemptions for Islamic funds, allowing managers of Sharī'ah-compliant funds to invest up to 50 % of the market value of total assets in a particular portfolio, from the previous 10 % limit.[105] More importantly, the Taxation Laws was amended in 2010 to remove some tax anomalies with regard to Islamic financial products. It has been admitted that "The proposed amendments will level the playing field in respect of certain Islamic financial products."[106]

The recent important development in South Africa with regard to Islamic finance was the successful launch of its debut US$500 million 5.75-year *ṣukūk* in September 2014. The *sukuk* was priced at a coupon rate of 3.90 %, representing a spread of 180 basis points above the corresponding mid-swap (benchmark) rate. The transaction was more than four times oversubscribed, with an order book of US$2.2 billion and listed on the Luxembourg Stock Exchange. The investor distribution of the transaction comprised 59 % from the Middle East and Asia, 25 % from Europe, 8 % from the USA, and the balance from the rest of the world. Investor distribution represents a resounding success in building a more diversified investor base for South Africa. The lead arrangers for the transaction were BNP Paribas, KFH Investment, and Standard Bank. Reflecting on the rationale behind the *sukuk* issuance, South Africa's National Treasury noted that it was intended, "to broaden the investor base and to set a benchmark for state-owned companies seeking diversified sources of funding for infrastructure development."[107]

### *Islamic Finance in Zambia*

The Bank of Zambia hosted the first Islamic Banking Conference in Zambia in October 2008. Since then, efforts have been ongoing to develop a regulatory framework for Islamic banking. The Central Bank has held several consultations, both internally and externally, and subjected the Islamic Banking framework to expert review by internationally renowned experts.[108] Referring to the country's interest in Islamic finance, the governor of the Central Bank of Zambia noted that despite the fact that the Muslim community is estimated at 12 % of country's population, the community constitutes high-value businessmen who control a very significant share of the Zambian economy in various sectors. Their exclusion from the financial sector, according to the governor, has significant impact on the Bank of Zambia efforts towards financial inclusion. The majority of the Muslim community shuns the use of commercial banks due to lack of banking products and services that are compliant with their religious tenets. The introduction of Islamic finance may provide a solution to injecting the much-needed liquidity currently being kept at homes due to the lack of Islamic banking products and services.[109]

Banks and non-banking financial institutions are being encouraged to increase the availability of and access to financial services to the population through the design of new and affordable products The Bank of Zambia undertook a survey to determine the extent of the knowledge and demand for Islamic banking among banks as a way of enhancing the regulatory preparedness. The results indicated that 80 % of the respondents intended to introduce Islamic banking products in the near future. Furthermore, most banks received enquiries from their clients on Islamic banking products.[110] The Bank of Zambia has joined the IFSB as an associate member, in a move which is perceived as a positive step to learn more about the system, and directly interact with the organisation's members.

Under the Banking and Financial Services Act (BFSA), a banking licence enables a bank to engage in various financial services. However, it is not entirely clear from the provisions of the BFSA whether a Zambian bank can, for example, enter into Sharī'ah-compliant transactions involving sale and purchase, and whether this, in principle, is permitted and recognised under the law. One major challenge in this connection will once again be the tax issue and the application of value-added tax (VAT) and whether the tax authority would recognise that the underlying nature of the transaction is, in fact, a financing arrangement[111] and therefore, exempted from taxation.[112]

## *Islamic Finance in Zimbabwe*

Zimbabwe is another country seeking to attract its Muslim community into the banking and financial system. Talks between the central bank, the finance ministry, and the Islamic community have already started. The majority of people in Zimbabwe's Muslim community do not use banks and are prone to robberies. Some observers believe that the introduction of Islamic finance in the country will provide the opportunity to bring a large section of the Muslim population into the mainstream banking system.[113]

If the numbers of countries interested in Islamic banking and finance in the southern region is limited to three countries, it is worth mentioning that almost seven countries in the eastern part of Africa have some form of Islamic finance.

## Islamic Finance in East Africa

The East African region is characterised by its significant Muslim minority, its vicinity to the GCC region, the home of Islamic finance, and the eternal commercial and trade interaction between the two regions. Besides the rapid economic growth registered by a number of countries in East Africa, these factors make the region very attractive to Islamic finance and its opportunities.

### *Islamic Finance in Sudan*

When talking about Islamic finance in East Africa or in the continent, Sudan represents an exceptional case. The country is an international player in Islamic finance and a pioneer in many aspects of the industry. The banking system in Sudan has passed through six stages. The first stage, from 1903 to 1956, during the British colonial rule, was characterised by the domination of foreign banks branches in Sudan. The second stage from 1956 to 1976, following the independence of the country, witnessed the establishment of the Central Bank of Sudan (CBOS) and other national banks, which operated, hand in hand, with the then existing branches of foreign banks until their nationalisation and amalgamation into national banks between 1970 and 1975. The third stage, from 1976 to 1989, was marked by the declaration of Sharī'ah law in Sudan, Islamisation of financial legislations, and establishment of many Islamic banks. The fourth stage, from 1989 to 2002, witnessed the strengthening of Islamisation of financial institutions and legislation. The fifth stage, from 2002 to 2011, following the Comprehensive Peace Agreement (CPA), signed in 2002 between the Government of Sudan and the Sudan People Liberation Movement (SPLM) of South Sudan, has been embodied in the Transitional Constitution of The Republic of Sudan, and the financial system witnessed the establishment of two banking systems in Sudan. An Islamic banking system existed in the North of Sudan, whilst it was agreed in the Nevasha agreement that a conventional banking system would be implemented in the South of Sudan. The Central Bank of South Sudan (CBSS) was established as a branch of CBOS to look after the conventional banking system, while CBOS carries on its responsibilities as supervisor of the Islamic banking system operating in the North of Sudan.[114] The sixth stage was the return to a full Sharī'ah-compliant financial system following the declaration of independence of South Sudan.

The emergence of Islamic banks has helped in attracting considerable funds to the banking system. Customers had previously shied away from conventional banking services.[115] Recently, some Sudanese banks have started expanding into other markets in Africa. For instance, the Islamic Bank of Khartoum is trying to expand its customer base to East Africa in the medium-term, beginning with Kenya. The Islamic Bank of Khartoum was privatised in 2002, and is now 60 % owned by Dubai Islamic Bank.[116]

In 1992, the state established the High Sharī'ah Supervisory Board to oversee the progress of the reforms and their compliance with Sharī'ah. The body comprises scholars, jurists, and economists and is subject to the terms of the law regulating the banking activities. The council consists of eleven people, the majority of whom are Sharī'ah scholars. All members are Sudanese citizens and are appointed by the president of the country upon recommendation of the governor of the Bank of Sudan and the minister of finance. There is no time restriction on the mandate, so theoretically, it can be a lifelong post. The members are allowed to combine their membership at the council with the membership of the Sharī'ah boards of commercial banks. The decisions of the council are based on the majority of votes if agreement cannot be reached.[117] The High Sharī'ah Supervisory Board also acts as an appeal authority for disputes between the various Islamic banks, or between Islamic banks and the Bank of Sudan, or an Islamic bank and its customers. As such, the council's functions are not limited to the direct supervision over the country's banking sector. A bank can also turn to the High Sharī'ah Supervisory Board as the ultimate authority if it does not agree with a decision of its internal Sharī'ah board.

The insurance sector is also based on Sharī'ah principles and is stipulated in state legislation. The insurance sector was given a range of incentives, including tax exemption on all of its assets and profits, and the firm's assets cannot be confiscated or nationalised.

In 1994, the Khartoum Stock Exchange (KSE) was set up. The exchange trades shares of 58 Sudanese companies as of May 10, 2012,[118] some investment funds, and a number of government *ṣukūk*. KSE requires full information disclosure, which ensures a high level of transparency. The stock exchange has its own Sharī'ah board, which screens and approves the products prior to their trading. IMF played a significant role in supporting Sudan's endeavours. Amongst other things, the IMF specialists helped to devise government bonds, based on the mechanism of *mushārakah*. In 2003, KSE launched the Khartoum Index, developed with the assistance of the IMF. In 5 years, it grew from 1000 to 2500 points. Today, KSE is one of the top five African stock exchanges—it ranks fifth, with a trade volume of trading US$5 billion (not including *ṣukūk* trading). Government *mushārakah* certificates (GMCs), also known as *Shahama*, are short-term securities. Through *Shahama*, the state raises money in the domestic market instead of printing more banknotes. After 1 year, holders of GMCs can either cash or extend them. These certificates are backed by the stocks and shares portfolio of various companies owned by the Ministry of Finance, and are therefore, asset-backed. The profitability of GMCs can reach 33 % per annum and depends on the financial results of the companies involved. Hence, the profit of a GMC varies and is not fixed. The government issues these certificates on a quarterly basis.[119]

Government investment certificates (GICs) are medium-term securities based on various contracts financed by the Ministry of Finance of Sudan via the *istisnā'*, *murābaḥah*, and *ijārah* tools. The Ministry of Finance acts as the originator of the certificates. GICs are based on restricted *mudārabah*, which means that the raised money is invested solely in the projects stipulated in the original contract. *Ijārah* certificates of the Bank of Sudan (CICs) are backed by the buildings owned by the central bank. According to the law, Sudanese banks must invest up to 30 % of deposits in CICs. These bonds use *ijārah* as the method of financing. At the end of each term, an independent surveyor evaluates the buildings.[120] Sudan's latest issue of *ṣukūk* was fully subscribed and the country was able to raise the equivalent of US$160 million. More such issues are planned for the coming years. The *ṣukūk* issues are designed to help make up for the loss of oil revenue.[121]

### *Islamic Finance in Kenya*

Besides the unique case of Sudan, Kenya seems to be taking the lead in the promotion of Islamic finance in East Africa. So far, the Kenyan authorities have licensed the Gulf African Bank and First Community Bank, both backed by Gulf investment. The Gulf African Bank, for instance, is registered and headquartered in Kenya, but is owned by a consortium that comprises Bank Muscat International (BMI) (55 %); Istithmar, which is an investment organisation owned by the government of Dubai (30 %); the World Bank's financial arm, the International Finance Corporation (10 %); and PTA Bank (5 %). The IFC's participation is particularly interesting, considering the fact that such an initiative is in line with its aims of encouraging the creation of a modern financial system in all African states. Besides the two banks, the Islamic industry also consists of several Islamic windows of local commercial banks, a *Takāful* company, and a Sharī'ah-compliant funds management company. It is interesting to note that Western banks operating in Kenya are also involved in Islamic finance. For instance, Barclays was the first to offer an Islamic bank account, appropriately named La Ribā, which means "no interest." More importantly, Kenyan regulators have explicitly acknowledged that Sharī'ah-compliant banking has emerged as an alternative vehicle for the mobilisation and supply of finance and that Islamic financial institutions have already contributed to the development agenda of the country through their participation in Sharī'ah-compliant components of infrastructure bonds, issued by the Central Bank of Kenya on behalf of the government of Kenya.[122]

One of the latest positive developments in the Kenyan Islamic financial sector is the new recommendation by the Capital Market Authority (CMA) regarding *ṣukūk*. Following a study by a group appointed by the Capital Markets Authority on *ṣukūk* issuance and regulation, it has been recommended that all future bond issues have to have a Sharī'ah-compliant component, targeting Islamic institutions and retail investors. This means that Islamic finance institutions, especially the growing *Takāful* market, will have an ever-expanding pool of liquidity from which to develop. The ruling will also allow retail customers to participate in the Sharī'ah-compliant *ṣukūk* market. The Kenyan government is the largest domestic issuer of bonds through the Central Bank of Kenya. The debt instruments are traded on the Nairobi Stock Exchange as are those issued by the private sector and non-profit organisations.[123]

Another recommendation by the CMA is the need to accelerate public education of Muslim and non-Muslims alike on Islamic capital markets, products, and services. It has also proposed the establishment of a national Sharī'ah advisory board to provide guidance on product authenticity throughout the entire Islamic finance industry in Kenya and to ensure consistent interpretation of the Sharī'ah. It is acknowledged that for a fair, efficient, and transparent Islamic capital market, certain prerequisites need to be in place. These prerequisites include, among others, a sound regulatory framework, a robust accounting framework, a facilitative tax environment, and an appropriate Sharī'ah compliance process.[124]

According to the Central Bank governor, as of the financial year ending December 31, 2010, the two fully fledged Sharī'ah-compliant banks collectively commanded a market share of 0.9 % of the banking sector, with gross assets of Ksh.16.54 billion, net loans and advances of Ksh.9.23 billion, and deposits of Ksh.13.76 billion. The two banks had 58,101 deposit accounts and 2609 loan accounts as at the end of December 2010—in less than 4 years of operation.[125] These developments have enabled formerly unbanked Kenyans, specifically the Muslim communities in remote areas, access to financial services, adding to the wealth creation in the economy. This is also a solid testimony of the vast potential of Islamic finance in Kenya, which should be tapped. This will open the doors for other opportunities that could be explored, such as the Islamic insurance (*Takāful*) and capital market segments using Sharī'ah-compliant vehicles.[126] Kenya is presenting itself with the potential to be the regional Islamic finance hub in tandem with the country's vision 2030 aspirations, under which one of the key aspirations for the financial sector is the positioning of Nairobi as a regional financial hub by 2030.[127]

The Islamic banking industry in Kenya is doing well. For instance, Gulf African Bank has reported a 230 % increase in profit before tax to KES155 million (US$1.8 million) for the financial year ended December 1, 2011, as net income rose 29 % to KES95.3 million (US$1.13 million). The bank's total assets amounted to KES12.9 billion (US$152.6 million), 35 % higher than a year earlier, as its financing portfolio rose 19 % to KES7.4 billion (US$87.54 million).[128] The trend continued for the first half of 2012, with the bank announcing a pre-tax profit of KES195 million (US$2.28 million) for the first half ended the June 30, 2012. Meanwhile, its financing portfolio rose 37 % year-on-year to KES8.54 billion (US$99.75 million), while customer deposits increased 20.7 % to KES11.1 billion (US$129.65 million).[129]

One particular positive development regarding Islamic finance in Kenya is regarding the Nairobi-based commercial Equity Bank, which has been authorised by the Central Bank of Kenya to open an Islamic banking window. The bank has more than seven million customers, more than 170 branches across East Africa, and is the largest bank in the region. Some observers consider the entry of Equity Bank into the Islamic market as a game changer in eastern Africa. The bank has a presence in Kenya, South

Sudan, Uganda, Tanzania, and Rwanda, all of which are in the process of amending their financial laws to allow Islamic banking. Equity Bank also has a reputation for aggressive marketing. The two Islamic financial institutions are classified as urban-based and commercially focused entities while Equity Bank, on the contrary, has its focus on rural areas and has maintained its microfinance philosophy. Its entry into Islamic banking is seen by some observers as a step towards maintaining the loyalty of its Muslim customers in the face of the newly created Islamic banks.[130]

Another notable development in the Kenyan market is the announcement by the Nairobi-based reinsurer, Kenya Re, of its plan to set up a dedicated *reTakāful* window to snap up business in Africa and the Middle East. The company already has *reTakāful* experience from working with 10 *Takāful* companies in Sudan and is eyeing opportunities across the whole of Africa. It recently announced a new venture in West Africa, a market with a greater Muslim population than Kenya Re's East African homelands. Kenya Re is listed on the Nairobi Stock Exchange and is majority-owned (60 %) by the Kenyan government. It reinsures companies in 23 African countries and 11 countries in the Middle East and Asia.[131]

Although many inquiries were received from local entities as well as foreign insurance companies looking forward to set up *Takāful* companies and to expand into the rapidly developing markets of East Africa, tipped by many as one of the hotspots for the development of the Islamic financial system, the licensing of new *Takāful* companies was frozen until a proper law to regulate the industry was completed. The two *Takāful* operators in Kenya are *Takāful* Insurance of Africa (TIA) and First Community Bank's Takāful window. Kenyan regulators think that the move is necessary so that they can understand the dynamics of *Takāful* operations with the two companies.[132]

Although the move offers an unexpected advantage to Kenya's existing *Takāful* companies in terms of competition, according to some observers, the regulator's strategy may be counterproductive as Kenya risks losing its position as the leading Islamic finance hub in East Africa to neighbouring countries such as Tanzania and Uganda, who have put no such restrictions on new local and foreign firms entering their markets.[133] Some have also criticised the move as coming in a vital time in the development of the regional industry, arguing that *Takāful* is a model that has been successful elsewhere, and therefore, there is no harm in adapting regulations and operational procedures from other countries that already have a flourishing *Takāful* sector, and adapt them for local conditions. The insurance regulatory authorities have been criticised for not involving Kenya *Takāful* expertise at the advisory level. Currently, Kenya's insurance law does not recognise *Takāful* as a standalone product, although according to some experts, the law empowers the IRA to issue ad hoc regulations authorising individual operators on a case-by-case basis to sell *Takāful* products. It is also observed that Kenya's capital markets do not yet have Sharī'ah-compliant financial products such as *ṣukūk*, which limits the avenues where *Takāful* companies can invest their premium. Moreover, the insurance regulations do not allow companies to invest in offshore assets, which is preventing Kenyan *Takāful* entities from established capital markets in the Middle East and Asia. *Takāful* companies are also facing double taxation, as Sharī'ah requires them to pay *zakah* while the national insurance law in Kenya requires that they also pay corporate taxes.[134]

The legal aspects need to be clear for the smooth operation and functioning of the Islamic finance industry. This is what the Kenyan regulators seem to be committed to. The Banking Act and the Central Bank of Kenya Act regulate the country's banking industry. There is a general prohibition against banks engaging in wholesale or retail trade, or purchasing or holding any land or any interest or right in land. The nature of Islamic finance transactions are such that banks will be required to own goods or land (in the case of land, the bank will usually not be registered as owner in the Land Registry, but will be recognised as beneficial owner and take risks attendant to ownership). In order to conduct such transactions in Islamic banking in Kenya, a bank would need to obtain from the Central Bank exemptions from the provisions of the Banking Act prohibiting banks from engaging in trade, acquiring, or holding land.

Tax is another outstanding issue that requires clear understanding and proper implementation. For instance, a *murābaḥah* transaction entails the purchase of the assets by a bank and the subsequent sale of the assets by the bank to the customer. The question arises whether a *murābaḥah* transaction would be subject to VAT. It is also necessary to consider other tax and accounting treatment of other payments and receipts in the hands of the bank and the customer. Another popular Islamic banking product is *ijārah*, which can be classified in conventional terms as a leasing arrangement. Certain *ijārah* transactions could be deemed to be hire purchase transactions, and would accordingly require a licence issued under the Hire Purchase Act (HPA) to conduct such business. Islamic banks must therefore be aware of the implications that the HPA would have on the conduct of their business. Islamic banks are perceived as sellers under the Sale of Goods Act (SGA),[135] and therefore, a bank undertaking *murābaḥah* transactions should, as a seller of goods, consider the application of the Sale of Goods Act (SGA). The SGA places by a number of legal obligations on a seller of goods. Some of these obligations include an implied warranty that the relevant goods are of merchantable quality and fit for their purpose. A bank undertaking a *murābaḥah* transaction should therefore consider the application of the SGA and consider how to limit its exposure accordingly.[136]

The latest development with regard to Islamic finance in Kenya is the launch of the Regional Certificate in Participatory/Islamic Banking Programme, designed to develop human capital. The programme is conducted by the Kenya School of Monetary Studies in collaboration with the International Centre for Education in Islamic Finance (INCEIF), based in Malaysia. Launching the programme, the Kenya Central Bank Governor noted that the programme will enhance financial inclusion since the focus is now on Africa, where consumer awareness and demand of Islamic Banking and finance are growing.[137]

The appetite for Islamic banking and finance in Kenya was reinforced by the entry of international Islamic finance players such as Standard Chartered Saadiq and Dubai Islamic Bank.[138] Dubai Islamic Bank received principle approval from the Kenyan regulator in January 2015 to start operating Islamic banking in Kenya, according to DIB Chief Executive Officer, Adnan Chilwan. The bank still need to get its final licence to be operational. The new bank will operate under the name DIB Kenya. DIB will hold 70 % of the bank, with 30 % owned by local partners.[139]

### *Islamic Finance in Mauritius*

Mauritius is working towards having a regulatory framework that accommodates both conventional and Islamic financial institutions. The country has drawn guidance from the experience of other countries that have embarked on Islamic finance to map its own route. According to the governor of the Bank of Mauritius, "the sound ethical principles underlying Islamic finance represent an attractive alternative to conventional financial products. Islamic finance offers advantages to Muslims and non-Muslims alike."[140] Outlining the country's strategy towards Islamic finance and becoming a world-class financial centre, the Governor of the Central Bank notes that:

> Islamic finance can encourage new levels of dynamism in the sector and attract more foreign direct investment and portfolio flows… It can smooth out the disparities between levels of financial development and capability, as well as foster deeper regional ties in Africa.[141]

Mauritius has already amended its legislation and issued the necessary guidelines and is moving aggressively towards the next challenge of marketing the country as a destination of choice for Islamic finance.[142] Mauritius has taken some concrete measures towards embracing Islamic finance. These include:

- In October 2005, the government set up a steering committee to explore the possibility of establishing Islamic financial services in Mauritius. The committee proposed to have the legislative framework reviewed and amended to facilitate the introduction of the Islamic finance industry. The proposals were finalised and the Finance Act 2007 brought the necessary amendments into legislation in June 2007. It made provision for banks to operate either as a fully-fledged Islamic bank or alternatively, to offer Islamic banking services through a window operation.
- A working group on Islamic banking was then set up to work on guidelines for conducting Islamic banking in Mauritius. The objective was to design a simple and standard regulatory framework, within which Islamic banking could develop and integrate with the conventional financial system. The working group was broadly based and included representatives from the banking industry. Those guidelines were finalised and issued to the industry in June 2008.
- The Bank of Mauritius, the country's central bank, also sought affiliation with the Islamic Financial Services Board (IFSB). The bank is a full member of the standard setting body while The Financial Services Commission of Mauritius, which regulates non-banking financial services, is an associate member of IFSB.
- With the IFSB, the Bank of Mauritius hosted seminars on Islamic capital markets in Mauritius in joint collaboration with the Financial Services Commission (FSC). This events aimed to bring Mauritius to the attention of the global Islamic finance community, as well as the Mauritian community in general.
- On May 5, 2009, HSBC Mauritius in collaboration with HSBC Amanah, launched its Islamic banking window to cater to the growing demand of Islamic banking services from global business clients.

- In April 2010, a Statement of Standard Practice SP5/10 was issued by the Mauritius Revenue Authority on VAT on *murābaḥah* transactions.
- In October 2010, the IFSB coordinated the establishment of an International Islamic Liquidity Management Corporation (IILM) and the Bank of Mauritius became a founding member, along with ten other central banks and two multilateral organisations (the Islamic Development Bank and the Islamic Corporation for the Development of the Private Sector). The IILM would issue investment-grade instruments to facilitate liquidity management for institutions offering Islamic financial services and cross-border investment flows. The Government of Mauritius contributed US$5 million to the capital of this supranational body, a clear demonstration of its commitment to creating an environment conducive to the development of this new Sharī'ah-compliant platform in the banking landscape.
- In October 2010, the Bank of Mauritius also entered into a Memorandum of Understanding (MOU) with Bank Negara or Central Bank of Malaysia to establish a collaborative framework for mutual cooperation in capacity building and human capital development in the financial services industry with the expectation of creating a pool of high-calibre professionals in the field.
- On March 31, 2011, the Century Banking Corporation, the first Islamic Bank licensed by the Bank of Mauritius, was launched. Born from a strategic partnership between Qatari investors through Domasol Limited and British American Investment Group, Century Banking Corporation would focus on wholesale banking, treasury and wealth management, targeting Africa, Asia, Mauritius, and the Middle East. Bait al Mashura Finance Consultations, a consultancy firm licensed by the Central Bank of Qatar, provides Sharī'ah advisory services to the bank.[143]
- The country is also embarking on a project to develop Sharī'ah-compliant money market products for the emergence of an active Inter-bank money market for Islamic financial institutions.[144]
- A range of Islamic trusts has already been issued on the island, whereby trustees allocate managed funds on behalf of Muslim investors.

From the Mauritian case as well as previous experiences in Malaysia and the Gulf region, whenever both regulators and political leaders share the same wish to enhance the entrenchment of Islamic finance in the domestic market, the chances of success are higher and Islamic finance would subsequently rapidly expand. Mauritian Muslim consumers of financial services appear to have the full backing and support of both their government and regulators.[145]

## *Islamic Finance in Uganda*

In the 2010/11 budget, the Government of Uganda announced that due to demands from the private sector, it would introduce new products, including Islamic banking. This will allow banks to move into previously untapped markets. Towards achieving that objective, the government would be submitting amendments to the Financial Institutions Act 2004 to Parliament, which would allow commercial banks to offer financial Islamic banking products. The decision by the government caps a decision by the Bank of Uganda to allow Islamic banking.[146]

Licensing of Islamic banking will follow the amendment of the Bank of Uganda Act 2000, the Financial Institutions Act 2004, and the Micro Finance Deposit Taking Institutions Act 2003. These acts are the basis under which the central bank licenses commercial banks and microfinance institutions to take deposits. The amendments are being pushed to be formulated into law so that the central bank can license Islamic banking. The proposed amendments will address legal as well as tax issues. In order to accommodate Islamic banking, it would first be necessary to amend the following sections of the Financial Institutions Act (Act 2 of 2004):

1. Section 37 of the FIA prohibits a financial institution from engaging directly or indirectly for its own account or with others in trade, commerce, industry, insurance, or agriculture except in the course of the satisfaction of debts, in which case all such activities and interests shall be disposed of at the earliest reasonable opportunity. Amending this section is necessary to allow the purchasing of goods for onward selling to customers at a mark-up cost on a *murābaḥah* basis.
2. Section 38 of FIA prohibits a financial institution from purchasing or acquiring any immovable property or any right in it except as may reasonably be necessary for the purpose of conducting its business or for housing or providing amenities for its staff. In such a case, the cost of the property in aggregate must not exceed 100 % of its core

capital. This provision would prohibit real estate transactions by Islamic financial institutions, whether they are *murābaḥah*, *ijārah*, or *mushārakahh* transactions since all these products include the Islamic bank owning property.

3. Section 37 of FIA prohibits a financial institution from acquiring or holding, directly or indirectly, any part of the share capital or interest of an enterprise engaged in trade, commerce, industry, or agriculture, in excess of 25 % of its core capital except in the course of satisfaction of debts due to it. This section, if not amended, would limit the Sharī'ah-compliant transactions described above and would only allow the bank's interest in such business to a 25 % of its core capital.
4. The Sharī'ah-compliant transactions undertaken by the bank, to the extent that they involve transfer of title of the goods to the customer, would be characterised as a "contract of sale" within the meaning of the Sale of Goods Act with the consequence that the obligations of a seller of goods under the Act would also fall on the bank.
5. *Ijārah* transactions, which operate as hire purchase agreements, could also be affected in many respects by the proposed Hire Purchase Bill, which, among other provisions, implies certain conditions and warranties similar to those in the Sale of Goods Act. The Bill also seeks to criminalise carrying on "hire purchase business" without a licence issued under the Act.
6. Sharī'ah compliant transactions involving sale or "supply" of goods would be subject to payment of VAT under the Value Added Tax regulation, which is currently at the rate of 18 % unless such supply of goods qualifies as "an exempt supply."[147]

According to the central bank, Islamic banking in Uganda would first operate through the existing commercial banks that have shown interest in having Islamic banking windows. They will provide Islamic products alongside conventional banking. The second category would be the initiatives of investors who wish to establish Islamic banking institutions as a separate arrangement. As noted earlier, in East Africa, Islamic banking is already practised in Sudan, Kenya, Djibouti, Mauritius, Uganda, and Tanzania. The anticipated east African common market could have driven the central bank to open up to the system.[148] The east African common market is set to promote the growth of the insurance market and the market for Islamic financial products, which should benefit bank customers in other sectors of the economy. Permitting banks in Uganda to offer these products will also align the Ugandan banking laws with those in other African countries which have already moved, or are moving, in a similar direction.[149] It will also increase the depth, breadth, and range of finance products bank customers can use to access banking services.[150]

The direct result of the above regulatory changes was the creation of the National Islamic Bank of Uganda (NIBoU). A merger between the National Bank of Commerce and International Investment House (IIH), a local subsidiary of the Abu Dhabi-based investment firm, has been given the green light to offer Islamic banking products.[151] Perhaps more importantly, the Jeddah-based Islamic Corporation for the Development of the Private Sector (ICD), the private sector funding arm of the Islamic Development Bank (IDB) Group, is in the process of applying for an Islamic banking licence in Uganda. The rationale, according to the ICD general manager and CEO, is to establish the bank in a member country which is a pre-condition under the ICD articles of memorandum, which could then enter other countries in the region in order to finance or to do business in these countries, irrespective of whether they are member countries or not.[152]

### *Islamic Finance in Ethiopia*

As noted earlier, the sustainability and attractiveness of Islamic finance as an alternative financial management model in a post-global financial crisis continues to flourish in new regions and countries. Many governments and regulators are trying to change banking regulations and laws to facilitate the introduction of such institutions and products in their respective jurisdictions. The latest country in East Africa trying to open up to Islamic finance is Ethiopia. The National Bank of Ethiopia (NBE) is in the process of finalising a banking regulation and business directive that would allow the authorisation of a bank operating under Islamic finance principles.[153]

It should be noted that the Christian–Muslim relations—in Ethiopia, in particular—can be a sensitive issue despite the fact that Muslims form a large minority, if not half of the population. However, some non-Muslim groups perceive the entry of Islamic finance in religious terms and a service exclusive to Muslims. Ethiopia is home to one of the oldest Christian churches and to an ancient Islamic heritage. Not surprisingly, the Ethiopian government is cautiously promoting the establishment of a home-grown nascent Islamic banking industry. The idea is to authorise the first local Islamic bank restricted only to Ethiopian shareholders. As such, no foreign investors or Islamic banks would be allowed to have shares in any proposed bank. The Bank of Ethiopia published the 2008 banking business proclamation, which is a draft consultation document outlining the introduction of interest-free banks in Ethiopia. After the consultation period, in June 2010, the Bank of Ethiopia published the directives for conducting interest-free banking. The directives would pave the way for the launching of the country's first Islamic bank. It should be noted that, in 2008, local Ethiopian Muslim investors set up the ZamZam Bank Share Company, and it was hinted that this company could become the first Islamic bank in Ethiopia.[154]

Unfortunately, the Ethiopian government has denied accreditation to what would have been the country's first Islamic bank following new banking and terrorism laws. The National Bank of Ethiopia (NBE) directive was ratified in September 2011, barring full–fledged Islamic banking. The refusal to licence the service is also killing the hopes of 6800 shareholders of the intended new Islamic bank after years of dispute with the National Bank. The "interest-free" banking project has an initial capitalisation of US$57 million.

The board reportedly offered three options for the shareholders—ranging from injecting their capital in other banks and opening a window, dissolving the bank and disbursing the raised capital, or investing in other investments. Most of the shareholders supported the idea of investing the capital elsewhere. However, there are complaints that NBE's decision is not helping a sizable number of Ethiopians to be part of the banking system and could be impede religious rights while also inhibiting the development of businesses in the country.[155] It is believed that the introduction of new commercial banks compatible with Sharī'ah will attract new bank customers currently operating outside the mainstream bank services.

As noted by one local observer, the Muslim community generally believes that their government has clearly neglected their cause for a just financial service that is compatible with their religion. The Ethiopian Muslims and the Muslim business community feel that they are economically disadvantaged and marginalised by the current conventional banking system. It is considered to be against their religious faith, and thus, a very large number of potential Muslim customers are not using the conventional banking system available.[156]

It should be noted that the financial system in Ethiopia is one of the fastest growing in the continent. The expansion was dramatic, according to a study by Standard Bank, whereby the financial services sector grew at 30 % between 2004 and 2008, contributing 11 % to GDP.[157] Unfortunately, unbanked Muslims are not yet benefiting from this huge potential in the financial sector by expediting the adoption and implementation of alternative banking products through Islamic banking and finance, largely due to a lack of appropriate regulatory and policy regimes to cater to a full-fledged non-interest-bearing banking system.

It is hoped that the Ethiopian authorities would revise their position, reform the new legislation, and ease restrictions so that a large section of the population is served by the introduction of new commercial banks that are compatible with Islamic law. This will stimulate new waves of bank customers that were not previously catered to by mainstream bank services.[158]

### *Islamic Finance in Tanzania*

The central Bank of Tanzania has so far received a number of applications from local and international promoters expressing interest in establishing Islamic banking windows or full-fledged Islamic banks.[159] Regulators believe that the time is appropriate to start the process of developing the required legal, institutional, regulatory, and governance framework for an Islamic financial system in the country.[160] However, as is the case with most legislation in the region, there is no specific reference to Islamic financing in the Tanzanian Banking Act 2006 (the "Banking Act"). The Act sets out the activities that a licensed bank can carry out. For instance, finance leasing is a specified activity and since that requires the financial institution to have title to the assets in order to act as lessor, the concept of a bank having ownership of assets for a finance transaction is not entirely unacceptable and this may assist in any required consent from the Bank of Tanzania. It should be noted that the Banking Act specifically prohibits a bank from acquiring or leasing any fixed assets, except where it is necessary for the purpose of conducting its business as a bank or financial institution and stipulates that the Bank of Tanzania shall prescribe limits under which a bank or financial institution shall invest in fixed assets. It requires a bank to dispose as soon as is practicable any property that it acquires or takes possession of as a result of enforcing a security interest. In order to address the legal issues under the Tanzanian law, it is necessary to consider the issue of agency and its implication under the law of Tanzania. More importantly, there is the issue of taxes where VAT of 20 % payable in Tanzania on supplies of goods or services, unless the supply is either zero-rated or exempted, needs to be considered. This obligation on the supplier (i.e. the seller or the bank) to account for VAT arises, irrespective of the receipt of VAT payment from the purchaser.[161]

The appetite for Islamic Banking in Tanzania has attracted a number of financial institutions to enter the market. By the end of 2014, there were five banks offering Islamic banking services in the country—of which one is a full-fledge bank.[162] More than 50 % of the population in Tanzania is Muslim, and as such, it is a ripe market for the region's Islamic banking.[163]

Tanzania launched its first Islamic bank Amana Bank, in early December 2011, in the capital, Dar es Salam. The bank aims at meeting the demands for an ethical and interest-free alternative to conventional banking of all Tanzanians who want to bank in an ethical and transparent way. As maintained by its chairman, Amana Bank is for all Tanzanians—not just Muslims—but would be run under Sharī'ah principles, which he says are fair and open to all. The founding shareholders of Amana Bank include prominent Tanzanian Muslims.[164]

Close economic cooperation among the states of the East African Community (Burundi, Kenya, Rwanda, Tanzania, and Uganda) has allowed banking groups that operate in the region's largest economy, Kenya, to expand across the borders and quickly set up operations in the country. However, until now, Tanzania's banking regulations have not made provisions for Islamic banking. Regulatory changes have been driven by the banking industry in consultation with the National Muslim Council of Tanzania.[165]

Just days after the mainland witnessed the launch of the country's first fully-fledged Islamic bank, Amana Bank, The People's Bank of Zanzibar, a state-owned commercial bank and 100 % owned by the Government of Zanzibar, launched an Islamic banking window. The island's population is 99 % Muslim, which represents a conducive environment in which the Islamic banking model can strive. Other Tanzanian banks that have launched Islamic finance windows include National Bank of Commerce, Stanbic Bank Tanzania, and KCB Tanzania.[166]

### *Islamic Finance in Rwanda*

Rwanda has one microfinance company that complies with Islamic law. Started in May 2005, Al Halaal is a microfinance institution operating on

Islamic banking principles, with plans to grow into a fully-fledged bank.[167] However, what is important is the consideration of the industry by the regulators in Kigali. The governor of the Central Bank of Rwanda was quoted saying that "Emerging issues like Sharī'ah/Islamic banking, convergence of financial services and financial inclusion are being taken on board seriously and the BNR will keep supporting and participating in key initiatives.".[168]

### *Islamic Finance in Djibouti*

Djibouti has four Islamic financial institutions operating on a Sharī'ah basis. These are Saba Bank, Salaam African Bank, and Dahabshil Bank. Saba Bank, a Yemeni bank by origin, opened a branch in Djibouti in June 2006. It was the first to introduce international ATM machines to the country. Salaam African Bank on the contrary, is a joint venture between some businessmen from Somalia and Djibouti. The bank was the first to offer customer e-banking, mobile banking, and debit cards. The newest Islamic bank is the Dahabshil Bank,[169] which is part of a remittance company in Somalia.

Despite its recent presence in the country, the Islamic finance industry in Djibouti has been able to double its market share in the last 5 years and controls around 10 % of the country's deposits, according to the governor of the Central Bank of Djibouti.[170]

The banking penetration in the country had risen in 2013 from 10 % of the population 6 years ago to 17 % or 18 %. Regulators acknowledge that a large portion of the population is still not part of the conventional banking system due to religious reasons. The increased bankability associated with Islamic banking could attract new sources of investment and increase the pool of deposits. By mid-2013, Islamic banks accounted for approximately 15 % of the country's total banking assets and 12 % of deposits. Moreover, an Islamic banking law was introduced in 2011 and seven guidance notes from Djibouti's central bank have been issued in order to help develop the industry.[171]

### *Islamic Finance in Somalia*

The potential of Islamic finance in Somalia is huge, given the fact that the country is almost entirely Muslim and there is strong desire for Islamic finance. Moreover, the experiences of Islamic finance in neighbouring countries, such as Djibouti, Kenya, or Ethiopia, are backed by resident Somali communities. Thus, the development of Islamic finance in Somalia is just a matter of time and premised on the country achieving a satisfactory level of peace and stability.

The International Bank of Somalia (IBS) was the first Islamic bank that started operations in Mogadishu. It was initiated and financed by Somali business people. IBS would offer several services, including mortgages, deposits, overdraft, project funds, trade finance, and service to non-resident customers.[172]

## Islamic Finance in the West African Region

The West African region first experienced Islamic finance in 1983, when six subsidiaries were established by Dar Al-Mal Islami (DMI) in Guinea, Niger, and Senegal. The six subsidiaries were three Islamic banks and three investment companies. Subsequently, for better functioning of these subsidiaries and in order to make them commercially viable and financially profitable, the three investment companies merged with the existing banks in the three countries. This would also allow avoiding duplication of activities between the banks and the investment companies.

In a recent move, the Islamic Corporation for the Development of the Private Sector (ICD), the private sector funding arm of the IDB Group, launched a joint venture holding company with Turkey's Asya Participation Bank, called Tamweel Africa SA, whose main aim is to support Islamic financial institutions in Sub-Saharan Africa and to extend financing to SMEs. Tamweel Africa has a capital of US$50 million and is based in Senegal. The company bought the shares of the three former banks in West Africa owned by Dar Al-Maal Al-Islami (DMI). The company started operations in January 2010. ICD holds 60 % of the equity and Asya Participation Bank owns 40 %, for which it paid US$15 million. Tamweel Africa owns a reported 66 % of the Islamic Bank of Niger, 77.5 % of the Islamic Bank of Senegal, 100 % of the Islamic Bank of Guinea, and 100 % of the Islamic Bank of Mauritania. Asya Participation Bank provides the technical expertise, management system, and the knowledge base for Tamweel Africa.[173]

Islamic finance experience in this region has not made any significant breakthrough, perhaps due to the lack of political and regulatory support, and the failure of local religious leaders to do educate the public on the negative effects of *ribā* and interest and the necessity to look for an Islamic alternative. However, if some countries in West Africa such as Senegal, Guinea, Niger, and Mauritania have had some form of Islamic banking since the 1980s, it is Nigeria that is strongly emerging as the West African hub for Islamic finance in the region, backed by the size of the economy and its large population.

### *Islamic Finance in Nigeria*

Nigeria is Sub-Saharan Africa's largest economy, with a population estimated at more than 160 million. It is arguably the largest consumer market in Africa. The country holds one of the most attractive outlets for the marketability and profitability of financial services. Between 2000 and 2004, average return on equity in the banking sector was 35–40 %, which was, without a doubt, one of the best in the world. The Nigerian financial services sector comprises banking, insurance and capital markets, and pension funds sub-sectors.[174] The banking sector can look forward to tremendous opportunities in Nigeria, with an estimated 70 % of the nation's citizens not having access to banks.[175]

The history of Islamic banking and finance in Nigeria could be traced to the early 1990s with the enactment of the Bankers and Other Financial Institutions Decree of 1991. This decree recognises banks based on profit and loss sharing. However, it prohibits the incorporation or registration of any bank with a name that includes the words "Islamic," "Christian," "Qur'anic," "Biblical" and so on. Sometime later, Habib Bank Plc opened a non-interest banking window, offering a limited number of Sharī'ah-compliant products. However, since there was no framework for non-interest banking in the country, the attempt did not register significant success or growth. Nonetheless, interest in Islamic finance did not stop and Nigeria joined the Islamic Development Bank as a full member. The IDB later offered the Central Bank of Nigeria a technical aid grant for training central bank examiners for the development of a framework for the regulation and supervision of Islamic finance in Nigeria, and for the organisation of an International Conference on Islamic Finance. This was followed by an Approval-in-Principle (AIP), which was granted to Jaiz Bank Plc to operate a full-fledged Islamic bank on meeting the mandatory capital requirement of NGN 25 billion.

A major financial development in the Nigerian financial system was the launch of the Financial System Strategy (FSS) 2020. This blueprint aims to engineer Nigeria's evolution into Africa's major International Financial

Centre (IFC) and enable Nigeria's transformation into one of the 20 largest economies in the world by 2020. Among its initiatives regarding the Money Market are: (a) to create institutions to attract the huge unbanked informal sector and (b) create non-interest banking instruments to capture huge unbanked segments of the society. This was followed by a number of initiatives with direct implications for the development of Islamic finance in the country, including the following:

- In January 2009, the Central Bank of Nigeria joined the International Financial Services Board (IFSB) as a full member.
- In March 2009, the Banking Supervision Department of the Central Bank of Nigeria (CBN) released the exposure draft of the Framework for the Regulation and Supervision of Non-Interest Banks in Nigeria for comments, suggestions, or inputs by stakeholders.
- In October 2009, the University of Ilorin held an International Conference on Islamic Finance jointly organised by the Department of Islamic Law of the University, and the Islamic Research and Training Institute (IRT) of the IDB.
- In January 2010, the CBN set up a non-interest banking unit in the Financial Policy and Regulation.
- Conventional banks are requesting regulatory approval to introduce Islamic financial products into their market offerings. Some banks have even gone ahead to appoint Sharī'ah Advisory Committees in accordance with international governance standards for Islamic financial institutions.
- In July 2010, CBN was represented in the Technical Committee of the IFSB.
- In August 2010, the CBN released the new banking model, which designated non-interest banks among the specialised banks. The non-interest banks were to be categorised into two, namely: National Non-Interest Bank, which shall have a capital based of NGN10 billion and will operate in every state of the federation, including the Federal Capital Territory (FCT).

  The other is regional non-interest bank, which shall have a capital base of NGN5 billion, and will operate in a minimum of six states and a maximum of 12 contiguous states of the federation, lying within not more than two geopolitical zones as well as within the FCT.

- In September 2010, the Nigeria Deposit Insurance Scheme (NDIC) released its draft framework for a Non-interest (Islamic) Deposit Insurance Scheme for stakeholders' comments and inputs.
- The Security and Exchange Commission posted on its website regulations guiding funds and securities, which included Islamic fund management.
- The Debt Management Office (DMO) set a tentative timetable for the development of the first *ṣukūk*.
- In October 2010, the CBN joined 11 other central banks and two multilateral organisations to form the International Islamic Liquidity Management Corporation (IILM), based in Malaysia.
  The IILM aim is to provide treasury instruments that are Sharī'ah-compliant to address the liquidity management issue of Islamic banks and serve as instruments for open market operations involving Islamic financial institutions.[176]
- In early March 2013, Nigeria amended the rules of the regulations of the Securities and Exchange Commission to regulate the issuance of *ṣukūk*. In April 2013, the country issued new guidelines to oversee the operation of its *takāful* (Islamic insurance) industry. Among other issues, the guidelines state that: (1) Firms must have advisory boards with at least two scholars, (2) Scholars must meet eligibility criteria, code of conduct, (3) Regulator to set up central Sharī'ah advisory board of its own, and (4) Allows the use of *takaful* windows by conventional insurers. Nigeria's insurance commission will, in turn, establish a *takāful* advisory council of its own to oversee industry products and practices, mirroring the centralised approach favoured by countries such as Malaysia and Oman. It should be noted that Nigeria currently has a total of 58 insurance companies, which posted gross premiums of 233 billion naira in 2011, a 16.6 % increase from a year earlier. Regulators opted to allow three *takāful* operating models under the new guidelines: *mudārabah*, *wakālah*, and hybrid. Firms are also encouraged to consider guidelines issued by the Malaysian-based Islamic Financial Services Board and the Bahrain-based Accounting and Auditing Organisation for Islamic Financial Institutions, though they are not legally binding.[177]
- In early March 2013, Nigeria's Securities and Exchange Commission approved new rules facilitating the issuance of *ṣukūk*.

The introduction of non-interest banking in Nigeria would deepen the Nigerian financial market through the entry of new market and institutional players such as the Islamic Money Market, Islamic asset management companies, and *Takāful*. This introduction is also expected to enable a larger proportion of the Nigerian population to actively participate and contribute to the country's economic development. Nigeria has a very large Muslim population, estimated to be around 80 million, the majority of whom are either underbanked or totally unbanked, and have turned away from conventional banking service due to their rejection of interest-based products and services. The financial inclusion of such a sizeable number into the economy, and winning their trust and confidence in the financial institutions, based on their religious beliefs, will go a long way in strengthening the resilience and stability of the financial system. This is expected to replace informal markets with formal and regulated ones. The entry of Islamic banks is also expected to engender a wave of healthy competition in the banking industry. Business minded non-Muslims in Nigeria are expected to join and support the system, either based on the ethical and social values of Islamic finance principles or based on their desire to explore an alternative to conventional finance. Islamic finance is not a religious activity restricted to Muslims, but is open to all segments of the society.[178]

Nigeria is looking beyond its borders and hopes to become Africa's Islamic financial hub. This would translate to multiple benefits for Nigeria, such as increased foreign direct investments (FDI), infrastructure development, increased employment, and development of the real sector of the economy. The CBN has sponsored and organised local and overseas training programmes for its officials to address the knowledge and capacity gaps. Equally, the Islamic Development Bank recently granted a Technical Assistance programme for the CBN for the purpose of capacity building and creation of awareness of Islamic banking in Nigeria. Furthermore, the CBN is leveraging its membership and/or relationship with international organisations and other regulatory agencies such as the Islamic Financial Services Board (IFSB), Bank Negara Malaysia, and Bank of Sudan to further address these challenges. The CBN recently issued a draft framework for the regulation and supervision of non-interest banks in Nigeria for comments by stakeholders.[179] The framework and reference to non-interest financial institution (NIFIs) applies to a wide range of financial institutions, including a full-fledged non-interest deposit money bank or subsidiary, a fully-fledged non-interest microfinance bank or subsidiary, a non-interest branch of a conventional bank or financial institution, a non-interest window of a conventional bank or financial institution, a development finance institution registered with the CBN to offer non-interest financial services either full-fledged or as a subsidiary, a primary mortgage institution registered with the CBN to offer non-interest financial services either full-fledged or as a subsidiary, and a finance company registered with the CBN to provide non-interest financial services, either full-fledged or as a subsidiary. This makes the framework arguably one of the most comprehensive in terms of the reference to the types of enabling non-interest financial institutions.[180]

The framework details the legal basis for authorising NIFIs in Nigeria, including the licensing requirements, non-interest financial instruments, commissions and fees; the establishment of NIFI branches and/or subsidiaries, cross-selling of products/services and shared facilities (the non-interest subsidiaries, and that windows or branches may operate using the existing facilities or branch network of the conventional bank. The non-interest subsidiaries, windows, or branches shall not sell non-Sharī'ah compliant products/services on behalf of the parent conventional bank. Rather, it should engage in the execution of service-level agreements in respect of shared services, intra-group transactions and exposures, corporate governance, conduct of business standards, profit sharing investment accounts, audit, accounting and disclosure requirements, prudential requirements, risk management, and anti-money laundering, and combating of terrorism financing.[181]

As far as Sharī'ah governance is concerned, the CBN is reported to be following the model adopted by countries such as Malaysia, Sudan, Indonesia, and Pakistan by having an advisory body on Sharī'ah compliance at the central bank, called the CBN Sharī'ah Council (CSC). The CSC shall advise the CBN on Sharī'ah matters pertaining to Islamic law relating to financial transactions and assist the CBN to effectively regulate and supervise NIFIs in Nigeria.[182]

The IFC, which is the private sector arm of the World Bank Group, has recently indicated its willingness to support Islamic banking in Nigeria. The new push for increased patronage for Islamic banking in the country and the world, noted IFC, is part of its strategies to deepen the growth of Islamic finance across the world through the introduction of new financial products in emerging markets. IFC believes that making Islamic finance products more available could help develop financial markets and promote economic growth, especially by increasing access to education, small business financing, and housing finance. It observed that Islamic finance represents an untapped source of capital and a new frontier of business opportunities that will help it meet the goals for increasing investment in the world's poorest countries. IFC's goal for Islamic banking in Nigeria is to innovatively channel the Muslim world's growing financial resources towards meeting development challenges in the country and the world at large.[183]

During the early days of the attempt to introduce Islamic finance into Nigeria, there were allegations that Islamic finance is "Sharī'ah implementation through the backdoor," "financing terrorism," or "favouring one section of the population over the other" and so on.[184] Yet, as will be elaborated in Chap. 8, such claims have no basis in reality. With regard to the claim that Islamic finance is favouring one section of the population over the other, it stands in sharp contrast with the reception of Islamic finance in many countries with Muslim minorities, as earlier elaborated, or the strong participation by non-Muslims in Islamic finance in countries such as Malaysia.

### *Islamic Finance in Senegal*

With Muslims comprising almost 94 % of its population, the potential for Islamic banking is strong within the West African nation. Senegal remains underbanked, with only 6 % of the population holding bank accounts, creating a big opportunity for Islamic finance. The passage of an Islamic banking law will pave the way for Islamic banks to set up operations.[185] The country has one Islamic bank, which was part of the Dar Al Mal Islami before being acquired by Tamweel Africa Holding.

Senegal started seriously thinking about Islamic finance in 2010, when the Dakar-based African Institute of Islamic Finance (AIIF-Advisory and Training) co-organised with the ministry of finance the first International Islamic Finance Forum for the Monetary Union Zone in Dakar in January 2010, with the presence of IDB President Ahmad Mohamad Ali and former President Wade of Senegal. With major players of the Islamic finance industry being present, including the IDB, AAOIFI, World Bank, and IMF, this forum became the kick-off for major strides towards the building of a solid Islamic finance industry in Senegal and in the region.

In June 2011, the African Institute of Islamic Finance partnered with the Dubai-based IIR Middle East to organise the second Islamic Finance Forum West Africa targeting the 15 ECOWAS states with the participation of Governor of Nigeria's central bank, the vice-governor of the Central Bank of Lebanon, and high-level speakers, including the CEO of the Islamic Corporation for the Development of the Private Sector (ICD).

In 2011, the ministry of finance of Senegal appointed a foreign firm to advice on necessary regulatory changes needed with the Central Bank of West African States (BCEAO) to create a favourable legal environment for the implementation of Islamic banks and the attraction of Islamic foreign direct investment (FDI). In 2011, the central bank common to the eight West African countries sharing the same currency sent a mission in London and Paris to learn about necessary steps to develop an Islamic financial system with favourable legal and regulatory environment for Senegal and its neighbouring partners.[186]

An important development in Senegal was when its Ministry of Finance announced in 2011 its intention to issue its first *ṣukūk*. This objective materialised in 2014. This inaugural CFA100 billion (approximately US$200 million) *ṣukūk* issuance was the first major *ṣukūk* issuance by a sovereign nation in Africa. The *ṣukūk* was structured as *ṣukūk al-ijara,* whereby the Republic of Senegal granted a 99-year usufruct over certain of its assets and agreed to lease them back in return for making rental payments to investors. The transaction was guaranteed by the Republic of Senegal. The *ṣukūk* provided the Government of Senegal with access to a more diversified investor base and encouraged a number of other African nations to look more closely at this alternative funding source. The Islamic Corporation for Private Sector Development (member of the Islamic Development Bank Group) and Citi Group arranged the deal.

Below are some of main features of the transaction:

- The FCTC as the issuer will issue asset-leasing certificates "*Ṣukūk*" to investors in return for cash proceeds.
- The FCTC uses the proceeds from the issuance to purchase the usufruct of the real estate assets (the *ṣukūk* assets) and to lease it to the Republic of Senegal.
- The Republic of Senegal as Lessee will pay rent to the Issuer on Real Estate Assets. The Issuer uses these proceeds to make payments of the Periodic Distributions to the *Ṣukūk* holders.
- Upon redemption or the occurrence of a dissolution event, the Republic of Senegal buys back the *Ṣukūk* assets from the Issuer, as set out in the Purchase Undertaking.

The *ṣukūk* assets consist of the usufruct of three (3) building complexes:

1. The "BUILDING ADMINISTRATIF" is the headquarters of the Government of Senegal and is located on the Avenue President Leopold Sedar Senghor, consisting of land having a total capacity of 10,181 square metres and a construction of 11 floors;
2. The "Building Peytavin" housing the Ministry of Economy and Finance is located at Place George Washington, Boulevard de la République angle rue de Carde, consisting of land having a total capacity of 3265 square metres and three (3) block constructions having respectively 6 floors, 11 floors, and 5 floors;
3. The building called "Direction du Trésor" is located on the Avenue George Pompidou Rue Docteur THEZE, consisting of land having a total capacity of 1608 square metres and constructions, having five floors, a basement, and a patio.

The evaluation of these properties has been performed by a licensed real estate expert and the auditor of the FCTC. The auditor concluded that the value of the *ṣukūk* assets is at least the value of the parts. Senegal's *sukuk* offering was seven times oversubscribed, with proceeds expected to be invested in public infrastructure, especially power.[187] According to Standard & Poor's, the Central Bank of West African States (BCEAO) in Sub-Saharan Africa, has agreed that banks can use *ṣukūk* issued by Senegal in their repurchase transactions. The Senegalese *ṣukūk* is the first of a series that will be issued by West African states and sponsored by the IDB.[188]

Another development in this area that needs to be noted is that the ICD owns Tamweel Africa Holding, which has gained control of the majority shares of the Islamic banks of Senegal, Guinea, and Niger. With Bank Asya of Turkey as a partner, the ICD has pumped in over €30 million (US$38.7 million) into the new institution, with a plan to expand into the West African market over the coming years. Senegal lacks trained staffs in Islamic finance. However, there are efforts to address the situation. The African Institute of Islamic Finance (AIIF-), for instance, is trying to build relations with countries having better experiences, such as Bahrain and Malaysia.[189]

Microfinance can also attract Islamic finance with a major microfinance entity in Senegal opening Islamic windows for pilot branches in order to tap the huge potential for Islamic microfinance in Senegal. There is also a large potential for the *Takāful* market, but this is impeded by major regulatory barriers, which need to be lifted at the regional level to allow the licensing of insurance companies to tap into that market.[190]

Senegal and members of the West African Economic and Monetary Union (UEMOA), which include Benin, Burkina Faso, Cote d'Ivoire, Guinea-Bissau, Mali, Niger, Senegal, and Togo, completed a major step towards the introduction of Islamic financial services in the region. This followed a review of the region's financial regulations. The review was completed by IFAAS (Islamic Finance Advisory & Assurance Services), which was commissioned by the Senegal Ministry of Finance with the support of the Islamic Development Bank (IDB). With the support of local taxation and legal experts, IFAAS undertook a review of the region's financial sector and the regulations pertaining to the banking, insurance, microfinance, securities, and capital markets industries. Senegalese tax laws were also reviewed to identify potential barriers that may impede the development of Islamic finance in Senegal and the UEMOA region.[191]

### *Islamic Finance in Gambia*

Gambia has one Islamic bank and *Takāful* company. The Arab Gambian Islamic Bank is one of West Africa's most dynamic Islamic financial institutions. The bank was incorporated under the Companies Act 1955 and has been licensed by the Central Bank of Gambia to operate on the basis of Islamic principles under the Financial Institutions Act 1992, as amended in 1993. The amendment was enacted by the Parliament to enable the operations of Islamic banks in Gambia. The bank commenced operations in January 1997 to carry on banking business in all its departments and branches in accordance with Islamic Sharī'ah principles and practices. The bank is mandated to carry out both commercial and development banking activities as well as trade in commodities. The Jeddah-based Islamic Development Bank holds 20 % paid-up capital in the bank, with the rest split among the Gambian National Insurance Company, Social Security and Housing Finance Corporation, and Arab and Gambian businessmen.[192]

The single *Takāful* company is the *Takāful* Insurance Company of The Gambia, which started operations in 2008. Its business plan at inception projected that it would be making profits within 5 years. However, at the close of the first financial year in 2009, the company was already in profit—a clear indication that *Takāful* is a sustainable business in the country. The annual growth rate of the company has been 85 %. The company was helped by the fact that more that 90 % of the population of The Gambia is Muslim. Since its establishment, the *Takāful* firm has so far shared profits with its clients twice.[193]

The Gambian government has been proactive in promoting Islamic finance, with regulations amended to facilitate the *Takāful* industry. For instance, local municipalities have begun offering their workers *Takāful* coverage through the *Takāful* Insurance Company Gambia. Moreover, the Gambian government has been issuing *salam ṣukūk* since 2008 as part of their liquidity management programmes. Based on government support and the rising demand for Islamic finance from the Gambian population, the future of Islamic finance in this country is very promising.[194]

### *Islamic Finance in Ghana*

Ghana has embraced Islamic finance through Islamic microfinance with the establishment of the Ghana Islamic Microfinance Company, which started its operations in September 2010. The company's CEO, Kwaku Yamoah Kyei upheld that the firm started as a response to demand, especially from rural collectives in Ghana for small business loans and for the reason that other microfinance organisations operating in the country were charging prohibitively high interest rates on microfinance loans. The Ghana Islamic Microfinance Company offers microfinance financing to Muslims and non-Muslims alike and structures its savings and current account products on *wadiah* contract. Its investment products are based on *mudārabahh* and *ijārah* contracts and its debt product is based on a contract of *Bay' Bithaman Ajil*.[195]

The company won the 2014 Islamic Development Bank Prize for Women's Contribution to Development Award for its innovative package of products aimed specifically at female smallholder farmers. Through its micro *ijarah* scheme, it rents agricultural land, and then, subleases it to farmers for an agreed period, which they pay back in the form of crops. The Ghana Islamic Microfinance also offers an interest-free loan scheme to female smallholder farmers in the form of high-quality inputs, private extension services, and tractor services against a guaranteed purchase price for their crops.[196]

The appetite for Islamic finance in the West African region is rapidly growing. One of the recent moves in that direction is that of Turkish participation bank, Bank Asya, which operates according to Islamic principles. The bank is reported to be planning acquisitions in Mali and Benin.[197] The bank is already in partnership with the ICD investing in Niger Senegal, Guinea, and Mauritania, as noted above.

### *Islamic Finance in Burkina Faso*

Burkina Faso's Coris Bank International (CBI) announced its decision to launch a Sharī'ah-compliant window in 2015. According to the bank, this will be possible due to the support of the Islamic Corporation for the Development of Private Sector (ICD), an affiliate of the Islamic Development Bank (BID). The CBI would be the first Burkinabe bank to introduce Islamic banking. According to the bank, this would enable it to set up parallel institutions for the provision of financial products to its customers on the basis of Islamic regulations.[198]

## Islamic Finance in the Central African Region

To date, the Economic and Monetary Community of Central Africa (CEMAC) has shown little to no interest in Islamic finance. This group includes Cameroon, Congo, Gabon, Equatorial Guinea, the Central African Republic, and Chad. Nevertheless, some local banks have launched private initiatives, such as Pan African Bank, Ecobank, and Banque Chari in Chad to have Islamic banking windows. More importantly, Ecobank is planning to use its branch in Chad as a pilot project for its experience with Islamic finance across the continent through its presence in 32 African countries. However, these initiatives have yet to make any real progress.

In February 2015, Cameroon's Afriland First Bank, the country's largest financial group, launched the first Islamic window of Sharī'ah-compliant financial products in the country. Afriland has offered an Islamic deposit account since 2000 to help Muslims perform their pilgrimage to Mecca, but it is now planning to offer a range of common types of Islamic financing contracts. The bank developed the Islamic window with assistance from the Islamic Corporation for the Development of the Private Sector (ICD), a unit of the Jeddah-based Islamic Development Bank through a memorandum agreement in December 2012. It should be noted that Afriland, founded in 1987, now operates subsidiaries in Equatorial Guinea, Sao Tome and Principe, Democratic Republic of Congo, Liberia, Zambia, South Sudan, and Guinea.[199]

Nevertheless, what is certain is that the prospect of Islamic finance in the region is very promising. The business communities in some of these countries are keen to adopt Islamic finance and ready to go into partnership with any foreign player willing to do business in the region. However, the region's public sector and regulators seem to have no clear strategy on the issue while the private sector has yet to develop a clear plan as it lacks concrete guidance. The only public move in the Central African region towards Islamic finance is that by the government of Gabon. It has been reported that the government is to change its financial laws to authorise Islamic finance in order to attract Sharī'ah-compliant FDI as part of the economic reforms it is currently implementing. Part of the reason for encouraging Islamic finance is to pave the way for the country to issue instruments such as sovereign *ṣukūk* in the international capital markets to help finance its infrastructure projects. As part of the planned reforms in the financial law, the country recently hosted a conference to ascertain how Islamic finance can be rolled out across the CEMAC. The region uses a common central bank and common currency known as CFA.[200]

Calling upon Islamic financial institutions to enter the African market is not a call for charity or aid, but to take advantage of the immense opportunities in the African market. These opportunities are evident in the GDP growth in the past decade or the expected GDP growth in the next decade, with both being among the highest worldwide. Economic players from around the world, including China, India Brazil, Japan, the West, and others, are rushing into Africa to gain access to the African market. In the financial sector in particular, African banks have registered double digit growth during the last decade and similar performance in the next decade is expected with international banks such as Citi, Standard Chartered, and Barclays expanding their presence in the continent.

For sceptics about Islamic finance in Africa, it is time to be realistic and not be left behind. As pointed out by KPMG, the Islamic finance industry is no longer a marginal business activity, but a real alternative financial management system. Although it is relatively young industry, there is a real potential for expansion in retail banking and consumer finance. The industry is gaining new markets and attracting new customers, including non-Muslim customers. However, the challenge, according to the consultancy firm, is how to obtain a suitable level of support from the governments and regulators in these markets towards the sector.[201]

## Notes

1. Alaa Shahine and Dana El Baltaji, "Egypt Delays Sukūk, Africa Lures Muslim Funds: Islamic Finance", *Bloomberg Businessweek*, www.bx.businessweek.com, April 11, 2011, retrieved August 2011.
2. International Monetary Fund, *World Economic Outlook April 2013 Hopes, Realities, Risks*, IMF 2013, www.imf.org, retrieved April 2013, p. 68.
3. James Watson & Others, *Into Africa Institutional investor intentions to 2016*, p. 7.

4. Ibid.
5. Helen Nyambura-Mwaura and Enos Phosa, "StanChart eyes $2.5 billion of Africa revenue in five years", www.reuters.com, April 18, 2012, retrieved December 2012; *Islamic Finance News*, "StanChart in African push", vol. 9, Issue 16, April 19, 2012.
6. Rene Kim & Ethn B Kapstein, *Banking on Africa Standard Chartered Social and Economic Impact*, Standard Chartered, www.sc.com, 2014, p. 27.
7. Islamic Finance News, *Africa the Sleeping Giant*, p. 1.
8. KPMG *Frontiers in Finance Supplement–Islamic Finance the New Agenda* 2010, p. 6.
9. Anouar Hassoune & Adel Satel, "Islamic Finance Explores New Horizons in Africa", p. 4.
10. Mohamed Damak, "Islamic Finance Could Make Inroads into North Africa, in Standard & Poor's Islamic Finance Outlook 2015, February 2014.
11. Mohamed Damak, "Islamic Finance Could Make Inroads into North Africa, in Standard & Poor's Islamic Finance Outlook 2015, February 2014.
12. Kurian Thomas, "Egypt Islamic finance sector faces uphill struggle", *Khalij Times,* June 30, 2010, www.khaleejtimes.com, retrieved March 2011; *Islamic Finance Asia*, "A Phoenix from the Ashes? The Future of Islamic Finance in Egypt", Special Report, March 2011, pp. 9–11.
13. *Islamic Finance Asia*, "A Phoenix from the Ashes? The Future of Islamic Finance in Egypt, p. 10.
14. Reinhard Klarmann, "Islamic Finance in Egypt" *Islamic Finance News Guide 2007*, pp. 92–93.
15. *Islamic Finance Asia*, "A Phoenix from the Ashes? The Future of Islamic Finance in. Egypt, p. 11.
16. Ibid, p. 9.
17. Ibid.
18. Ibid.
19. Gautam Bandyopadhyay, "Banking the Unbanked: Going Mobile in Africa", *Standard Chartered Asia, Africa and Middle East The Guide to Woking Capital Management* 2009/2010, pp. 59–67.
20. *Islamic Finance Asia*, "A Phoenix from the Ashes? The Future of Islamic Finance in Egypt", p. 10.
21. Ibid.
22. Melisa Hancok, "A Region Transformed North Africa", *The Banker* Special Supplement, *Top Islamic Financial Institutions*, November, 2012, p. 24.
23. Gerrit Seidel and others, "Islamic Finance Comes of Age Joint Opportunities for Western and Arabic Financial Institutions", Arthur

D. Little Financial Services Viewpoint, www.adlittle.se, 2009, retrieved June 2010, p. 2.

24. "Islamic Banking & Finance—Morocco's Mixed Welcome for *Sharī'ah* Financing, Special Report", www.executive-magazine.com, *Executive Magazine,* Issue 107, June 2008.
25. Mawassi Lahcen, "Morocco Permits Commercial Banks to Market Islamic Banking Products", *Magharebia*—March 23, 2007, www.magharebia.com, retrieved March 2010.
26. "Islamic Banking & Finance—Morocco's Mixed Welcome for Sharī'ah Financing, p. 1.
27. Ibid.
28. Thomson Reuters and Zawya, *Morocco Islamic Finance 2014: Unlocking the Kingdom's Potential*, 2014.
29. Aziz El Yaakoubi, "Morocco central bank plans central Sharia Board", Zawya, www.zawya.com, retrieved March 17, 2013.
30. Aziz El Yaakoubi, "Moroccan parliament approves Islamic finance legislation", Reuters, November 25, 2014.
31. Thomson Reuters and Zawya, *Morocco Islamic Finance 2014: Unlocking the Kingdom's Potential*, 2014.
32. Sherelle Jacobs, "Morocco inches towards Islamic finance", *The Banker*, July 1, 2014.
33. Aziz El Yaakoubi, "Moroccan parliament approves Islamic finance legislation", Reuters, November 25, 2014.
34. See, *The Morocco Islamic Finance 2014: Unlocking The kingdom's Potential* a Report written and produced by Thomson Reuters, Islamic Research and Training Institute (IRTI), and the General Council for Islamic Banks and Financial Institutions (CIBAFI), May 2014
35. Ibid.
36. Sherelle Jacobs, "Morocco inches towards Islamic finance", *The Banker*, July 1, 2014.
37. Business Islamica, "Moroccan consumer market ready to take-up Islamic Finance products", businessislamica.com, July 10, 2012, retrieved March 17, 2013.
38. Chiara Francavilla, "Morocco to enact sukuk law", This is Africa, May 17, 2013, www.thisisafricaonline.com, retrieved May 18, 2013.; Al-Khawarizmi Group, *Les Sukuks Une nouvelle alternative de financement pour le Maroc*, Décembre 28, 2012, www.al-khawarizmi-group.com, retrieved May 18, 2013.
39. Nouria Bourihane, "La Finance Islamique se Répand en Algérie", *Le Temps d'Algerie*, November 6, 2010. www.letempsdz.com, retrieved May 2011.
40. Patrick Abu Habib, *Islamic Finance Capturing the African Opportunity –North Africa Opportunity and Challenges*, Paper presented at the World Islamic Banking Conference Bahrain, November 21, 2011, p. 2.

41. BMB Islamic, *Global Islamic Finance Report 2011*, p. 251.
42. "Tunisia Opens First Islamic Bank in North Africa" Monday, www.Africa-investor.com, May 31, 2010.
43. Melisa Hancok, "A Region Transformed North Africa", p. 24.
44. Ibid.
45. Patrick Abu Habib, *Islamic Finance Capturing the African Opportunity –North Africa Opportunity and Challenges*, p. 5.
46. Rodney Wilson and others, *Islamic Banking and Finance in North Africa Past Development and Future Potential*, African development Bank, October 2011, p. 48.
47. Melissa Hancock "After the Arab Spring …Capital Markets" *The Banker*, September 2012, pp. 128–129.
48. Times, "Mauritania Gets its First Exclusive Islamic Bank", *Times*, Sunday, March 28, 2008.
49. Path Solutions, "Mauritania's second Islamic bank signs for Path Solutions' iMAL" *Path Bulletin*, Issue 18, December 2012.
50. Alsadek Hesain Gait, "The Impact of Demographic Variables on Libya Retail Consumer Attitudes towards Islamic Methods of Finance", *Islamic Economic Studies*, vol. 17, no. 1, June 2009, p. 2.
51. Ibid.
52. Alsadek H. Gait and Andrew C. Worthington, "Libyan Business Firm Attitudes towards Islamic Methods of Finance", Griffic Business School, Discussion Paper Finance, 2009, www.equella.rcs.griffith.edu.au, retrieved January 2011, p. 2.
53. See *Dawabit Wa Ussus Taqdim al-Muntajat Al-Masrfiyya Al-Badilah Al-Mutwafiqah Wa Ahkam Al-Sharīʿah al-Islamiyyah Fi al-Masarif Al-Tiijariyyah Fi Libiya*.
54. Rodney Wilson and others, *Islamic Banking and Finance in North Africa Past Development and Future Potential*, p. 51.
55. Patrick Abu Habib, *Islamic Finance Capturing the African Opportunity –North Africa Opportunity and Challenges*, p. 4.
56. See, Wil Crisp, Libya's banks struggle to escape Gaddafi's shadow, May 29, 2013, www.euromoney.com, retrieved June 2014; Wil Crisp, "Libya's banks Struggle to escape Gaddafi shadow"; Saleh Sarrar and Caroline Alexander "Libya Bank Lending Paralyzed Amid Interest Ban: Islamic Finance", Bloomberg, May 15, 2013 www.bloomberg.com, retrieved May 2013; International Monetary Fund, *Libya—2013 Article IV Consultation Concluding Statement Preliminary Conclusions of the IMF Mission*, March 6, 2013, www.imf.org, retrieved May 2013.
57. Ibid.
58. International Monetary Fund, *Libya—2013 Article IV Consultation Concluding Statement Preliminary Conclusions of the IMF Mission*, March 6, 2013, www.imf.org, retrieved May 2013.

59. Mohamed Damak, "Le pont de la finance islamique" Les Afriques, February 22, 2010, www.lesafriques.com, retrieved May 2011.
60. Melisa Hancok, "A Region Transformed North Africa", p. 24.
61. Rodney Wilson and others, *Islamic Banking and Finance in North Africa Past development and Future Potential*, p. 51.
62. Tripoli Post, "Islamic Finance Moves Slowly Moves into North Africa", *Tripoli Post*, June 7, 2008, www.tripolipost.com, retrieved June 2011.
63. Anouar Hassoune & Adel Satel, "Islamic Finance Explores New Horizons in Africa, p. 4.
64. Thorsten Beck & others, *Financing Africa Through the Crisis and Beyond*, The World Bank, September 2011, p. 101.
65. Mohamed Akram Laldin, "The Generation Game", *Islamic Business and Finance*, Issue 32, July 2008, pp. 8–10.
66. Thorsten Beck & others, *Financing Africa through the Crisis and Beyond*, The World Bank 2011, pp. 111–113.
67. Ibid.
68. Ibid.
69. Ibid.
70. Mushtak Parker, "World Bank declares Islamic finance a priority area", *Arab News*, May 16, 2011, www.arabnews.com, retrieved June 2011.
71. Ibid.
72. Douglas Pearce, *Financial Inclusion in the Middle East and North Africa: Analysis and Roadmap Recommendations*, Policy Research Working Papers 5610, World Bank, March 2011; Mahmoud Mohieldin, Zamir Iqbal, Ahmed Rostom and Xiaochen Fu, *The Role of Islamic Finance in Enhancing Financial Inclusion in Organization of Islamic Cooperation (OIC) Countries*, Policy Research Working Paper 5920, The World Bank, Islamic Economics and Finance Working Group, December 2011, p. 3.
73. Douglas Pearce, *Financial Inclusion in the Middle East and North Africa: Analysis and Roadmap Recommendations*, p. 33.
74. IFSB-IRTI-IDB, *Islamic Finance: Global Financial Stability*, 2010, www.ifsb.org, retrieved April 2011, p. 40.
75. Zeti Zeti Akhtar Aziz, "The New Islamic Finance Landscape", Keynote address by the Governor of the Central Bank of Malaysia, at the Islamic Financial Intelligence Summit (IFIS) 2011, "The New Islamic Finance Landscape", Kuala Lumpur, November 15, 2011. BIS central bankers' speeches, www.bis.org, p. 4.
76. See, www.ifsb.org
77. Ibid.
78. Mushtak Parker, "Ex-IFSB chief sheds light on Islamic finance issues", *Arab News*, May 29, 2011, www.arabnews.com, retrieved June 2011.
79. See, www.ifsb.org
80. Ibid.

81. Umer Chapra, "The Global Financial Crisis: Can Islamic Finance Help minimizing the Severity and Frequency of such crisis in the Future?", A paper prepared for presentation at the Forum on the Global Financial Crisis to be held at the Islamic Development Bank on 25 October 2008, pp. 14–15.
82. M. Kabir Hassan and Rasem N. Kayed, "The Global Financial Crisis, Risk Management and Social Justice in Islamic Finance" *ISRA International Journal of Islamic Finance*, vol. 1, Issue 1, 2009, pp. 33–34.; Zeti Akhtar Azizi, Governor's speech at the 7th Islamic Financial Services Board Summit—Global Financial Architecture: Challenges for Islamic Finance, Manama Bahrain, May 4, 2011.
83. Thorsten Beck, Asli Demirgüç-Kunt and Ouarda Merrouche, *Islamic* vs. *Conventional Banking Business Model, Efficiency and Stability*, The World Bank Development Research Group Finance and Private Sector Development Team, October 2010, pp. 2–4.
84. Juan Solé, *Introducing Islamic Banks into Conventional Banking Systems*, IMF Working Paper, 2007, www.imf.org, p. 2.
85. Patrick Imam and Kangni Kpodar, *Islamic Banking: How Has it diffused?*, p. 20.
86. Anouar Hassoune & Adel Satel, *Islamic Finance Explores New Horizons in Africa*, p. 2.
87. The Economist, "Turning towards Mecca Islamic banks join in the race for Africa".
88. Ibid.
89. Keynote address by Prof Njuguna Ndung'u, Governor of the Central Bank of Kenya, at the 5th Joint CMA/CBK/RBA/IRA Board Members retreat on collaboration among domestic financial sector regulators, Mombasa, October 13, 2011, "Financial stability and financial inclusion" BIS central bankers' speeches, www.bis.org, retrieved January 2012, p. 2.
90. Ibid, p. 1.
91. Njuguna Ndung'u, "Islamic Finance, A Paradigm Shift in Africa", Remarks by the Central Bank of Kenya, at the 3rd Gulf African Bank Annual East & Central Africa Islamic Finance Conference, Nairobi, 28 March 2011, BIS central bankers' speeches, www.bis.org, retrieved December 2011, p. 1.
92. Michael Gondwe, "Talking Notes at the Launch of the Islamic Finance Guidelines", A Key Note Address by the Governor, Bank of Zambia, December 30, 2014.
93. ZaidIbrahim & Co, *Demystifying Islamic Finance: Correcting Misconceptions Advancing Value Proposition*, June 2010, www.zaidibrahim.com, retrieved January 2011, p. 11.
94. Njuguna Ndung'u, Keynote address by the Governor of the Central Bank of Kenya, at the 5th Joint CMA/CBK/RBA/IRA Board Members

retreat on collaboration among domestic financial sector regulators, Mombasa, October 13, 2011, www.bis.org, p. 2.

95. Maher Hasan and Jemma Dridil, *The Effects of the Global Crisis on Islamic and Conventional Banks: A Comparative Study*, IMF Working Paper, September 2010, p. 5; KPMG, *Development of an Islamic Bond Market in Hong Kong what are the tax implications?*, p. 3; IMF, *Islamic Banks: More Resilient to Crisis?* IMF Survey Magazine: IMF Research, October 4, 2010 retrieved June 2011; Deloitte, *Understanding Islamic Finance*, www.deloitte.com, retrieved April 2011; Oxford Analytica, "Islamic Finance Moves Toward Common Standards" October3, 2010; Aziz Tayyebi, *Islamic Finance: An ethical alternative to conventional finance?* Discussion paper, The Association of Chartered Certified Accountants, August 2008. Zeti, Governor's Keynote Address at State Street Islamic Finance Congress 2008, Boston USA- "Islamic Finance: A Global Growth Opportunity Amidst a Challenging Environment".
96. Ernst &Young, The World Islamic Banking Competiveness Report 2012–2013, p. 4.
97. Oxford Analytica, "Islamic Finance Moves Toward Common Standards", October 3, 2010.
98. The Economist, "Turning towards Mecca Islamic banks join in the race for Africa".
99. Mushtak Parker, "Winds of change in S. African tax laws for Islamic finance products", *Arab News*, www.arabnews.com, September 26, 2010, retrieved June 2011.
100. Anouar Hassoune & Adel Satel, *Islamic Finance Explores New Horizons in Africa*, p. 7.
101. Mushtak Parker, "Takāful market set to grow in S. Africa and beyond", *Arab News*, September 18, 2011, www.arabnews.com, retrieved December 2012.
102. Ibid.
103. *Islamic Finance News*, Special Supplement, *Africa: The Sleeping Giant*, "Asset management in South Africa" August 2011, p. 11.
104. Ibid.
105. Ibid, p. 12.
106. Global Islamic Finance Magazine, "Change on the Horizon for Islamic Finance Tax Law in South Africa", www.globalislamicfinancemagazine.com also See, www.polity.org.za for the full Address by the Minister of Finance, on the Taxation Laws Amendment Bill, National Assembly, Cape Town, August 24, 2010.
107. See, National Treasury "South Africa concludes debut sukuk bond", September 17, 2014, www.treasury.gov.za
108. Opening Remarks by Governor, Bank of Zambia Dr. Michael Gondwe at the Islamic Commerce and Finance workshop on 24th march 2013 Courtyard Hotel, Lusaka, BIS central bankers' speeches, www.bis.org

109. Ibid.
110. Caleb Fundanga, Governor, Bank of Zambia "Opening Remark to the Islamic Banking Conference under the Theme "Building Partnership For Development", October 20, 2008, Taj Pamodzi Hotel Lusaka, *BIS Review*, 31/2008, p. 1.2.
111. Mwila Chibiliti, "Islamic Trade Financing: Challenges in Zambia", *Legal Notes*, vol. 5, no. 2, July 2008, pp. 7–8.
112. *Islamic Finance News*, "Islamic finance regulations", vol. 9, Issue 26, June 29, 2012.
113. The Africa Report, "Zimbabwe to introduce Islamic banking", November 06, 2013, www.theafricareport.com, retrieved November 2013.
114. Elsamawal A.Idris, "Islamic Finance in Sudan: An Overview", Emerging Market Africa, Sj berwin, Issue 3, 2009, pp. 19–20.
115. Anouar Hassoune & Adel Satel, "Islamic Finance Explores New Horizons in Africa", p. 6.
116. *Islamic Finance News* Special Supplement.
117. Renat Bekkin, "Sudan—Forgotten Centre of Islamic finance", *New Horizon*, April 1, 2009.
118. See www.kse.com.sd
119. Ibid.
120. Renat Bekkin, "Sudan—Forgotten Centre of Islamic finance", *New Horizon*, April 1, 2009.
121. Reuters, "Sudan Sells 160 million work of ṣukūk", Wednesday, July 4, 2012 www.reuters.com
122. Njuguna Ndung'u: Islamic finance—the African experience", Remarks by Prof Njuguna Ndung'u, Governor of the Central Bank of Kenya, at the 2nd Gulf African Bank Annual East & Central Africa Islamic conference, Nairobi, May 3–4, 2010. BIS Review 69/2010, pp. 1–2.
123. Islamic Globe, "Kenya's CMA in ṣukūk call", Issue 37, October 26, 2011, www.theislamicglobe.com, retrieved October 2011.
124. Ibid.
125. Njuguna Ndung'u, "Islamic Finance, A Paradigm Shift in Africa", p. 1.
126. Islamic Globe," Kenya's CMA in ṣukūk call", Issue 37, October 26, 2011.
127. Njuguna Ndung'u, "Islamic finance—the African experience", pp. 1–2.
128. *Islamic Finance news*, "230 % increase in net profit", vol. 9, Issue 1, April 2, 2012, www.islamicfinancenews.com
129. *Islamic Finance News*, "Glowing results for GAB", vol. 9, Issue 34, August 27, 2012, www.islamicfinancenews.com
130. See The Islamic Globe, "E. Africa's largest bank opens Islamic window, January 18, 2012, www.theislamicglobe.com, retrieved January 2012.
131. The Islamic Globe, "Kenya Re moves into pan-Africa reTakaful", May 4, 2011, www.theislamicglobe.com, retrieved May 2011.

132. See *The Islamic Globe*, "Kenya Freeze Takaful" January 12, 2012, www.theislamicglobe.com, retrieved January 2012.
133. Ibid.
134. Ibid.
135. Juliet Mazera," Islamic Banking in Kenya", *Legal Notes*, vol. 5, no. 2, July 2008, pp. 3–4.
136. Ibid.
137. "Essential groundwork for competing effectively in the Islamic banking environment" Remarks by Prof Njuguna Ndung'u, Governor of the Central Bank of Kenya, at the launch of the Regional Certificate in Participatory/Islamic Banking, Kenya School of Monetary Studies, Nairobi, February 25, 2014. March 13, 2014, www.bis.org
138. See, "Kenya is our first African market to offer Islamic Banking", March 19, 2014, www.sc.com, retrieved January 2015.
139. Robin Amlot, "Coming to Africa", February17, 2015, www.cpifinancial.net, retrieved February 2015.
140. Rundheersing Bheenick, "Putting Mauritius on the world's Islamic finance map" Address by Mr. Rundheersing Bheenick, Governor of the Bank of Mauritius, at the Official Launching of HSBC Amanah Islamic Banking Mauritius, Les Guibies, Pailles, May 5, 2009. *BIS Review 552,009*, pp. 1–5.
141. Rundheersing Bheenick Address by the Governor, Bank of Mauritius, at the Opening Ceremony of the Seminar on Islamic Capital Markets, "Islamic finance and its developments in Mauritius" May 19, 2009, Mauritius. BIS Review 62/2009, p. 4.
142. Rundheersing Bheenick, "Putting Mauritius on the world's Islamic finance map", pp. 1 5.
143. Najmul Rassool, "Mauritius—An Emerging Centre for Islamic Finance", *New Horizon*, July1, 2011, www.newhorizon-islamicbanking.com
144. Ibid.
145. Anouar Hassoune & Adel Satel "Islamic Finance Explores New Horizons in Africa", p. 8.
146. Patrick Kagenda, "Islamic banking will bring minor change", *The Independent*, June 21, 2010, www.independent.co.ug, retrieved July 2010.
147. Christopher Walugembe, "Islamic Banking in Uganda", *Legal Notes*, vol. 6, no. 1, January 2009, pp. 6–7.
148. Patrick Kagenda, "Islamic banking will bring minor change "*The Independent*, June 21, 2010. Emmanuel Tumusiime-Mutebile: "Banking issues in Uganda, *BIS Review* 130/2009, "The progress made on the introduction of Islamic banking in Uganda", Speech by Prof. Emmanuel Tumusiime-Mutebile, Governor, Bank of Uganda, on the occasion of

Eid-El-Fitri Celebrations at BoU Western Gardens, Kampala, September 25, 2009. BIS Review 119/2010.

149. David G Opiokello, "The Aftermath of the financial crisis and the way Forward", Closing remarks by Mr. David G Opiokello, Deputy Governor of the Bank of Uganda, at the 3rd Annual Bankers' Dinner, Kampala, May 7, 2010. *BIS Review* 65/2010, p. 4 (1–6).
150. Emmanuel Tumusiime-Mutebile, "Banking issues in Uganda, *BIS Review* 130/2009, "The progress made on the introduction of Islamic banking in Uganda", p. 1.
151. Summit Business Review, "Islamic Banking: No Riba Here?' August 28, 2010, www.sbreview.net
152. Mushtak Parker, "East Africa Catching up with Islamic Finance", *Arab News*, September 26, 2010 www.arabnews.com, retrieved June 2011.
153. Ibid.
154. Ibid.
155. Africa Review, "Ethiopian government slams door on Islamic bank", June 5, 2012; Daily Ethiopia, "*ZamZam*, the under formation Islamic bank failed to launch its operation", June 7, 2012. Tigrai Online "A newly formed Islamic bank, Zamzam failed", June 10, 2012, www.tigraionline.com, retrieved December 2012.
156. Mohamed M. Olad, "Islamic Banking: Banking the unbanked", *The Reporter*, December 12, 2011.
157. Simon Freemantle, *Africa Macro Insight, The Five Trends Powering Africa's Enduring Allure, Trend 5 Africa Deepening Financial Sector*, p. 3.
158. Ibid.
159. Jumah.Reli, Deputy Governor Bank of Tanzania speech at a high Level Seminar on the Oversight of Islamic finance, Tanzania, Dares Salaam, July 15–17, 2009, www.eastafritac.org, p. 3, retrieved March 2010.
160. Ibid.
161. Ringo & Associates, "Islamic Banking in Tanzania", *Legal Notes*, vol. 5, no. 2. July 2008, p. 6.
162. The Citizen, "Tanzania Poised to be East Africa's Islamic Banking Hub", September 20, 2014, www.thecitizen.co.tz, retrieved January 2015.
163. The Islamic Globe, "KCB rolls out retail account in Tanzania", Issue 34, October 5, 2011, www.theislamicglobe.com, retrieved October 2011.
164. *The Islamic Globe*, "Tanzania's first Islamic bank takes off", December 2011, www.theislamicglobe.com, retrieved December 2011.
165. *The Islamic Globe*, "KCB rolls out retail account in Tanzania".
166. *The Islamic Globe*, "Zanzibar's People's Bank opens Islamic window", December 21, 2011,www.theislamicglobe.com, retrieved December 2011.

167. Summit Business Review, Islamic Banking: No Riba Here?', August 28, 2010, www.sbreview.net
168. Opening Remarks by Mr. Frabcois Kanimba, The Governor, National Bank of Rwanda at the Meeting of East African Community IEAC) Monetary Affairs Committee (MAC) Arusha Tanzania 10th May, 2010, www.eac.int, p. 3.
169. Mohamed Farah Mead, *Islamic Banking in Djibouti Challenges and Opportunities*, Project Submitted for the fulfilment of the requirement of Master in Business Administration Open University Malaysia –Bahrain 2010, p. 12.
170. Djama M. Haid, Governor of the Central Bank of Djibouti speech at the Inaugural Islamic Banking Summit Africa (IBSA 2012) held on the 6th and 7th of November 2012. p. 4.
171. Bernardo Vizcaino, "Djibouti enlists Islamic finance to boost banking penetration", *Reuters*, November 7, 2013
172. Abdulkadir Khalif, "International Bank of Somalia opens in Mogadishu, Africa Review, October 11, 2014, www.africareview.com, retrieved January 2015.
173. Mushtak Parker, "IDB joins hands with AfDB to boost development", *Arab News*, December 26, 2010, www.arabnews.com, retrieved June 2011; Mushtak Parker, "Asya Bank makes mark in cards", *Arab News*, February 22, 2010, www.arabnews.com, retrieved June 2011.
174. Femi Sunmonu & Associates, Barristers & Solicitors, "Islamic Financial Services in Nigeria", *Islamic Finance News Guide 2007*, pp. 90–92.
175. Gautam Bandyopadhyay, "Banking the Unbanked: Going Mobile in Africa", *Standard Chartered Asia, Africa and Middle East the Guide to Working Capital Management* 2009/2010, pp. 59–67.
176. Bashir Aliyu Umar, "Islamic Finance in Nigeria: Issues and Challenges" *The Guardian*, January 5, 2011.
177. Bernardo Vizcaino, "Nigeria Favors Centralized Approach for Takaful Firms", Reuters, May 3, 2013, www.reutersreprints.com retrieved June 2013.
178. Bashir Aliyu Umar, "Islamic Finance in Nigeria: Issues and Challenges".
179. *Gulf News*, "Nigeria on track to be Africa's Islamic finance hub", June 14, 2010, www.gulfnews.com, retrieved June 2011.
180. Mustak Parker, "Islamic banking gaining foothold in Nigeria", *Arab News*, Jan. 31, 2011, www.arabnews.com, retrieved June 2011.
181. Ibid.
182. Ibid.
183. Uhomoibhi Toni Aburime and Felix Alio, "Islamic Banking: Theories, Practices and Insights For Nigeria", *International Review of Business Research Papers*, vol. 5, no. 1, January 2009, pp. 321–339; Amechi

Ogbonna, "IFC to support Islamic banking services in Nigeria", Sunday, August 25, 2008, *The Sun News On-line*, retrieved August 29, 2008.

184. *The Islamic Globe*, "If not now, when", *The Islamic Globe*, Issue 31, September 14, 2011, www.theislamicglobe.com, retrieved September 2011.
185. Shaheen Pasha, "Senegal Eye First Sukūk as Africa look to Islamic finance", Reuters, November 11, 2011, www.reuters.com, retrieved January 2012.
186. Lamine Mbacke, "Senegal: Human capital a main concern", *Islamic Finance News Guide 2012*, February 16, 2012, www.islamicfinancenews.com, retrieved April 2012.
187. The Economist Intelligence Unit, Risk and Reward: The Gulf Push into African Infrastructure, commissioned by Dubai Chamber, 2014.
188. Samira Mensah, *After A Mixed 2013, The Global Sukuk Market Looks Promising In 2014*, February 4, 2014 in Standard & Poor's Islamic Finance Outlook 2015.
189. Ibid.
190. Ibid.
191. Robin Amlôt, "West Africa moves towards the introduction of Islamic finance", www.cpifinancial.net, July 09, 2012.
192. *Islamic Business and Finance*, Issue, 64, p. 23.
193. Steve Mbogo, "TIC ups presence in the Gambia", *The Islamic Globe*, Issue 31, September 14, 2011 www.theislamicglobe.com, retrieved May 2012.
194. BMB Islamic, *Global Islamic Finance Report 2011*, p. 251.
195. Steve Mbogo, "Out of Africa", *The Islamic Globe*, Issue 17, June 8, 2011, www.theislamicglobe.com, pp. 1–3.
196. Ghana Islamic Microfinance, "Islamic Development Bank To Honor Ghana Islamic Microfinance", June 20, 2014, www.businessghana.com
197. *Reuters*, "Bank Asya says plans acquisitions in Mali and Benin", May 23, 2011, www.reuters.com, retrieved March 2012.
198. *Islamic Finance News*, –October 8, 2014, vol. 11, Issue 41.
199. Reuters, "Cameroon's Afriland First Bank launches Islamic window", February 22, 2015, www.reuters.com; Yuh Timchia, "Saudis to launch Islamic banking in Cameroon", www.africareview.com, December 21, 2012.
200. Steve Mbogo, "Gabon Court Islamic Finance", *The Islamic Globe*, Issue 31, September 14, 2011, www.theislamicglobe.com, retrieved May 2012.
201. KPMG, *Growth and Diversification in Islamic Finance* 2007, www.kpmg.com, retrieved June 2011, p. 19.

CHAPTER 4

# Africa's Economic Growth: Indicators and Investment Opportunities

## Economic Growth

Over the past decade and half, Sub-Saharan Africa's real GDP growth rate has jumped to an annual average of 5.7 %, with forecasts that Africa's economy will grow at an average annual rate of 7 % over the next 20 years—slightly faster than China.[1] Few people know that from 2000 to 2010, the fastest growing country in the world was Angola, with far stronger growth than China.[2] *The Economist* noted that over the 10 years from 2000 to 2010, six of the world's ten fastest growing economies were in Sub-Saharan Africa while the IMF forecasts that Africa will grab seven of the top ten places.[3] The trend is continuing and Africa was home to eight of the world's 15 fastest growing economies between 2000 and 2013.[4]

On a similar note, the global management consulting, technology service, and outsourcing company Accenture stressed that "13 African countries already have a higher per capita GDP than China, and 22 are higher than India."[5]

This optimistic view is also shared by former Goldman Sachs' Asset Management Chief Jim O'Neill, known for spotting opportunities in Brazil, Russia, India, and China and coining the term BRIC. He stressed that people are increasingly concentrating on the opportunities in the continent. Foreign companies have significantly raised their presence and more investment is expected. Besides the traditional areas of focus, such as commodities and mining, other sectors, such as retail and financial services, are also attracting greater attention.[6]



M. Al Bashir M. Al Amine, *Islamic Finance and Africa's Economic Resurgence*, DOI 10.1007/978-3-319-28835-2_4

Prior to the global economic crisis, economic growth in the continent was averaging 5 % a year for a decade and had accelerated to 6 % between 2006 and 2008. This growth was widespread and not limited to countries relying on oil and its high prices. In fact, 22 non-oil exporting countries had 4 % or higher growth during 1998–2008. While Africa was affected by the global crisis, the continent avoided a worse growth shortfall in 2009, and had rebounded in 2010 as a result of prudent macroeconomic policies and financial support from multilateral agencies. Moreover, Africa's poverty rate was falling one percentage point a year, from 59 % in 1995 to 50 % in 2005, with the trend expected to continue.[7] A recent study by the Federal Reserve Bank of New York pointed out that the poverty rate for these countries in 1990 was 34 %. It rose to a maximum of 36.5 % in 1992, and then began a sustained decline that continued even after the crisis. By 2011, US$1/day poverty had fallen to under 21 %."[8]

Similarly, child mortality rates are declining and have been a tremendous success story that has only barely been recognised. According to the World Bank, 16 of the 20 African countries which have had detailed surveys of living conditions since 2005 reported falls in their child mortality rates. Twelve had falls of over 4.4 % a year, which is the rate of decline that is needed to meet the millennium development goal (MDG) of cutting the child mortality rate by two-thirds between 1990 and 2015.[9] The decline in African child mortality is speeding up. In most countries, it is now falling about twice as fast as during the early 2000s and 1990s. More strikingly, the average fall is faster than it was in China in the early 1980s, when child mortality was declining around 3 % a year, admittedly from a lower base. *The Economist* pointed out that the top rates of decline in African child mortality are the fastest seen in the world for at least 30 years. What is striking, according to the magazine, is that the falls have been widespread—with falls recorded in large and small countries, in Muslim and Christian majority, and in every corner of the continent. The three biggest successes are in east, west, and central Africa.[10] Despite the fact that Sub-Saharan Africa witnessed unprecedented declines in child mortality over the past two decades, more still needs to be done. The average child mortality rate decreased from 174 per 1000 in 1990 to 92 per 1000 in 2014, according to a recent report by the United Nations Children's Fund (UNICEF). Sub-Saharan Africa has reduced the under-five mortality rate by 48 % since 1990, the report said; however, the region still has the world's highest rate. When considering birth rates, if current demographic trends continue, an estimated five billion children will be born worldwide between 2015 and 2050, 1.6 billion of them in Sub-Saharan Africa. By 2050, 37 % of the global under-five population will be living in Sub-Saharan Africa, compared to just 9 % in 1950.[11]

Moreover, HIV/AIDS is sharply declining. According to a report by the United Nations in Sub-Saharan Africa, one million fewer people acquired HIV in 2012—a drop of almost 40 %. At the same time, there were an estimated 22 % fewer AIDS-related deaths in Sub-Saharan Africa between 2001 and 2012.[12] Moreover, primary education completion rates are rising faster in Africa than anywhere else. Furthermore, Africa's private sector is increasingly attracting investment, with much of the funding coming from domestic banks and investors. Returns on investment in Africa are among the highest in the world. Moreover, success of Information Technology—especially mobile phone penetration—shows how rapidly the sector can grow. Private capital flows are higher than official development assistance and Foreign Direct Investment (FDI) is higher than in India. Moreover, the climate for market-oriented, pro-poor reforms is proving robust. Although the payoffs to economic reforms fell during the global crisis, policymakers continued with prudent economic policies, even in the face of contradictory policies elsewhere. The voice of civil society is increasing and various groups are demanding more accountability for resource revenues.[13] As rightly observed by Ernst & Young, "there is an increasing recognition that the continent is on an upward trajectory; economically, politically and socially."[14]

Similar optimism has been stressed by Kofi Annan, the former Secretary General of the United Nations, who noted that "feeding a remarkable 'can-do spirit' and what was termed 'the hopeless continent' 10 years ago has now unquestionably become the continent of hope."[15] In parallel, *The Economist*—which, a decade ago, depicted Africa as the "hopeless continent" —acknowledged in 2011 that "since The Economist regrettably labelled Africa 'the hopeless continent' a decade ago, a profound change has taken hold."[16]

After decades of poor performance, Africa has worked its way into the global dialogue on economic opportunity and growth. Africa's reputation as a viable and profitable investment destination has grown rapidly. Its population presents a new market for many products and services.[17] Over the past decade, Sub-Saharan Africa's real GDP growth rate jumped to an annual average of 5.7 %—up from only 2.4 % over the previous two decades. That beats Latin America's 3.3 %, but falls short of Asia's 7.9 %. Asia's stunning performance largely reflects the vast weight of China and

India, if we take into consideration that most other economies saw much slower growth—such as 4 % in South Korea and Taiwan. The simple unweighted average of countries' growth rates in Africa and Asia was virtually identical.[18] As rightly observed by *The Economist,* although the rise of the BRICs and Asia's impressive economic performance have been frequently highlighted, analysis show that over the 10 years to 2010, six of the world's ten fastest growing economies were in Sub-Saharan Africa.[19] Similar observations were reported in 2010 by *Newsweek,* which stressed that despite the recognition of China and India as economic powers and the media headlines, "there's another global growth story that is easily overlooked: Africa."[20]

More surprisingly, according to the magazine, much of Africa's growth is driven not by the sale of raw materials, but by a burgeoning domestic market—the largest outside India and China. In recent years, the surge in private consumption of goods and services has accounted for two-thirds of Africa's GDP growth. The rapidly emerging African middle class could number as many as 300 million, out of a total population of one billion, according to development expert Vijay Majahan, author of the 2009 book, *Africa Rising.* While a few of them have the kind of disposable income found in Asia and the West, they are driving up demands for goods and services such as cell phones, bank accounts, foodstuff, and real estate. In Africa's 10 largest economies, the service sector makes up 40 % of GDP, not too far from India's 53 %. Much of the boom in this new consumer class can be attributed to outside forces, evolving trade patterns—particularly from increased demand coming out of China—and technological innovation abroad that spurs local productivity and growth, such as the multibillion-dollar fibre-optic lines that are being laid out between Africa and the developed world. Other changes are domestic and deliberate. Despite Africa's well-founded reputation for corruption and poor governance, a substantial chunk of the continent has quietly experienced this economic renaissance by dint of its virtually unprecedented political stability. Encouraged by eager investors, governments have steadily deregulated industries and developed infrastructure. A study by the World Bank found that improvements in Africa's telecommunication infrastructure have contributed as much as 1 % to per capita GDP growth—a bigger role than changes in monetary or fiscal policies.[21]

Looking further ahead, Standard Chartered forecasts that Africa's economy will grow at an average annual rate of 7 % over the next 20 years, slightly faster than China.[22] Standard Chartered Group Chief Executive articulated his stand on Africa and its economic growth, saying:

> All eyes are on Africa. Over the past decade, the continent has consistently grown faster than the world as a whole. And unlike previous resource-driven booms, this time Africa's success is built on foundations that should be sustainable for the long term.[23]

Among these, according to the Chief Executive, we have the emergence of a confident African middle class, the expansion of trade, and the acceptance of the digital revolution. In fact, the opportunities are compelling across Africa. However, this does not deny the fact that there are also challenges that face the continent.[24]

The above facts are echoed by a number of other observers. McKinney Global Institute, for instance, in its pioneer and well-acclaimed report entitled *Lion on the Move: The Progress and Potential of African Economies,* emphasises that the continent is currently among the world's most rapidly growing economic regions. This acceleration is a sign of hard-earned progress and promise. Africa's economic pulse has accelerated in recent years, infusing the continent with a new commercial vibrancy and enthusiasm. Real GDP rose 4.9 % per year from 2008—more than twice its pace in the 1980s and 1990s. Telecom, banking, and retail are flourishing while construction is booming and foreign investment is surging.[25] Thus, many investors around the globe will find it difficult to ignore the region, despite the region's reputation, though sometimes exaggerated, as a tough place for business.[26] Sub-Saharan Africa, in particular, will be more than just a commodity play. With recovery in Western economies still looking fragile, there will be a growing appetite to invest in Africa, adding to the forays already made by China and India.[27]

Even some of the slightly less bullish observers, such as *The Economist Intelligence Unit*, still forecast average real GDP growth of 4.9 % for the 2012–2016 period. This growth far outweighs Western Europe, North America, and even Asia, where much investor attention is focused,[28] thereby placing African markets ahead of other emerging markets in terms of investor interest.

However, there are challenges that need to be confronted. These include regulatory and logistical issues, the challenge of providing banking services to rural populations, and the need to educate clients about the benefits of handing over their wages/salaries to banks for safe-keeping. In some cases, formal banking through branches has been successful, but in other cases, mobile banking has dominated public interest.[29]

In a much longer forecast of global economic growth, including Africa until 2050, Citibank maintained that the fastest growing region will be Africa (7.0 % pa growth in real GDP between 2010 and 2050), followed by developing Asia (5.4 % pa).[30] From its side, the African Development Bank, in making projections for Africa for the next 50 years, noted that while Africa's growth projection in 50 years from now is by no means easy or assured, given the extremely dynamic social and economic regional and global conditions, the current economic performance suggests a positive future. The bank estimates that Africa's GDP could increase to over US$15 trillion in 2060, from a base of US$1.7 trillion in 2010. Consequently, income per capita expressed in current US$ terms should grow from US$1,667 in 2010 to over US$5,600 by 2060.[31]

These positive figures are supported by a report by the United Nations Economic Commission for Africa, which stressed that Africa has strengthened the recovery that it started after the global financial and economic crisis.[32] The IMF, with particular reference to Sub-Saharan Africa, noted that Sub-Saharan Africa's recovery from the crisis-induced slowdown is well under way, with growth in most countries now fairly close to the high levels of the mid-2000s.[33]

The recovery was supported by various factors. Although commodity revenue still represents around 50 % of sources of growth in Africa, other growth factors are also contributing significantly, and vary in importance across countries. These factors include increasing inflows of FDI, debt relief, aid, increased productivity, the return of tourists after the crisis, higher infrastructure investment associated with sound policies adopted by many African countries, and a notable rise in revenue from trade services. Two distinguishing features of the current recovery have been its swiftness and strength.[34] Pointing out some of the reasons behind this growth, *The Economist* noted that "the commodities boom is partly responsible…But the growth also has a lot to do with the manufacturing and service economies that African countries are beginning to develop."[35]

African economies are expected to continue strengthening and broadening their economic performance. This upturn reflects strong economic performance in both oil-exporting and oil-importing countries that will benefit from the growth factors discussed above. Continued investment in infrastructure and in the production of metals and minerals for export is expected to underpin economic growth in some oil importing countries.[36]

The World Bank pointed out that growth was widespread, whereby some 22 non-oil exporters had 4 % or higher growth during 1998–2008.[37] In the same vein, International Business Machines (IBM) expects Africa to be a strong growth area for the information technology business, particularly over the next 5 years due to growth in banking and telecoms. IBM, which signed a deal in September 2010 to manage Bharti Airtel's IT operations in 16 African countries, has embarked on an expansion programme across the continent. There is intense focus on Africa as there are growth opportunities in the banking, telecommunications, and public sectors.[38] Ernst & Young pointed out the African growth is supported by economic and regulatory reforms, inflation has been brought under control, foreign debt and budget deficits reduced, state-owned enterprises privatised, regulatory and legal systems strengthened, and many African economies opened up to international trade and investment.[39]

In his insightful book, *Emerging Africa*, Steven Radelet joins the growing chorus of voices explaining how and why Africa has turned the corner. In Radelet's view, five main factors have worked together to turn Africa around. First of all, democratisation has opened up governments and reinforced accountability. Second, improved economic policies have curbed the worst tax and regulatory policies and debt reduction has freed up resources for development use. Thirdly ever increased number of educated people represent a valuable asset for development. Fourthly the mastering of new technologies boosted Africans' access to markets. Finally, the rise of a new generation of energetic leaders has brought new ideas and attitudes to the fore.[40] Africa no longer suffers from the problems of the 1980s and 1990s. There has been a sea of change—the continent is on the move.[41]

The upturn in national growth rates is clearly reflected in the increased profitability of companies operating in Africa. Three distinct sources of data indicate that returns on investment are higher in Africa than in other regions. A comprehensive study of publicly traded companies, mostly in the manufacturing and services sectors operating in Africa for the 2002–2007 period, found that average return on capital was around two-thirds higher than that of comparable companies in China, India, Indonesia, and Vietnam. Foreign direct investment of US companies received higher returns from their African investments than from those in other regions. Finally, a series of surveys of several thousand manufacturing firms around the developing world found that capital investment had a higher return in Africa.[42] McKinney Global Institute, in one of its researches, concluded that "global executives and investors cannot afford to ignore the continent's immense potential" as the rate of return on foreign investment in

Africa is higher than in any other developing region. Therefore, early entry into African economies will help creating markets, establishing brands, shaping industry structure, and influencing customer preferences and long-term relationships.[43]

Similar observations have been stressed by Standard & Poor's, with particular reference to sovereign rating. The agency stressed that Sub-Saharan Africa, in particular, has had to deal with two major shocks, which are the oil and food price shock of 2008; and then the global financial and economic crises of 2008 and 2009. Although we witnessed some deterioration in SSA sovereign creditworthiness, on the whole, the region has managed these challenges reasonably well. SSA's performance, according to the agency, partly reflects the past decade of macroeconomic reforms, which have put SSA countries in a better position to respond to external shocks through countercyclical fiscal and monetary policies.[44]

Moody's Investors Service, on the contrary, observed improving credit dynamics among both rated and unrated sovereigns in Sub-Saharan Africa. The rating agency noted that the pick-up in growth is sustained by a strengthening of governance, liberalisation of domestic industries, better public finance and debt management, and a boom in the region's commodities spurred by growing demand from other emerging markets. Political stability has also improved and a growing middle class has emerged, both of which are leading to profound societal changes that are helping to bolster the region's resilience. Moreover, the emerging virtuous circle of politics and economics has, in turn, improved risk perceptions of Sub-Saharan Africa among investors consequently, triggering greater demand for the region's financial assets. Moody's noted that, as a result, an increasing number of African countries are beginning to borrow from the international capital markets in response to increasing developmental financing needs driven by their rapidly growing economies. While Moody's expects these favourable trends to continue and believes that the region's dynamism is sustainable, it also recognises that progress will not be even across all countries. Considerable structural challenges remain, and the credit risk trajectories of specific countries will depend on their individual starting points, factor endowments, and political contexts.[45]

In reference to foreign direct investment, Ernst & Young maintained that "We are confident that the region is on a sustainable growth curve and that FDI rates will steadily grow."[46] Likewise, Credit Suisse noted that "Africa's promising growth outlook is based on a number of growth drivers, ranging from the continent's enormous natural resources to mobile telephony and even to agriculture."[47]

Similarly, the American giant Merrill Lynch was one of the earliest to point out the new reality in Africa, stressing in one of its reports that the African economy is expanding at rates that exceed global growth and is expected to continue doing so for the next few years. Countries are monetising their natural resources, diversifying their economies, becoming more productive and more involved in the global economy. Although a number of constraints are still in place and could hinder current and future prospects of development, the good news is that in recent years, much work has been done, and Africa's global standing on many of these issues has improved.[48]

Société Générale shares the same positive assessment of Africa's economic growth. The French conglomerate stressed that economic growth in Africa has increased markedly since the start of this century. Several factors have contributed towards this performance, such as the rise in commodities prices, increased trade and capital flows with emerging markets, but also improvement in macroeconomic policy and political stabilisation. Although strong growth does not automatically translate into true social development, this growth is expected to continue.[49]

Another leading professional services firm that has put its stamp on the promising future of investing in Africa and translating it into concrete action is PricewaterhouseCoopers (PwC). The firm has been operating in the continent for 65 years, with firms in 31 countries. It works with most of the continent's leading businesses and public sector organisations and is confident about its future in Africa. The firm recently announced an ambitious growth strategy for the region with a US$100 million investment in people and infrastructure, in order to build an integrated advisory business in the continent. The advisory firm plans to recruit 8000 additional partners and staff over the next 5 years.[50] The chairman of PwC International, commenting on a CEO survey, stressed that the regional economy could double by 2020 to nearly US$3 trillion and is increasingly seen as an important market. The survey shows that 69 % of CEOs in Africa are very confident of revenue growth over the next 3 years, compared to 51 % of CEOs globally.[51]

By the same token, Accenture noted that despite the challenges facing the continent, it believes that the recent growth is indeed lasting and should increase. The consulting company's optimism is based on the positive changes noticeable in key dimensions: consumers, resources, talent, capital, and innovation.[52] These five dimensions of growth coincide with the critical aspects of successful business operations: gaining customers, sourcing high-quality and affordable inputs, building a workforce to convert inputs into value, acquiring capital to fund ongoing growth, and developing innovations to support long-term success.[53]

Advisory firm Deloitte shared a similar positive assessment when its Director for Corporate Finance remarked that there is a general recognition that Africa is poised for growth in the twenty-first century, with some commentators even calling it the African century. The debate, according to the advisory firm, is no longer about whether there will be significant growth on the continent or not, but rather about the scale of the growth.[54]

The *Economist Intelligence Unit* stresses that, "Overall, 51 % of investors polled—regardless of their size—agree that Africa's frontier markets will offer the best overall prospects for investment growth in the next decade."[55]

Another survey conducted by Ernst & Young deduced that the continent is high on the agenda of investors, with 43 % considering investing further in the region with an additional 19 % confirming they will maintain their operations on the continent. However, almost one-third of investors surveyed are still not considering investing in Africa.[56] Moreover, according to E&Y, a critically important aspect of the changing character of activities in the region is the fact that there has been significant growth in intra-African investment in new FDI projects. This underlines the optimism and growing self-confidence of Africans, according to the accountancy firm. By contrast, new investment activity from emerging economies outside of Africa grew by only 9 % although it is recognised that this growth tends to be far less capital-intensive than investment by other emerging economies as it represents only 27 % of the total capital invested by emerging economies.[57]

A number of reasons are behind the optimistic view that Africa's growth surge was based on improved political and macroeconomic stability and reforms. Several African countries halted their hostilities, creating the political stability necessary to foster economic growth. Moreover, governments lowered inflation, trimmed their foreign debt, and shrunk their budget deficits. Finally, many African governments adopted policies to energise markets by privatising state-owned enterprises, reducing trade barriers, cutting corporate taxes, and strengthening regulatory and legal systems. Although some governments still have a long way to go, these important first steps enable a private business sector to emerge.

There is growing and diverse hard evidence to support the fact that the economic and broader developmental prospects for Africa have improved considerably over the past decade and that the continent is on a sustainable longer-term growth trajectory. African economic output has more than doubled over the past decade. More importantly, growth has not simply been a factor of resources and commodity boom, as many African economies are diversifying beyond resources, with very high growth levels in sectors such as telecommunications, financial services, and consumer products.[58]

## Africa Investment Potential

Many observers rightly uphold that the present African economic surge is real and not a one-time event. The following are some of the indicators that support this assumption:

1. **Abundance of Riches:** The continent boasts an abundance of riches and it is structurally well-placed to leverage these to its economic advantage. It is the world's most resource-rich continent, holding 10 % of the world's oil reserves, 40 % of its gold, and 80–90 % of the chromium and the platinum reserves, to name a few, coupled with high demands for raw materials.[59]

The continent also hold 85 % of phosphate rock reserves and more than half of the world's cobalt.[60] At the same time, what is important is that these figures are likely to increase in the coming years as much of the continent has not been explored for its hydrocarbon reserves or other resources.[61] Credit Suisse observed that African yearly oil production increased by 3.4 % per year, which is double the global rate of 1.4 %. Africa also holds 8.2 % of the world's total natural gas reserves. Moreover, the continent's proven oil and gas reserves have risen by 15 % in the past 10 years, compared to only 8 % for the rest of the world However, given the fact that exploration in Africa has been so limited, Credit Suisse expects a lot more oil and gas to be found on the continent. Recent discoveries seem to support this view.[62] These discoveries are merely the beginning. As articulated by Paul Collier in his seminal book, *The Plundered Planet*,[63] Africa is the last major region that remains largely unexplored. In the long-explored countries of the OECD, the average square kilometre of the territory has beneath it around US$114,000 of known sub-soil assets, despite two centuries of intense extraction. In contrast, the average square kilometre of Sub-Saharan Africa has a mere US$23,000 of known sub-soil assets. It is highly unlikely that this massive difference is due to a corresponding difference in what is actually there. Rather, the difference in known assets is likely to indicate an offsetting difference in what is awaiting discovery. The author argues that it is reasonable to suppose that what is actually under the soil in the average square kilometre of Africa is at least as valuable as what is known still to be available in the OECD. An implication is that once these untapped resources have been discovered, Africa's commodity exports will be around five times their present level. In turn, this has three profound implications. One is that many of the countries in which resources are discovered will be those that are not currently significant resource exporters; the economic map of Africa will change quite drastically as new opportunities open. The second implication is that such a radically high level of commodity exports across the region will support correspondingly larger economies. The final implication is that in the process of getting to this much higher level, Africa will have a prolonged phase of rapid growth.[64] With regard to mining, Ernst & Young noted that "Africa's share of global deal-flow tripled from 5 % in 2009 to 15 % in 2010."[65]

Africa's mining and metal economies are in the spotlight again. The return to profitability of global industries such as automotive, technology, and telecommunications works well for the continent, with an expected increase in demand for minerals and metals. This will result in positive changes in developed economies, and ultimately, lead to greater interest and activity in Africa's mining industry.[66]

It is an undeniable fact that the recent acceleration of economic growth in the continent is, to some extent, related to the rise in commodity prices recorded since 2003. For example, after having stagnated at around US$ 20 between 1990 and 2003, the oil barrel price shot up to US$ 145 during the summer of 2008, and since then, it has averaged US$ 100 until the recent decline. Africa has profited from this boom. The continent's oil production has also risen by 24 % since 2000. It is the biggest regional increase. However, this growth could not be solely attributed to a commodities boom. The McKinsey Global Institute believes that natural resources accounted for only about one-third of the continent's growth during 2000–2008. Even African countries without substantial natural resources have recorded an annual growth of 4.2 % on average over the same period, which is not very far from that of African countries exporting commodities (6.6 %). Commenting on the role of commodities in the current economic growth in Africa, *The Economist* pointed to the fact that despite being the main source of growth in some African countries, it cannot be generalised due to realities on the ground. Growth in East Africa, with little oil and only a sprinkling of minerals, is a good example.[67] The magazine added that there is no doubt that a long-term decline in commodity prices would undoubtedly hurt the economy of many African countries, but the present growth on the continent is not as reversible as it used to be. This is based on the fact that African governments have invested more wisely this time round, and Africa's commodities now have a wider range of buyers, particularly from the BRIC countries....[68] On a similar note, Deloitte stressed that "a surprising fact is that natural resources generate only a third of Africa's GDP growth. The remainder comes from other sectors such as wholesale and retail, transportation, telecommunications and manufacturing."[69] Similar conclusions have been reached by other institutions. PwC pointed out that, interestingly, Africa's recent performers have been low-income countries and not the oil-exporting countries of the continent. Although mining and oil remain big business, there are significant emerging growth areas such as infrastructure and the consumer market, with allied industries developing around both. Telecom, financial services, pharmaceuticals, and clean-tech are among such emerging sectors.[70] Based on such consensus, the *Economic intelligence Unit* showed that commodities will take a back seat as the main asset class attracting investors to the African markets in the few coming years.[71]

2. **Foreign Direct Investment (FDI):** Foreign direct investment (FDI) is among the major sources of economic development. It offers multiple benefits, such as funds expertise and know-how, ideas, talent, and connections to the wider world. It is often considered the single most effective source of investment in contributing to economic growth, strengthening companies and sectors, and increasing employment and income. In the case of Africa, FDI originates not only from outside the continent but also, increasingly, from within the continent itself as comparatively more advanced economies invest in Africa's future beyond their own borders.[72] FDI in Africa has increased from US$9 billion in 2000 to US$62 billion in 2008. When measured relative to GDP, this is almost as large as the flow into China.[73] At the same time, FDI by African companies has risen by 81 % annually since 2002—more than double the

> growth rates of Latin America and Asia.[74] In particular, FDI from Africa's new trading partners in Asia—mainly China and India—is expected to strengthen Africa's economic growth. Such diversification of financing sources for much-needed public investment would be welcome, but extra care is needed, given the fact that such investments would also require a coherent macroeconomic policy and foreign exchange regime to cope with capital flow surges.[75] Foreign direct investment into Africa will reach US$ 150 billion a year by 2015, according to a report by Ernst & Young. The report points out that the continent, which received US$84 billion in FDI in 2010, is becoming a magnet for investors seeking higher returns as local governments work to improve risk perceptions. Over 40 % of the 562 global executives polled by Ernst & Young said they were considering increasing investments in Africa over the next decade. Consumer goods, construction, telecommunications, financial services, and mining are among the sectors perceived to have the greatest potential. Ernst & Young expects African GDP to rise from US$1.6 trillion in 2008 to US$2.6 trillion in 2020.[76] The global accounting firm observed that Africa currently attracts less than 5 % of global FDI projects, which is not reflective of the attractiveness of the African growth story. Although Africa's FDI has grown to some extent over the last decade, it does not accurately reflect the potential of a region that has one of the fastest economic growth rates and highest returns on investment in the world.[77]

It is extremely important for investors seeking to realise the high returns on offer from the continent to understand that it will make less and less sense to compare investment in Africa with investment in developed regions in terms of risk/reward factors. The factors are fundamentally different. Levels of risk can be high, but levels of profitability are also high, with competition in some sectors comparatively low. This investment window may not remain open for long. Africa appears to be relatively well-positioned, while the only emerging region clearly ahead of the continent in terms of investor perceptions at this time is Asia.[78]

What is also noticeable is the fact that intra-African investment continues to steadily rise and investors are looking beyond the more established markets of the continent by expanding their operations and moving into more consumer-related sectors as Africa's middle class expands. African investors nearly tripled their share of FDI projects over the last decade—

from 8 % in 2003 to 22.8 % in 2013. However, it must be acknowledged that despite the fact that Africa's share of global FDI projects has grown steadily in the past decade, it remains around 5 % of global flows, and therefore, efforts are needed to improve the situation. In 2013, Africa received 5.7 % of global FDI projects. This is up from just 3.6 % in 2003 and represents its highest share in the past decade.[79]

3. **Demography and Urbanisation:** Another factor concerning Africa's positive outlook as a suitable destination for investment is the social and demographic trends that are creating new engines of domestic growth, such as urbanisation and the rise of the middle-class African consumer. For instance, in the 1980s, just 28 % of Africans lived in cities, while today, 40 % do so. This share is projected to increase.[80] Building on current growth rates, which are the fastest in the world, Standard Bank projects that more than half of Africa's population will be urbanised by 2030. Further ahead, by 2050, more than 60 % of Africans will live in urban areas. By that time, Africa's total population will exceed two billion, which suggests that around 800 million Africans will either migrate to, or be born in, urban areas in the next four decades.[81] Moreover, as more Africans move to urban jobs, their incomes are rising. By 2030, the continent's top 18 cities could have a combined purchasing power of US$1.3 trillion.[82] As of 2010, Africa had 49 cities with populations of over one million, compared to 42 in the United States (US), and 48 in India.[83] More positive estimates suggest that Africa today has a level of urbanisation nearly as high as China's, with 52 cities of more than one million people.[84]

Africa's large population creates a readymade market. Although most Africans are still poor, the collective purchasing power of the continent is rising. Between 2000 and 2008, GDP per capita increased by 51 %.[85] The continent will have the youngest, fastest-growing, and fastest-urbanising population in the world. Its population has increased from around 110 million in the mid-nineteenth century to an estimated one billion people today. This is set to double before 2050. Global executives cite Africa's demographic position as one of the continent's biggest competitive advantages, although it could also be a source of political risk if not well-managed, especially in countries where the job market, infrastructure, and public services cannot keep up with rapid population growth.[86]

Throughout history, cities have been the engines of economic growth and Africa will be no exception. Thus, some observers stressed that the economic future of Africa, particularly Sub-Saharan Africa, is more connected to the success of its cities, and the competitive clusters based there, than to its nation states. Cities today generate most of the subcontinent's wealth, with many thriving despite obvious challenges. Rapid urbanisation fuels economic growth and diversification, enhances productivity, increases employment opportunities, and improves standards of living.[87] While population growth can create intense pressure on resources, public institutions, and social stability, it also provides an enormous opportunity for the continent.[88] Africa's high urbanisation rate exceeds that of any other region and can be a great asset, boosting productivity, demand, and investment by creating economies of scale. The link between economic growth and urbanisation is clear. Urban-based enterprises are generally more productive than rural. This is clearly reflected in the rate of poverty, which in African cities, stands at around 35 %, compared to 52 % for rural areas, while African urban household incomes are more than double the rural incomes. Urbanisation means greater access to basic infrastructure, allowing more fluid commercial gains.[89] Pointing to the demographic factor in Africa's future economic growth, *The Economist* noted that "This 'demographic dividend' was crucial to the growth of East Asian economies a generation ago. It offers a huge opportunity to Africa today."[90]

4. **Consumer Sectors and the Rise of Middle Class:** Africa's consumer sectors—which include consumer goods, telecom, and banking, among others—present one of the largest opportunities. These sectors are already growing two to three times faster than member countries of the Organisation for Economic Co-operation and Development (OECD).[91] In the banking sector, in particular, although many on the continent do not have a bank account, the banking systems in some countries are growing increasingly sophisticated.[92] By 2010, it is estimated that 59 million African households are projected to earn $5000 or more and it is generally acknowledged that this is the level above which most people will start spending roughly half of their incomes on items other than food. By 2015, the number of households in Sub-Saharan Africa with this level of discretionary income is expected to hit 76 million. In terms of household consumption, the region's total expenditures grew from US$385 billion in 1995 to US$762 billion in 2010.[93]

This growth in consumption accompanies an equally spectacular rise in collective GDP, which is estimated at US$1.6 trillion in 2010. The consumer dimension forms a critical part of an economy's growth: consumer spending in Africa accounted for more than 60 % of GDP in 2008, according to Accenture.[94] Moreover, consumer spending increased by more than 100 % from 2000 to 2007, growing from US$376 billion to US$761 billion.[95] It is expected to reach US$1 trillion by 2020[96] *The Wall Street Journal* also noted that sustained economic growth in Africa has produced for the first time a broad middle class. It is a dramatic marker for the global economy. At a time when industrialised countries are struggling to grow, Africa is transforming into a consumer hub due to a young population.[97] Concurring to the above facts, Deloitte pointed out that many Africans are yet to be offered the products or services that correspond to their lifestyles and aspirations, and therefore, there are enormous opportunities in areas such as telecommunications, banking and financial services, freight and logistics, retail, and many more.[98]

The continent's prospects have proved alluring for giant companies such as Wal-Mart Stores Inc. that plan to use the discount retailer as a foothold for continental expansion. Yum Brands Inc. wants to double its KFC outlets in the next few years to 1200. In South Africa alone, Google Inc. and Microsoft Corp. are behind efforts to fund local entrepreneurs, with the hope that seeding African technology firms will grow their own businesses.[99]

Another sign of how multinational companies are paying more attention to Africa's emerging consumer class was Unilever's decision to turn the continent into one of its eight global operating regions in September 2011 to cater for an average 10 % revenue growth in the region, compared with 4 % across the firm as a whole.[100] This explains why institutional investors are showing particular interest in rising consumerism in the continent and its emerging middle class rating this as the most attractive aspect overall for investing in African markets, ahead of raw economic growth, and high commodity prices. This view is held by both the largest and the smallest funds surveyed by the *Economist Intelligence Unit*, whereas mid-sized funds lean more towards growth and commodities.[101]

5. **Expanding Labour Force:** Africa's labour force is expanding more rapidly than anywhere in the world. The region has more than 470 million people of working age (15–64 years old)—more than Brazil and Russia combined. By 2050, that number is projected to reach

1.2 billion, surpassing that of China and India. Not only is the labour force growing, but its productivity has experienced a noticeable improvement from negative growth in the 1980s and 1990s to more than 3 % over the last 10 years.[102] *The Economist* reported that "productivity is growing by nearly 3 % a year, compared with 2.3 % in America."[103] Over the past 20 years, three-quarters of the continent has increased its GDP per capita, which came from an expanding workforce with the reminder from higher labour productivity.[104] Between 2000 and 2008, labour productivity increased at a compound annual rate of 2.8 % in Africa, compared to 1.5 % in the USA and 1 % in Western Europe, but Africa still lags behind Brazil, China, and India, which enjoyed annual growth in labour productivity of 7.7 % over the same period.[105]

6. **Vast Potential in Agriculture:** Africa's agriculture holds enormous potential for companies across the value chain. Africa has almost 600 million hectares of potentially suitable land that is currently undercultivated. This represents around 60 % of the world's uncultivated arable land.[106]

Africa is well-positioned to experience a "green revolution" similar to those that transformed agriculture in Asia and Brazil.[107] An African "green revolution" in agriculture, based on the use of new technology and infrastructure, would have potentially enormous implications.[108] Africa has the potential to increase the value of its annual agricultural output from US$280 billion today to around US$500 billion by 2020 and to US$880 billion by 2030. This would also increase demand and stimulate the growth of other related activities, such as fertilisers production, grain refining, and other types of food processing. The total value of these additional markets could reach US$275 billion per year by 2030. An agricultural revolution on this scale would bring more land into cultivation, raise yields on key crops, and help shift cultivation from lower-value crops such as bulk cereals, to higher-value crops such as fruits and vegetables. Over the past decade, many African countries have begun expanding their cultivated lands, but more can be done. Brazil provides an example in this area. From 1987 to 1996, Brazil added one million hectares annually to land under cultivation. If Africa could achieve half that rate, it would raise production by US$225 billion annually by 2030. If Africa could raise yields on key crops to 80 % of the world average, similar to the achievements of other countries that experienced a green revolution in agriculture, the continent would increase the value of its agricultural production by US$235 billion over the next two decades. Kenya, for example, has tripled its horticulture exports to US$700 million annually through such efforts. If African countries shifted 20 % of the land now devoted to low-value crops such as cereals to higher-value horticulture and biofuels, they would raise the value of agricultural production by US$140 billion annually by 2030.[109] The above facts caused Merrill Lynch to stress that Africa could become a major food exporter, especially to countries such as China that are struggling to feed their people.[110]

As is the case with other sectors that require financing, for Africa to harness its indisputably vast agricultural potential, financing is necessary and financial institutions need to get involved. Thus, the financial and the agricultural sectors need to work closely together. According to estimates, the need for sustainable and reliable agricultural production needs to increase by 70 % by 2050 to be able to feed the world's population. Access to finance is a widely considered key to agricultural growth and agricultural finance is, therefore, a national and international development priority.[111] Access to finance is necessary to unleashing Africa's agricultural potential and growth of the sector. However, as agriculture is subject to high systemic risks, engaging with the sector has been challenging for financial institutions. Financial institutions are often unable to adequately conceptualise and assess risk, and therefore, are unable, or reluctant, to develop sustainable financial products for actors in the agricultural value chain. Consequently, agricultural clients—from smallholders to large agricultural businesses—often lack access to adequate financial services, and therefore, face severe growth constraints. An adequate policy framework is a major building block to creating a conducive environment for financial institutions to develop and put in operation effective financial products for agricultural clients.[112]

The agricultural sector could also become a catalyst for the continent's development by providing business and employment opportunities. In Sub-Saharan Africa, for instance, agriculture generates, on average, 34 % of Gross Domestic Product (GDP) and employs 64 % of the labour force, making it the largest source of employment. Furthermore, agriculture is twice as effective at reducing poverty as other sectors.[113] As is rightly pointed out by Crédit Agricole, progress in the agricultural base will continue to be decisive for development in the coming decades. Agriculture provides not only opportunities for inclusive growth, driven by rapidly increasing urban demand, but can also drive other industries, notably in the area of processing.[114]

Developing the agriculture sector in Africa is not without its challenges, such as funding constraints, market access, inadequate agricultural education or the widely publicised issue of "land grab" in the continent. Given the fact that one of the main reasons behind the underdevelopment of Africa's agriculture sector is lack of access to credit, Islamic finance should play a role in developing the sector. However, as pointed out by Standard Bank, "the introduction of new capital, skills, and technology is an essential component in unlocking the continent's ultimate allure."[115]

7. **Infrastructure Opportunities:** The continent has the lowest regional infrastructure capacity in the world,[116] underscoring the urgent need for these infrastructures to be improved. Consequently, there are great opportunities for investors in this sector. Currently, African governments and private sources are investing about US$72 billion a year in new infrastructure across the continent. However, Africa still faces huge unmet needs, particularly in the provision of power, water, and transportation that will require at least US$46 billion more in spending per year.[117] Shortcomings in the infrastructure sector represent the core issues retarding economic development in Africa. It has been reported that 40 % of the Sub-Saharan African population lives in landlocked countries with the lowest road densities in the world. As a result of this and other factors, Africa's trade costs are double those of comparable emerging markets and act as a major obstacle to intra-regional trade.[118] The World Bank estimates that US$93 billion needs to be spent on improving the energy, transport, and water sectors. One area of infrastructure illustrating Africa's potential is mobile telephony. In the past 5 years, there has been a growth rate of 49 % in mobile telephony in Africa, compared to 20 % or less in the developed world. African mobile companies have been at the forefront of the development of value-added services such as mobile banking.[119] According to *the Guardian*, perhaps the most tangible catalyst is technology. The mobile phone is fast becoming as much an African symbol as the leopard or baobab tree. A Gallup poll in 2011 found that 71 % of adults in Nigeria, 62 % in Botswana, and more than half the populations of Ghana and Kenya have mobile phones. The continent is the world's fastest-growing mobile phone market, according to the industry group,

> Groupe Spéciale Mobile Association, with Africa's 600 million users making it second only to Asia. Subscriber levels have grown by almost 20 % for each of the past 5 years,. Moreover, around a tenth of Africa's land mass is covered by mobile internet services—a higher proportion than in India. This has allowed Africans to leapfrog poor landline infrastructure. Many will get their first internet experience on a mobile rather than a desktop computer, using services that are revolutionising commerce, farming, and healthcare. Almost 18 million Kenyans use their mobiles as a bank account to deposit or transfer money and pay their accounts—contributing 8 % of GDP.[120]

Technology start-up companies are flourishing in many parts of the continent. Internet penetration is still relatively low at 120 million users, but catching up fast: the growth rate between 2000 and 2011 was 2527 %, compared with a world average of 480 %. This includes around 32 million Facebook users.[121]

It should be noted that as infrastructure improves, so will economic growth expand. Thus, "If countries can achieve 6 % annual GDP growth without good infrastructure, think what they will be able to achieve with it!"[122] Some have even gone further to suggest that it is poor infrastructure not volatile politics that could be the biggest threat to Africa's long-term economic health and growth. For years, investors have been bothered over political risks when the lack of adequate roads and ports may be a bigger long-term hindrance for the continent. Infrastructure is one of the top challenges facing many nations in Africa, given the massive investment required for road-building, development of ports and bridges, railway construction, and energy generation projects.[123] If all African countries were to catch up with Mauritius, the regional leader in infrastructure in the region, per capita growth could increase by 2.2 %. Moreover, if the region were to catch up with the Republic of South Korea, this would increase per capita growth by 2.6 % a year according to the World Bank,[124] and the figure could be even higher according to other analyses.[125] Some observers have gone even further, asserting that poor infrastructure in SSA is estimated to reduce economic growth by an average of 4.7 %[126] A study by the World Bank on Africa infrastructure pointed out to the following main findings:

- Infrastructure has been responsible for more than half of Africa's recent improved growth performance and has the potential to contribute more in the future.

- Africa's infrastructure networks lag behind those of other developing countries and are characterised by missing regional links and stagnant household access.
- Africa's difficult economic geography presents a particular challenge for the region.
- Africa's infrastructure services are twice as expensive as elsewhere.
- Power is, by far, Africa's largest infrastructure challenge.
- The cost of addressing Africa's infrastructure needs is around US$93 billion a year, about one-third of which is for maintenance.
- The infrastructure challenge varies greatly by country type—fragile states face an impossible burden and resource-rich countries lag despite their wealth.
- A large share of Africa's infrastructure is domestically financed, with the central government budget being the main driver of infrastructure investment.
- Even if major potential efficiency gains are captured, Africa would still face an infrastructure funding gap of US$31 billion a year, mainly in power.
- Africa's institutional, regulatory, and administrative reforms are only halfway along, but they are already proving their effect on operational efficiency.[127]

Energy investments are crucial to meet Africa's energy requirements, with a particular focus on generating renewable and sustainable power supplies. The African continent only consumes 3 % of the world's electricity, which is five times less than the world average. Progress in accessing modern energy has been unsatisfactory. The future of energy lies in developing sustainable alternative sources. However, policymakers must be aware of the hidden costs when deciding which types of alternative energy to use. There are alternative projects, such as the INGA dam in the Democratic Republic of Congo, which is a major hydroelectric project, that will have the capacity to generate 40,000 to 44,000 MW of energy that will be able to meet the needs of the African continent and export the surplus. It aims at making the environmentally friendly electricity generated accessible to the poorest. It is a trans-African project that many hope could foster greater cooperation between countries. The project has the potential to power the region and promises to provide good returns to investors. Whilst the project already has funding of US$2.4 billion, another US$4 billion is needed. There are still opportunities for investors to invest in this particular project and many other power-generation projects. Desertec is another alternative energy project whose advantage lies in the use of solar and wind power. Solar power is useful not just for electricity generation.[128] Power is the source of all production. Africa has a lot of power resources, and yet, on average, only 10 % of its population has access to energy. Dependence on a single energy source needs to be reduced and electricity must be produced in sufficient quantity to make it available to the masses.[129] Companies doing business on the continent lose, on average, 6 % of their revenue due to lack of electricity.[130] According to KMPG, the three sectors with the biggest infrastructure investment needs include Energy, WWS (water, waste and sewage), and Irrigation.[131]

Another important infrastructure requirement is transportation, particularly railways. The coming decade could be Africa's opportunity for investment. Although Africa is also affected by global risks, the prospect of sustaining the current growth throughout the next decade will rest on further resource discoveries and agricultural development. New transportation infrastructure, especially railways, is vital to harness these two potential sources of growth. By radically reducing transportation costs, railways could open up vast tracts of Africa to economic opportunities, especially in agriculture and mining, which represent the building blocks for future growth for many countries.[132] Paul Collier commented, "The continent needs a decade of massive investment in rail networks."[133] Such railways should be international in nature so that many of the landlocked countries would benefit. It is also very important that such a rail network is a regulated private monopoly with both financing and managerial expertise from a private company. Such projects should also be regulated by an international dispute settlement board whose members are approved by governments, investors, and customers.[134] Stressing the suitability of Islamic finance in funding infrastructure projects, Standard & and Poor's noted that "we also believe that infrastructure projects are a logical fit for Islamic finance."[135] The agency added that *ṣukūk*, in particular, given their longer tenures, stable and predictable cash flow traits that are typically associated with infrastructure projects, are ideal. Therefore, according to Standard & Poor's, the principles of Sharī'ah are a good fit with infrastructure spending, and Islamic financing—particularly *ṣukūk* financing—could play a key role in financing infrastructure projects.[136]

8. **Healthcare Needs:** According to Merrill Lynch the health sector is one of Africa's most urgent necessities and represents a great

> opportunity for investors as most African countries still have not met many of the basic healthcare needs.[137]

In its 2006 report, The International Finance Corporation (IFC) drew the conclusion that it was both financially impossible and impractical for the public sector (even with donor support) to fund all of the necessary investment in health systems in emerging economies. They forecasted a US$25–30 billion investment need in the sector over the next 10 years, of which US$11–20 billion is likely to come from the private sector. Approximately half of these investments are expected to be made by for-profit entities, with NGOs and social enterprises accounting for the rest. It is the IFC/McKinsey forecast that US$5–10 billion will be invested in health systems by the private sector over the next 10 years.[138]

The current unprecedented economic growth in Africa is expected to expand the health care gap, as higher incomes will create new demand. The biggest individual investment opportunities, according to the IFC, will be in building and improving the sector's physical assets. It estimated that the market for health care will more than double by 2016, going up to US$35 billion. Around 550,000–650,000 additional hospital beds will need to be added to the existing base. An approximated additional 90,000 physicians, 500,000 nurses, and 300,000 community health workers will be required over and above the numbers that will graduate from the existing medical colleges and training institutions. Demand for better distribution and retail systems and for pharmaceutical and medical supply production facilities will also be strong. A broad range of investment opportunities exists across all components of the healthcare industry throughout the region. These opportunities can deliver compelling financial returns and have an enormous potential development impact. Healthcare provision, distribution and retail, pharmaceutical and medical product manufacturing, insurance, and medical education are main sectors that will absorb such an investment. These investments will fund capacity expansion, new businesses, and renovation of existing assets. According to the report, only a quarter of the opportunities are expected to have a project size larger than US$3 million.[139]

The landscape of private healthcare in Sub-Saharan Africa is as diverse as that of the continent itself. In a region where public resources are limited, the private sector is already a significant player. Around 60 % of healthcare financing in Africa comes from private sources, and about 50 % of total health expenditure goes to private providers. Just as important, the vast majority of the region's poor people, both urban and rural, rely on private healthcare.[140]

Few countries in Africa are able to afford the US$34–40 per person annual spending, recommended as a minimum by the World Health Organisation. The huge need presents opportunities for investors looking to leverage growing African consumer spending power.[141] One specific example of an equity fund interested in investing in the African health sector is TLG Capital, a London-based emerging markets private equity investor. Justifying this interest in the health sector, the company maintains that while there are a lot of investors chasing the telecoms sector, it is worth looking at the sector that not many people are focused on. In 2010, the company acquired a 40 % stake in Liberian healthcare provider Snapper Hill Clinic, which offers general healthcare services and consultations, including general practitioner diagnoses, referrals, minor surgical procedures, prescriptions, pharmacy, and laboratory services. After the capital injection, the clinic expanded into medical diagnostics, X-ray scanning, ultrasound and echo cardiography, PAP tests, and child immunisation services.[142]

Other investors are looking beyond primary healthcare provisions, and moving into medical-related manufacturing, information technology, distribution, and risk pooling. Aureos Advisers, for instance, is in the process of raising US$100 million for its Africa Health Care fund to invest in companies requiring early stage and growth capital funding. They identified 26 companies to which it is looking to commit a total of US$69 million, investing between US$250,000 and US$5 million per company.[143] The market is huge, with Nigeria alone estimated to be spending over US$1 billion on foreign medical services a year. Therefore, there is a huge amount of income that can be generated in their country of origin if a company is able to provide equal services.[144]

The combination of economic strength and an expanding middle class is already driving a demand for medicines across Africa. By 2016, according to a recent IMS Health report, pharmaceutical spending in Africa is expected to reach US$30 billion. This value is driven by a 10.6 % compound annual growth rate through 2016, second only to Asia Pacific (12.5 %) and in line with Latin America (10.5 %).[145] By 2020, the market, as per the same estimates, represents a US$45 billion opportunity to be driven by stability in the region, economic growth, and demographic changes.[146] According to the report, the appeal of Africa lies not in its size—the continent accounts for just 3 % of the global economy—but in the dynamics that drive sustainable growth at a time when the major established pharmaceutical markets face a more uncertain future. Africa is demonstrating more predictable growth and its economy is still maturing, rather than being in a point of over-saturation. IMS also illustrates that Africa's rising middle class, which accounts for 34 % of the continent's inhabitants, is another factor that will accelerate this growth.[147] Real gross domestic product (GDP) is expected to grow at 5 % per annum through 2017 in SSA and rising healthcare spending is expected to continue.[148]

Healthcare spending in Africa has grown at a rate of 9.6 % across 49 countries over the last decade, and the demand for medicine in Sub-Saharan part of the continent is expected to outpace any other region of the world, with cities focusing on as much as 20–30 % of the total market share.[149]

The key elements underpinning a successful market strategy in Africa are similar to those elsewhere in the world, such as choice of location, operational strategy, and portfolio selection. When selecting target markets, a consideration for economic strength, the adequacy of the healthcare environment, demographic transitions towards a larger population of working age, and therapy potential are critical. However, according to IMS Health report, there are three differentiating attributes to Africa when it comes to assessing what it takes to succeed. Firstly, to really fulfil pharmaceutical opportunity potential, a strategy needs to be tailored for different areas within a large heterogeneous market. Pharmaceutical companies need to understand the similarities and differences across the continent that hinge on geographic, economic, and cultural attributes. Secondly, unlike Western markets, most African markets have nascent market access capabilities. This is predominantly manifested in the hurdles companies must overcome when registering, pricing, and distributing their product and in ensuring their product is accessible and usable by the patient. Finally, African markets are still poorly understood, with information on medicine consumption yet to be systematically collected. Consequently, market players need to work with local partners to strengthen and leverage data collection to inform the opportunity. Information is also crucial to sustain and build the opportunity, moving forward.

The pharmaceutical market growth in African countries has already generated interest from multinational companies (MNCs), Indian and Chinese pharmaceutical companies, as well as local manufacturers in Northern and South Africa.[150] Most of the major pharmaceutical companies have had a presence in Africa for a number of years. Among the first companies to enter the continent were Abbott (South Africa, 1930s), Sanofi-Aventis (Morocco, 1953), Novartis (Egypt, 1962), Pfizer (Morocco, 1963), and GSK (Nigeria, 1971). MNCs have predominantly focused on, and succeeded in marketing, branded innovative, and generics drugs to the private sector in urban areas.[151]

9. **Improved Macroeconomic Stability:** Governments in Africa have significantly improved the continent's macroeconomic stability. The continent has managed to reduce its collective inflation rate.[152] They have also cut their combined foreign debt from 82 % of GDP to 59 % and shrunk their budget deficits from 4.6 % of GDP to 1.8 %. Moreover, external debt as a percentage of GDP has fallen.[153] Finally, African governments have begun adopting economic policies aimed at energising markets. They have privatised state-owned enterprises, allowed more business competition, opened trade, lowered taxes, and strengthened regulatory and legal systems.[154] The World Bank acknowledged that over the last decade, many African countries have been focusing on getting the economic fundamentals right. They have put in place more sustainable fiscal policies, controlled inflation, and managed their debt. Some countries have gone further, addressing fundamental structural rigidities by divesting from private-sector activity, opening up some publicly dominated sectors—such as telecommunications—and reducing public-sector borrowing from the banking sector, which is crowding out private investment. These reforms have paid off. Both domestic and foreign investors welcomed these reforms, and FDI has increased significantly.[155] Related to that is the fact that the average annual consumer price inflation in Sub-Saharan Africa has fallen from nearly 50 % in the mid-1990s to 7.5 % in 2010—a sign of improving economic management.[156] The latest figures from the IMF indicate that inflation in Africa will decline to 6.8 % in 2016, owing to increasingly prudent monetary policies as well as moderating import prices.
10. Africa's economic potential extends well beyond commodity exporting. The continent is soon expected to be the last remaining major low-wage region. Per capita GDP in China is already above the global average, so its days as the low-wage factory of the world are limited. Africa has an enormous coastline and closer proximity to both European and North American markets than Asia.[157] Over

the past three decades, offshoring has shifted labour-intensive manufacturing from the OECD countries to Asia. In the next decade, expect the same process to begin shifting these activities from Asia to Africa.

11. Africa is also gaining increased access to international capital flows. Total capital flows to the continent including FDI, bank lending, and investor purchases of equity and debt securities from African issuers have increased from just US$15 billion in 2000 to a peak of US$87 billion in 2007, surpassing both aid and remittances in scale. While Africa's oil, gas, and mining sectors have historically attracted the majority of new foreign capital, new investments are also being made in banking, tourism, textiles, construction, telecommunications, and other sectors.[158] Since 2010, and considering the global financial conditions, combined with sustained high growth and improved economic prospects, there has been a significant increase in private capital inflows, particularly to Sub-Saharan African countries. A recent research by IMF noted that "over the 2010–2012 period, net private flows to Sub-Saharan African countries doubled, from a low base, compared with the 2000–2007 period; in the case of Sub-Saharan African frontier markets, there has been a fivefold increase."[159] A number of factors contributed to this capital flow, including weak economic growth, excess liquidity, low bond yields in advanced economies, and the better economic prospects in Sub-Saharan African frontier markets, coupled with improved macroeconomic policy management, low debt levels, and structural reforms in a very large number of African countries.[160]
12. Africa is a young continent. In 2009, 43 % of the people in Sub-Saharan Africa were below the age of 14, compared to 20 % in China and 17 % in high-income countries.[161] Africa's population is a youthful one, with one in every seven of the world's young persons living in the continent. The median age in Sub-Saharan Africa is 19 years, compared to China's 34. This young population is choosing to urbanise at a rapid rate. By 2030, the proportion of Africa's population living in cities is projected to hit 48 %.
13. Perhaps one of the strongest evidence of the readiness of the continent for investment comes from the performance of African stock markets which, in the last decade, have undergone a transformation in terms of number, size, and depth. There are **29 formal**

**stock markets in Africa** as of 2012, from just 18 by the end of 2002, with further proposals to open new ones in a number of African countries.[162] Capitalisation for the continent has also rapidly increased, from US$245 billion in 2002 to approximately US$1 trillion at the end of 2009.[163]

14. Conflict has decreased. The total number of refugees in Africa has fallen to almost half from the number registered a decade earlier.[164] Political governance has been steadily improving across the continent, despite sporadic disturbances. At least two-thirds of African countries now have presidential term limits. Some 14 leaders have been compelled to step down from office in the last decade. As noted by *The Economist*, change of regime through election has been on the rise in Africa, "since Benin set the mainland trend in 1991, it has happened more than 30 times—far more often than in the Arab world."[165] Multiparty political systems and the discourse of political accountability are gaining wider acceptability among key stakeholders, while the media has become less gagged with the rapid spread of the internet and mobile phones.[166] As pointed out by *The Economist*, the electoral agenda in Sub-Saharan Africa becomes more common, and most posts, from the presidency to seats in the National Assembly or mayorships, are contested, rather than seized or bestowed.

The magazine added that although coups d'état have become more infrequent and despite the fact that cases failed governments and human-rights abuses remain widespread, for every two steps forward over the past 20 years, there has been at least one step back, but the overall trend appears to be in the right direction.[167]

Standard Bank stressed that "Africa's reputation, tinged by decades of instability, is gradually being altered with each election which takes place in a manner befitting of maturing democratic systems."[168] Evidence of this fluidity is found in Freedom House rankings of Africa's political systems where, in 2011, 18 % of African countries were deemed to be "free," 42 % "partly free," and 40 % "not free."[169] However, this does not deny the fact that challenges are still there and need to be overcome. Remaining in step with Africa's changing political landscape is critical for those engaged in the continent's ongoing renaissance, and an analysis of fluctuations brought about at the ballot box provides one such steer.[170]

In the 1990s, 22 African heads of state were deposed in coups, while in the 2000s, this number was reduced to seven.[171] Democracy is not by itself an end, but a means, and therefore, should not be implemented in all countries with exact similarities. There are greater values that need to be observed through democracy. Values such as justice, equality rule of law, transparency, accountability, and prosperity are the ends and objectives. Thus, a multiparty system is just a means and not an end. Paul Collier stressed:

> As in Asia, I doubt that there will be a close correspondence between the struggles for democracy and the struggles for economic transformation. The struggles for democracy do indeed have an important economic dimension.[172]

Thus, democracy through a multiparty system and elections needs to be managed carefully as multiparty system could having adverse effects. Elections have sometimes further polarised ethnic groups, resulting in violent conflicts. Elections have also sometimes allowed specific groups to continue their dominance over others by excluding smaller ethnic groups. It has sometimes been marred by widespread vote buying, bribery, and voter intimidation. Probably the worst aspect of competitive elections in Africa has been their influence on ethnic politics. Rather than uniting various groups, electoral politics in Africa have tended to divide the different ethnic groups and erode trust among them. Such negative outcomes do not bode well for creating the key social networks that are conducive for economic development in Africa.[173]

Thus, new criteria need to be designed in order to avoid dictatorships, with their consequent harmful impacts. Such criteria should help eliminate the negative effects of mere implementation of multiparty systems while preserving continued growth and economic development.

15. Many Sub-Saharan African countries have liberalised trade since the early 1980s, and since then, the continent's fiscal soundness and monetary discipline have been increasing. Debt as a share of exports has declined dramatically to levels comparable to those of other regions, and sovereign credit ratings in parts of the continent enjoy a positive outlook. More countries are now regarded as frontier emerging economies with relatively developed financial markets. The list includes, among others, Botswana, Cape Verde,

Ghana, Kenya, Mauritius, Mozambique, Namibia, Nigeria, Seychelles, South Africa, Tanzania, Uganda, and Zambia.[174]

16. The rate of poverty is falling. Since 1995, the rate of poverty throughout the continent has been falling steadily, and much faster than previously thought, according to a study released in February 2010 by the National Bureau of Economic Research, stressing that "The conventional wisdom that Africa is not reducing poverty is wrong." The study shows that:

1. African poverty is falling and is falling rapidly;
2. If present trends continue, the poverty Millennium Development Goal could be achieved on time;
3. Economic growth decreased African income inequality instead of increasing it;
4. African poverty reduction is remarkably general. All classes of countries, including those with disadvantageous geography and history, experience reductions in poverty. In particular, poverty fell for both landlocked as well as coastal countries; for mineral-rich as well as mineral-poor countries; for countries with favourable or with unfavourable agriculture.[175]

A similar positive assessment of the falling poverty rate in Africa is given by Accenture, which estimates that by 2020 poverty levels in Africa will fall to 20 % from nearly 45 % in the 1980s.[176]

Many African countries have taken bold steps to break the cycle of corruption and poverty by moving towards political stability and economic openness. This, in turn, has brought economic and social advancement as well as unprecedented receptiveness to foreign direct investment.[177] However, despite the progress made so far, the issue of governance remains a central issue to the future of Africa. This is rightly observed by the Coca Cola CEO, who said

> Whether the next decade becomes the decade of Africa or not, in my opinion, will depend upon one single thing—and everything is right there to have it happen—and that is better governance. And it is improving, there's no question.[178]

Africa's economic growth is creating substantial new business opportunities that are often overlooked by global companies. If the continent maintains its hard-won political and macroeconomic stability, and if governments continue to create a more attractive business environment, four groups of industries could together generate as much as US$2.6 trillion in revenue annually by 2020, or US$1 trillion more than today. The four groups are consumer goods and services financing, natural resources, agriculture, and infrastructure.[179]

Concluding its seminal report on the African's economy, McKinney Global Institute stated that if recent trends continue, Africa is expected to play an important role in the global economy. McKinsey's advice for companies already operating in Africa is to expand their business and urging those still on the sidelines to consider early entry in order to be able to create markets, establish brands, shape industry structures, influence customer preferences, and establish long-term relationships. And working together, business, governments, and civil society can confront the continent's many challenges and lift the living standards of its people.[180]

Beside the above listed indicators about the economic growth in Africa and the investment opportunities in the continent in the different sectors, the financial sector, in particular, holds a very promising future for investors.

## Notes

1. *The Economist*, "The Lion Kings?", January 6, 2011 www.economist.com, retrieved May 2012; Sarona Asset Management, "Roaring African Lions", *Quarterly Report 1*, 2011, www.saronafund.com, retrieved March 2012, p. 1.
2. Ernst & Young's 2011 *Africa Attractiveness Survey, It is Time for Africa*, p. 8.
3. *The Economist*, "Africa's Impressive Growth", January 10, 2011, www.economist.com, retrieved December, 2011.
4. Acha Leke, & others Lions go global: Deepening Africa's ties to the United States, August 2014, http://www.mckinsey.com, retrieved January 2015.
5. Accenture, *Africa the New Frontier for Growth*, 2010, p. 5, www.accenture.com, retrieved May 2011.
6. Jim O'Neill and Anna Stupnystka, *How Exiting is Africa Potential*, Goldman Sachs Asset Management Strategy Series, October 14, 2010, p. 1.
7. See, The World Bank, *Africa's Future and the World Bank's Support to It*, March 2011.

8. *Maxim Pinkovskiy* & *Xavier Sala-i-Martin*, "*Africa Is on Time*", *Federal Reserve Bank of New York Staff Reports, Staff Report No. 686*, August 2014, www.newyorkfed.org, retrieved February 2015.
9. The Economist, "African Child Mortality The Best Story in Development", *The Economist*, May 17, 2012, www.economist.com, retrieved December, 2012.
10. Ibid.
11. *United Nations Children's Fund* (*UNICEF*), Committing to Child Survival: A Promise Renewed Progress Report 2014, September 2014, www.files.unicef.org, retrieved January 2015.
12. *UNAIDS*, AIDS by the Numbers, www.unaids.org, 2013, retrieved January 2015.
13. See, The World Bank, *Africa's Future and the World Bank's Support to It*, March 2011, pp. 3–4.
14. Ernst & Young's 2011 *Africa Attractiveness Survey, It is Time for Africa*, p. 8.
15. Koffi Annan in his forward to *Africa Progress Report* 2011 The Transformative Power of Partnership, www.africaprogresspanel.org, retrieved January 2012, p. 6.
16. *The Economist*, "Africa's hopeful economies The sun shines bright", December 3, 2011.
17. JP van der Merwe, "Africa: Local Banks Capturing the Market", www.allafrica.com, September 30, 2010.
18. *The Economist*, "Africa's impressive growth", January 6, 2011.
19. Ibid.
20. Jerry Guo, "How Africa is Becoming the New Asia", *Newsweek Magazine*, vol. 155, no. 09, February 18, 2010, retrieved April 2011.
21. Ibid.
22. *The Economist*, "*The Lions Kings*", January 6, 2011, www.economist.com, retrieved June 2011, & *The Economist*, "Africa's impressive growth", January 6, 2011.
23. Rene Kim & Ethn B Kapstein, *Banking on Africa, Standard Chartered Social and Economic Impact*, Standard Chartered, www.sc.com, 2014, p. 1.
24. Ibid.
25. Charles Roxburgh, *Lion on the Move: The Progress and Potential of African Economies*, p. 1.
26. *The Economist*, "South of the Sahara: Boom Times, at least in Part", November 22, 2010, www.economist.com, retrieved June 2011.
27. Ibid.
28. James Watson & Others, *Into Africa Institutional Investor Intentions to 2016*, p. 6.

29. Ibid.
30. Willem Buiter & Ebrahim Rahbari, *Global Economics View Global Growth Generators: Moving beyond 'Emerging Markets' and 'BRIC'*, p. 4.
31. African Development Bank, *Africa in 50 Years Time: The Road Towards Inclusive Growth*, African Development Bank Group, Tunis, Tunisia, September 2011, www.afdb.org, retrieved December 2011, p. 12.
32. United Nations Economic Commission for Africa, "Economic and Social Conditions in Africa in 2010 and Prospects for 2011", p. 29.
33. IMF, *Regional Economic Outlook. Sub-Saharan Africa*, April 2011, www.imf.org, retrieved June 2012, p. 11.
34. United Nations Economic Commission for Africa, "Economic and Social Conditions in Africa in 2010 and Prospects for 2011", p. 29.
35. *The Economist*, "The hopeful continent Africa rising", December 3, 2011.
36. Ibid.
37. The World Bank, *Africa's Future and the World Bank's Support to It* March 2011, p. 3.
38. Reuters, "IBM Sees Strong Growth In Africa For IT Sector", June 2, 2011, www.reuters.com, retrieved December 2011.
39. Paul Collier, "The case for investing in Africa", *McKinsey Quarterly*, June 2010, www.mckinsey.com, retrieved June 2011.
40. Edward Miguel, "Africa Unleashed", *Foreign Affairs*, November–December, 2011, www.foreignaffairs.com, retrieved March 2012.
41. Paul Collier, "The case for investing in Africa".
42. Ibid.
43. Charles Roxburgh & Others *Lion on the Move: The progress and Potential of African Economies*, p. 1.
44. Christian Esters, "Sub-Saharan African Sovereigns Have Withstood External Shocks Well, But Volatile Commodity Prices Remain A Risk", pp. 33–37.
45. Oritseweyimi Omamuli, "Improving credit dynamics among sovereigns in Sub-Saharan Africa, despite challenges", Moody's Global Credit Research, June 8, 2011; David Berman "Moody's upbeat on Africa", www.theglobeandmail.com, retrieved June 2012.
46. Ernst & Young's 2011 Africa Attractiveness Survey, *It is Time for Africa*, May 2011, p. 8.
47. Robert Ruthann, *Africa's Development Prospects Remain Intact*, Equity Research, Credit Suisse, January 11, 2011, www.credit-suisse.com, retrieved June 2011, p. 1.
48. Richard Bernstein, *Africa: The Final Frontier*, Merrill Lynch Investment Strategy, July 23, 2007, www.ml.com, p. 1.
49. Clement Gillet, "Is Africa About to Take Off", p. 1.
50. "Pwc Announces Ambitious Growth Strategy for Africa", Press Release, www.pwc.com.mu

51. Ibid.
52. Accenture, *Africa The New Frontier for Growth*, 2010, p. 1.
53. Ibid.
54. Lwazi Bam, "Africa Poised for Growth", www.deloittesa.wordpress.com, retrieved March 2012.
55. James Watson & Others, *Into Africa Institutional investor intentions to 2016*, p. 10.
56. Ernst & Young's 2011 *Africa Attractiveness Survey, It is Time for Africa*, May 2011, p. 23.
57. Ibid.
58. Zahid Torres –Rahman & Michel Lalor, *The New Africa Emerging Opportunities for Business and Africa* Business Action for Africa, www.businessactionforafrica.org, retrieved December 2011, p. 5.
59. McKinsey Global Institute, *Lion on the Move: the Progress and Potential of African Economies*, p. 3.
60. Simon Freemantle, *Africa Macro Insight, The Five Trends Powering Africa's Enduring Allure, Trend 4 Africa, Africa Dormant Resources Potential*, Standard Bank, October 6, 2011, www.standardbank.com, retrieved January 2012, p. 1.
61. David McIlroy, "Africa Rising" *Quantum Finance in Perspective*, Issue 12, July 2010, pp. 23–25.
62. Robert Ruthann, "Africa's Development Prospects Remain Intact", p. 1.
63. Paul Collier *The Plundered Planet: Why We Must—and How We Can—Manage Nature for Global Prosperity*, Oxford University Press, April 2010.
64. Paul Collier, "The case for investing in Africa", p. 2.
65. Andrian Macartney, "Africa Still Golden", Eye on Africa, vol. 3, March 2011, Ernst & Young 2011, p. 10.
66. Ibid.
67. *The Economist*, "The Sun. Shines bright", www.economist.com, December 3, 2011, retrieved January 2012, p. 69.
68. Ibid.
69. Deloitte, *Investments into Africa Tackling Tax and Regulatory Challenges*, March 2010, www.deloitte.com, retrieved June 2011, p. 3.
70. PricewaterhouseCoopers, "10 Minutes on Investing in Africa", pp. 1–4.
71. James Watson & Others, *Into Africa Institutional investor intentions to 2016*, p. 8.
72. Monitor Company Group, "Africa from the Bottom up: Cities, Economic Growth and Prosperity in Sub-Saharan Africa", paper presented at *Gulf-Africa Investment Conference 2010: Fostering Economic Relations*, December 4–5, 2010, Riyadh, Kingdom of Saudi Arabia, p. 59.
73. McKinsey Global Institute, *Lion on the Move: the Progress and Potential of African Economies*, p. 3.

74. Lionel Are and others, *The African Challengers Global Competitors Emerges from the Overlooked Continent*, the Boston Consulting Group, 2010, p. 2.
75. Shawn Ladd "Emerging Africa Expected to See Rise in Investment", *IMF Survey Magazine: Countries & Regions*, January 12, 2011, www.imf.org, retrieved June 2011.
76. Ernst & Young's 2011 Africa Attractiveness Survey, *It is Time for Africa*, May 2011, p. 8; Antonio Guerrero, "Investors Fall for Africa's Charms", *Global Finance*, vol. 25, no. 6, June 2011, p. 8.
77. Ernst & Young's 2011 Africa Attractiveness Survey, *It is Time for Africa*, May 2011, p. 8.
78. Ibid, p. 9.
79. Ernst & Young, "FDI in Africa in 2013: a mixed picture", EY's attractiveness survey Africa 2014, pp. 62–63.
80. McKinsey Global Institute, *Lion on the Move: the Progress and Potential of African Economies*, p. 3. Fiona Rintoul, "Vibrant Africa beckons investors", *Financial Times*, July 18, 2010.
81. Simon Freemantle, *Africa Macro Insight, Five Trends Powering Africa's Enduring Allure, Trend 2 Africa Transformational Urban Swell*, Standard Bank, September 21, 2011, p. 1.
82. McKinsey Global Institute, *Lion on the Move: the Progress and Potential of African Economies*, p. 3.
83. Simon Freemantle, *Africa Macro Insight, Five Trends Powering Africa's Enduring Allure, Trend 2 Africa Transformational Urban Swell*, Standard Bank, September 21, 2011, p. 1.
84. Fiona Rintoul, "Vibrant Africa beckons investors", *Financial Times*, July 18, 2010.
85. Lionel Are and others, *The African Challengers Global Competitors Emerges from the Overlooked Continent*, the Boston Consulting Group, 2010, p. 6.
86. Ayesha Sabavala and Ali al-Saffar, *GCC Trade and Investment Flows: The Emerging-Market Surge*, p. 17.
87. Monitor Company Group, "Africa from the Bottom up: Cities, Economic Growth and Prosperity in Sub-Saharan Africa", paper presented at *Gulf-Africa Investment Conference 2010: Fostering Economic Relations*, December 4–5, 2010, Riyadh, Kingdom of Saudi Arabia, p. 57.
88. Africa Progress Panel, *Africa Progress Report 2011 The Transformative Power of Partnership*, p. 19.
89. Simon Freemantle, *Africa Macro Insight, The Five Trends Powering Africa's Enduring Allure, Trend 2 Africa Transformational Urban Swell*, p. 1.
90. *The Economist*, "Africa's hopeful economies the sun shines bright, p. 68.

91. McKinsey Global Institute, *Lion on the Move: the Progress and Potential of African Economies*, p. 7.
92. The Economist, "Turning towards Mecca Islamic banks join in the race for Africa".
93. Pieter Becker and Michelle van Zyl (2011). *The Dynamic African Consumer Market: Exploring Growth Opportunities in Sub-Saharan Africa* Accenture, www.accenture.com, retrieved January 2012, pp. 1–44.
94. Accenture *Africa the New Frontier for Growth*, 2010, p. 5.
95. Ibid, p. 6.
96. The Wall Street Journal, African Consumer Spending Expected to Double by 2020, August 3, 2014, www.online.wsj.com, retrieved January 2015.
97. Peter Wanacott, "A New Class of Consumers Grows in Africa", *The Wall Street Journal*, May 2, 2011.
98. Deloitte, *Investments into Africa Tackling Tax and Regulatory Challenges*, p. 1.
99. Peter Wanacott, "A New Class of Consumers Grows in Africa", *The Wall Street Journal*, May 2, 2011.
100. James Watson & Others, *Into Africa Institutional investor intentions to 2016*, p. 8.; Stefan Wagstyl, "Unilever: Mr. Africa, I presume?" *Financial Times*, October 4, 2011, www.ft.com, retrieved August 2012.
101. Ibid.
102. Kenneth Ngwa Anye "Telecommunication Markets and Trends in Sub-Saharan Africa", paper presented at Gulf-Africa Investment Conference 2010: Fostering Economic Relations, December 4–5, 2010, Riyadh, Kingdom of Saudi Arabia, p. 6.
103. *The Economist*, "The hopeful continent Africa rising", December 3, 2011.
104. Ibid, p. 19.
105. Lionel Are and others, *The African Challengers Global Competitors Emerges from the Overlooked Continent*, p. 7.
106. Simon Freemantle, *Africa Macro Insight*, *The Five Trends Powering Africa's Enduring Allure*, *Trend 4 Africa*, *Africa Dormant Resources Potential*, p. 4.
107. McKinsey Global Institute, *Lion on the Move: the Progress and Potential of African Economies*, p. 7.
108. Ibid, p. 22.
109. McKinsey Global Institute, *Lion on the Move: the Progress and Potential of African Economies*, p. 41.
110. Richard Bernstein, *Africa: The Final Frontier*, p. 10.
111. Making Finance Work for Africa (MFW4A) Conference, *Zipping Finance and Farming in Africa–Harnessing the Continent's Potential*, p. 3.
112. Ibid, p. 3.
113. Ibid, p. 4.

114. Nanou Keita, *Sub-Saharan Africa: a Challenging New Frontier*, p. 3.
115. Simon Freemantle, *Africa Macro Insight, The Five Trends Powering Africa's Enduring Allure, Trend 4 Africa, Africa Dormant Resources Potential*, p. 2.
116. Robert Ruthann, *Africa's Development Prospects Remain Intac*, Equity Research, Credit Suisse, January 11, www.credit-suisse.com, 2011, retrieved February 2012.
117. McKinsey Global Institute, *Lion on the Move: the Progress and Potential of African Economies*, p. 8.
118. Ibid.
119. David McIlroy "Africa Rising" *Quantum Finance in Perspective*, Issue 12, July 2010, pp. 23–25.
120. David Smith and Lucy Lamble, "Africa's burgeoning middle class brings hope to a continent", *The Guardian*, December 25, 2011, www.guardian.co.uk, retrieved March 2012.
121. Ibid.
122. Fiona Rintoul, "Vibrant Africa beckons investors", *Financial Times*, July 18, 2010.
123. Tiisetso Motsoeneng, "Shoddy infrastructure biggest obstacle for Africa", *Reuters*, March 8, 2011.
124. The World Bank, *Africa's Infrastructure: A Time for Transformation*, 2010, p. 2.
125. Charles Robertson, Yvonne Mhango and Nothando Ndebele, "Africa: The bottom billion becomes the fastest billion," Renaissance Capital, July 2011, p. 29.
126. Monitor Company Group, "Africa from the Bottom up: Cities, Economic Growth and Prosperity in Sub-Saharan Africa", *Gulf-Africa Investment Conference* 2010: Fostering Economic Relations, December 4–5, 2010 Riyadh, Kingdom of Saudi Arabia, p. 57.
127. The World Bank, Africa's *Infrastructure: A Time for Transformation*, 2010, p. 1.
128. *The 3rd COMESA Investment Forum: Connecting Africa to the World*, April 12–13, 2010, Sharm El Sheikh, Egypt, Conference Report, p. 7. Conference Report on the 4th COMESA Investment Forum "Dubai to Africa Unlocking the Market of the Future", March 23–24, 2011, p. 6.
129. Conference Report on the 4th COMESA Investment Forum, "Dubai to Africa Unlocking the Market of the Future", March 23–24, 2011, p. 6.
130. Accenture *Africa The New Frontier for Growth*, 2010, p. 7.
131. KPMG, *KPMG Survey of Current Economic and Business Conditions in Africa*, December 2010, www.kpmg.com, p. 6.
132. Paul Collier "Building an African Infrastructure", *Finance & Development*, International Monetary Fund (IMF), December 2011, vol. 48, no. 4, p. 18.

133. Ibid.
134. Ibid, p. 19.
135. Standard and Poor's, *Will Islamic Finance Play a Key Role in Funding Asia's Huge Infrastructure Task?*, October 13, 2011, www.standardandpoors.com, p. 2.
136. Ibid.
137. Richard Bernstein, *Africa: The Final Frontier*, p. 11.
138. International Finance Corporation (IFC), *The Business of Health in Africa Partnering with the Private Sector to Improve People's Lives* 2007, www.ifc.org, retrieved January 2012, p. 14.
139. Ibid, p. 9.
140. Ibid, p. 50.
141. Ibid.
142. Ibid.
143. Ibid.
144. Ibid.
145. IMS Health, "Africa: A ripe opportunity Understanding the pharmaceutical market opportunity and developing sustainable business models in Africa", 2013, www.imshealth.com
146. ICICI Securities Limited (ICICI Securities, Ajanta Pharmaceuticals (AJAPHA), September 22, 2014, www.ajantapharma.com
147. IMS Health, "Africa: A ripe opportunity Understanding the pharmaceutical market opportunity and developing sustainable business models in Africa", 2013, www.imshealth.com; Zuzanna, Fiminska, The Next Emerging Market–30 Billion Reasons to Focus on Africa, February 13, 2013, http://social.eyeforpharma.com
148. Ibid.
149. Elyse Lichtenthal, "Africa Moves Center Stage As Next Emerging Market in Pharmaceuticals: New Challenges Global Health Partnerships," July 4, 2013, http://www.foreignpolicyblogs.com
150. IMS Health, "Africa: A ripe opportunity Understanding the pharmaceutical market opportunity and developing sustainable business models in Africa", 2013, www.imshealth.com
151. Ibid.
152. Juan Trevino "Sub-Saharan Africa Maintains Growth in an Uncertain World", IMF African Department, October 12, 2012, www.imf.org, retrieved January 2013.
153. Ocean Equities Limited, "Factbox: Changing Africa" Weekly Review, March 9, 2011, www.oceanequities.co.uk, retrieved June 2011, p. 12.
154. McKinsey Global Institute, *Lion on the Move: the Progress and Potential of African Economies*, p. 12.
155. The World Bank, *Africa Competiveness Report* 2011.

156. Ocean Equities Limited: Changing Africa, p. 12.
157. Paul Collier, "The case for investing in Africa", *McKinsey Quarterly*, June 2010, www.mckinsey.com, retrieved June 2011.
158. McKinsey Global Institute, *Lion on the Move: the Progress and Potential of African Economies*, p. 16.
159. Alleyne, Trevor Serge Coleridge, "Managing volatile capital flows: experiences and lessons for Sub-Saharan African frontier markets", International Monetary Fund, 2014, www.imf.org
160. Ibid.
161. Ocean Equities Limited, "Factbox: Changing Africa", p. 12.
162. Collins G. Ntim, "Why African Stock Markets Should Formally Harmonise and Integrate their Operations", *African Review of Economics and Finance*, vol. 4, no. 1, December 2012, p. 54.
163. David McIlroy, "Africa Rising" *Quantum Finance in Perspective*, Issue 12, July 2010, pp. 23–25.
164. Ocean Equities Limited, "Factbox: Changing Africa", p. 12.
165. *The Economist*, "The hopeful continent Africa rising", December 3, 2011, p. 13.
166. Meeting of the Committee of Experts of the 4th Joint Annual Meetings of the AU Conference of Ministers of Economy and Finance and ECA Conference of African Ministers of Finance, Planning and Economic Development *Leveraging Opportunities for Accelerated Growth in Africa: Prospects and Challenges for the Next Decade*, E/ECA/COE/30/6 AU/CAMEF/EXP/6(VI), March 15, 2011, p. 4.
167. *The Economist*, Democracy in Africa: Democratization and its Discontents, January 7, 2011, www.economist.com, retrieved December, 2011.
168. Simon Freemantle, *Africa Macro Insight and Strategy African Election Map 2011/2012*, Standard Bank 15 December, 2011, p. 1.
169. Ibid.
170. Ibid.
171. Clement Gillet, "Is Africa About to Take Off", Societe Generale Economic Study Department, May 10, 2011, pp. 1–10.
172. Paul Collier, "The case for investing in Africa", *Mckinesy Quarterly*, June 2010.
173. Mwangi S. Kimenyi, "Africa's 2011 Election" in *Foresight Africa: The Continent's Greatest Challenges and Opportunities for 2011*, p. 4.
174. Ngozi Okonjo-Iweala, "Fulfilling the promise of sub-Saharan Africa", *McKinsey Quarterly* June 2010, www.mckinsey.com, retrieved June 2011.
175. Xavier Sala-i- Martin Pinkovskiy, *African Poverty is Falling...Much Faster than You Think!*, Working Paper No. 15775, Issued in February 2010, www.columbia.edu, retrieved June 2011, p. 1.

176. Pieter Becker and Michelle van Zyl, *The Dynamic African Consumer Market: Exploring Growth Opportunities in Sub-Saharan Africa*, p. 11.
177. Kieran Loughran and Sonia Xavier, "Private Equity Investment into Africa: The Cayman and Mauritius Route" Cayman Financial Review, Second Quarter 2011, no. 23, pp. 43–45.
178. *Bloomberg Businessweek*, "Africa: Coke's Last Frontier", October 28, 2010, www.businessweek.com, retrieved June 2011.
179. McKinsey Global Institute, *Lion on the Move: the Progress and Potential of African Economies*, p. 37.
180. Ibid, p. 50.

CHAPTER 5

# Financial Sector as a Backbone of Economic Growth: *The Banking Sector*

## Financial and Banking Sector

After spending decades at the periphery of the mainstream global financial system, Africa is now becoming one of the world's fastest growing emerging markets and an increasingly popular investment destination. There are clear reasons for this reassessment, as illustrated in the previous chapter. African economies are expanding on the back of increasing commodity prices, trade, and foreign investment, while increasing consumer affluence is helping to drive the demand for goods and services.[1]

Recent development theories see the lack of access to finance as a critical mechanism for generating persistent income inequality as well as slower growth. Without inclusive financial systems, poor individuals and small enterprises need to rely on their own limited savings and earnings to invest in their education in order to become entrepreneurs or take advantage of some of the promising growth opportunities. The World Bank Group has long recognised that well-functioning financial systems are essential for economic development. The evidence suggests that developing the financial sector and improving access to finance will not only accelerate economic growth, but also reduce income inequality and poverty.[2] The main reason why finance matters is that financial development and intermediation have been shown empirically to be key drivers of economic growth and development. Finance motivates savers to save by offering them a range of instruments to fit their financial needs, channels savings to



M. Al Bashir M. Al Amine, *Islamic Finance and Africa's Economic Resurgence*, DOI 10.1007/978-3-319-28835-2_5

investors, and in the process, broadens investment opportunities, increases investment, ameliorates risk sharing, increases growth of the real sector, enables individuals and business entities to smooth income and consumption profiles over time, and there is some evidence that this process it not only leading to economic development, but that it may also play a positive role in reducing poverty and income inequality.[3]

The financial sector is central to any meaningful economic development worldwide, especially given the current globalised world. A strong financial sector can provide the capital needed for other sectors. At the same time, there is a need for innovative financial services to reach out to the masses. Innovation and technology represent a great opportunity for African banking and other financial sectors waiting to be tapped. Technical advancements have already led to mobile phone banking growing faster than traditional banking in the continent. Thinking outside the box is imperative to the development of new innovative products catering to the needs of the African market.[4]

There is convincing evidence of a close correlation between financial sector development and growth. Banks, in particular, perform a fundamental economic role as financial intermediaries and as facilitators of payments. They help stimulate savings and allocate resources efficiently. Banks also allow diversification of risk, monitor managers, and exert control. Moreover, evidence suggests that domestic savings and investment rates are highly correlated.[5]

At the same time, there is growing realisation that financial development should emphasise the need to expand accessibility to finance. According to many development economists, improving access and making basic financial services available to all members of the society in order to build an inclusive financial system should be the goal. However, availability of financial services may not automatically result in financial inclusion, as many people may voluntarily exclude themselves from the financial services for religious or cultural reasons, even though they have access and can afford the services.[6] Therefore, there is a need for a mechanism of financial inclusion that will satisfy the needs of such people. This is the precise role of Islamic finance.

Increased innovation will help Africa increase its GDP by impacting on gross investment and private consumption. The demand for mobile telephony is a good example. It has led to investment in wireless communication infrastructure and services. The consumer demand for mobiles has opened the doors for a wide range of companies to invest in innovative solutions such as mobile banking. In Kenya for example, more than six million people use mobile banking services,[7] and as is rightly pointed out by the *Economist Intelligence Unit*, "the continent's industry is a leader in mobile banking and other innovative approaches to reaching new customers."[8] Other analyses on the effect of mobile banking in Kenya have suggested even higher figures, whereby nearly 70 % of Kenyan adults now access financial services, compared with below 5 % in 2006.[9] Based on this innovative use of technology, banks have done away with the need for extensive branch networks and greatly reduced their operating expenses. It now costs little to take on customers, particularly those who are only able to deposit very small amounts of money.[10]

Another successful experience of using mobiles for banking and financial services is that of Tanzania, where mobile financial services have halved the number of financially excluded people to 27 % of adults as of 2013, compared with 55 % in 2009. According to Benno Ndulu, the governor of the Central Bank of Tanzania, mobile finance offers greater access to financial services to millions of Tanzanians. As of July 2014, 55 % of adults now use active mobile accounts in the country. In addition to being used for payment and remittance services, mobile financial services have enabled more than six million people to store value or save credit in their mobile wallets, thus enhancing the potential to migrate the unbanked to the banking system. This service is not limited to urban populations, with rural populations also active in using the service. Moreover, 41 % of women and 45 % of men are active users of mobile financial services.[11]

Due to a combination of mobile financial services, agents, and bank agents using mobile technology, a recent geographical mapping exercise undertaken in Tanzania shows that at the end of 2013, 45 % of (or 20.1 million) Tanzanians lived within five kilometres of a financial access point, compared with 35 % in 2012.

However, in the process of developing mobile financial services, some key prerequisites are needed:

1. A flexible regulatory framework that imbued proportionate risk management measures;
2. Balanced financial stability considerations;
3. Innovations for financial inclusion;
4. Collaboration between financial institutions and MNOs is imperative as the latter are only allowed to offer money transfer services, leaving other financial services to financial institutions.[12]

Experience has shown that economic development is inextricably linked to a strong banking sector. Banking—through its inherently dynamic role in financing an economy—can play an important role in boosting economic activities. This does not deny the fact that other financial service sectors also have an important role to play, as providers of services and developers of financial infrastructure. To deliver these benefits more effectively in Africa, major banks and other financial institutions are now actively investigating how best to expand their footprint there.[13]

Africa's banking sector has grown rapidly in the last decade. Developments in the banking sector have been most dramatic. **In 2008, total assets of Africa's top 200 banks amounted to US$935 billion,** 72 % of which was generated by corporate banking.[14] The continent has become a substantial player in emerging-market banking, with Africa's banking assets comparing favourably to those in other emerging markets, such as Russia. More importantly, almost 50 % of the growth in Africa's largest banks came from portfolio momentum or the market's natural increase and not from inorganic (or M&A-driven) factors. Underpinning this portfolio momentum is strong overall market expansion, and the financial sector is outgrowing GDP in most of the continent's main markets.[15]

The banking sector in many African countries is either dominated by state-owned banks or by a few large—sometimes foreign—banks. In Algeria, for example, state-owned banks control over 90 % of total banking deposits and assets. However, as part of the restructuring programme, the banking industry in Africa is undergoing reforms. Privatisation is playing an important role with the aim of restructuring state-owned banks in order to improve their quality. Foreign banks, on the contrary, have played an important role in banking development in Africa and their share of total African banking has increased significantly.[16] Opportunities in the sector are tremendous if we take into consideration that just 25 % of the population have bank accounts. The continent has the largest unbanked population with around 230 million unbanked households and this represent enormous profit potential for banks.[17]

Moreover, some specific financial products are not attractive to some customers on ethical or religious grounds; non-usage, in this case, cannot be attributed to lack of access—although access might be an issue here if acceptable alternatives are not being offered. The case of Sharī'ah-compliant financial products can be relevant here.[18] Thus, the introduction of Islamic banking and finance in African countries is part of this required innovation in the banking and financial system to attract those who are still unbanked due to religious or ethical considerations. It represents another source of funding for various infrastructure projects. Finally, it is another means of trading with others in a globalised world.

Despite the rapid growth of African banking systems, indicators of financial depth in Africa are the lowest in the world, which means wider room for growth. On average, bank credit to the private sector represents no more than 15 % of GDP in Africa, while in developed economies, it is more than 100 %. Moreover, compared with their counterparts in emerging markets, African banks have a limited role in the economy. Banking services penetration is as low as 5 % in some countries in the continent and access in most countries is limited to the urban centres. Financial intermediation is hampered by the slow execution of due process, as manifested in slow court proceedings, the absence of credit assessment information, and little protection for property rights.[19]

However, despite its small size compared to other economies, African banking systems are reasonably sound. Improved macroeconomic conditions and less government intervention seem to have diminished the ratio of non-performing loans in the banking system, even though the characteristics of a specific country, such as current or past conflict and the implication for the government, can cause differences between countries. The capital adequacy ratio is at an average of 16 % of risk-weighted assets and is widely respected. Banks are profitable even though they are less efficient than in other countries. Overhead costs and net interest rate margins are better than in other low-income countries. Perhaps due to the size of the market, the banking system is generally very concentrated and often dominated by foreign banks. More importantly, the legal environment tends to be less conducive and represents a real challenge for sector development.[20]

Despite the high percentage of unbanked in Africa, many of those who are still unbanked are not among the poorest of the poor. The unbanked can include owners of micro-businesses, traders, tradesmen, workers, and employees of state or private sector organisations who do not have a bank account and have unmet needs for financial services. Thus, the opportunities are real and waiting for the right investor. These unbanked members of the society remain without a bank account generally because of geographical inaccessibility, lack of infrastructure, the high cost of banking services, and lack of financial understanding or a viable alternative that suits their religious beliefs. These people, however, clearly represent a market that is underserved.[21] As noted by *Time Magazine*, 95 % of the nearly 500 million adults in Sub-Saharan Africa earning less than US$10 a day have no access to bank accounts. If these people are included into the formal banking system, they could bring as much as US$59 billion in new deposits.[22]

Although many find it hard to imagine how more than 300 million adults in Africa making less than US$ 2 a day can save any money, the reality, according to the consultancy firm Roland Berger, is that low-income Africans already save and desperately need a safe and convenient way to store and access their money to help smooth often volatile income flows. Given the absence of formal alternatives, many resort to some classical avenues and means for their savings, such as buying goods that have a relatively stable value such as gold, goats, or cows, or creating their own lending pools, bypassing institutions altogether by lending money to friends and family so they do not have to stuff savings under a bed despite the risk of huge losses. Thus, according to the consultancy firm, the need for formal savings services creates huge business opportunities for commercial banks in Africa. The estimated potential for annual savings mobilisation in Sub-Saharan Africa from clients earning less than US$10 per day is US$60 billion per year.[23]

Any potential investor willing to operate in the region and achieve success in the African market needs to understand the special needs of this market. The unbanked often require:

1. Flexibility in savings and repayment schedules
2. Simplicity and speed in processing
3. Small product sizes when it comes to loans and low-balance savings accounts
4. Proximity and ease of access
5. Basic financial education or information.[24]

In one of its studies, consultancy firm Bain & Company found that Africa's financial services industry will be growing at 15 % annually due to a boom in retail banking. The consultancy stresses that banking growth will outperform economic expansion in the coming years, as demands for deposit accounts and sophisticated products will increase amid urbanisation. The study comes up with some interesting findings regarding the financial sector in Africa. It found that the industry is currently dominated by corporate banking, followed by retail banking, and the insurance and wealth management products. The financial services industry is predicted to register an impressive growth for the rest of the decade as more banks target the continent's emerging middle class. The industry has already expanded by 15 % annually between 2004 and 2008, with a return on equity of 15 % and it is forecast to continue expanding by 15 % to 2020, making up 19 % of the continent's GDP, up from 11 % in 2009. The contribution of financial services to GDP varies tremendously in the continent. Retail banking is expected to grow faster than corporate banking at 18 % between 2009 and 2020, representing 38 % of banking revenue by 2020. It is up from 28 % in 2009, helped by rapid adoption of mobile phone banking, which has exploded between 2005 and 2009 and is growing 35 % annually. There is a tremendous growth of mobile phone subscribers in the continent, as noted above, and it is forecast that over the next 5 years, there will be additional mobile phone users. This will help spread the adoption of banking services among the hundreds of millions of Africans currently without bank accounts. The biggest opportunities will be in the "mass retail segment," serving customers with low incomes and the rural poor, many of whom did not previously have bank accounts. The African banking industry is highly fragmented, except for South Africa, which suggests consolidation will gather pace in the coming years. Thus, innovative approaches to target the unbanked in rural areas will be much needed in the near future.[25] Some of the above facts have also been echoed by consultancy firm Roland Berger, which forecasts Sub-Saharan financial institutions to grow from US$90 billion in 2010 to US$390 billion in net revenues by the end of this decade.[26]

The *Banker* in a comment entitled "*African Returns make it the Place to be*" stressed that:

> The potential for growth in Sub-Saharan Africa's banking sector over the coming years seems phenomenal. And foreign institutions especially those from western Europe looking to expand outside their sluggish home market are well placed to take advantage…there is plenty scope for the under developed banking industry to develop.[27]

Much of this potential stems from concrete realities, such as the fact that the continent is starting from a lower base; macroeconomic conditions are favourable; the continent came out of the financial crisis strongly; there is a steady increase in real gross domestic products; and a high level of returns can be made without taking big risks in terms of liquidity.[28] Outlining the basis of this growth, *The Economist Intelligence Unit* maintained that a surge in the banking industry in Sub-Saharan Africa will be based on three main drivers—very high rates of economic growth, financial deepening that fulfils huge unmet needs for basic financial services, and new technologies that facilitate this transformation. The magazine added that "the conditions are in place for a doubling of banking assets and deposits, a proliferation of outlets and the extension of services to swathes of the continent's unbanked majority over the next decade."[29]

In a similar note, PricewaterhouseCoopers stressed Sub-Saharan Africa is now one of the world's fastest growing emerging banking markets and an increasingly sought-after investment destination. Increasing consumer affluence is creating fresh demand for banking services while M&A activity has been growing as groups seek to increase their strategic coverage and tap into this demand.[30]

African banks are generally still small when it comes to size. However, they are among the world's most profitable and dominate their peers from other regions of the world, according to *The Banker's* survey of lenders outside the top 1000 World Banks in 2011[31] and 2014.[32] African banks stand out; however, they are still small, with only two featuring among the top 50. They punch far above their weight when it comes to profitability. Of the top 10 lenders measured by return on capital (ROC), five are African, while seven of the ten with the highest return on assets (ROA) are also African. Overall, African banks (17 banks) have made an average ROA of 3.65 % (on weighted basis) and ROC of 35 %. These levels are far higher than the next most profitable region, South America, where banks made returns of 1.95 % on their assets and 19.6 % on their capital.[33] These banks have been able to achieve high levels of profitability without taking substantial risks. Their capital adequacy ratios (CARs) are, on average, 11.3 %—only slightly below those of banks in South America, which have CARs of 12.3 %. African banks have the lowest average cost-to-income ratios (49 %) while those in Asia–Pacific and South America have respective ratios of 57 % and 64 %. Despite the success of African banks, they seem unlikely to increase their ranking in the upcoming Top 1000 World Banks rankings due to the fact that most of these banks are still far from the US$250–260 million Tier 1 threshold needed to enter those rankings. At the same time, they are growing slower than their peers in other regions.[34] However, considering the existing growth in the industry and based on the 2010 results, 19 of them have Tier 1 capital of more than US$1 billion—a level that roughly marks the cut-off point for the world's biggest 500 banks. This represents an impressive rise for Africa, which had only 10 banks with US$1billion of tier capital or more at the end of 2007. Moreover, 31 banks on the continent now have capital strengths of US$500 million or more, compared with just 13 in 2007, according to *The Banker*. This ranking, according to the magazine, suggests that it will not be long before banks in Africa, only 30 of which made it into *the Banker's* 2011 Top 1000, collectively become a significant part of the global banking system.[35]

In addressing the reasons behind this positive outlook, *The Banker* points out to the favourable macroeconomic conditions, the continent's resilience in coming out of the recent financial crisis, and the steady growth of 5.5 % in 2011 and 5.9 % in 2012, reported by international financial institutions such as the IMF. Africa's positive financial growth is also based on the rapidly rising demand for consumer and corporate credit, and more attractively, the levels of return that can be made without lenders taking big risks with their liquidity. Moreover, operating in the region does not require much expertise beyond retail banking, as capital market products such as debt or equity are generally small or even non-existent in some African countries.[36]

Although the region is trailing the rest of the world in developing the banking systems as vital sources for stronger economic development and growth, in some key aspects, the region is leading other countries in ways that will allow it to rapidly catch up, or even leapfrog forward in the next decade and beyond. In particular, the continent's industry is a leader in mobile banking and other innovative approaches to reach new customers. Most of its markets are unusually among emerging markets and open to foreign banks and microfinance firms. More than anything, it offers huge unmet financial needs. The boom in the banking system will vary markedly across the continent.[37] In short, the continent could be "the most exciting opportunity" worldwide.[38]

*The Economist Intelligence Unit* forecasts that banking assets and deposits in 16 key African countries will expand rapidly between 2010 and 2020. In one scenario, based on economic growth it is anticipated that total assets will expand by 178 % to US$980 billion while deposits will grow by 188 % to US$766 billion. In a second scenario, combining high levels of economic growth and financial sector deepening, it is forecast that assets will grow by 248 % to US$1.37 trillion, while deposits will expand by 270 % to US$1.1 trillion by 2020.[39] Based on similar figures and optimism, Accenture stressed that the financial services markets in several African countries are either already well-established, or nearing the "tipping point" of rapid growth. Therefore, firms that seize these opportunities now will build a lasting competitive advantage in these markets.[40]

Mergers and Acquisitions in the financial sector have also been one of the signs of reforms that the continent has undertaken in the last few years with smaller and less-efficient institutions being acquired by larger ones. From 2004 to 2009, some 430 M&A deals involved financial institutions in Africa, and about 40 % were cross-border, with the acquirer originating elsewhere in Africa or outside it. Banks in South Africa are especially active in gaining footholds outside their home market. Further market consolidation is taking place within countries.[41] The average annual value of M&A transactions has increased strongly since 2004, rising more than threefold from US$2.4 billion in 2000–2004 to US$7.4 billion in 2005–2009.[42]

Interest in Africa's banking system is rapidly growing, whether through local financial institutions or big international financial conglomerates. This growth is reflected in and increased by the expanding number of active players. A number of European banks have long-established presences in Africa, and the past 5 years have seen them strengthening their involvement by leading a new wave of investment in Sub-Saharan Africa.[43] We have Citigroup, for instance, planning to expand into new African countries to strengthen its corporate and investment banking business. The corporation has an established banking presence in 16 countries in Africa and conducts business in an additional 40 countries. The bank is expected to continue focusing on corporate and investment banking on the continent. Citigroup, which has a history in Africa dating back to the 1950s, faces increased competition on the continent as more of its rivals target rising trade between emerging markets.[44] Citi has also pledged to source US$2.5 billion in incremental capital to improve access to electricity across Africa as part of the "Power Africa" initiative. Power Africa is a multi-stakeholder partnership between the US government, governments of several African countries, and other public and private sector entities, working to accelerate investment in Africa's power sector over the next coming years.

The bank is also reported to be leveraging its financing expertise in renewable energy to encourage the adoption and implementation of the appropriate technologies for specific markets. The bank will be working with key stakeholders in local capital markets to introduce innovative debt securities and to enhance financial infrastructure. Accelerating the development of local capital markets will mobilise domestic savings and attract greater international financial resources to the power sector in Africa. By deploying its systems and technology to enhance the payment and collection capabilities of the various providers in the "Power Africa" markets, Citi aims to increase efficiency and transparency along the entire supply chain. Over the past 2 years, Citi has enabled over US$1.5 billion in funding for the power sector in Africa.[45]

Given the fact that Citi is also a leader in Islamic capital market, in particular, it can use its expertise in attracting the needed fund for ambitious projects such as "Power Africa." Citi's recent involvement as a lead arranger in the first sovereign *Ṣukūk* by Senegal testifies to its commitment to investing in Africa.

Another giant financial institution choosing to directly operate from the continent is JP Morgan, which began offering rand clearing services in South Africa for the first time in November 2011. The firm's presence currently extends across South Africa, Nigeria, and Ghana. The company is reportedly looking at establishing representative offices in Kenya. JP Morgan managed the Kenyan government's debut US$2 billion bonds, along with Citigroup Inc. JP Morgan's African operations date back more than 100 years. It offers clients both local and global services, including asset management, private banking, and corporate and investment banking.[46] John Coulter, JP Morgan's senior country officer for Sub-Saharan Africa, asserted that "If we invest now, then we will reap the upturn in Africa, whether it's in 5 years, 10 years or 20 years, but we recognise that we need to make that investment now."[47]

Barclays is another international bank with a presence in the continent. Having bought a majority in Absa of South Africa, the bank has widened its presence in the continent. Thus, if we combine the operation of the two banks, we find a presence in 12 countries in Sub-Saharan Africa, with 15 million customers and 1600 points of distribution.[48] Absa Group and Barclays Africa Chief Executive Maria Ramos says its African business accounts for more than 16 % of Barclays' adjusted group revenue, making a significant contribution to its overall operations.

In line with the trend, Credit Suisse set up a wholly-owned subsidiary in South Africa in January 2011 as its first standalone presence on the continent in order to establish a broader investment banking business to serve the continent. For Credit Suisse, a key reason for increasing its presence in Africa is about bolstering its emerging markets coverage as trade patterns shift. It is common that "the dialogue these days with clients is about emerging markets to an increasing extent and they talk about Asia and then they want to talk about Africa," according to Leo Reif, head of the Investment Banking Department at Credit Suisse South Africa. He also adds, "If you can't talk about Africa, then they'll find another bank."[49]

UBS AG, the world's biggest wealth manager, is another Swiss bank targeting millionaire clients in Africa, particularly in oil-rich countries such as Nigeria and Angola. The strategy is built on the background that the number of people on the continent that fall within the wealth management of the bank is increasing every day, and therefore, there are opportunities that need to be untapped. The number of Africans with at least US$1 million of investable assets climbed 9.9 % to 140,000 in 2012. It is the fastest rate of increase outside North America.[50]

Standard Chartered, on the contrary, has a unique profile in Africa with its business balanced across 37 markets in East, West, and Southern Africa—including 15 countries in which the bank has a full presence as a substantial local bank, and 22 in which it operates on a transaction basis,[51] with total assets worth almost US$16 billion.[52] As stressed by Standard Chartered Bank Zambia's managing director, "Africa is very much core to our business activities and strategy and we have confidence in our strategy for long-term sustainable growth."[53] The bank is very active in facilitating trade flows between Africa and Asia, financing major infrastructure projects or Agri-financing deals.[54] Operating profit in Africa rose almost 10 % to US$103 million in 2010.[55] Standard Chartered's wholesale operation, on the contrary, is now contributing 80 % of its African profits—up from 60 % a decade ago. It got there by bulking up its energy and commodities teams and using its global network to win African business from European and Indian clients.[56]

Singapore-based Templeton Asset Management's Emerging Market Group has a strong presence in Africa. It has been buying shares in Nigerian banks as the first step towards reaching Africa's growing middle class. The company's US$1 billion Frontier Market Fund had 12.3 % of its investment in Nigeria at the end of 2010. The fund, which returned 74 % from its inception in 2008 to the end of 2010, owns shares in Nigeria's United Bank for Africa Plc and Zenith Bank Plc.[57]

Perhaps the most recent significant push was when the Industrial and Commercial Bank of China (ICBC), paid US$5.5 billion for a 20 % stake in Standard Bank of South Africa in 2007. The deal with South Africa's largest lender suggests that Africa is no longer a curiosity, but a potentially big source of profit.[58] Standard Bank operates in 18 African countries. The deal is considered a landmark transaction for Africa, South Africa, and the

Standard Bank Group. It will place Standard Bank at the crossroads of economic interaction between China and the African continent and will represent a strong vote of confidence in future relationships between the two regions. It also cements the impression that China is seeking to move beyond its standard strategy of the past few years of offering cheap loans in return for access to the continent's mineral wealth.[59]

By the same token, in January 2010, Bank of China, the country's most international outfit, entered into a pact with Ecobank, which operates in 31 African countries. In August of the same year, Brazil's Bradesco and state-controlled Banco do Brasil announced a new African holding company with Banco Espirito Santo (BES), a Portuguese bank active in Angola.[60]

Meanwhile, Portugal's three largest listed banks—Millennium BCP, Bank Espirrito Santo (BES), and Banco BPI—are the dominant foreign banks in Angola, a market that, in 2010, contributed 4 %, 19 %, and 53 %, respectively, to the three banks' net income and which is forecast to continue driving banking activity with strong economic growth.[61] Banco BPI, through its subsidiary Banco de Fomento Angola, has 138 branches and was ranked fourth and second in terms of deposit and loan, respectively, in 2009. BES has 28 branches in Angola while BCP group operates 38 branches in the country. Portuguese banks have discovered Angola as a growing alternative to their own small domestic market facing recession. Portuguese firms are estimated to have invested more than US$1 billion in Angola over the past few years, helping to make Portugal the country's biggest foreign supplier, accounting for 17 % of imports that totalled almost US$16 billion in 2009. As a result, Angola has become Portugal's fourth biggest export market, ahead of the USA.[62] Thus, Portugal's banks have re-entered Angola after the civil war and are enjoying its oil bonanza. BES, Banco BPI, and Banco Millennium BCP, together have over 170 branches in Angola, and made a staggering US$440 million profit in 2009.[63] Despite their troubles, Portugal's banks are continuing to invest in their Angolan operations and push for expansion, given the gloomy prospects in their homeland.

It is worth mentioning that all three Portugal big private banks—Millennium, BCP, BPI, and BES—together with CGD investment bank, have 49 % or close to that percentage of their Angolan operations in local hands. BEC's ownership, for instance, has fallen to around 52 % from 76 % in 2009 after selling a 24 % stake to an Angolan institutional investor in December 2009. This diminution in Portuguese influence is another example of how the balance of power between the former imperial master and its colony has turned.[64]

The Angolan–Portuguese relationship has another dimension with Angolan investment in Portugal as the dominant theme in a sign of how emerging markets are gaining the upper hand in the competition for economic power. The trend is still in its early stages, but is expected to intensify, especially with Portugal on the verge of bankruptcy and Angola reaping windfall oil profits. It also demonstrates, according to *Euromoney*, how things have changed and could change further in the future. The tables have turned for the country that built Europe's first global empire. Not all Portuguese are pleased with Angolan investments as Angolan investors want large stakes in telecoms energy and banks, and therefore, many fear that these investors will 1 day dominate the country.[65] These investments have led one observer to point out that, "in relative terms, Angolan investment in Portugal's corporation and financial institutions is much bigger than, say, Middle East sovereign wealth fund investment in UK banks."[66] Angola is the biggest producer of crude oil in Africa, having overtaken Nigeria in 2009. With surplus liquidity, Angola is in a prime position to invest in ailing European economies as a way to gain credibility, access to markets, and cheap assets.[67]

Another sign of the booming banking sector is the plan by Société Générale's international retail activities to add 100 branches in Sub-Saharan Africa to the existing 300, using plain buildings and a regional back-office system to keep a lid on costs.[68] The French giant operates in North Africa, West Africa, and Central Africa. It is one of the biggest banking networks on the African continent. The group holds market shares in excess of 20 % in Cameroon, Côte d'Ivoire, Guinea, Equatorial Guinea, Madagascar, Senegal, and Chad, for example. With a total of 15,000 employees and a network of 1000 branches, its African subsidiaries had 3.5 million customers at the end of 2012. The group's African network continues to generate growing revenues and sustained profitability. Although the 2008 financial crisis and Basel III have forced European banks' African subsidiaries to be more selective and prudent, Société Générale's commitment to Africa remains unchanged. This is because Africa is considered to be a traditional field of operations for the group, and more importantly, the continent remains a profitable market that fulfils the group's selection criteria for expansion. Despite the economic and political conditions of the continent, growth has been sustained over several years. The continent is connected with its dynamic population growth and the presence of significant natural resources. These three parameters—economic growth, an expanding population, and low banking penetration rates—represent significant growth drivers for the group. Political stability, a healthy business environment, and security for people and property will main the criteria to be taken into consideration by the group. Société Générale is implementing an ambitious expansion plan for its branch networks and its customer base across the continent, with the goal of having 1.7 million personal customers in Sub-Saharan Africa by the end of 2015. In some countries, the bank is already opening new branches at a rate of 10–15 per year, while in others, the rate of expansion is that of 2–3 new branches per year.[69]

The main business logic behind this interest in the African financial sector is that Africa's growing trade links with other emerging markets have raised its strategic importance in banking. The Export-Import Bank of China, a state entity which promotes trade and investment, has provided approximately US$20 billion worth of loans in Africa. Western private banks in Sub-Saharan Africa, on the contrary, have loans of US$50 billion, excluding South Africa and Liberia. As stressed by Jacko Maree, Standard Bank's boss, "Now everyone's looking at Africa." William Mills, who runs Citigroup in Africa, Europe, and the Middle East, echoed that the continent is becoming more and more competitive.[70]

Some asset managers have even gone to the extent of emphasising the fact that China is already a "very discovered market and investors should be looking at other regions in the world which looked like China in the late 90s."[71] Plamen Monovski, the Chief Investment Officer at Russia's Renaissance Asset Manager, in an interview with Reuters, said investors should forget China and place their money in Sub-Saharan Africa if they wish to benefit from the growth in emerging markets. He added, "Africa reminds me of China back in 1999. If you missed China then, do not do that now… It's the last place in the world that is due for that rapid change and advancement." Renaissance is more bullish on Africa's infrastructure, consumer-related, and financial sectors, which will benefit from the region's growing prosperity, rather than commodities. "The real appeal of Africa is the rise of the consumer society. Africa has got a population the size of India and consumer force as big as India."[72]

The African banking and financial sector will undoubtedly benefit from the increased presence of international banks and asset management companies in the continent. The increased interest of Asian and Western banks in servicing the African market will help increase the liquidity projects on the continent and create competition that will lead to an improvement in the services that banks provide to customers. It addition, it will create the right environment for consolidation to continue gathering pace whereby some of the local banks become global players as a result of tie-ups with international counterparts. Moreover, international banks will play a vital role in implementing global best practice in the retail banking sector, facilitating the flow of international trade and the leveraging of global resources.[73] Islamic financial institutions are under an obligation to be part of this transformation and competition for new markets.

Besides the international players, we also have the local big players who are doing very well on the continent. The emergence of dominant cross-border financial institutions, which are owned, controlled, and managed by African entrepreneurs and professionals is a case in point. The list of African cross-border banks is growing, but it is important to mention a few examples. These include, among others, Ecobank, Standard Bank, United Bank for Africa, Attijārahwafa, First National Bank (FNB), First Bank of Nigeria, Zenith Bank, and Access Bank. African cross-border banks have brought significant benefits to host and home countries. These banks have been involved in grassroot banking in their host communities, helping finance the real sectors of the economy, bringing the unbanked population into the formal banking system, and contributing towards job creation. However, the emergence and extension of these cross-border banks also come with its own challenges. Some of these challenges, as outlined by Nigeria's Central Bank governor, include:

- First, we have regulatory and compliance issues that will arise as a result of the operation in multiple jurisdictions. These banks are expected to report to both the home and host country supervisors, who may have different regulatory reporting standards and requirements. This may require that the same information be formatted using different templates to meet the needs of each supervisor, which may result in duplication of efforts and increased costs in terms of time and other resources.
- Second, the differences in the roles and responsibilities of the home and host country supervisors may create challenges and frictions, which may result in achieving goals that are at variance with the economic objectives of the host or home countries. For example, in some jurisdictions, the central bank is responsible for banking, securities, and insurance supervision, while in others, the responsibility for securities and insurance rests with different regulators.

- Third, the possible restrictions in the movement of capital and labour through various exchange controls and restrictive labour laws exert undue pressure on technical and executive capacity in some host countries.
- Fourth, the non-convertibility of currencies between the host and home countries would compel these banks to denominate their cross-border trade transactions in major international currencies, such as the US dollar, thus aggravating exchange risks.[74]
- To address these challenges, there is a need for a partnership and effective cooperation among the regulatory and supervisory authorities in these jurisdictions. Some of the necessary steps to follow towards that end are outlined by the Governor of the Central Bank of Nigeria and summarised as follows:
- Working towards achieving convergence of regulatory and supervisory standards and reporting across member states;
- Creating a level playing field for African indigenous and foreign banks by reviewing all existing requirements that tend to discriminate against foreign banks, particularly on minimum regulatory capital and foreign exchange remittances;
- Collaborating with other stakeholders to develop and deepen the money and capital markets in member countries so as to broaden the range of investment opportunities for banks in the domestic economies;
- Working with relevant stakeholders to review laws that impede effective loan recovery and provide loopholes for fraudulent customers and employees;
- Implement the policy of "naming and shaming" for bank loan defaulters and barring them from accessing further credit from the entire financial services industry;
- Working with relevant stakeholders to constantly review labour laws so as to ensure improved staff productivity and promote healthy employer–employee relations;
- Implementing joint crisis preparedness and management framework, which will include joint crisis simulation exercises, to mitigate the impact of crisis;
- Implementing common accounting standards, such as the International Financial Reporting Standards, for all banks in the region, except in situations where the scale of operations dictates

otherwise, such as community, rural, savings associations, and microfinance banks;

- Communicate and share supervisory and relevant financial and macroeconomic information with each other and respect the provisions of established agreement.[75]

One of the typical examples of these local banks with a presence in most African countries is Ecobank. Established in 1985 under a private sector initiative spearheaded by the Federation of West African Chambers of Commerce and Industry (FEWACCI), with the support of the Economic Community of West African States (ECOWAS), Ecobank Transnational Incorporated (ETI) was established in Togo as a bank holding company with a dual mandate of building a world-class African bank and contributing to the economic integration and development of Africa. ETI was incorporated as a public limited liability company with an authorised capital of US$100 million. ETI's initial paid-up capital of US$32 million was raised from more than 1500 individuals and institutions from West African countries. The largest shareholder was the ECOWAS Fund, the development finance arm of the ECOWAS.[76] In early 2010, ETI's paid-up capital amounted to US$775 million, owned by about 175,000 shareholders, most of whom are African, and of whom, more than 170,000 are individuals. Geographically, the shareholding base spreads across Africa and Europe. Ecobank group currently has operations in 32 countries with 800 branches and offices and a staff complement of more than 11,000 professionals. It generates more than US$1 billion in gross revenues and has a balance sheet of approximately US$9 billion.[77] Some of the biggest non-African shareholders of the bank include IFC and Russian investment firm Renaissance Capital. In 2010, IFC lent the bank US$175 million, US$150 million of which was convertible debt instruments.[78]Africans make up an overwhelming majority of Ecobank's Board as well as its senior management employees.[79] The bank increased retail lending more than fivefold from 2005 to 2010 to US$5.3 billion. By early 2011, the assets of the bank reached US$10 billion,[80] and by the middle of the same year, the number was reported to be around US$11.8 billion.[81] In terms of income, the bank's net income in the first half of 2011 grew impressively at 34 % year-on-year, following 104 % net income growth in 2010.[82] The bank's capital adequacy was healthy in the second quarter of 2011 at 19.5 % and the shareholders' equity totalled US$1.4 billion.[83]

In 2006, for strategic reasons, the Ecobank Group undertook simultaneous multiple listing of its shares on three stock exchanges in West Africa: the Ghana Stock Exchange (GSE), the Nigerian Stock exchange (NSE), and the Bourse Régionale des Valeurs Mobilières (BRVM), the regional stock exchange for Francophone West Africa. Ecobank's performance to-date, along with that of other banks in Africa, confirms once again that Africa is a good investment destination despite perceived risks.[84] Building on its strong presence in the continent, the bank agreed to acquire Nigeria Oceanic Bank in July 2011. There is also discussion on a potential merger in Ghana with Accra-based Trust Bank, which could make Ecobank the biggest bank by assets in Ghana.

Another African bank that has made great strides in expanding its services beyond the borders of its country of origin is Standard Bank of South Africa, under the banner of Stanbic Bank. It has operations in 17 countries. First National Bank (FNB), another South African bank, has a presence in six countries.[85] South African banks have also realised the demands for Islamic banking services. In May 2010, both Absa and Standard Bank launched Islamic banking services in Tanzania—Absa through its shares in the National Bank of Commerce, and Standard Bank through its Stanbic operation.[86] Moreover, the Nigerian unit of South African lender Standard Bank has won approval to set up an Islamic banking arm.[87]

Morocco's Attijārahwafa Bank, which is Africa's sixth largest bank and second biggest overall outside of the South African market, is also expanding into other African countries, relying on Morocco's relative maturity and banking penetration. It has been eyeing future growth in its less-developed neighbours. Since 2005, it has expanded its retail banking into new markets capturing market share in Tunisia, Senegal, and Côte d'Ivoire.[88] The bank has also expanded in countries such as Mauritania, Mali, Cameroon, and Gabon. The bank increased its operation and presence by the end of 2015 in 22 countries with three new African countries in the list that Burkina-Faso, Guinee Bissau and Congo.[89] The bank's investment in pan-African ventures totals US$800 million, or about 25 % of consolidated equity. A significant part of its business strategy is aimed at reaching the continent's unbanked masses, as well as initiatives that include partnering with SMEs to finance trade and underwriting large-scale development and infrastructure projects. For example, the bank financed an international airport in Mali, a major mining project in Gabon, and highways in Senegal.[90]

There are broadly two sorts of banks operating in the Sub-Saharan region. First, the large local banks, such as Standard Bank and Ecobank, and the big international banks, which tend to operate where there are historical links. Thus, Société Générale is largely present in French-speaking West and Central African countries. Barclays and Standard Chartered are dominant in former British colonies or English-speaking countries, Portuguese banks are in Angola and Mozambique, while Citigroup has run a skeletal network since the mid-1960s.[91] Local and Western banks' profits in Sub-Saharan Africa, excluding South Africa, were about US$2.6 billion in 2009, not far off the sum Western firms made in India or China.[92]

Traditionally, all these banks used variants of the same basic business model of serving well-off consumers, state entities, and medium-sized and big businesses. The banks typically gathered more in deposits than they lent, which meant excess liquidity was parked with governments and central banks. There were usually limits on how much profit could be sent home. But with high interest rates on private loans, the returns on equity were pretty good.[93]

Although telecommunications has thus far been the biggest success story in Africa, it is strongly maintained that the figures are clear and independent forecasts suggest that the largest growth can be seen in the financial area, even ahead of the commodities sector. As stressed by Ernst & Young, one of the main factors for the continued growth of economies in a functioning financial system is that only 20 % of the population of Sub-Saharan Africa currently has access to the formal financial sector. Therefore, the sector is well-suited for development with the rise of a middle class and a gross national product that continues to grow.[94]

Developing the banking and financial system is also an essential prerequisite to financing SMEs. SME financing is critical to any development. However, many obstacles need to be addressed. These include reforming the underlying infrastructure needed to support SME financing, e.g. the legal, collateral, contract enforcement frameworks, and the ownership problem. The above concerns are challenges primarily related to governments, and therefore, it is the responsibility of governments to ensure a favourable environment for SME financing to thrive. Nurturing SME growth is a slow and long-term process and governments should not be reluctant to invest in reforming the sector. A lot needs to be spent on training, as well as collecting information on borrowers, e.g. credit scorecards, credit analysis, or reliable financial statements. Investment in fostering and enabling the helpful environment for SME growth will reap its rewards in the long run. Moreover, SMEs generally borrow at low rates due to their size. This means that there are not enough cushions against losses in a lender's portfolio. Furthermore, lenders need to have a good credit rating, which is an additional burden. Hence, there are constraints on the supply side as well. Lenders are therefore urged to provide private equity to SMEs, not just loans, and to be more creative in designing financial products for SMEs that will create a win-win situation for all.[95] The great potential of the banking sector is also emphasised by PricewaterhouseCoopers maintaining that "demand for banking services is likely to expand and become more sophisticated" as economies are growing and there is a need to satisfy the desires of a growing consumer class. Banks are enhancing their product and distribution capabilities and market development is likely to include new innovative strategies such as mobile/e-banking.[96] The advisory services company added that acquisition offers the fastest way to develop a competitive presence in these markets. Potential investors need to grasp these opportunities quickly as international groups are set to deal with a stronger competition from regional and pan-African players.[97] While investment in the banking sector in Africa is promising, investors naturally need to consider the risks of a volatile region. Yet, the potential rewards certainly merit a fresh look and make investment ultimately worthwhile.[98]

Although the African financial system is still dominated by the banking sector, one area that needs special attention is the area of Islamic microfinance.

## Microfinance and Islamic Finance Opportunities in Africa

With low bank penetration and a very large informal sector, Africa is a fertile ground for microfinance.[99] Microfinance is the provision of financial services such as savings, deposits, and credit services to the entrepreneurial poor.[100] Pointing out the potential of Islamic microfinance in the African context, Moody's noted that one area where the industry appears to have a promising capability to add value in Africa countries is microfinance. This is based, according to the rating agency, on the nature of microfinance to meet the financing needs of the poor segments of the society, but also adequately fitting with the "ethical" nature of Islamic finance. Therefore, microfinance is undoubtedly a field that Islamic finance could further explore at a time where the objective of financing the least wealthy and combating poverty has received tremendous support from a vast number of international organisations and multilateral financial institutions.[101]

Islamic microfinance represents the convergence of two rapidly growing industries of microfinance and Islamic finance. It has the potential to not only respond to unmet demands, but also to combine the Islamic social principles of caring for the less fortunate with microfinance's power to provide financial access. Unlocking this potential could be the key to providing financial access to millions of Muslim poor, who currently reject microfinance products that do not comply with Islamic law.[102] Approximately 44 % of conventional microfinance clients worldwide reside in Muslim countries. Yet, as is well articulated in a study by the Consultative Group to Assist the Poor (CGAP):

> Conventional microfinance products do not fulfil the needs of many Muslim clients. Just as there are mainstream banking clients who demand Islamic financial products, there are also many poor people who insist on these products.[103]

Similarly, a report by the Africa Microfinance Action Forum (AMAF) and Women's World Banking (WWB) recognised that, "the development of Islamic finance products has the potential to bring many unbanked into the financial sector."[104] The report acknowledged that many elements of microfinance are consistent with Islamic finance, such as entrepreneurship advocacy and risk sharing, and the industry could address the needs of those who, because of religious beliefs, are still unbanked. The report added that "a large proportion of the population, mostly poor, had chosen not to use products based on interest rates (Ribā), but has naturally accepted Islamic products."[105]

The report recommends that MFIs in Muslim countries and Muslim communities should realise the importance of introducing products based on Islamic law, given the large number of people who refuse, for religious reasons, to take out traditional microfinance products. Preparing for the future and the road ahead, the report noted that "this is a vast reservoir of people on the African continent, which hosts a Muslim population of more than 400 million, the second largest continent, after Asia."[106]

A higher percentage of poor Muslims demand Islamic financial services, regardless of price, while some conventional micro borrowers tend to switch over once Islamic products become available.[107] Thus, a 2006 study by Frankfurt School of Finance and Management reported that in Algeria, 20.7 % of microenterprise owners did not apply for loans primarily because of religious reasons.[108] Furthermore, an estimated 72 % of people living in Muslim-majority countries do not use formal financial services, even when available, as many view conventional products as incompatible with the financial principles set forth in Islamic law.[109] These figures could be even higher with Muslims and non-Muslims in Africa. This is supported by a study by the World Bank with particular reference to the MENA region, but its result could also be applicable to Africa, especially nations with a sizable Muslim population. The study revealed that between 20 % and 60 % of those interviewed preferred Sharī'ah-compliant products. For some, the non-existence of such products is an absolute constraint to financial access, while others are continuing to use conventional finance in the absence of competitive Islamic ones.[110]

The study recommended that barriers to the growth of Islamic financial services should be removed and highlighted the need to enable growth in Islamic financial services to meet market demand. Industry players believe that Islamic microfinance could play a significant role in Sub-Saharan Africa's economic growth and development due to its low cost and ability to attract small entrepreneurs and allow the large unbanked African population to fully participate in the economy. Based purely on volume, Africa's Islamic microfinance initiatives have incredible potential. As Benjamin Nkungi, CEO of the Association of Microfinance Institutions in Kenya, states:

> The next big thing we are likely to see is the establishment of exclusive Islamic microfinance institutions across Sub-Saharan Africa as a result of outstanding grassroots demand.[111]

The Sudanese experience represents a unique experiment of Islamic microfinance market development. According to the Consultative Group to Assist the Poor (CGAP) of the World Bank in 2006, Sudan had only a few institutions serving the microfinance market and had a very limited penetration of only 9500 clients. By the first quarter of 2013, Islamic microfinance reached more than 400,000 customers. This qualifies Sudan as the second largest market in terms of outreach, after Bangladesh. The rapid expansion of the Sudanese market, according to CGAP, is largely due to: (i) an active Central Bank that prioritised microfinance through a dedicated unit, and (ii) priority sector lending requirements obligating banks to lend to the micro, small, and medium enterprise development sector. The growth of the Islamic microfinance sector reflects the government's push to provide financial services to the underserved—and Sudan has become a laboratory for Islamic microfinance delivery where developments could shed light on effective Islamic microfinance practices.[112]

Even in Sudan, where Islamic finance has been in existence for decades, the amount that microfinance contributes to total lending is still tiny, with the sector currently only fulfilling a minuscule 3 % of its demand. In 2010, the Central Bank of Sudan committed itself to the continued development of microfinance, ruling that all banks operating in Sudan have to allocate a minimum of 12 % of their portfolios to microfinance and instructed the banks to establish specialised units that must submit annual microfinance plans to the Central Bank. Banks are also required to carry out public education through the media on the opportunities available from Islamic microfinance.[113]

One of the many experiments of Sharī'ah-compliant credit, savings, and microinsurance is the Agricultural Bank of Sudan Microfinance Initiative (ABSUMI), created within the Agricultural Bank of Sudan (ABS) through a pilot phase in two localities in North and South Kordofan. Starting in 2010, ABSUMI was supported by three key stakeholders: the IFAD-funded Western Sudan Resources Management Programme, ABS, and the Microfinance Unit of the Central Bank of Sudan. ABSUMI entered the microfinance market at the bottom layers of the economic pyramid, providing much smaller loans (on average US$130) than those of other microfinance programmes in the country (on average US$650), benefiting the most disadvantaged segments of the population. The International Fund for Agriculture Development (IFDA) reported that the risk carried by the financing service is zero, while the model has cultivated strong credit discipline among rural poor people with a repayment rate of 100 %. As of May 2012, ABSUMI had reached 36,000 members of 6000 households through 350 women groups. It had mobilised savings worth US$72,000 with a client base of 4500 borrowers and a loan portfolio of US$700,000. Its loans, based on *murabahah* and *musharakah,* are supporting small agricultural activities, livestock fattening and rearing, and a range of microenterprises such as petty trading, tea stalls, and brick-making. ABSUMI is scaling up the initiative by establishing six new units between 2012 and 2013 with the objective of reaching 150,000 households over 5 years and mobilising US$10 million of savings.[114]

Among the recent developments of Islamic microfinance in Africa is the initiative by Kenya's Equity Bank, a conventional bank built on microlending, which recently introduced a Sharī'ah-compliant microfinance lending product in Kenya, although it has yet to launch on a big scale. Another experience is that of Ghana Islamic Microfinance Company, which started its operations in September 2010. The firm started as a response to the demands, especially from rural collectives in Ghana and for small business loans, and because other microfinance organisations are operating on high interest rates on microfinance loans. The firm offers microfinance financing to Muslims and non-Muslims alike.[115] Although there is a small microfinance presence in Tanzania, the volume of the industry throughout the continent is still very small.[116]

Despite the overwhelming demand for Islamic microfinance products, meeting such demand requires clients to be comfortable that the products offered are authentically Islamic. Therefore, Islamic financial institutions willing to introduce microfinance in Africa are creating working relationships with local religious leaders to address questions of Islamic law, given the fact that the rural and low-income populations often rely on the opinion of their Sheikhs, who must be convinced of the authenticity of Islamic financial products if Islamic microfinance is to reach its full potential. Greater efforts should be explored to: (i) increase collaboration between financial experts and Sharī'ah experts on product authenticity, (ii) encourage exchange of experiences among religious leaders (particularly those serving poor populations at the local level) relating to Sharī'ah compliance of microfinance products, and (iii) educate low-income populations, in collaboration with local religious leaders, on how financial products comply with Islamic law.[117]

Among the first Islamic microfinance institutions in Sub-Saharan Africa was Azaouad Finances, resulting from a development project by the German Technical Cooperation and German Financial Cooperation after the eruption of fierce conflicts in the three poorest northern regions of Mali, spanning Timbuktu, Gao, and Kidal, beginning in 1990 and ending in 1995. The project aimed to provide financial services to all the tribes in Northern Mali. Based on general consensus, it was decided that an Islamic bank would be most appealing to them.[118]

Despite the fact that microfinance has a long history in Africa, the industry has experienced high growth in recent years and is becoming an important driver in the development of the economies in Africa. Yet, it continues to play a key role as a grassroots financial tool, given the challenges. The high transaction costs cause firms in the industry to operate in urban and semi-urban areas, making it hard to reach the rural communities, as microfinance institutions are mostly concentrated around big cities. Microfinance in rural areas is underrepresented, making it difficult for entrepreneurs in rural areas to undertake small businesses.[119]

Among the many areas that could be covered through microfinance is agriculture. Africa's agriculture holds enormous potential of investment for Islamic financial institutions across the value chain. With 60 % of the world's uncultivated arable land and low crop yields, agriculture in Africa is expected to contribute a lot to the development of the continent. It is estimated that agricultural output could increase from US$280 billion per year today to as much as US$880 billion by 2030.[120] The agrarian sector is at the heart of the majority of African livelihoods and opportunities within agriculture are tremendous. Investing, improving, and increasing trade in this sector is paramount to Africa's development initiative. Africa has the potential to not only feed itself, but the world. However, there is the need for greater regional cooperation and harmonisation of policies in order to facilitate the growth of the agrarian sector and benefit the farmers.[121]

It is worth noting that the majority of farmers in Africa are smallholders in need of assistance in accessing funds, formulating commercial business plans, accessing the market, and adding value. There is also a need for innovation and technology to increase productivity and reduce costs, which will empower the farmers. Increasing productivity is crucial, but it is not sufficient in transforming the sector unless the smallholders are included in the value chain. Additionally, the farmers need to identify what the consumers want and cater to those demands by supplying consumer-specific produce.[122]

Agriculture must be seen as an industry. Despite the challenges of investing in the agrarian sector—taking into account its uncertainty and instability, exacerbated by climate change, energy shortages, and increasing urbanisation—it is still a growing sector in the African economy. The public sector needs to champion agriculture in order to mobilise the private sector. One sector that many African governments are actively promoting and where the Islamic finance industry can play a positive role is the cotton sector. It plays an important role in the socio-economic development of more than 20 OIC member states. They constitute a share of 28 % of total global cotton production, 24 % of total global cotton consumption, 36 % of global cotton export, and 27 % of global cotton imports. Cotton is particularly important for the socio-economic well-being and development of the Central and West African member states. The development of the cotton sector in these countries is of prime importance. Its production is an important economic activity, and cotton farming provides employment for the majority of the rural population.[123]

Investing in the agriculture sector needs to be backed by fair trade. One concrete step that advanced economies can take to help Africa get started on the road to higher growth is to open their markets to products, including agricultural commodities that Africa is capable of exporting at this nascent stage of industrial development. More importantly, they have to rid themselves of their own massive domestic agricultural subsidies, which would be sensible for advanced economies and do a world of good for underdeveloped economies in Africa and elsewhere. Sadly, piety and aid flows seem to be easier solutions for advanced economies to muster, holding back rather than helping Africa in the long run.[124] Credit Agricole stressed:

> Africa could move from being the poor relative in global finance to the sector's new frontier, if it succeeds in nurturing the growth of well-managed institutions that are true to the social mission of microfinance.[125]

More importantly, Africa's MFIs must give priority to factors that limit their profitability. They must first deal with largely inefficient infrastructures for roads, telecoms, and electricity, along with wages that, stated as a percentage of Net Banking Income (NBI), are higher than elsewhere. More importantly, they have to adapt to low population density, mainly in rural areas, which are therefore harder to cover. Another factor holding back growth of microfinance in Africa is the lack of qualified personnel. Not only are experienced managers lacking, there is an insufficient number of technicians with skills in IT, accounting, and marketing.[126]

Africa's stock markets, debt or bonds market, the insurance industry, and the private equity market are all doing well and Islamic financiers are invited to grasp these opportunities.

## Notes

1. Noel Gordon & Others, *At the Tipping Point: Financial Services in Africa comes of age How Financial Institutions can Capitalise on the Growth Opportunities in Africa*, Accenture, 2011, www.mckinsey.com, p. 3.
2. World Bank, *Finance for All? Policies and Pitfalls in Expanding Access*, World Bank Policy Research Report. Washington World Bank, 2008, p. 2.

3. Mahmoud Mohieldin, Zamir Iqbal, Ahmed Rostom and Xiaochen Fu, *The Role of Islamic Finance in Enhancing Financial Inclusion in Organization of Islamic Cooperation (OIC) Countries*, p. 2.
4. Ibid, p. 6.
5. Patrick Imam and Kangni Kpodar, *Islamic Banking: How Has it Diffused?*, p. 3.
6. Mahmoud Mohieldin, Zamir Iqbal, Ahmed Rostom and Xiaochen Fu, *The Role of Islamic Finance in Enhancing Financial Inclusion in Organization of Islamic Cooperation (OIC) Countries*, p. 3.
7. Accenture, *Africa The New Frontier for Growth*, 2010, p. 8.
8. The Economist Intelligence Unit, *Banking in Sub Saharah Africa to 2020 Promising Frontiers*, p. 1.
9. William Wallis, Andrew England and Katrina Manson, "Africa: Ripe for Appraisal", *Financial Times* May 18, 2011; Simon Freemantle, *Africa Macro Insight, The Five Trends Powering Africa's Enduring Allure, Trend 5 Africa Deepening Financial Sector*, p. 5.
10. Paul Wallace, "What Kenya can teach the world about banking to the masses", *The Banker*, February, 2012, p. 6.
11. Benno Ndulu, Tanzania's mobile-fuelled banking revolution, The Banker October 2014, p. 197.
12. Ibid.
13. Noel Gordon & Others, *At the Tipping Point: Financial Services in Africa comes of age How Financial Institutions can Capitalise on the Growth Opportunities in Africa*, Accenture, 2011, p. 3.
14. Simon Freemantle, *Africa Macro Insight, The Five Trends Powering Africa's Enduring Allure, Trend 5 Africa Deepening Financial Sector*, p. 1.
15. Hilary De Grandis and Gary Pinshaw, "Banking Building on Success", in *Africa's Path to Growth Sector by Sector* McKinnsey, June 2010, www.mckinseyquarterly.com, retrieved January 2011.
16. Franklin Allen & Others, "African Financial Systems: A Review" *Review of Development Finance*, vol. 1, Issue 2 April–June, pp. 79–113.
17. Gautam Bandyopadhyay, "Banking the Unbanked: Going Mobile in Africa", *Standard Chartered Asia, Africa and Middle East The Guide to Working Capital Management* 2009/2010, pp. 59–67; Robert Ruthann, *Africa's Development Prospects Remain Intact*, p. 5.
18. World Bank, *Finance for All Policies and Pitfalls in Expanding Access*, World Bank Policy Research Report. Washington World Bank, 2008, p. 28.
19. Andrianaivo and Charles Amo Yartey, *Understanding the Growth of African Financial Markets*, p. 5.
20. Ibid, pp. 6–7.

21. Gautam Bandyopadhyay, "Banking the Unbanked: Going Mobile in Africa", *Standard Chartered Asia, Africa and Middle East The Guide to Working Capital Management* 2009/2010, pp. 59–67.
22. Erik Heinrich, "The Secret of Africa's Banking Boom: Mobility", *Time Magazine*, www.techland.time.com, August, 16, 2012, retrieved December 2012.
23. Chriatian Wessels and others, *Inside Africa*, *Think: act study*, p. 43.
24. Infosys Technologies Limited, "Banking the Unbanked: Going Mobile in Africa", www.infosys.com, retrieved January 2013, p. 8.
25. Sid Verma, "Africa's decade-long banking bull run in pictures", *Financial Times* 03/07/11, www.ft.com, retrieved December 2011.
26. Chriatian Wessels and others, *Inside Africa*, *Think: act study*, p. 16.
27. *The Banker*, "African Returns Make it the Place to be", June 2011, p. 6.
28. Ibid.
29. The Economist Intelligence Unit, *Banking in Sub Saharah Africa to 2020 Promising Frontiers*, p. 1.
30. Nick Page & Others, *Into Africa: Investment Prospects in the Sub-Saharan Banking Sector*, PricewaterhouseCoopers, 2008, p. 1.
31. Paul Wallace, "Banks on the Climb", *The Banker*, August 2011, pp. 16–18.
32. See Brian Caplen, "Top 100 Banks in Africa Ranking: Africa Continues to Outperform", *The Banker*, January 5, 2015, p. 54.
33. Ibid.
34. Ibid.
35. Paul Wallace, "Africa's Banks on the Brink of the Big Time", *The Banker*, January, 2012, p. 114.
36. Paul Wallace, "Banks on the Climb", *The Banker*, August 2011, p. 16–18.
37. The Economist Intelligence Unit, *Banking in Sub Sahara Africa to 2020 Promising Frontiers*, p. 1.
38. William Wallis, Andrew England and Katrina Manson, "Africa: Ripe for Appraisal", *Financial Times* May 18, 2011.
39. Ibid.
40. Noel Gordon & Others, *At the Tipping Point: Financial Services in Africa comes of age How Financial Institutions can Capitalise on the Growth Opportunities in Africa*, Accenture, 2011, p. 3.
41. Hilary De Grandis and Gary Pinshaw, "Banking Building on Success", in *Africa's Path to Growth Sector by Sector* June 2010, www.mckinseyquarterly.com retrieved January 2011.
42. Noel Gordon & Others, *At the Tipping Point: Financial Services in Africa comes of age How Financial Institutions can Capitalise on the Growth Opportunities in Africa*, p. 23.
43. Ibid.

44. David Dolan, "Citi eyes three new Africa markets", *Reuters*, March 7, 2011, www.reuters.com, retrieved June 2011.
45. Citigroup Inc. (NYSE: C), Citi to Source $2.5 Billion to "Power Africa", August 5, 2014, www.citigroup.com
46. Bloomberg, "JPMorgan Says Kenya May Be Part of Future Africa Expansion", November 25, 2014, www.bloomberg.com
47. Andrew England, "International banks ramp up presence in Africa" *Financial Times*, January 2, 2012 www.ft.com, retrieved June 2012.
48. Autumn St John, "Islamic Wealth Management Opportunities in Africa", *Global Islamic Finance*, November, 2010, pp. 32–36.
49. Andrew England, "International banks ramp up presence in Africa" *Financial Times*, January 2, 2012, www.ft.com, retrieved June 2012.
50. Bloomberg, UBS Targets African Wealthy as Credit Suisse Takes Step Back, November 22, 2013, www.bloomberg.com
51. Diana Layfield, "Seeking the opportunity, managing the risk", in *Ernst & Young's attractiveness surveys Africa 2013 Getting Down to Business*, www.ey.com, retrieved May 2013, p. 3.
52. Bonorchis &Nasreen Seria, "The Rise of Middle Africa", *Bloomberg Markets*, June 2011, vol. 6, no. 6, pp. 107–111.
53. Chongo Kabange, "Standard Chartered Top African banks" *Africa news*, www.africanews.com, March 30, 2010.
54. Ibid.
55. Bonorchis &Nasreen Seria. The Rise of Middle Africa", pp. 107–111.
56. *The Economist*, "Africa's banking boom, Scrambled in Africa "Chinese and Western banks are flocking to Africa but finding a strategy that works isn't easy", September 16, 2010, www.economist.com, retrieved January 2011.
57. Bonorchis &Nasreen Seria, "The Rise of Middle Africa", pp. 107–111.
58. *The Economist*, "Africa's banking boom, Scrambled in Africa", September 16, 2010, www.economist.com, retrieved January 2011.
59. Alec Russell and William MacNamara, "ICBC Pays $5.5bn for Standard Bank stake", *Financial Times*, October 25, 2007, www.ft.com, retrieved June 2012.
60. *The Economist*, "Africa's banking boom, Scrambled in Africa", September 16, 2010, www.economist.com, retrieved January 2011.
61. Peter Wise, "A Colonial Lifeline? "*The Banker*, May 2011, p. 84.
62. Ibid.
63. *The Economist*, "Africa's banking boom, Scrambled in Africa", September 16, 2010, www.economist.com, retrieved January 2011.
64. *EUROMONNEY Magazine*, "The Scramble for Angola", March 2011, vol. 42, Number 503, p. 60.
65. Sudip Roy "Angola's Elite Looks to Clean up In Portugal" EUROMONEY March 2011, vol. 42, Number 503, pp. 55–61.

66. Ibid.
67. Ibid.
68. *The Economist*, "Africa's banking boom, Scrambled in Africa", September 16 2010, www.economist.com, retrieved January 2011.
69. Jean-Louis Mattei, "A French bank's vision of the African banking sector's evolution," *Private Sector* & *Development*, www.proparco.fr, issue 16, May 2013, pp. 26–28.
70. *The Economist*, "Africa's banking boom, Scrambled in Africa", September 16 2010, www.economist.com, retrieved January 2011.
71. Reuters, "Forget China, Invest in Africa says Russia Renaissance" Dec2, 2011, www.reuters.com, retrieved February 2012.
72. Reuters, "Forget China, Invest in Africa says Russia Renaissance" www.reuters.com, retrieved February 2012.
73. This is Africa, "The Future of African Banking", *This is Africa*, www.thisisafricaonline.com, retrieved January 2012.
74. Godwin, I Emefiele, "Thoughts on Building Effective Supervision in the Era of Cross- Border Banks in Africa", Keynote Speech by Governor Central Bank of Nigeria on the Occasion of the 17th Regular Meeting of the College of Supervisors of the West African Monetary Zone (CSWAMZ), CBN International Training Institute, July 2014.
75. Ibid.
76. Arnold Ekpe, "Motives for a Multiple Listing on African Stock Exchanges: The Ecobank Experience", Private Sector Development, *Proparco's Magazine*, Issue 5–March 2010–Africa's Financial Markets: A Real Development Tool?, pp. 14–16.
77. Ibid.
78. Dominic O′ Neil, "Ecobank: Africa Banking Champion Leaps Forward", *Euromoney*, September, 2011, vol. 42, no. 509, p. 336.
79. Ibid.
80. Renee Bonorchis & Nasreen Seria "The Rise of Middle Africa", pp. 107–111.
81. Dominic O′ Neil, "Ecobank: Africa Banking Champion Leaps Forward", p. 332.
82. Ibid.
83. Ibid, p. 336.
84. Ibid.
85. Autumn St John, "Islamic Wealth Management Opportunities in Africa" *Global Islamic Finance*, November, 2010, pp. 32–36.
86. Ibid.
87. Reuters, "Nigeria's Stanbic wins approval for Islamic banking", July 4, 2011, www.reuters.com, retrieved December 2011.
88. James Watson & Others, *Into Africa Institutional investor intentions to 2016*, p. 11.

89. See Groupe Attijariwafa bank, www.attijaribank.com as of April 2016.
90. Erik Heinrich, "Africa: Growth of Pan –African Banks" *Global Finance*, February 2011, www.gfmag.com, retrieved May 2011.
91. *The Economist*, "Africa's banking boom, Scrambled", September 16, 2010, www.economist.com, retrieved January 2011.
92. Ibid.
93. Ibid.
94. Olaf Meier, "It is still possible to Gain Access To Attractive Investment Targets with Relatively Low Capital Input" in Ernst & Young's 2011 Africa Attractiveness Survey, *It is Time for Africa*, May 2011, p. 18.
95. *The 3rd COMESA Investment Forum Connecting Africa to the World* 12–13 April, 2010, Sharm El Sheikh, Egypt, Conference Report, p. 22.
96. Nick Page & Others, *Into Africa: Investment Prospects in the Sub-Saharan Banking Sector*, PricewaterhouseCoopers, 2008, p. 13.
97. Ibid.
98. Ibid.
99. Mariama Olatunde Ashcroft, *Microfinance in Africa the Challenges Realities and Success*, Micro Banking Bulletin Issue 17 Autumn 2008, www.themix.org, retrieved March 2012, p. 6.
100. Bransdma. Judith and Laurence Hart, *Making Microfinance Work Better in the Middle East and North Africa*. World Bank Institute and Private and Financial Sector Development Group, Middle East and North Africa Region, World Bank, 2000,Washington, DC, p. 1.
101. Anouar Hassoune Adel Satel, *Islamic Finance Explores New Horizons in Africa*, p. 5.
102. Karim, Nimrah, Michael Tarazi, and Xavier Reille. "Islamic Microfinance: An Emerging Market Niche", p. 1.
103. Ibid, p. 5.
104. Africa Microfinance Action Forum, *Diagnostic to Action: Microfinance in Africa*, p. 8.
105. Ibid.
106. Ibid.
107. Karim, Nimrah, Michael Tarazi, and Xavier Reille. 2008. "Islamic Microfinance: An Emerging Market Niche.", p. 6.
108. Ibid, p. 5.
109. Ibid, p. 1.
110. Douglas Pearce, *Financial Inclusion in the Middle East and North Africa: Analysis and Roadmap Recommendations*, p. 14.
111. Nazneen Halim, "Banking on Microfinance," *Islamic Finance News Supplement -IFN Supplement Africa-* 29-July-2011, www.islamicfinance-news.com, retrieved December 2011.

112. Mayada El Zoghbi and Michael Tarazi, "Trends in Sharia-Compliant Financial Inclusion", Consultative Group to Assist the Poor (CGAP), no. 84, March 2013, www.cgap.org, p. 7.
113. Nazneen Halim, "Banking on Microfinance," *Islamic Finance News*, special Supplement *Africa the Sleeping Giant*, August 2011, p. 10.
114. International Fund for Agriculture Development (IFDA), *Islamic Microfinance: Unlocking New Potential to Fight Rural Poverty*, December 2012 www.ifad.org, pp. 2–4.
115. Nazneen Halim, "Banking on Microfinance," *Islamic Finance News*, special Supplement *Africa the Sleeping Giant*, August 2011, p. 10.
116. Ibid.
117. Karim, Nimrah, Michael Tarazi, and Xavier Reille. 2008. Islamic Microfinance: An Emerging Market Niche, pp. 12–13.
118. Nazneen Halim, "Banking on Microfinance", p. 10.
119. Franklin Allen & Others, "African Financial Systems: A Review" *Review of Development Finance*, vol. 1 issue 2 April–June, pp. 79–113.
120. Charles Roxburgh & Others, *Lion on the Move: The progress and Potential of African Economies*, p. 8.
121. The 3rd COMESA Investment Forum Connecting Africa to the World 12–13 April, 2010, Sharm El Sheikh, Egypt, Conference Report, p. 7.
122. Ibid.
123. Ekmeleddin Ihsanoglu, Keynote Address on *Enhancing Economic Cooperation Among Muslim Countries- The Role of OIC* H.E. by the Secretary General, Organization of Islamic Cooperation *IIUM Journal of Economics and Management* The International Islamic University Malaysia 17, no. 1 (2009): 13–30.
124. Eswar Prasad "Is Africa Poised to Steady, Rapid Growth?" *The Economist*, September 7, 2010, www.economist.com, retrieved May 2011.
125. Nanou Keita, "Sub-Saharan Africa: a Challenging New Frontier", Credit Agricole Bimonthly No. 139 January–February 2010, p. 5.
126. Ibid.

CHAPTER 6

# Financial Sector as the Backbone of Economic Growth: *The Non-banking Sector*

## Stock Markets

Until recently, Africa remained a continent filled with under-followed companies and stock markets. While China, India, and other emerging markets got the lion's share of media and investor attention, Africa has received little notice for its recent run of solid economic performance. This is despite the fact that the continent is filled with resources to help fuel many of the booming economies that investors are clamouring for. Traditionally, Africa has not been a place where more risk-oriented emerging market investors would invest, but that is changing. Investors in search of higher returns have increased their risk tolerances and have begun to search for greater returns from so-called frontier markets.[1]

The situation started to change with the surge of interest in the establishment of stock exchanges, particularly in Sub-Sahara Africa. Stock exchanges have proliferated over the last two decades. There were only five stock exchanges in SSA 20 years ago and three in North Africa, but now, there are 20 in operation. The established markets in the continent are the South African and Egyptian markets. It is also interesting to note that SSA witnessed the establishment of a regional stock exchange domiciled in Abidjan, particularly serving the Francophone countries of West Africa. Similar initiatives are supposed to be underway in Southern and Eastern Africa in order to consolidate the thinly capitalised markets into regional markets[2].



M. Al Bashir M. Al Amine, *Islamic Finance and Africa's Economic Resurgence*, DOI 10.1007/978-3-319-28835-2_6

Despite the challenges associated with liquidity and infrastructure, African stock markets have performed well in terms of both absolute returns and on a risk-adjusted basis. The average annual return for these markets over the past 10 years was 25 % with the exception of 2008. The performance of the markets looks attractive even after adjusting for standard risk measures. Currency fluctuation could be a concern to global investors who might consider investing in Africa. Even in this area, African stock markets have performed well. When converted into dollar terms, the results remain an impressive average annual return of 21.8 %. Following the recent financial crisis, these markets have fared better than most other markets around the world. Surprisingly, some markets generate positive returns in the face of the crisis. Moreover, stock market volatility has been decreasing steadily prior to the global crisis. Thus, Africa offers growth and investment opportunities which currently appear under-exploited. However, the viability of these markets as investment opportunities depends on the extent to which they have the potential to improve risk-return trade-offs facing global investors. The historical track record points to this potential.[3]

Recent financial data showed that all Africa-based publicly traded companies were highly profitable. More importantly, the average annual return on capital of the sampled companies was 65–70 % higher than that of comparable firms in China, India, Indonesia, and Vietnam. The median profit margin was 11 % better than the comparable figures for Asia and South America. This is explained in part by the low labour costs and gains in operational efficiency.[4]

Nevertheless, this does not deny the fact that these markets are still suffering from a number of problems that need to be addressed in order to better attract foreign investors. The manual trading and clearing systems in some African markets are some of these problems. Although a number of African stock exchanges have adopted automated systems, the majority of SSA markets remain operationally inefficient as they use manual trading and clearing systems. This poses impediments to operational efficiency, as well as liquidity. Similarly, these markets face serious challenges in terms of depth measured by market capitalisation and listing. The liquidity problem is generally the result of limited trading activity by institutional investors, as well as governments which maintain minority stockholdings.

It should also be noted that previous changes and reforms at the macroeconomic level have translated into noticeable improvements in the business climate. Markets are becoming more efficient due to increased automation. The greater involvement by global custodian banks has encouraged more trading by international investment funds. Company news and stock prices have also become much more accessible via the internet. Finally, the creation of a Frontier Markets Index has "legitimised" less-developed markets as an investment destination, and Africa as the final frontier among them. It should be noted that some stereotypes still endure and they are not positive for the continent's markets. Pointing to this problem, one observer noted, "The perception of Africa tends to be a lot more negative than the reality. And that's not the case for other frontier markets like Vietnam and Mongolia, which face less of a stigma." Concerns revolve around political stability, a lack of regulation, and corruption. This has resulted in the market being off-limits to everyone "except the most sophisticated investors."[5] One key feature of the financial markets in Africa until recently is also the dearth of bond markets for both government and corporate bonds. The bond market is either not well-developed or, at best, is in its infancy except for a few exceptions in South Africa or Nigeria, where we have a secondary debt market and a bond index.[6] The following are some of the main features of the African market:

- Markets are still small compared to stock markets in other emerging markets.
- Markets are illiquid. There are large gaps between buy and sell orders.
- Returns have generally been high despite the problems of small size and low liquidity.
- Returns are similar to those realised in Latin America and Asia even when the results are converted into dollars. Therefore, the African markets represent unexploited opportunities for international investors. There are diversification opportunities that are minimally correlated with the global system and its risk.
- Total market capitalisation increased by 113 % between 1995 and 2005.
- Markets suffer from infrastructural bottlenecks. Trading, clearing, and settlement systems are so slow and many of the exchanges still operate through the manual systems.[7]

Some banks are tracking the African market by developing specific pan-African indexes, as is the case with Société Générale Pan African Index (SGI) in collaboration with Standard and Poor's. The SGI Pan Africa

Index attempts to capture the performance of stocks listed in Africa or stocks of companies predominantly exploring African assets. The index is evenly exposed to three zones: South Africa, Northern Africa including Morocco and Egypt, and Sub-Saharan Africa excluding South Africa. SGI Pan Africa is calculated and published by Standard & Poor's and is composed by Société Générale. The index is calculated real-time. The index components are reviewed by Société Générale every 6 months in order to reflect changes due to new entrants, corporate actions, and potential changes in the core activities of companies to ensure the stock selection remains relevant. The number of stocks is equal to 30, with the largest 10 eligible stocks selected as components in each zone, provided that at least 10 stocks can be selected from each zone. By construction, each zone is given a weight representing a third of the index. The weight of each component is then adjusted accordingly, depending on its market capitalisation. The largest constituents are capped at 10 %. The regional breakdown may change slightly due to liquidity constraints, but no zone can represent less than 25 % and more than 50 % of the index by market capitalisation.[8]

Attracting Islamic funds to the market will definitely help in developing these markets and constitute a source of diversification and better return for these funds. One of the early Sharī'ah-compliant funds to enter the African market is Saudi-based Jadwa Africa Equity Freestyle Fund. The fund was the best performing fund in Saudi Arabia in 2010, with a return of 31.74 %.[9] Reporting the news concerning the approval of the fund by the Capital Market Authority, the *Saudi Gazette* stated the following:

> The African continent provides some very exciting opportunities... A number of African markets have provided some of the world's strongest returns over the past three years, despite being perceived as historically too risky. Investors may be surprised to know that several African markets outperformed the major world indices during this period.[10]

In fact, it is widely acknowledged that the best investment opportunities lie where perception differs from reality and Africa perfectly fits that.[11] Commenting on the move by the company into the African market in 2008, the Managing Director and CEO of Jadwa Investment said:

> We are bringing to our investors an opportunity that is special and not many international investors have been alerted to it as yet. We believe our investors will benefit from the early mover advantage and expectedly enjoy substantial gains.[12]

During the 2011 political changes in Egypt and Tunisia, some investors started to look very carefully at their African investments. The Egyptian market, for instance, was down to 20 %. However, if an African investor had been holding a diversified portfolio across various African stock markets, the numbers would tell a different story. It would be very simplistic to judge all African markets based on the retreat or performance of one market. Although Egypt and Tunisia have had negative returns during that period, other African markets have produced exceptionally good returns over the past year. Kenya and Nigeria have performed particularly well.[13] *The Banker* stressed:

> The relative resilience of Africa's financial markets to social and political unrest in the north, and to the default of Côte d'Ivoire on last year's global bond, suggest that the continent's markets have taken one more step towards greater sophistication. Investors are increasingly differentiating one from another.[14]

Thus, investors are reminded of the importance of portfolio diversification across countries and stocks in order to reduce risk. Even political risk can be diversified because it is often localised as each country has different political dynamics. A sharp downturn in a particular market, possibly from irrational panic selling, may also provide an opportunity to enter the market at lower prices.[15] Africa remains at the centre of the global investment stage.

However, investing in equity markets from an Islamic perspective is governed by some specific rules that need to observed by investors, and therefore, require positive attention from regulators by creating a conducive environment. Investing in Sharī'ah-compliant equities remains a cornerstone of Islamic finance. The industry has developed its own methodology of screening and selecting equities and shares that comply with Islamic principles and Islamic equity indices have accordingly become an important part of the industry's investment universe. Islamic equity indices cover nearly all countries, regions, and industry segments which do not contradict Islamic values. These benchmarks indicate to investors how a region or country performs over time and which sectors are driving index trends. They also offer a measure of comparison. Sharī'ah-compliant indices are offered by a number of index providers, including Dow Jones Indexes,[16] Standard and Poor's (S&P),[17] FTSE Group,[18]Morgan Stanley Capital International (MSCI),[19] Thomson Reuters IdealRatings Islamic

Indices,[20] and Russell Investments.[21] Indices have various functions. They are used in asset management as benchmarks. They form the basis for calculating market risk, and they allow professional and retail investors to track the economic performance of a region, country, or industry.[22]

Muslim investors are not permitted to invest in firms producing alcohol, tobacco, or pornography, nor may they invest in conventional banks or insurance operations. These kinds of businesses are regarded as impermissible or *haram* for Muslims. Firms with a debt-to-market capitalisation ratio of over one-third are also are considered to be non-Sharī'ah-compliant as well as companies that hoard money. However, firms which generate no more than 5 % of the aforementioned *haram* goods or services can be included in an Islamic index, while companies with primary or secondary business activity in an impermissible area will be excluded.

Considering the fact that most Muslim capital markets are part of the emerging markets, investing only in these markets would inevitably lead to a volatile equity portfolio. A reported 99 % of all Sharī'ah-compliant stocks are located in non-Muslim countries. The importance of regional diversification as a means or risk management is well-known and the African equity market could be another destination for these Sharī'ah-compliant investors. This is particularly relevant in a time where desires for raw materials and industrial metals or oil and gas, for instance, will continue to fuel the underlying firms and indices, offering wealthy clients an opportunity to participate in rising commodity prices, without compromising the Islamic principles.[23]

With African stock markets still small and illiquid, private equity is another way for investors to take advantage of the opportunities in African emerging economies. Private Equity (PE) funds in Africa are still small by international standards. However, Africa can offer unique investment opportunities as it accounts for 36 % of potential growth and 25 % of the world population. Portfolio assets need to increase in Africa and PE is one way towards restructuring companies, cutting costs, and driving top-line profits. PE comes with tenure and is not a short-term fix, but "PE is about developing partnerships."[24]

## Private Equity in Africa

Private equity could play a crucial role in financing the growth of the private sector in Africa, including the SME sector. PE can offer a win-win situation for Africa as it provides funding to entrepreneurs in a way that local banks are not in a position to provide. However, the industry needs to be understood within a regional context, especially as the focus has changed since the financial crisis. PE today is about creating value. At the same time, the returns need to be good to encourage PE investors and to understand the environment investors operate in, particularly as there are risk-adjusted returns for interested investors.[25]

It is a very promising asset class that is expected to gain prominence and importance in the coming years. Commodities as an investment class are expected to decline in popularity, from being the most popular asset today, to third place overall, while PE and infrastructure will gain more ground, becoming the two most popular asset classes. Equities will remain part of the mix, as the fourth most popular asset class. In terms of the investment vehicles favoured, 40 % of investors expect to use equity funds in the coming 3 years.[26]

PE firms operating in the continent are active in a wide range of asset classes that include areas such as infrastructure, banking and financial services, industrial and manufacturing, energy and natural resources, media and telecoms, agribusiness, and others.

A better macroeconomic environment characterised by high growth and low inflation has been a primary factor in the growth of PE in Africa. Even though there are shortcomings that work against market development in some countries, such as developed systems and institutions to facilitate deal flows and exit strategy, poor governance, and political instability, foreign investors are attracted by the high returns in African markets over the last 5 years due to cheap labour, little competition, low rents, and higher margins. However, the institutional environment and the quality of regulations remain important impediments to the proper functioning of the PE market in Africa.[27]

Although PE activity in Africa is presently limited, the industry has been active for many years, with solid track records emerging in the last decade. Africa has a long history of private ownership and relatively well-developed institutional settings compared with Eastern Europe, for instance. The continent benefits from UK and French-based legal systems, increasingly sophisticated securities commissions, and improved banking oversight. PE capital commitments across the continent are steadily increasing. In the past few years, Goldman Sachs and RSA-based Pamodzi each launched US$1.3 billion funds, while Actic, Ethos, Emerging Capital Partners, and Renaissance Capital, each launched roughly US$1 billion funds, and HSBC Kingdom Africa, Citigroup, and Global Environmental

Fund (GEF) respectively launched a US$400 million, a US$200 million, and a US$150 million fund for Africa. In addition to institutional investors, international financial institutions (IFIs), African and non-African development finance institutions (DFIs), among them, the African Development Bank (AfDB), the Development Bank of Southern Africa (DBSA), the British Colonial Development Corporation (CDC), the Dutch FMO (Development Finance Company), and the French PROPARCO (Investment and Promotions Company for Economic Cooperation) have participated in PE activities in Africa.[28]

Africa's image is fast changing from being a humanitarian cause to the latest frontier for financial returns. Approximately 44 % of the global LPs surveyed by Coller Capital's 2011 annual survey said they found Africa as an attractive investment region, compared to only 21 % in 2010. In the 2011 survey, Africa surpassed key frontier markets such as Turkey, the Middle East and North Africa region, Russia, and Central and Eastern Europe.[29]

In terms of return, the number of investors expecting 16 % and above is higher in Sub-Saharan Africa than in other regions such as the Middle East and North Africa region, Russia, and Central and Eastern Europe.[30]

Africa's rapid ascent of LPs ladder of preferred investment regions is also evidenced in the rate at which fundraising for the region has grown. Year-on-year fundraising for the African Sub-Saharan region grew at the rate of 56 % in 2009, while Russia, the Middle East and North Africa, India, emerging Asia, and the collective Central and Eastern European region, and Commonwealth of Independent States suffered decline in their fundraising figures in the same year.

Investors nevertheless continue to be wary of the low number of established fund managers in the African market, with 47 % citing this as a primary deterrent to committing capital to the region. Interestingly, this concern ranked above political risk, which was singled out by 39 % of the group. Almost a quarter of the LPs expressed worries over the scale of opportunity to invest, believing that, for Africa, this is still too small.

Surprisingly, the poor choice of exits was not a huge concern for the LPs, with only 14 % of the respondents saying it was a discouraging factor. Valuations were the least concern for investors, with only 2 % listing this as a deterrent. This is compared to India, where 58 % of the investors believed the market is becoming overheated in terms of asset valuations.[31]

Carlyle recently announced its strategy for the African private equity market with plans to deploy US$750 million to the continent. The move is considered by observers as a landmark occurrence, given the respect and recognition Carlyle commands in global PE circles. Its commitment to the continent signals a stamp of approval, creating a path for other global investors to follow.[32]

For many years, numerous PE funds have been active on the continent and have developed strong track records in a number of different industry sectors, such as telecoms and the financial services sectors, and have to some extent enjoyed the benefits of an uncrowded market. However, we are now seeing a growing recognition of the opportunities in Africa from a broad range of funds ranging from pan-African funds, South African-based GPs, country or regionally focused funds in the larger markets in West and East Africa as well as funds with a higher appetite for risk in more frontier markets.[33]

In terms of return and looking at this history, the most successful deployment of PE in Africa has applied best practices that have been tested and proven in both emerging and developed markets alike. Three important areas of application need to be taken into consideration, identifying risks, defining the path to liquidity, and anticipating changes in judicial and regulatory frameworks. Understanding how these factors affect a company is critical to ensure that PE investments in Africa will generate attractive returns over time. The Managing Director of Emerging Capital Partners analysed these factors and maintained that every opportunity in PE comes with risks that must be mitigated and those in Africa are no exception.[34]

The global financial crisis has shown that the developing world no longer holds a monopoly on investment risk. A new risk reality has emerged that is ever present and less associated with the developing regions of the world. Combined with other factors affecting the global economic landscape, businesses are now looking for new markets in which to invest.[35]

Many of the perceived risks, such as political risk, corporate governance, transparency and the like, are not necessarily peculiar to Africa and are generally found in all emerging markets. However, there are some fundamental "must haves" when considering any investment. Choosing the right local partner is key to any investment in Africa. Extensive due diligence on the industry, the market, and your partner is vital, and conducting background checks on individuals, their position, and reputation in the local business community through the use of risk consultancy advisers is advisable.[36]

Portfolio company risk analysis often begins with local factors, which are specific to each country, industry, and currency. With regard to country risk, although this type of risk has been steadily subsiding in many African countries, with successive democratic elections and improving rule of law, it is often advisable to look for companies that operate across country borders as that will naturally diversify risks specific to a single country. Where politics pose a risk, investments should be structured to transfer country risk outside of the zone or onto the sponsors who may be more adept at handling sudden developments. With regard to industry risk, the industries that are among the first to feel the shocks of a crisis or downturn are similar to those in the rest of the world—such as consumer goods, transportation, commodities, and hospitality/travel. Portfolio managers should assess just how much a company will be directly impacted in various economic scenarios and how they will plan for secondary complications such as the loss of a major vendor or client due to bankruptcy. Concerning currency risk, African currencies have appreciated slightly against the US dollar in the past 10 years. Nevertheless, it remains an important consideration, as currency depreciation or inflation can significantly change investment yields over a typical 3–5 year holding period. This risk can be reduced through diversification across currencies and by using hard currency convertible loans and investing in companies with hard currency revenues such as those in export industries and companies in primary material export countries.[37]

It is important to point out here that "while the perceived risk in Africa is generally greater than the actual risk, investing across the continent does require a significant level of risk tolerance and an honest assessment of how a company operates within its environment."[38]

Liquidity and exit options are important considerations when investing in African companies due to the limited number of stock exchanges in Africa with a reasonable market capitalisation. Most of these markets do not have the liquidity to absorb IPOs in excess of about US$100 million. In addition, local institutions tend to be the primary investors in these markets. Thus, before investing, fund managers need to consider whether a listing on one or multiple African exchanges—or even on a foreign exchange—is feasible. Trade sales are also common in Africa, particularly as countries in the Middle East and Asia have increased their interest in the continent. Africa also offers opportunities to enter into structured investments, pursuant to which, cash flow is paid disproportionately to one or more investors or one or more sponsors commit upfront to repurchase an investor's stake.[39] Although exit activities remain sluggish in the last few years , however, 2014 for instance was a record year for exits on the continent with 40 exits announced by private equity firms.[40]

On the judicial and regulatory framework front, African governments are increasingly backing open market philosophies, and improvements in regulation have encouraged outside investment. However, inefficiencies remain in the continent's judicial and regulatory systems. Fiscal conventions standard in other regions of the world may be absent in Africa, and differences in judicial systems must be accounted for in planning. It is also important to consider how various countries approach taxation, repatriation of dividends, and capital gains; accordingly, investors should take local policies into consideration in structuring an investment in a tax-efficient manner. Thus, applying the best practices in corporate governance and requiring documentation based on international standards from a target company before investment makes sense in any market, particularly in Africa.[41]

African countries tend to impose high levels of withholding tax on cross-border cash flows, including dividends, interest, and management or advisory fees. Minimising these taxes through the use of appropriate tax treaties can present challenges because, with a few notable exceptions, most African countries have very few tax treaties. As with the legal systems, the influence of the colonial past can often be discerned in the choice of treaty partners and many of the treaties are very old.[42]

Another constraint facing fund managers is the absence of a robust intermediary network—advisors, bankers, brokers, and data providers—making sourcing and evaluating opportunities labour-intensive. The financial crisis may result in many Western-trained African professionals returning home to fill this void.[43]

While the African PE market is yet to achieve landmark status on the global alternatives map or to pull the investment that other emerging PE markets attract, the sector is most definitely growing, with expansion taking place at a quick pace and new funds rapidly increasing in both size and reach. As the fastest growing region in the world, the benefits of investing in Africa-focused funds cannot be ignored, especially as traditional barriers to entry, such as poorly developed financial markets, political instability, and the fragmentation of the economy, are gradually being broken down. Although not immune to risks, the market proved its resilience between 2008 and 2009. Increased disposable income has led to growth in the consumer sector, and this, along with greater political stability, has helped to improve macroeconomic conditions in Africa and raised the region's profile as an attractive investment option. Global firms are already investing or showing an interest to invest in the region and there has been growth in the domestic industry in recent years.[44]

Some 172 fund managers worldwide include Africa in their regional focus, with Preqin data showing that there are currently 71 Africa-focused funds seeking a combined aggregate of US$24.9 billion in capital commitments, according to the alternative assets industry's leading source of data and intelligence.

Fund raising in Africa peaked in 2007, when 31 funds raised an aggregate capital of US$11.4 billion. Although the market was affected by the global economic slump in 2008, it has proved to be relatively robust as 20 funds still raised an aggregate capital of US$5.65 billion in that year—a little more than the combined total raised by the 40 funds that closed between 2005 and 2006. This resilience continued through 2009. While only 14 funds were raised, accumulating an aggregate capital of US$3.41 billion, it was almost double the amount raised by the same number of funds in 2005. One the largest funds to close between 2009 and 2010 was the Pan African Infrastructure Development Fund, managed by South Africa-based Harith, which closed at US$630 million.[45]

Preqin's Investor Intelligence database also shows that there are 981 LPs currently expressing an active interest in investing in PE in the emerging markets—a category in which Africa is included. More specifically, the database reveals that 176 fund managers state Africa as a particular geographical investment preference. Thirty seven of these firms are Africa-based and the rest are headquartered elsewhere. Africa needs a strong infrastructure if the economy is to continue to grow—a need which presents an excellent opportunity for PE infrastructure investment in the region.[46]

Pan-African PE group Helios Investment Partners raised US$900 million to form the largest ever amount of money for a new PE fund targeting Africa and is among the latest signs of burgeoning investor appetite for the continent. The new fund attracted orders of more than US$1 billion. Approximately 70 % of the financing came from outside development finance institutions—the highest proportion yet for an Africa fund and illustrative of a broadening spread of interest in the potential for private equity on the continent.[47]

Among the noted PE funds that have raised funds during 2010, is industry veteran Emerging Capital Partners' third fund, which closed at US$613 million in July 2010, which was the largest pan-African growth capital fund raised. Kingdom Zephyr Africa Management captured

US$492 million in February 2010 for its second Pan African Investment Partners Fund, and pan-emerging markets investor Aureos Capital raised US$381 million in February 2010 for its latest Africa-focused fund. Recent developments point to the region's growing ability to attract capital from an increasingly diverse group of investors and the potential for eclipsing even pre-crisis fund sizes.[48] Moreover, in the spring of 2011, global PE house The Carlyle Group announced the launch of a fund dedicated to Sub-Saharan Africa, targeting commitments of at least US$500 million.[49]

The Emerging Markets Private Equity Association (EMPEA) concluded that there has been improvements in the region's branding, with 67 % of LPs surveyed viewing Africa as attractive in 2011 and 39 % planning to begin or expand their investments in Sub-Saharan African funds. Between 2008 and 2010, PE-backed investment in Sub-Saharan African countries accounted for approximately 0.17 % of GDP, versus 0.16 % for China and 0.10 % across Latin America, accordingly.[50]

Investors are more open-minded after realising that returns can be found in other places, not just in the largely developed markets. Helios closed its fund at a time when investors' optimism about Africa's prospects was high, with more than 10 African economies forecast by the African Development Bank to grow at more than 7 % in 2011 at a time when the developed world faced overall sluggish performance. Growth has been spurred by soaring prices for commodities as well as the rapid expansion of banking, telecoms, and other services. Helios sourced its funding from US university endowments, Asian sovereign wealth funds, large African corporate pension funds, European and American funds, as well as development finance institutions.[51]

*The Wall Street Journal* reported Africa as the top performing region over the past 10 years in terms of equity investments, with a 31 % return, compared to 25 % globally, according to the International Finance Corporation, the corporate investment arm of the World Bank.[52]

The African market already presents an attractive size with the African Securities Exchanges Association estimating the total market cap of the continent's larger exchanges, such as South Africa, Egypt, Morocco, Botswana, Nigeria, Kenya, Tunisia, and Mauritius, at US$1.3 trillion.[53]

For example, PE firm Satya Capital, which started as a US$200 million fund in 2009, has almost doubled its investment 3 years later, as pointed out by chairman Ibrahim Moo, who added, "nowhere in the world you can have that return of investment as in Africa."[54]

### *Islamic Private Equity*

Although many of the principles and methods used in conventional PE can be used and adopted in Islamic PE, some additional specific requirements need to be observed, such as the underlying asset and the structure should be Sharī'ah-compliant. The underlying asset must be an asset which is permissible and not prohibited by Islamic law. For instance, a real estate investment fund needs to take into consideration that the occupancy of the real estate must be Sharī'ah-compliant. Non- Sharī'ah-compliant activities include, among others, activities such as conventional financial services, pornography, gambling, and the sale of alcohol or pork. Moreover, the proposed contract, financing, and instrument structure have to be Sharī'ah-compliant. Thus, funds must be invested in a vehicle that has been structured in a Sharī'ah-compliant manner. This, in particular, takes into account that the activities of the vehicle are based on tangible assets, which are not speculative in nature (*gharar*). The constitution of the vehicle provides for a prohibition on *haram* activities. Furthermore, the activities of the directors and officers are acceptable in nature and it is possible to ensure that their activities are conducted in a Sharī'ah-compliant manner such as not to seek any financing in interest-based instruments.[55] Besides, Sharī'ah-compliant investment in private equity requires additional requirements in term of conventional leverage of the company against its total market capitalisation and the same in term of its cash and receivables. The following are the main financial filters that the fund manager would be required to employ:

- Exclude companies if Total Conventional Debt divided by the Trailing 12-Month Average Market Capitalisation is greater than or equal to 33 %. (Note: Total Debt = Conventional Short-Term Debt + Current Portion of Conventional Long-Term Debt + Conventional Long-Term Debt)
- Exclude companies if the sum of Cash and Interest-Bearing Securities divided by Trailing 12-Month Average Market Capitalisation is greater than or equal to 33 %.
- Exclude companies if Accounts Receivables divided by Trailing 12-Month Average Market Capitalisation is greater than or equal to 33 %. (Note: Accounts Receivables = Current Receivables + Long-Term Receivables)
- Companies that are engaged in permissible activities but have a small percentage of non-permissible element could be included in the

universe. However, the amount of income generated from prohibited component should not exceed 5 % of the total revenues of the company.

The amount of income generated from the prohibited component would be subject to purification by setting it aside to be disposed in charitable activities. Although this would not affect the management of the portfolio, the fund manager would be required to report this component to the fund's Sharī'ah-board so that it could take appropriate measures to purify the income of the fund.

The growing importance of the African stock markets and the complementary nature of the PE industry in strengthening financial markets make a strong case for investors to enter the African financial markets. However, the real potential of the African financial markets will not be achieved until we address the status of the African bond market and the prospect for *ṣukūk*.

## Project Financing and *Sukūk* Prospects in Africa

It is a basic fact that as infrastructure improves, so will economic growth expand. Thus, it is rightly upheld that, "If countries can achieve 6 % annual GDP growth without infrastructure, think what they will be able to achieve with it!"[56] Project financing in Africa can be funded through different modes of financing. Among others, it is strongly believed that *ṣukūk* issuance can play an important role in that direction.

## *Sukūk* Definition

The concept of *ṣukūk* is defined in different ways, based on the institution concerned and its understanding.[57] Perhaps the most widely circulated and accepted definition are those by the Accounting and Auditing Organisation of Islamic financial institutions (AAOIFI) and the Securities Commission Malaysia (SC).

The AAOIFI defines *ṣukūk* as:

> Investment *ṣukūk* are certificates of equal value representing undivided shares in ownership of tangible assets, usufructs and services (in the ownership of) the assets of particular projects or special investment activity…[58]

The IFSB, on the contrary, defines *ṣukūk* as:

*Ṣukūk* (plural of *sakk*), frequently referred to as "Islamic bonds", are certificates with each sakk representing a proportional undivided ownership right in tangible assets, or a pool of predominantly tangible assets, or a business venture. These assets may be in a specific project or investment activity in accordance with *Sharī'ah* rules and principles.[59]

### *Ṣukūk Market Growth and Development*

Although *ṣukūk* started being issued in the 1990s, the global *ṣukūk* was inaugurated by Malaysia's global *ṣukūk* in 2002. From that day, the market has witnessed exceptional double-digit growth until the recent financial and economic crisis, wherein we witnessed a short period of limited decline. The *ṣukūk* market, as was case with the Islamic finance industry, was less affected by the financial crisis than its conventional counterpart, though it was not completely immune to its consequences. The industry faced difficult times during the financial meltdown, as reflected in the reduction of *ṣukūk* issuance at the pick of the crisis. However, the *ṣukūk* market emerged from the worst of the financial crisis more rapidly than expected.[60] Thus, in 2010, *ṣukūk* issuances hit a record of US$47.78 billion. If compared to the last few years, the market in 2010 managed to surpass the 2007 peak level by around 7 % and 50 %, when compared to 2009. This was a clear sign of increasing confidence in the global markets. According to *Dow Jones Islamic Markets Indices December 2010 Commentary*, the DJIM Citigroup *ṣukūk* Index gained 9.1 % in 2010, finishing at 125.32 points.[61] From its side, Standard & Poor's posted a marginally higher figure for the issuance in 2010 that reached a record high of US$51.2 billion in 2010, including those issued and matured that same year, beating the previous peak in 2007 by 34 %.[62]

This positive development continued throughout 2011 with a surge in *ṣukūk* issuance with a total of US$85.1 billion issued—a 78 % increase over the US$47.8 billion raised in 2010.[63] Another *ṣukūk* record for issuances was in 2012, when US$137.1 billion was raised. However, issuance dropped to US$111.3 billion in 2013 and picked up to US$116.4 billion in 2014. According to Standard & Poor's 2015 forecast, despite some emerging headwinds such as the collapsing oil prices or the expected increase in US Fed interest rates, which is likely to reduce global liquidity that could all slow the growth of the *ṣukūk* market in 2015, the market is still expected to cross the US$100 billion mark again in 2015, in another solid year supported by economic performance in core countries, increasing interest from new countries, and regulatory developments. In 2014 alone, according to the agency, the UK, Luxembourg, South Africa, Hong Kong, Senegal, and others went to the market with their first *ṣukūk* issuances. The rationale for sovereign *ṣukūk* issuance can vary for different governments. It is believed that creating benchmarks and diversifying the investor base have been among the most important reasons for new sovereign *ṣukūk* issuance in 2014. New sovereigns could join the club of *ṣukūk* issuers in the coming years. Tunisia, Nigeria, Korea, Egypt, Mexico, Kazakhstan, Kenya, Philippines, and Thailand figure among governments that announced issuance plans in the past, but have yet to actually issue any *ṣukūk*. *Ṣukūk* issuance can give a government access to a new investor class, thereby diversifying sources of funding. For countries with both fiscal and trade deficits, attracting foreign investors to sovereign *ṣukūk* could provide fiscal funding, as well as help cover external financing needs and support reserve-building. In some cases, governments plan to issue sovereign *ṣukūk* not with a view to funding needs, but to establish a benchmark for the development of an Islamic finance market.[64]

The African *ṣukūk* market was tested in 2007, when Sudan-based Berber Cement Co. issued the first-ever African *ṣukūk* in a US$130 million transaction for the financing of a cement project on the River Nile. Funding will be required going forward, especially for African sovereigns, in light of: (i) the current unprecedented economic growth; (ii) the active debt repayments by a number of African states, especially those with material oil reserves, contributing to reducing their risk profiles, and (iii) the populations' tremendous need for housing, infrastructure, and jobs across the region. Sovereign *ṣukūk* issued by African states may find a range of buyers, especially from investors with an appetite for higher-yielding non-investment-grade Islamic paper.[65] The *ṣukūk* market could also act as a bridge between Africa, where there is an immense need for financing, and the Gulf countries, for instance, which have a wealth of financing resources due to their strong oil-based economies.[66] It should be noted that with *ṣukūk*, one can have more diverse financing sources rather than simply having access to less expensive financing options.[67]

Gambia started issuing Al Salam *ṣukūk*, ending in 2008. The dollar amount raised from these issues was small when compared to the total ṣukūk market, but the high number of Gambian *ṣukūk* shows that there is an overwhelming demand for financial instruments that are in compliance with Sharī'ah.

Nigeria's Osun State issued a 10 billion naira *ṣukūk* yielding 14.75 %. It received 11.4 billion naira in total subscriptions for its 7-year paper. The yield offered was the same Osun State paid last year to sell a conventional 7-year bond worth 30 billion naira. Nigeria's profile as Africa's most liquid debt market after South Africa has been rising since JP Morgan and Barclays included its bonds in their sovereign bond indices in the last year, encouraging greater foreign participation in its debt market. The *ṣukūk* is based on an *ijārah* structure. Local credit rating agency Agusto & Co gave an A rating to the *ṣukūk*, suggesting it will attract ample investor demand. Bankers earlier said that Osun hoped the issue, which is expected to be listed on the Nigerian Stock Exchange, would be bought by both local pension funds and international investors.[68]

Senegal, through its inaugural CFA 100 billion (approximately US$200 million) *ṣukūk* issuance, was the first major *ṣukūk* issuance by a sovereign in Africa. The *ṣukūk* was structured as *ṣukūk al-ijāra,* whereby the Republic of Senegal granted a 99-year usufruct over certain of its assets and agreed to lease them back in return for making rental payments to investors. The transaction was guaranteed by the Republic of Senegal. The *ṣukūk* provides the Government of Senegal access to a more diversified investor base and is likely to encourage a number of other African sovereigns to look more closely at this alternative funding source. The Islamic Corporation for Private Sector Development (ICD) (member of the Islamic Development Bank Group) and Citi were the arrangers of the deal.

An interesting development following the Senegal *ṣukūk* is that the Central Bank of West African States (BCEAO) allowed banks in the regions to use *ṣukūk* issued by Senegal in their repurchase transactions. The move aims at encouraging banks to invest in *ṣukūk,* as highlighted by a report by Standard & Poor's.[69] It is believed that the move will have several implications, such as

1. Equalising the treatment of the *ṣukūk* with the regional government's conventional bonds.
2. Offsetting any liquidity disadvantage that the banks would face if they invested in *ṣukūk* instead of conventional bonds.
3. Encouraging conventional banks to invest in *ṣukūk* and support *ṣukūk* primary market issuance.

4. Supporting the development of more robust pricing data by ensuring that the *ṣukūk* can be a source of liquidity if needed and will enhance the pricing benchmark for *ṣukūk*.
5. Supporting corporate issuance as well as to move out on the yield curve.[70]

South Africa debuted in the sovereign *ṣukūk* market with a deal worth US$500 million in September 2014. The *ṣukūk*, which was listed on the Luxembourg Stock Exchange, was oversubscribed by 4.4 times, with nearly 50 % orders originating from the Middle East while Senegal's debut issuance was a first for Islamic capital markets in the Sub-Saharan Africa region. The issue was priced at a coupon rate of 3.9 %, representing a spread of 180 basis points above the corresponding mid-swap benchmark rate. There was a very big appetite and this was very aggressive priced, given that most issuers come at a 20 and 40 basis point premium over their conventional *Eurobond*, rendering it one of the lowest new issue premiums ever paid for a debut *ṣukūk*. The bond, which matures in June 2020, is a *Ṣukūk Al-Ijāra* structure with cash flows based on infrastructure assets. It is the first non-Muslim emerging market country to sell an international Islamic bond and the first in Africa, thereby setting a precedent. Analysts say other countries will be watching the South African *ṣukūk* with interest and may follow suit, given their already expressed interest in issuing *ṣukūk*. The South African sovereign *ṣukūk* represented an important milestone for the development of Islamic finance in African markets.[71]

Some financial institutions in South Africa are considering the issuance of *ṣukūk*. Although most South African banks enjoy investment-grade ratings, two constraints have emerged when exploring the *ṣukūk* option. On the one hand, a prerequisite remains to build enough underlying Sharī'ah-compliant assets to back the *ṣukūk* transactions, which Southern African banks might not have already achieved. On the other hand, such *ṣukūk* would still be subject to foreign exchange risks, as banks in South Africa generate the bulk of their returns from domestic rand-based businesses.[72]

Several other African countries are planning to test the market. The World Bank reported that several countries are revamping their laws to tap into the Islamic financial market.[73] There is a growing appetite for *ṣukūk* issuance from different countries in the continent.[74]

Investment-grade bond and *ṣukūk* are definitely more attractive to many market players. However, it is also a market reality that the debt market is composed of investment grade and high-yield papers and each category has its customers and investors. Thus, its investment-grade paper considerably limits investors' capacity to diversify their *ṣukūk* portfolios across underlying asset classes, geographies, sectors, and rating levels. Although the average investment-grade *ṣukūk* portfolios carry relatively low credit risks, they tend to be weakened by the high volume of issuers operating in the same economic environment, and are, therefore, prone to cyclicality. Accordingly, *ṣukūk* issuances by African sovereigns, and subsequently, by African corporates, might fit investors' diversification strategies, while bringing further depth and liquidity to the Islamic capital markets. One desirable prerequisite to issuing *ṣukūk* out of Africa is the wider use of credit ratings by African issuers—be they sovereign or corporate entities.[75] This will give possible investors some comfort and help in attract global attention to issuances from the continent.

As stated above, Nigeria is another country planning to sell its first *ṣukūk*. The initiative is believed to be part of the country's bid to become the continent's centre for Sharī'ah-compliant financing. The government has yet to decide on the size of the *ṣukūk* sale. Nigeria is rated B+ by Standard and Poor's and has a BB- from Fitch Ratings. It is expected that Nigeria's *ṣukūk* "will generate some interest among Gulf investors."[76]

At the same time, the government of Kenya is studying the possibility of issuing the country's debut sovereign *ṣukūk*.[77] However, some observers pointed out that such a step from the Kenyan government or other African state will require time, given the fact that key laws need to be amended. Such initiatives require political will and parliamentary approval. These changes can only be effected, as far as Kenya is concerned, if the Ministry of Finance and the Central Bank push these legal amendments robustly. At the same time, the Debt Management Office at the Kenyan Treasury is studying ways of introducing tax neutrality measures for the issuance of *ṣukūk*. It is likely that some local corporates may issue local-currency *ṣukūk* before a sovereign issuance. The positive thing is that there is agreement among major players in the country that the business case for Islamic finance in Kenya and East Africa is proven and that *ṣukūk* could be a vital tool for local corporates to raise funds to finance local projects and for balance sheet purposes.[78]

Sovereign ṣukūk can be issued for various reasons.[79] Governments can issue *ṣukūk* in order to access new investor classes and to diversify sources of fiscal funding. For countries with both fiscal and current account deficits, attracting foreign investors to sovereign *ṣukūk* could provide fiscal funding, as well as help cover external financing needs and support reserve-building. In some cases, governments will issue sovereign *ṣukūk* not with a view to fiscal or external funding needs, but to establish a benchmark for the development of an Islamic finance market. Governments could also be responding to the desires of a significant Muslim population or aiming to become a hub for the global Islamic finance market.[80] *Ṣukūk* issued by African sovereigns could address an investor base in GCC countries or at the Islamic Development Bank (ISDB), which may be looking for Sharīʿah-compliant investment opportunities. Countries in the GCC generally benefit from strong current account surpluses that could make them potential investors in *sukuk* issued in other regions, according to Standard & Poor's.[81]

Sovereign *Ṣukūk* are mostly *ṣukūk al-ijārah* based on leases or rents while government-owned entities, such as development banks, tend to use profit-sharing *ṣukūk* structures. The assets underlying sovereign *ṣukūk* tend to be public real estate, such as schools, hospitals, or administrative buildings. However, given the limited availability of such sovereigns, Sukuk might use other types of government assets, such as infrastructure, especially if the proceeds of *sukūk* are used to help finance infrastructure construction.[82]

The Public Private Infrastructure Advisory Facility (PPIAF) of the World Bank in its December 2009 Newsletter stressed that while the global financial crisis has generally slowed the development of emerging bond markets, interest in bond financing of infrastructure in Africa continues to grow in anticipation of the recovery. Across the region, governments are increasingly cognisant of the role of large infrastructure investments as a stimulus to support economic growth. For utilities or local authorities in Africa seeking to raise financing to meet the pressing demands for infrastructure, the discipline and transparency inherent in a robust bond market can reduce risk and lower the cost of capital.[83]

Thus, as stated above, the encouraging prospect of *ṣukūk* issuance by African sovereigns and corporations is linked to the growing appetite among African issuers to tap the international market for conventional bond issuance. A dozen African countries have already issued Eurobonds for ambitious infrastructure investment programmes. This development will directly contribute to building critically needed African infrastructure. Establishing a benchmark bond yield will also help speed the development of capital markets and financial services for the African private sector.[84]

Until recently, the African bond markets were largely underdeveloped. In most African countries, the public sector dominates debt issuance. These debt instruments are generally characterised as being very short-tenured, with activities focusing on the domestic primary market and limited secondary trading despite the fact that several countries have listed the bonds on the stock exchange. This is mainly due to the "buy and hold" strategy of domestic banks who hold the bulk of these instruments, the limited lending opportunities, and some prudential requirements such as liquid asset ratios in some countries that require banks to hold a certain amount of their assets in government-issued paper.[85]

Thus, while bond markets at a national and regional level, or rather, the continent level remain largely underdeveloped, several initiatives are underway by governments, private sectors, and donors. These initiatives are aimed at addressing deficiencies in the legal system, enhancing bond issuance, broadening and diversifying the investor base, strengthening market infrastructure, developing supranational, and corporate bond markets and the promotion of regional initiatives.[86]

Capital market conditions are increasingly encouraging governments in Sub-Saharan Africa to turn to the international markets for fund raising. Several African sovereigns have launched debut global debt issues in recent years.

The African Eurobonds enjoyed remarkable growth throughout 2014. Analysts are expecting the trend to continue for the foreseeable future. Although the renewed strength of the US dollar should have made things difficult for emerging market bonds, African debt held firm. Total returns on JPMorgan's global Emerging Market Bond Index fell by 1.05 %, and losses were particularly significant in Venezuela, Russia, and Ukraine while Africa Eurobonds performed relatively well, losing just 0.48 %. The buoyant African Eurobonds market is not limited to sovereign debt as there is a noticeable rise in corporate Eurobond as well. The notional amount of outstanding African sovereign Eurobond debt, which stood at US$4 billion in 2005, has now reached more than US$60 billion. In the same period, the Eurobonds issued by African corporates increased from US$7 billion to US$42 billion.[87]

According to Standard & Poor's, some of the reasons behind this growing interest in the international bond market by African countries can be summarised as follows:

1. Low returns on investments in Europe and the USA appear to be attracting international investors to emerging markets such as Africa.

2. Higher funding rates at home currently make it cheaper for many African countries to issue debt on the international markets than domestically. This is generally due to less developed domestic markets and uncertainty on inflation rates and exchange rates in many countries.
3. Austerity measures in developed countries since the onset of the global financial crisis slowed the flow of bilateral and multilateral financing that has traditionally been a key funding source for many African sovereigns

However, the issuance of this Eurobond sovereign issues has its downside:

1. It could contribute to peaks in debt maturities once these bonds come due and this will require governments to undertake some careful fiscal management.
2. Government issuers also bear exchange-rate risk on the service of foreign currency debt. If repayment of the bullet maturity of the Eurobond coincides with a sharp depreciation of the exchange rate, the fiscal cost of repaying will be even higher.[88]
3. There are also fears that its growth will impede the development of liquid, local currency-denominated assets.[89]

Caution is needed despite the growing appetite for African sovereign debt and the issuance of several Eurobonds by a number of African countries. The International Monetary Fund warned African countries against rushing to issue Eurobonds due to problems of exchange-rate risks that might create problems in repaying debts. Africa must be aware of the fact that whereas the costs to issue these bonds seems to be lower than what they would pay on domestic borrowing, the real cost in the final analysis will depend on the evolution of exchange rates in the course of the life of the bond issuance.

The renewed investor appetite for African sovereign credit to raise bonds in the international market is apparent in some of the sovereign bonds recently issued out of the continent. The Government of Ghana raised US$750 million in debt sovereign bonds in 2007. The issue was sold with a coupon of 8.5 % that tightened in the secondary market and was quoted at 5.8 % in early June 2011. The country could build on this to lengthen its curve by selling a second Eurobond. Similarly, the Republic of Gabon successfully raised a US$1 billion 10-year bond on the international market. The Government of Seychelles, on its part, raised a US$230 million 3-year bond. In effect, these flows enhanced governments' financing capacities and constituted fresh money for public investments. The rise in African financial markets was underpinned by improved macroeconomic fundamentals in the region, as well as by a good performance of African stock markets during that period.[90] Since then, Senegal, Nigeria, Zambia, Rwanda, Cote d'Ivoire (Ivory Coast), and Kenya have all joined in. The Tanzanian government is expected to sign for credit rating services agreements with two rating agencies in November 2016 in preparation of the issuance of their sovereign Eurobond in 2017.[91] On the other hand, Ethiopia completed raising $1 billion with its debut Eurobond. The 10 years issue was oversubscribed.[92] Ethiopia aims to make its first foray into the international bond markets by early 2015, while Rwanda is planning another sovereign bond. According to the IMF, foreign investors were interested in Sub-Saharan Africa's "good economic prospects" and "sound macro-economic policies" and Sub-Saharan Africa's economy to grow by 5 % in 2014 and accelerate to 5.8 % in 2015 on infrastructure investments.[93]

In June 2014, Kenya's US$2 billion Eurobond was the largest for an African sovereign, excluding South Africa. The issue was spread over two tranches and was more than four times oversubscribed, with an order book of US$8.8 billion. The 5-year, US$500 million bond yielded 5.875 % and the 10-year US$1.5 billion issue yielded 6.875 %. Barclays, Standard Bank, JPMorgan, and Qatar National Bank were lead managers.

Kenya's top-tier corporates and financial institutions are primed to follow hot on the heels of the sovereign's Eurobond issue. Many corporates in Kenya eagerly anticipated the debut sovereign Eurobond, as it set an important benchmark, which will enable them to more easily access funding from international capital markets.[94]

Another issue is Rwanda's US$400 million issue in April 2013. The Rwandan government plans to use the proceeds to repay loans related to the Kigali Convention Centre and the RwandAir strategic development plan, as well as for financing the completion of the Kigali Convention Centre.[95] The 10-year bond was sold at a yield of 6.875 %. The order book for the bond was US$3.5 billion, more than 8.5 times the issue size, underscoring the huge investor appetite for high-yielding African sovereign debt and reflecting high global liquidity. Fitch assigned the bond a B rating, in line with the country rating.[96] At less than US$500 million, Rwanda's bond was ineligible for JP Morgan's emerging market bond indices that would have automatically triggered demand from index track-ers and ensured increased secondary market liquidity.[97] However, some observers noted that investors were undeterred by the fact that the size of the bond would exclude it from influential bond indices.

Another African Eurobond is the one issued by Zambia in 2012. Again, demand far outstripped supply. The 10-year bond was priced at 5.625 %. The government originally planned to raise US$500 million, but high levels of interest led it to increase the target to US$750 million. Barclays and Deutsche Bank were the joint lead managers and book runners. The issue received more than 425 orders worth US$12 billion. Buyers from the USA took up 56 % of the bond issue after an investor roadshow in London, Los Angeles, San Francisco, Boston, and New York. The remainder was bought by European investors (40 %), Asian (3 %) and others at 1 %. In terms of sectors, fund managers received 85 % of allocations, followed by banks with 8 %, pension and insurance funds with 5 %, and others at 2 %. As well as the interest in emerging markets, demand was also fuelled by Zambia's own buoyant economy, which the IMF expects to grow by 7.7 % this year.[98]

Zambia went to the international bond market once again in 2014 with the proceeds of the new offer planned to be used for transportation and energy infrastructure. The new issue was 10-year bonds with a 8.5 % coupon. Like the first, the second bond was significantly oversubscribed by about 330 %, reflecting strong confidence in the economy despite ongoing fiscally and externally induced challenges and rising US Treasury yields. This positive development could be due partly to prospects of a potential rise in copper production over the medium term and the reassurance of real positive returns on sovereign yield curve in light of ongoing monetary tightening. The country sold its first dollar bond in 2012 at a coupon of 5.375 %. Deutsche Bank AG and Barclays once again led the issue.[99] The final allocation statistics showed that fund managers dominated the allocation of the bond, particularly US-based investors. Fund managers accounted for 84 % of total bond allocation, of which US-based investors accounted for 56 % of demand, followed by UK-based investors, 27 %; other European investors, 14 %; Asian-based investors, 2 %; and others, 1 %. Banks (both public and private) were the second main participants, accounting for 9 % of total bond allocation; followed by insurance and pension funds, 6 %; and others, 1 %.[100] Zambia was rated B+ by Standard & Poor's and B by Fitch.[101]

Nigeria was also among the African countries that raised Eurobond funds. Africa's largest economy raised US$1 billion in its return to the Eurobond market. The issue was four times oversubscribed, with just over

US$4 billion. Africa's top oil producer issued a US$500 million 5-year bond at a yield of 5.375 % and a US$500 million 10-year bond with a yield of 6.625 %, according to IFR, a Thomson Reuters news and analysis service. The 5-year paper received bids of US$1.77 billion and the 10-year of US$2.26 billion. By comparison, Nigeria's debut US$500 million 10-year Eurobond, which it issued in 2011, received bids worth two and a half times the amount on offer. The yield on the 10-year bond is less than the 7 % the West African country paid in 2011.[102]

After a lot of anticipation, Nigeria finally brought its much awaited debut US$500 million sovereign bond issue to market in January, the first time the sovereign has printed a note targeted at the global market. The 10-year bond carried a coupon of 6.75 %, and attracted investors from 18 countries across Europe, North America, Asia, and Africa. Investors clamoured to get a piece of the deal, resulting in the issuance being 2.5 times oversubscribed, despite concerns over Nigeria's management of its oil fund. The interest garnered by the bond demonstrates the wide gap between demand and supply of Sub-Saharan African debt created for international investors. Unlike local currency bonds, the Eurobonds pass international jurisdiction requirements and are traded and settled in non-African hard currencies. Global investors favour such bonds because they carry no currency risks and have lower counterparty risks than locally issued notes.

There is a positive dynamic in Eurobond issuances from Sub-Saharan African countries, but the volume of supply remains largely limited and thin. Many investors that have purchased bonds are using a "buy and hold" strategy. Investors have a strong appetite for sub-Saharan African bonds, but face the critical issue of currency risk.

The bulk of Sub-Saharan countries remain shy of the Eurobond market, deterred by the hurdles to listing such notes. Apart from the minimum US$500 m requirement per issuance for the notes to be included on the JP Morgan Emerging Markets Bonds Index, some countries simply do not have a high enough sovereign rating to attract investors.

Despite debt reductions, some countries still have relatively high levels of external debt and cannot realistically take on more. More importantly, while many countries could raise capital on global markets, the institutional capacity to spend the proceeds is limited, causing concern over the cost of having unused funds sitting in reserves.[103]

Besides the growing appetite for Eurobonds, Africa's local currency bond market is also experiencing increased activities and development.

If African dollar bonds are increasingly gaining mainstream acceptance, the excitement over Africa's growing role in international capital markets should not exclude the need to develop the local bond market. Some observers are beginning to question just how healthy the dollar borrowing spree is. It is believed that Eurobonds should be a short-term solution for African sovereigns, and therefore, developing local bond markets should be a priority. Although currently raising funds domestically can be expensive, with double-digit yields in many countries, compared to single digits on the Eurobond market, in the long-term, borrowing in dollars may not be as cheap as governments think. African local currency bond markets have been growing steadily, with total outstanding debt reaching more than US$400 billion in 2014, compared to less than US$150 billion a decade ago. However, there are currently only 15 investable local bond markets on the continent and foreign investors are believed to be deterred by the small size of many markets, limited liquidity, short yield curves, and currency volatility.[104]

Although local currency bond markets in Sub-Saharan African countries are still at a nascent stage of development with market capitalisation of both government securities and corporate bonds typically much lower than those of other developing, emerging, and advanced economies, there has been noticeable growth in recent years. The local currency bond market is generally dominated by government securities. However, the corporate bond market, although still at a nascent stage of development, has become an increasingly important component of the total bond market in the continent. The market has been expanding in a consistent fashion. Moreover, the growth of corporate bonds relative to government securities suggests that the corporate bonds could, in the future, be a very important source of finance for many Sub-Saharan African countries.[105]

One example of this growing interest is coming from Chad. The country launched its first local currency bond in June 2011. Chad aimed to raise CFA 100 billion (US$220 million) in 5-year notes.[106] The issue drew strong interests from Central African investors. The oil-producing nation is selling the 100 billion CFA 5-year bond with a yield of 6 % to raise money for infrastructure projects and to service domestic and foreign liabilities. Although not particularly attractive for offshore accounts, observers pointed out that the issue will prove appealing to Central African CFA investors, given the lack of listed securities in the Monetary and Economic Community of Central Africa (CEMAC) and the reasonable regional systemic liquidity position. Chad's bond is also attractive because it offers the highest regional sovereign yield.[107]

As expected, Chad's first local-currency bond was over-subscribed as local institutional and retail investors were attracted by both the structure of the transaction and the attractive yield in comparison to other sovereign bonds in the Monetary and Economic Community of the Central African region. Chad raised 107.6 billion CFA francs (US$232 million) in the issue. Ecobank Capital, the investment banking arm of the Ecobank Group, through its local subsidiary, EDC Investment Corporation, acted as the lead arranger for the issue. The 5-year bond had a yield of 6 % and was due to help the landlocked nation pay off internal debt and finance infrastructure projects. The transaction was structured around government receipts from the Chad-Cameroon oil export pipeline. Commenting on the issue, Chad's finance minister said, "This issue is a clear success and shows that Chad is not a risky country." In addition, the Group Head of Investment Banking, Ecobank Capital said, "This is a landmark deal for Chad, marking its entry into the capital market after a long, politically difficult period."[108]

On January 27, 2011, Afren, a FTSE 250 company based in the UK, launched a 450 million, 5-year senior secured bond. The bonds, rated B- by Standard and Poor's and B by Fitch, were priced to yield 11.75 % and carried a coupon of 11.5 %. These numbers proved attractive to investors desperate for yield, with the order book reaching US$1 billion. Dedicated emerging market funds accounted for about 85 % of the bonds with high-yield fund taking the rest. USA and UK investors bought 80 %, with the rest split between buyers from continental Europe, Africa, and Asia. The deal was co-led by Deutsche Bank, Goldman Sachs, and BNP Paribās. The company was profitable with revenues for the 12 months up to September 30, 2010 of approximately 350 million. The company, like many African companies, relied mostly on equity financing, but decided this time to tap the bond market to diversify its investor base,[109] and as pointed out by *Euromoney Magazine*, "the Afren transaction was not conditional on Nigeria's deal. Now all eyes are on the likely identity of the next Africa borrower."[110]

The rise of financial markets in Sub-Saharan Africa over the past few years has uncovered the importance of the often underestimated role of African investors eager to invest in financial assets.[111] At the same time, the demand by African sovereigns and corporates for large amounts of capital to finance infrastructure projects will not eclipse the high demand to finance small projects, which generally fall under microfinance.

Xavier Rolet, Chief Executive of the London Stock Exchange Group, stressed in an interview with *This Is Africa* that Africa has an outspoken proponent of its success in recent years. He stressed that before 2008, Africa was a net exporter of capital. With the recent financial and economic crisis, everything completely changed.[112] He added that "Africa always knew its potential, but now, for the first time, I think Africa has confidence in itself because it has seen the beginning of a much faster and independent path towards growth."[113]

However, African countries are advised to manage new debt carefully by limiting market financing to high-return projects to avoid the risk of future debt crises and confront the task of making their economies robust to capital flow surges in the face of historical volatility.[114] Yet, it should be noted that although volatility is a challenge in the African market, there is also a welcome side effect of this volatility because returns fluctuate wildly in Africa's frontier markets; 64 % of investors say that investing long-term, rather than short-term speculation, is the way to go.[115]

On the contrary, capital inflows to Africa's frontier markets have increased steadily over the past decade. According to investors polled by *Economist Intelligence Unit*, this trend is set to continue in the following 5 years. Most strikingly, while 21 % of institutional investors today have zero allocation in Africa, this dropped to just 1 % in 3 years' time and in 5 years' time, all say that they will have some allocations in Africa.[116]

### *Insurance and Prospects of* **Takāful** *or Islamic Insurance*

As a key pillar of the financial services sector, insurance is a central element of the trade and development matrix. Both an infrastructural and commercial service, a well-functioning insurance sector plays a crucial role in economic development not just at a macroeconomic level, but also, in terms of the activities of individuals and businesses. The world insurance market is dominated by industrialised countries, which in 2004, generated about 88 % of world life insurance premiums and accounted for 90 % of the world non-life market. Figures for real growth rate and insurance density, i.e. premium per capita, indicate the potential for substantial growth within the insurance sectors of emerging markets. The overall real growth rate of emerging markets for 2004 stood at 7.5 %, compared to 1.7 % in industrialised countries.[117]

The insurance sector is in its infancy in most African countries. It is generally characterised by low insurance penetration, which is below 1 % with few exceptions. The industry is dominated by non–life insurance business lines, such as automobile, health, and industrial insurance policies, while the life segment constitutes less than 30 % in most countries. This reflects the fact that in most countries, insurance development is driven by compulsory business lines such as the motor line. Another feature of Africa's insurance market is that many countries have fragmented insurance systems characterised by many small, underfunded, and weak companies. The lack of regulatory oversight, including in consumer protection, undermines the development of insurance markets. In many countries, insurance supervision is still undertaken by an office within the ministry of finance, although there is an increasing trend towards a separate non-banking financial institution supervisor. Notable is the development in francophone West and Central Africa of a joint insurance supervisor for 14 countries. In some North African countries, such as Algeria, Egypt, and Libya, the dominance of state-owned insurance companies may also explain the limited development of the insurance sector. Low incomes explain much of the low insurance penetration; monetary instability and the weak contractual framework contribute as well.[118]

Insurance markets in Africa are at varying stages of development. Their share of the total premium generated on the continent closely correlates with the level of economic development in their respective countries. African countries have some 650 insurance and reinsurance companies, which generate a gross premium income of US$38 billion. South Africa has the most developed economy and insurance industry on the continent and produces around US$30 billion (79 %) of the continent's total insurance output. There is substantial potential for growth and development in the insurance sector of the vast majority of African countries, but there are also serious difficulties and challenges.[119]

The continent has the lowest regional insurance penetration in the world, averaging below US$15 per capita, both for life and non-life insurance. The main reasons for this low penetration include the late introduction of insurance to the continent, monopolistic/closed markets in many countries until the latter part of the 1990s, the low personal and disposable incomes of African populations, lack of functional financial markets in the majority of countries, unhelpful legislation and tax regimes, limited awareness of the benefits of insurance by the general population, and outdated products and services in a number of countries.[120] Recent figures about life insurance in Africa shows that life insurance premiums fell by 2.4 % to 47 billion in 2010 after having increased by 1.7 % in 2009. At the same time, it has been noticed that non-life insurance has risen by 4.1 % during the same period. However, a number of *Takāful* companies have been established recently in several African countries, which is expected to increase the appeal for life insurance to the continent's significant Muslim population, according to a recent report by Swiss Re.[121]

However, the question is why look for *Takāful* or Islamic insurance in Africa. In a study on insurance in emerging markets and the lower penetration of insurance, particularly life insurance in Muslim countries, by Swiss Re, it was stated that:

> One reason for the lower penetration is that conventional insurance is not compatible with Islamic faith. In order to grow the insurance market in Muslim countries, it is important to understand the different Islamic insurance modes along with their unique challenges and opportunities.[122]

PricewaterhouseCoopers, in its assessment of the prospects of the global *Takāful* industry, noted that "the market opportunity represented by *Takāful* is too significant to ignore. The challenge is to enter the market quickly while minimising costs and risks."[123] The above statements are relevant to many African countries that are part of the emerging markets, and at the same time, they are classified as Muslim countries or countries with sizeable Muslim minority. Even in countries where Muslims are a minority, there is a real demand for Islamic insurance, with South Africa constituting the best example.

Similar to the case of Islamic banking, which originated in its modern form in Africa through The Mit Ghamr experience in Egypt, Africa is also the birthplace of *Takāful*, with Sudan introducing the world's first general *Takāful* product in 1979. According to Ernst & Young, *Takāful* is one per cent of the total global insurance market, but Muslims are more than 20 % of the world's population and, "If we continue with the 2009 growth rate of 31 % or higher, we will clearly touch the $25 billion mark in 2015."[124]

The *Takāful* industry is currently concentrated mainly in the GCC and Malaysia, with Saudi Arabia, Malaysia, and the UAE as the top three *Takāful* markets while Egypt, Sudan, Bangladesh, and Pakistan are growing at a rapid pace. However, future market growth areas are the populous countries of Indonesia and the Indian subcontinent, followed by the African subcontinent and the CIS countries. Legislation in Islamic countries to make *Takāful* products the preferred choice among insurance products can place the industry on a completely different level. For instance, growth in the GCC is primarily driven by compulsory insurance rather than voluntary policies.

The Islamic insurance industry is estimated to grow at an annual rate of between 15 % and 20 %, compared with a growth rate of below 10 % for conventional insurance.[125] The industry is based on principles of *Ta-awun* (mutual assistance) that is *Tabarru* (voluntarily). *Takāful* has similarities with conventional cooperative insurance, whereby participants pool their funds together to insure one another. *Takāful* is based on shared responsibility, solidarity, and co-operative risk-sharing. It is an Islamic form of financial protection established in its modern form for more than 25 years. The market now comprises some 130 companies in both Muslim and non-Muslim countries.

*Takāful* customers (policyholders) agree to pool their contributions and share the liability of each policyholder. If one policyholder has to be paid a claim, this is paid from the combined pool of the policyholders' contribution. The policyholders share in the profit and loss of the *Takāful* business, i.e. the policyholders all share the insurance risk—they do not transfer the risk to the *Takāful* company (as is the case in a conventional shareholder insurance company). Consequently, if at the end of a financial year, the *Takāful* business makes a surplus, this is shared between the *Takāful* policyholders. In contrast, if the policyholders' fund incurs a loss, this deficit is funded by an interest-free loan from the shareholders' fund. The shareholders' fund is then repaid the loan from any future surpluses of the policyholders' fund.[126]

The assets of the *Takāful* business have to be invested in Sharī'ah-compliant funds. Thus, investments cannot be made in any Sharī'ah prohibited businesses involving gambling, alcohol, casino, pork, or assets that pay interest, such as conventional financial institutions. The operators of the business are paid determined fees for setting up and running the company on behalf of the policyholders. These fees should cover all the setting-up costs, running costs, and profit loading of the shareholders, and are the only way that the shareholders are remunerated. After the fees are deducted, any surplus arising from the *Takāful* business is shared amongst the policyholders only. These fees are mentioned in the *Takāful* contract that each policyholder signs with the *Takāful* company and are fully transparent.

There are four major operating models for *Takāful* companies, which are: the *mudārabah* model, *wakālah*, hybrid model, and the *wakāla waqf* model.

**The *Mudārabah* model** is based on the profit–loss sharing concept. The shareholders share in the profit or loss with the policyholder. In this model, the shareholders are paid:

- A pre-agreed proportion of any surplus generated by the policyholders' fund in return for running the insurance operations of the *Takāful* business on behalf of the policyholders. If the policyholders' fund incurs a loss, the operator provides an interest-free loan, as explained above.
- A pre-agreed proportion of any investment income from investing the policyholders' fund's assets on behalf of the policyholders.

**In the *wakālah* model**, the operator acts as an agent of the participants. Thus, shareholders are paid a pre-agreed proportion of the contributions paid by the policyholders in return for running the insurance operations of the *Takāful* business on behalf of the policyholders. If the policyholders' fund incurs a loss, the operator provides an interest-free loan to the policyholders' fund, which is repaid from future surpluses in the fund.

**The hybrid model** is a mix of the *mudarabah* and *wakālah* models. In this model, the operator receives a wakāla fee for managing the insurance operation of the policyholders' fund as well as a *mudarabah* fee for managing the investment fund. This model, according to PwC, is widely used in the GCC countries, with the exception of Saudi Arabia.

**The *wakāla waqf* model** is widely used in Pakistan and South Africa. In this model, the policyholders' fund is replaced by a trust, which is the waqf fund. Part of the capital of the shareholders' fund is used to create this trust, which is considered charitable under local law.[127]

## Reasons for Global *Takāful* Growth

1. The global *Takāful* industry is growing at 20 % per year, far outstripping the 2.5 % annual growth for conventional insurance premiums.
2. One-third of the world's 1.5 billion Muslims represent a potential customer base that no insurer can afford to ignore.

3. 60 % of the global Muslim population is under 25 years of age, with those in Africa the youngest. This youthful population has started to achieve a certain level of affluence, and if it can be taped early, it has the potential of becoming a customer base that is sustainable for 40 years or more.
4. Under-insured status of most African Muslims is also a significant enticement to potential *Takāful* operators in the continent.
5. Insurers and customers are starting to realise that there is a significant market for *takāful.*
6. *Takāful* products can be price competitive with conventional insurance products.
7. *Takāful* is inherently ethical, and thus, obliges to invest in ethical products. This could also be a factor of attraction to non-Muslims in the continent.
8. Another factor is that if the *Takāful* business makes money, it gives a share of this surplus back to the policyholders.[128]

*Takāful* has not expanded materially in Africa, with very few exceptions in Sudan, Egypt, Kenya, Senegal, Gambia, Mauritius, South Africa, and recently, in Tunisia.[129] However, recent developments across the continent are very promising. In Egypt, where Islamic banking and finance companies still lag far behind mainstream commercial institutions, the acceptance of Sharī'ah-based financial solutions remains exceptionally low by standards of the Muslim world. The Egyptian Saudi Insurance House, a provider of general *Takāful* established in 2002, is the first to offer *Takāful* in the country. Five other *Takāful* companies have been licensed, the latest being a joint venture between Japan's Tokio Marine & Nichido Fire Insurance and Egypt Kuwait Holding Co, which will provide both family and general *Takāful* this year.

Elsewhere in North Africa, *Takāful* investment has been driven by the Salama Group in Tunisia (Best Re), Algeria (Salama Algeria), and Senegal (Salama Senegal). Signs of interest have also been reported in the Morocco market. *Takāful* products were introduced to South Africa last year by Al-Noor Risk Solutions, which is currently riding on the licence of an existing insurer (Lions). It expects to obtain a full *Takāful* licence within the next 5 years. In West Africa, *Takāful* Insurance Co opened in Gambia at the end of 2007.[130]

In East Africa, the first fully Sharī'ah-compliant insurance company was officially licensed and launched in Nairobi, Kenya in 2008. *Takāful*

Insurance of Africa was founded and registered by the Kenyan industry regulator, Insurance Regulatory Authority. It is backed by the Cooperative Insurance Company of Kenya. Kenya's population is put at 39 million, out of which more than 10 % is Muslim. The potential market for *takāful* products is projected to be around 25 % of the estimated four million Muslims in the country. The launch of *Takāful* Insurance of Africa follows the granting of two Islamic banking licences by Kenyan authorities in 2007 to Gulf African Bank and First Community Bank. The Kenyan insurance market is currently served by more than 45 conventional insurance companies.[131]

A recent sign of South Africa taking Islamic finance as a serious niche market business is clearly reflected in the acquisition of the local Islamic insurance company, Takafol SA, by Absa, one of the republic's largest banking groups. The deal is expected to have implications regarding *Takāful* beyond the borders of South Africa to Southern, Central, West, and East Africa. Absa Insurance Company Limited (AIC), a wholly owned subsidiary of Absa Financial Services Limited (AFS), bought the book of business of Takafol South Africa (Pty) Limited (Takafol SA), which is a subsidiary of the Hannover Reinsurance Group, a major global reinsurer. The *Takāful* premium market in South Africa is currently estimated at about three billion South African rands (about US$420 million), which is very modest compared to the conventional insurance market. As such, market penetration potential is huge because of the low base, especially in a country with a fast growing population of over 45 million of which only about three million are Muslims, but with a relatively largish affluent Muslim middle class.[132] It should be noted that the *Takāful* market in South Africa has recorded average annual growth of more than 40 % since Takaful products were launched in the country in, 2003.[133]

As is the case with banking, *Takāful* is not the exclusive domain of Muslim. It is opened to non-Muslims. The experience of countries such as Malaysia offers a good example. For instance, with its multicultural population, market friendly legislation, and tax incentives system, Malaysia continues to be a perfect ground for Sharī'ah-compliant insurance products. An estimated 20–30 % of *Takāful* participants in Malaysia are non-Muslims in a country where over 40 % of the population are non-Muslims.[134]

The country's *Takāful* market has witnessed significant growth during the last few years. More importantly, many Malaysian of ethnic Chinese origin, who are predominantly non-Muslims are buying *Takāful*, especially due to the transparency of the products and other attributes. Malaysia's Islamic insurance industry is growing very fast and is expected to surpass its conventional counterpart in 10 years with the entry of new players. HSBC Amanah Takāful Malaysia added, "The Islamic insurance market has expanded due to more interest in *Sharī'ah*-compliant investments, and the issuance of four new family *Takāful* licences in September would further drive growth." In Malaysia, this success is also due to the extended distribution network, with the country home to eight *Takāful* operators. In order to grow further, the *Takāful* industry will need more assets. But due to compliance with Islamic law, *Takāful* insurers are excessively dependent on regional equities and real estate for investments, which exposes them to the vulnerability of these markets.[135]

The African Reinsurance Corporation (Africa Re) has launched a new subsidiary called African *Takāful* Reinsurance Company (Africa *Retakāful*). The new company is a subsidiary of African Re to give the much-needed back-up to *Takāful* insurance companies around the globe. Africa ReTakāful is wholly owned by Africa Re and licensed in Egypt under the Investment and Free Zone Law. The Sharī'ah-compliant company of the reinsurer is expected to accept business from all regions in Africa, Middle East including GCC countries, and Asia and to provide the *reTakāful* protection for all *Takāful* and Sharī'ah-complaint clients. With Africa Re's outstanding experience of the traditional reinsurance business, and its unique position as the leader of the African reinsurance industry, the corporation will from inception support this Africa ReTakāful to become one of the important players in the industry. This step has been necessitated by the increasing need of Africa's *Takāful* Insurance companies for *Retakāful*, and the fact that Africa Re was established basically to support the needs of the African insurance markets. For a more balanced portfolio, it will extend its services to the *Takāful* players in the Middle East and Asia.

The company is considered the first *ReTakāful* Operator in Africa and is expected to form a milestone for the global *Takāful* industry by providing all Sharī'ah-compliant reTakāful products to the Islamic-based primary *Takāful* products, and to assist in developing the *Takāful* insurance business in Africa to more prosperous levels. The company is expected to provide the same quality service that Africa Re's clients are used to receiving and to use its existing capacity for all regions in Africa and Asia. Africa Re enjoys A- rating from S&P and AM Best, respectively, and it will provide all the required support for Africa *Retakāful*.[136]

Another *ReTakāful* company in Africa ZEP-RE set up a *ReTakāful* window in Khartoum, Sudan in September 2009. The window, which became operational in January 2010, aims at serving the needs of the Islamic community in Sudan and beyond. They recently asked for products and services that serve their needs, but at the same time, comply with the teachings of Islam. ZEP-RE is believed to be the first multinational company to do so in the African continent. To this end, the company intends to address the specific needs of the Islamic societies in Sudan and beyond by using its technical expertise to provide viable products that comply with the rules set by Sharī'ah commercial rules. ZEP-RE's *ReTakāful* Window in Khartoum, Sudan operates as a unit of ZEP-RE and has full and unconditional financial backing from ZEP-RE.[137]

Although the potential for *Takāful* is beyond any doubt, as is rightly emphasised by PricewaterhouseCoopers, there are many hurdles to overcome if this market is to realise its potential. These challenges are not only relevant in the African context, but also, to the industry as a whole.

1. Human resources pose a major obstacle to the growth of the industry in Africa. The market is facing a severe shortage of qualified staff who understand both the technical insurance principles and have an adequate awareness of Sharī'ah finance even in the regions where *Takāful* has existed for three decades now.
2. One of the biggest challenges is creating customer awareness. Many Muslims live under the misconception that insurance contradicts the principles of Islam, particularly with regard to life insurance. People have to be made aware that *Takāful* provides an acceptable religiously validated solution.
3. Non-Muslims need to be made aware of why *Takāful* is ethical and the industry is not limited to Muslims.
4. How *Takāful* business should be taxed is another challenge.
5. Creating a regulatory regime that does not treat *Takāful* less favourably than conventional insurance is a cornerstone to the development of the industry.
6. The limited availability of short-term non-equity financial instruments, such as *ṣukūk* and Sharī'ah-compliant money market instruments equivalent to treasury bills, represent a further challenge for *Takāful* companies, making managing their investment portfolio more challenging than for conventional insurers, who can simply invest in bonds and cash assets.
7. *Takāful* providers must enhance their product innovation and continue to offer a high level of customer service. They must be able to understand evolving customer and market-specific needs and be willing to renew or re-engineer product design and consumer ben-

efit packages, as well as expand customer reach across various distribution channels.[138]

## Financial Crisis

Despite the various crises Africa has had to cope with, such as food crises, fuel crises, and financial crises, the continent has still managed to emerge in far better shape than many other regions. After witnessing tremendous growth in the recent decade, Africa has become an attractive investment destination for investors as it offers the highest return on capital.

Concerning the recent financial and economic crisis, even though Africa was hit and growth slowed sharply in 2009 to 2.5 %, the continent avoided the recession. The impact of the crisis varied across regions and countries, though on the whole, the decline in growth was less severe than expected, allowing for a faster recovery.[139] With a number of African nations appearing to have escaped the hangover from the global credit crisis, the question we hear more and more frequently is whether Africans collectively share the same bright future as the Brazilians, Russians, Indians, and Chinese.[140] The head of the IMF's African department, Antoinette Sayeh, says that Africa had demonstrated considerable resilience during the recession, and the IMF is hopeful about future prospects for the continent.[141]

One key factor has been the considerable progress made by African countries, starting in the late 1990s and in the first decade of this century, in addressing their fiscal problems and reducing their fiscal deficits. When the crisis hit and despite the fact that many countries suffered from lower revenues as a result of the reduced demands for African exports, African countries were able to sustain spending on key priorities. Some of them made space for additional expenditure—in some cases, to protect the poor from the impact of the crisis. That was possible because previous efforts at reform had borne fruit in more sustainable fiscal positions. Another factor that helped in facing the crisis was inflation. It had come under control and countries in the region were also able to use interest rate policy and reduced interest rates as other means of mitigating the impact of the crisis. Where exchange rates were flexible, countries let them adjust and this helped them deal with the shocks. As a result, African countries did not begin to put up barriers. Instead, they continued to pursue policies broadly encouraging foreign investment and trade.

Taken together, all those factors meant this time around, Africa is able to better withstand the impact of the crisis. That gives us optimism that as the global economy recovers, the recovery in Africa will keep pace.[142]

Although growth across Sub-Saharan Africa plummeted during the global crisis to an average of 2 % in 2009 from 5.6 % the previous year, the IMF projects that it bounced back to 4.5 % in 2010 and 5 % in 2011. Sub-Saharan Africa was one of the regions least affected by recent financial turmoil and deterioration in the global market. The region has been surprisingly resilient to the European slowdown, reflecting an ongoing redirection of its economic linkages towards Asia.

Antoinette Sayeh pointed to several important factors that helped African economies weather the crisis:

1. *Improved policies.* Many African countries, from the late 1990s onward, ran better policies than in the past, which helped mitigate the impact of the downturn—with strengthened fiscal positions, reduced debt burdens, lower inflation, and better cushion for foreign exchange reserves.
2. *Fiscal policies.* Because fiscal deficits and debt positions had improved dramatically, many countries were able to use fiscal policy to counteract the crisis, rather than make it worse. They strived to preserve—and sometimes even increase—public spending, at a time when revenue was falling rapidly. Fiscal policy was countercyclical in two-thirds of Sub-Saharan African countries in 2009.
3. *Room for interest rate cuts.* Because inflation had come under control, they were also able to effectively use interest rate policy. They reduced interest rates as other means of mitigating the impact of the crisis, and where exchange rates were flexible, countries let them adjust and help them deal with the shocks, contributing to their resilience.
4. *Countries generally protected social spending during the crisis*, using a variety of strategies. In particular, countries maintained health and education expenditures at pre-crisis levels, with most countries increasing expenditures. A growing number of countries have also put in place conditional cash transfers and an increasing number are focusing on a more developmental approach to social protection, including public works programs and food security initiatives.

5. *Protectionism avoided.* African countries did not begin to put up barriers and look inwards, instead they continued to pursue policies broadly encouraging foreign investment and trade.[143]
6. Africa has strengthened the recovery that started after the global financial and economic crises, with GDP growth rising from 2.3 % in 2009 to 4.7 % in 2010.[144]

The recovery was supported by various factors, including the rebound of export demand and commodity prices; increased inflows of FDI in extractive industries and of aid; a return of tourists; higher infrastructure investment associated with the countercyclical policies adopted by many African countries; increased activity in the service sector, particularly telecommunications, on higher consumer demands; and good harvests in some sub-regions. Two distinguishing features of the current recovery have been its swiftness and strength.[145] Significant opportunity exists for Sub-Saharan Africa to emerge from the global economic downturn as a vibrant and growing region—the next development frontier. The subcontinent confronts serious economic, social, and human development challenges, but underlying drivers of long-term prosperity are gathering momentum.

Many countries in Africa seem to have learnt the right lessons of orthodox economics and have tightened up their monetary and fiscal policies before the global financial crisis hit. This gave them a lot of policy space to respond to the shock emanating from the advanced economies. On average, the economies of the Middle East and North Africa and even those of Sub-Saharan Africa did not fare too badly during the worst of the crisis, with many of them posting positive GDP growth even in 2008–09. This performance was better than most other emerging markets, excluding China and India, and certainly quite remarkable, given the historical record of these countries.[146] The African Development Bank stressed that the performance of most African economies during the global economic crisis of 2008–09 was a testimony to their underlying resilience and robust fundamentals.[147]

Ethan B. Kapstein in the *Foreign Affairs* articulated that at the time where the Western countries are nationalising their banks and adopting protectionist reforms initiatives, Africa is promoting trade, foreign direct investment, and domestic entrepreneurship. Africa is not much concerned about foreign aid flows due to the current recession, but about rising barriers to exports and diminishing private investment from abroad, which could impede the continuation of the impressive economic progress the continent has made over the past decade.[148] The journal stressed that "Africa may well emerge from the current global recession as the only region in the world that remains committed to global capitalism."[149]

Although the crisis has not affected much the continent, due to the resilience of the different economies in the continent, the crisis has turned out to be a blessing by focusing the attention of global investors on Africa. Many of the economies rebounded from the crisis faster than the rest of the world. Sub-Saharan Africa in particular is increasingly seen as an opportunity rather than a burden. It is rising rapidly up the agenda for global investment managers.[150]

The recent financial crisis has provided another common ground between Islamic finance and economic growth in Africa, whereby they have both performed much better than others during the crisis. Yet, there are some who would argue that the performance of African economies and that of Islamic finance are primarily due to the weak link of the African economies or Islamic finance to the global economy. However, the reality is that although this weak link could not be totally denied and could be one of many reasons, the resilience of the African economies is also the result of hard-earned economic reforms in last few decades. For Islamic finance, the resilience is generally attributed to its principles of avoiding excessive debt, trading debt, and avoiding investment in non-asset backed transactions.

## Notes

1. Richard Bernstein, *Africa: The Final Frontier*, p. 17.
2. Franklin Allen & Others, "African Financial Systems: A Review" *Review of Development Finance*, vol. 1, Issue 2 April–June 2011, pp. 79–113.
3. Ibid.
4. Paul Collier and Jean-Louis Warnholz, "Now's the Time to Invest in Africa," *Harvard Business Review* February 2009. p. 5.
5. Ibid.
6. Franklin Allen & Others, "African Financial Systems: A Review", p. 10.
7. Mihasonirina Andrianaivo and Charles Amo Yartey, *Understanding the Growth of African Financial Markets*, p. 8.
8. Société Générale Pan African Index.
9. *Global Finance*, June 2011, www.gfmag.com, retrieved January 2012.
10. Saudi Gazette "CMA approves Jadwa Africa Freestyle Fund", www.saudigazette.com

11. Ibid.
12. Zawya "CMA approves Jadwa Africa Equity Freestyle Fund", May 6, 2008, www.zawya.com, retrieved January 2011.
13. Jonathan Kruger, "Hidden Opportunities", In *Eye on Africa*, Ernst & Young, vol. 3. March 2011, pp. 15–16.
14. Geraldine Lambe, "Investors start to differentiate between African markets", *The Banker*, February 23, 2011, p. 23.
15. Jonathan Kruger, "Hidden Opportunities", In *Eye on Africa*, Ernst & Young vol. 3. March 2011, pp. 15–16.
16. See, http://www.djindexes.com/islamicmarket/
17. See, www.shariah.standardandpoors.com
18. See, http://www.ftse.com/
19. See, http://www.mscibarra.com
20. See, http://www.idealratings.com/news/thomson-reuters
21. See, http://www.russell.com/indexes
22. See, *Bank Sarasin* "Islamic equity indices mirror regional and expansion trends", In *Bank Sarasin Islamic Wealth Management Report 2011*, p. 27.
23. Ibid, p. 25.
24. The 3rd COMESA Investment Forum Connecting Africa to the World 12–13 April, 2010, Sharm El Sheikh, Egypt, Conference Report, p. 6.
25. Ibid.
26. See, James Watson & Others, *Into Africa Institutional investor intentions to 2016*, pp. 15–16.
27. Mihasonirina Andrianaivo and Charles Amo Yartey, *Understanding the Growth of African Financial Markets*, p. 9.
28. Olufemi Barbarinde, "Renaissance Africa", *Thunderbird Quarterly*, Issue 2 Spring 2009, www.thunderbird.edu, retrieved June 2011; Carolyn Campbell, "Private Equity In Africa— Lessons Learned", *Thunderbird Quarterly*, Issue 2, 2009, www.thunderbird.edu, retrieved June 2011.
29. Coller Capital & Emerging Markets Private Equity Association, *Emerging Markets Private Equity Association Survey 2011*; Private Equity Africa, "Global LPs interest in Africa spikes", April 25, 2011, www.privateequityafrica.com retrieved June 2012.
30. Ibid.
31. Coller Capital & Emerging Markets Private Equity Association, *Emerging Markets Private Equity Association Survey 2011*; Private Equity Africa, "Global LPs interest in Africa spikes", April 25, 2011, www.privateequityafrica.com, retrieved June 2012.
32. Private Equity Africa, "Giant at the Gate" April 8, 2011, www.privateequityafrica.com, retrieved June 2012.
33. Roddy McKean & Anne Bennett, "Structural Differences", *The African Handbook*, September, 2011.

34. Carolyn Campbell, "Private Equity In Africa— Lessons Learned", *Thunderbird Quarterly*, Issue 2, 2009.
35. Ngozi Okonjo-Iweala, "Fulfilling the promise of sub-Saharan Africa" *McKinsey Quarterly*, June 2010, www.mckinsey.com, retrieved June 2011.
36. McKean & Anne Bennett, "Structural Differences", *The African Handbook*, September, 2011.
37. Carolyn Campbell, "Private Equity In Africa— Lessons Learned", *Thunderbird Quarterly*, Issue 2, 2009.
38. Ibid.
39. Ibid
40. Hurley Doddy , "PE exits in Africa – a market gaining momentum", *Financier Worldwide Magazine*, September 2015, www.financierworld-wide.com, retrieved April 2016.
41. Carolyn Campbell, "Private Equity In Africa—Lessons Learned" Thunderbird Quarterly, Issue 2, 2009.
42. Roddy McKean & Anne Bennett, "Structural Differences", *The African Handbook*, September, 2011.
43. Jennifer Choi, "The Next Chapter for Private Equity in Sub-Saharan Africa", p. 4.
44. Preqin, The Private Equity Market in Africa, *Perqin Special Report*, October 2010, www.preqin.com, retrieved June 2011, pp. 1–4.
45. Ibid.
46. Ibid.
47. William Wallis, "Helios sets Record for African Private Equity", *Financial Times*, June 14 2011, www.ft.com, retrieved December, 2011.
48. Jennifer Choi, "The Next Chapter for Private Equity in sub-Saharan Africa", p. 3.
49. Ibid.
50. Ibid.
51. William Wallis, "Helios sets Record for African Private Equity", *Financial Times*, June 14, 2011.
52. Neanda Salvaterra, "Mobile Pioneer Sees Rich Promise in Africa", *The Wall Street Journal*, April 18, 2011, www.online.wsj.com, retrieved January 2012.
53. Ruth Sullivan, "Potentials of Africa growth outlook", *The Financial Times*, November 6, 2011, www.ft.com, retrieved June 2012.
54. Neanda Salvaterra, "Mobile Pioneer Sees Rich Promise in Africa".
55. Hamid Yunis, "Growth of Private Equity Fund Using Islamic Finance", *Islamic Finance News*, Guide 2006, pp. 67–68.
56. Fiona Rintoul, "Vibrant Africa beckons investors", *Financial Times*, July 18, 2010, www.ft.com

57. For a comprehensive and detailed research on Sukuk see Muhammad Al-Bashir Muhammad Al-Amine, *Global Sukuk and Islamic Securitization Market Financial Engineering and Product Innovation*, Brill 2012.
58. AAOIFI, (Accounting and Auditing Organization for Islamic Financial Institutions), *Sharī'ah Standards n.17 Investment Ṣukūk.*
59. IFSB, *Capital Adequacy Requirements for Ṣukūk Securitisations and Real Estate Investment, Standard 7, January 2009.*
60. KFH Research Limited, Sukūk Back on Tract" *KFH Research Limited*, July 20, 2010, www.mifc.com, retrieved June 2011, p. 3.
61. IFIS, Islamic Finance Information Service, *Global Sukūk Market H2-2010 Report*, www.securities.com, retrieved June 2011, p. 2.
62. Paul-Henri Pruvost, *Global Standards To Give Breadth And Depth To The Global ṣukūk Market*, Standard &Poor's, March 1, 2011, www.zawya.com, retrieved October 2011.
63. *Global Finance*, "Landmark Year", June 2012, p. 21.
64. Mohamed Damak, "For Sukuk Issuance, Emerging Headwinds May Cause Turbulence In 2015", January 2015, Standard & Poor's, www.standardandpoors.com, retrieved February 2015.
65. Anouar Hassoune Adel Satel, "Islamic Finance Explores New Horizons in Africa", p. 5.
66. Mohamed Damak "Sukūk: An African Opportunity Yet to be Explored" in an interview with *Les Afriques*, Saturday, September 27, 2008, www.lesafriques.com, retrieved January 2011.
67. Ibid.
68. Chijioke Ohuocha, "Osun State issues Nigeria's debut sukuk at 14.75 pct", *The Africa Report*, October 2, 2013, www.theafricareport.com, retrieved November 2013.
69. Samira Mensah & Others, *Regulations and Fiscal Incentives Could Speed Islamic Finance Development In Africa*, Standard & Poor's August 6, 2015, www.standardandpoors.com, pp. 1–9.
70. See, Conventional banks could lay foundation for sukuk secondary market in West Africa www.meglobaladvisors.com
71. Elaine Moore, Andrew England and Robin Wigglesworth, "South Africa Joins Sukuk Bond Rush", Financial Times, September 17, 2014.
72. Ibid.
73. World Bank, *Sub-Saharan Africa. Global Economic Prospects*: Regional Annex (Washington, DC: 2011, www.worldbank.org, retrieved January 2012, p. 131.
74. Global Investment House, *Sukuk Market—Down but Not Out*, February 2009, p. 3.
75. Ibid.

76. Dana El Baltaji, "Nigeria Plans ṣukūk Debut Targeting Role as Sharī'ah Hub: Islamic Finance", *Bloomberg*, September 28, 2010, www.bloomberg.com, retrieved February 2012.
77. Nagashi, "East Africa Catching up with Islamic Finance", *Arab News*, September 28, 2010, www.arabnews.com, retrieved June 2011.
78. Mustak Parker, "Kenya's Sukūk ambitions must be tempered with reality", *Arab News*, March 28, 2011, www.arabnews.com, retrieved June 2011.
79. Mohamed Damak, "Afrique: le pont de la finance islamique", Les Afriques February 22, 2010, www.lesafriques.com, retrieved January 2011.
80. Christian Esters & Paul-Henri M Pruvost, "Will African Sovereigns Turn To Islamic Finance To Fund Growth?", February 22, 2013.
81. Ibid.
82. Ibid.
83. Public-Private Infrastructure Advisory Facility (PPIAF), "Bond financing in Africa—the next big thing?" www.ppiaf.org, retrieved January 2012, p. 1.
84. Shawn Ladd, "Emerging Africa Expected To See Rise in Investment", *IMF Survey Magazine: Countries* & *Regions*, January 12, 2011, www.imf.org, retrieved June 2011.
85. Jennifer Moyo, *Mapping of Current Ongoing Initiatives related to Bond Market Development in African* Summary of Regional Studies, African Development Bank, Tunis Tunisia April 30–31, 2009, www.afdb.org, retrieved January 2011, p. 2.
86. Ibid, p. 11.
87. Michael Wat, "Eurobonds Ride High in Africa", *The Banker*, January 5, 2015, www.thebanker.com, retrieved January 2015.
88. Christian Esters, "The Growing Allure of Eurobonds for African Sovereigns", http://www.standardandpoors.com, May 6, 2013.
89. Michael Wat, "Eurobonds Ride High in Africa".
90. Cyrille Nkontchou, "Recent Evolution of the African Financial Markets" Private Sector Development, *Proparco's Magazine*, Issue 5—March 2010—Africa's Financial Markets: A Real Development Tool?, pp. 3–5; Paul Wallace, "Ghana Vows to Avoid Oil Curse", *The Banker Supplement*, Ghana's Rising Star, July 2011, p. 101.
91. Daily News Government Secures credit Rating Services for Eurobond issue, *Daily News*, February 9 2016, www.dailynews.co.tz, retrieved April 2016.
92. Reuters, "Ethiopia completes $1 bln debut Eurobond, says oversubscribed" Reuters Dec 6, 2014, www. af.reuters.com.
93. Fumbuka Ng'wanakilala, "IMF urges caution in Africa's Eurobond borrowing spree", www.reuters.com, retrieved January 2015.

94. Kanika Saigal, Kenyan corporates to raid Eurobond market, September 23, 2014, http://www.euromoney.com, retrieved January 2015.
95. Ibid.
96. Tosin Sulaiman, "Rwanda Eurobond "priced to perfection"—lead managers. April 26, 2013.
97. Robin Wigglesworth, "Rwanda issues first 10-year bond to international investors", Financial Times www.ft.com, April 25, 2013.
98. Dominic Dudley, "Africa: Zambia issues debut Eurobond", Euromoney, October, 2012, www.euromoney.com
99. Matthew Hill, "Zambia Says $1 Billion Eurobond Was Oversubscribed" Apr. 8, 2014, www.bloomberg.com
100. Ecobank Research, "Zambia: Successful Issuance of Eurobond despite Macroeconomic Challenges", Middle Africa Briefing Note—Fixed Income, April 2014, www.ecobank.com
101. SUDIP, ROY, "ZAMBIA LAUNCHES US$ 1BILLION 10 YEAR EUROBOND AT YEILD OF 8.625 %, APRIL 7, 2014. WWW.REUTERS.COM
102. Tosin, Sulaiman, Nigeria $1 billion Eurobonds four times oversubscribed, Reuters, Jul. 2, 2013; http://www.reuters.com
103. Gail Mwamba, "Structuring Local Solutions", *This is Africa*, 30 March, 2011, www.thisisafricaonline.com, retrieved June 2011.
104. *Tosin Sulaiman "African local bonds—an untapped opportunity?"*, Financial Times, *Oct. 15 2014.*
105. *Y*ibin Mu, Peter Phelps, and Janet G. Stotsky, "Bond Markets in Africa", IMF Working Paper, International Monetary Fund January 2013, www.imf.org
106. Dominic O'Neil, "Chad Joins Local -Currency Spree", *Euromonney Magazine*, July 2011 vol. 42, no. 507, p. 51.
107. Reuter, "Chad bond likely to draw domestic interest: analyst", June 23, 2011, www.reuters.com, retrieved January 2012.
108. Reuters, "Chad raises $232 million in bond issue—bank", July 20, 2011, www.reuters.com, retrieved January 2012; also see, Ecobank,"Chad's first local-currency bond, arranged by Ecobank Capital, oversubscribed", August 1–7, 2011, www.ecobank.com, retrieved January 2012.
109. Sudip Roy, "Afren Oils Wheels of African Bond Markets", *Euromoney*, vol. 42 Number 503 March 2011, pp. 49–51.
110. Ibid.
111. Cyrille Nkontchou, "Recent Evolution of the African Financial Markets", Private Sector Development, *Proparco's Magazine*, Issue 5—March 2010—Africa's Financial Markets: A Real Development Tool?, pp. 3–5.
112. Lanre, Akinola, "Xavier Rolet, Chief Executive of the London Stock Exchange Group", *This is Africa*, November 15, 2011. www.thisisafrica-

online.com, retrieved June 2012; Lanre Akinola, "Xavier Rolet, Chief Executive of the London Stock Exchange Group", www.allafrica.com, November 15, 2011.
113. Ibid.
114. Ibid.
115. Keyur Patel, "Africa: no longer a leap of faith", *Financial Times*, January 24, 2012, www.ft.com, retrieved June 2012.
116. James Watson & Others, *Into Africa Institutional investor intentions to 2016*, p. 9.
117. Mina Mashayekhi and Deepali Fernandes, *Trade and Development Aspects of Insurance Services and Regulatory Frameworks*, The United Nations, New York and Geneva, 2007, www.unctad.org, p. iii, retrieved January 2011.
118. Beck Thorsten, *Financing Africa through the Crisis and Beyond*, pp. 111–113.
119. Mina Mashayekhi and Deepali Fernandes, *Trade and development aspects of insurance Services and Regulatory Frameworks*, p. 8.
120. Yosef Aseffa, "Insurance services liberalization and capacity-building: the case of Africa", in *Trade and Development Aspects of Insurance Services and Regulatory Frameworks*, p. 199.
121. Daniel Staib& Lucia Bevere, *World Insurance in 2010 Premium Back to Growth Capital Increase*, no. 2 Swiss Reinsurance Company Limited May 2011, www.swissre.com, pp. 25–26.
122. Prudence Ho and Daniel Staib, *Sigma no. 5, Insurance in the Emerging Market: Overview and Prospects for Islamic Insurance*, Swiss, Reinsurance Company Limited October, 2008, www.swissre.com, *retrieved* December, 2011, p. 19.
123. PricewaterhouseCoopers, *Takaful: Growth Opportunities in a Dynamic Islamic Market*, 2008, www.pwc.com, retrieved January 2011, p. 13.
124. Ashar Nazim, "the default choice for Islamic countries" paper presented at the International Takāful Summit 2011 Jumeirah Carlton Towers, London UK, from 11th till 13th July 2011, p. 5.
125. Sohail Jaffer, "Growth opportunities for Takāful in Europe", *The European Financial Review*, December–January 2011, p. 2.
126. PricewaterhouseCoopers, *Takaful: Growth Opportunities in a Dynamic Islamic Market*, p. 4.
127. PricewaterhouseCoopers, *Takaful: Growth Opportunities in a Dynamic Islamic Market*, p. 7.
128. PricewaterhouseCoopers, *Takaful: Growth Opportunities in a Dynamic Islamic Market*, p. 9.
129. Anouar Hassoune & Adel Satel, "Islamic Finance Explores New Horizons in Africa", Moody's Investor Services Global Banking, March 2008, www.moodya.com, pp. 1–18.

130. Middle East Insurance Review, "Overview of the Global Takāful Market", May 2008. www.meinsurancereview.com
131. See, www.cpifinancial.net, January 25, 2011.
132. Mushtak Parker, "Takāful market set to grow in S. Africa and beyond", *Arab News*, September 18, 2011, www.arabnews.com, retrieved December 2012.
133. *Islamic Finance News*, "Regional expansion", vol. 9, Issue 36, September 11, 2012, www.islamicfinancenews.com, retrieved December 2012.
134. Zainal Abidin Mohd, "Takāful Concepts and Practice", *The African Reinsurer*, vol. 022, June 2008, pp. 5–12.
135. Sohail Jaffer, "Growth Opportunities for Takāful in Europe", The *European Financial Review*, December 18, 2010, www.europeanfinancialreview.com, retrieved June 2011.
136. Patience Saghana, "Africa Re Group launches Africa Retakaful", *Vanguard Online edition*, September 12, 2010, www.vanguardngr.com, retrieved January 2012.
137. See, www.zep-re.com
138. See, PricewaterhouseCoopers, *Takaful: Growth Opportunities in a Dynamic Islamic Market*, p. 12.
139. Donald Kaberuka, "Capturing Africa Business Opportunity", www.mckinsey.com, June 2010, retrieved August 2011.
140. Jim O'Neill and Anna Stupnystka, "How Exiting is Africa Potential", p. 1.
141. Simon Willson, "Private Sector Gains Ground in Africa", *IMF Survey Magazine*, March 4, 2010, www.imf.org, retrieved June 2011.
142. Ibid.
143. Jeremy Clift, "Africa Faces Twin Challenges After Global Crisis" *IMF Survey Magazine*, March 4, 2010, www.imf.org, retrieved June 2011.
144. Ibid.
145. Ibid
146. Eswar Prasad, "Is Africa Poised to Steady Growth?", *The Economist*, September 7, 2010, www.economist.com, retrieved June 2011.
147. African Development Bank, *Africa in 50 Years Time: The Road Towards Inclusive Growth*, p. 10.
148. Ethan B. Kapstein, "Africa Capitalist Revolution", *Foreign Affairs*, July–August 2009, vol. 88, no. 4, www.foreignaffairs.com, retrieved June 2011.
149. Ibid.
150. William Wallis, Andrew England and Katrina Manson, "Africa Ripe for Reappraisal", *Financial Times*, May 18, 2011.

CHAPTER 7

# The Rise of Global Interest in Africa

The world is now recognising that a new Africa is emerging. The predominant theme in the emerging narrative is no longer war, famine, and disease, but strong economic performance, abundance of resources, and better governance. Undeniably, resources have played an important role in this shift, but Africa is also becoming increasingly economically diverse. This is clearly reflected in an expanding consumer base that is fuelling growth in other sectors. Measurable improvements in governance and human development suggest that these changes are sustainable for the long term, backed by business friendly reforms and mature financial institutions. Moreover, foreign investment in Africa is showing strong growth and returns on investment in Africa, both foreign and domestic, are among the highest in the world.[1] PwC stressed that for many global investors, Africa is no longer about war, famine, and poverty, but rather, about opportunities and growth. Some of the world's fastest growing economies are in Africa and the continent offers the highest return on foreign direct investment among emerging markets.[2]

The recent interest in the continent is so diversified and from different players to the extent that it is described by some observers and analysts as "the new scramble for Africa."[3] Although BRIC countries are leading the way,[4] many other emerging economies are also doing their best. Commenting on the specific interests of the BRIC countries, some have gone to extend of claiming that these countries have literally invaded the continent, not with arms, but with money, goods, ideas, and drilling and



M. Al Bashir M. Al Amine, *Islamic Finance and Africa's Economic Resurgence*, DOI 10.1007/978-3-319-28835-2_7

mining equipment. BRIC countries are becoming major players in the continent, changing not only Africa's traditional trade and investment relations, but also, creating significant opportunities and challenges for Africa's economies.[5]

Pointing to Africa's new dynamism with its emerging powerful partners, Société Générale noted that Africa growing relation with its new partners represents a new challenge for the continent's traditional partners of Western Europe and the United States. The standard international aid mechanisms are also being challenged by the innovative practices of the emerging powers.[6]

On a similar note, the Indian Journal of African Affairs, *Africa Quarterly*, reported that the BRIC countries trade with the continent has grown from merely US$3.5 billion in 2000 to over US$250 billion in 2011. China has multiplied its trade with Africa, from US$3.5 billion in 1990 to around US$150 billion in 2011. India's trade with Africa is estimated to be over US$50 billion; Brazil's trade is estimated at around US$16 billion; and Russia's bilateral trade is around US$10 billion.[7]

The scramble is not only based on the exploitation of key natural resources by these emerging economic powers, but also the diversification of their investment portfolio in the continent, that includes textiles, SMEs, social services such as health and education, information communication technology, and automobiles. It also includes massive construction projects such as building roads, dams, hydroelectric power stations, and railways. Moreover, BRIC countries are also becoming important players in development aid to Africa through concessionary and soft loans, lines of credit, and grants. They are also providing project aid to expand and improve Africa's infrastructure.[8]

Despite the widely discussed interest and burgeoning relationship with the new emerging trading partner to Africa, especially China and India, Western countries still remain Africa's leading partners,[9] although things are gradually changing.[10]

## The West as a Major Economic Partner

Since the end of the Cold War, Western political engagement in Africa has tended to be static. In the past ten years, there has been significant growth in the dollar value of Africa's trade with countries such as the United States, France, Netherlands, Spain, and Sweden while the growth has been more modest in the case of Germany, the United Kingdom, and

Italy. Most of the increase in trade with the United States, for instance, was a result of importing more African oil.[11]

However, while most Western countries were still focusing on domestic issues or dealing with other pressing issues in other parts of the world, there has been a sharp increase in non-Western investment appetite in Africa, especially since the beginning of the twenty-first century. Most of this engagement has focused on trade and investment. There are more important non-Western actors who work hard to take advantage of this situation. China and India have become major donor nations to Africa.[12] Commenting on the European stand on the present African economic growth, *the Guardian* noted that European countries have been slow to adjust to the rise of Africa, its economic growth, or its burgeoning consumer boom while the African lions are finding their voice.[13]

Realising its retreating position in terms of investment in Africa and in a clear broad recognition that American companies are trailing behind those from China and India in tapping the continent's economic opportunities, in order to restructure its trade and investment in Africa, the USA is adopting a new strategy that is more practical and realistic. The new strategy, according to the *Wall Street Journal*, emphasises the need for more close collaboration with China. Embassies had been instructed to seek "areas of cooperation" with Chinese counterparts in Africa. Thus, it is widely recognised that a new approach is needed with a continent that is projected to grow faster than any other global region over the coming years. In the first 11 months of 2010, China's trade with Africa amounted to US$114.81 billion, according to the Chinese government's White Paper on the topic, while US trade with Africa for the period reached US$103 billion, according to the US Census Bureau.[14]

The USA is also looking at how to improve the African Growth and Opportunities Act, or Agoa, an 11-year-old piece of US legislation that provides preferential access to the American market for more than 1800 African products. It covers 37 countries in Sub-Saharan Africa, with a handful of others disqualified because of coups and corruption. Agoa boosted African exports to the USA ten times from its inception to 2008. However, it has failed to significantly broaden the trade relationship. Energy exports account for about 90 % of Sub-Saharan African trade to the USA That type of trade relationship is seen as too narrow to seize opportunities tied to Africa's accelerating economic growth and new consumers.[15]

Even if the trade and investment relationship between the West and Africa is still dominant, Africa's relationship with emerging markets is witnessing tremendous surge and growth. This is particularly evident with the case of BRIC countries. However, other emerging economies are also doing their best to get their share of African opportunities. Referring to Africa's relation with the emerging economies, *The Economist* noted that:

> China's arrival has improved Africa's infrastructure and boosted its manufacturing sector. Other non-Western countries, from Brazil and Turkey to Malaysia and India, are following its lead. Africa could break into the global market for light manufacturing and services such as call centres.[16]

Despite the different mentioned experiences, it is Africa's partnership with China that receives most attention.

## Africa–China Model

Although Africa has benefited in its recent economic growth from big inflows of foreign direct investment, foreign aid, debt relief, urbanisation, and rising incomes, among other factors,[17] its economic partnership with China has been singled out as one of the important external factors that have fuelled faster growth. African trade is already shifting towards the dynamic emerging markets, notably China. The Chinese–African trade and investment relationship has been widely debated in academic circles. It is also a hot topic in the media and a controversial political and diplomatic issue. China is Africa's second largest trading partner after the USA and is on track to soon move into first place. China obtains about one-third of its total oil imports from Africa. This constitutes only about 13 % of total African oil exports. The USA and Europe continue to be the larger importers of oil from Africa, with each purchasing about one-third of Africa's total oil exports. China also imports from Africa high percentages of strategic mineral requirements, such as cobalt, manganese, and tantalum that support its fast-growing economy. China's exports to Africa have also risen as impressively as its imports from Africa. However, while total Western involvement in Africa's oil and mineral sectors is much greater than that of China, Beijing's recent investments in Africa probably exceed that of any other individual Western country.[18]

China has become an important driver of Africa's resource sector growth. It increased its share of African oil exports from 1 % in 1995 to 13 % in 2008 and became the single largest contributor to Africa's oil export growth. If current trends continue, China could overtake Europe as Africa's second largest oil export market by 2020.[19]

Official Chinese economic engagement with Africa continues to stress two key political considerations: the adherence to the official principals of engagement, that engender equality among partners, mutual benefit, respect for sovereignty, use of interest-free grants and loans, beneficiary capacity building, compliance with obligations, provision of equipment made in China, the same living conditions for both Chinese and local experts, and the recognition of Taiwan as an integral part of China.[20]

Trade between China and Africa has been expanding rapidly, growing by an average of 30 % a year over the past decade. This new partnership is expected to continue to show strong demand for goods that Africa can supply, and will be a basis for opportunities to invest directly. For Africa, the key priorities will be negotiating fair and durable deals with big multinational firms and making the best use of the revenue windfalls, especially when most of these resources are non-renewable.[21] According to China's Ministry of Commerce, Sino–African trade reached US$106.8 billion in 2008, up from US$10 billion in 2000, and by 2010, trade between the two partners surpassed US$120 billion.[22] Standard Bank expects China–Africa trade to surpass US$300 billion by 2015 and accumulated investment to surpass US$50 billion.[23] China has a competitive advantage over other economic powers investing in faraway developing countries. The benefit from the particular lack of ancient hostility and colonial bitter legacy is a positive aspect.[24] Despite the media polemic about this trade relationship, China–Africa trade is still relatively modest. It comprises only 4 % of the total Chinese imports and exports. However, from an African perspective, China–Africa trade growth is more important as it represents close to 10 % of the continent's exports and imports.[25]

From Berlin to Tokyo, newspapers and parliaments have depicted China's economic engagement in Africa in alarmist terms. Some independent observers stressed that many of the fears about Chinese aid and engagement in Africa are misinformed and spread myths divorced from all reality.[26] Seven myths and illusion are generally advanced: (1) "China is a newcomer to Africa"; (2) "China targets pariah regimes"; (3) "China hurts the West's efforts to build democracy"; (4) "Chinese aid is huge"; (5) "Chinese aid is mainly used to win access to resources"; (6) "China is sending millions of farmers to Africa, leading the land grab"; and (7) "Chinese companies bring in all their own workers."

One recent analysis stressed that the Chinese extensive engagement in Africa is deeply rooted. Ethnic Chinese from families that arrived in the nineteenth and early twentieth centuries have risen to become cabinet ministers or parliamentarians in several countries, including Mauritius, Mozambique, Zimbabwe, Gabon, and South Africa. Chinese engagement is not seen as a new or temporary phenomenon in most parts of Africa.[27]

On the issue that China is targeting reclusive regimes that the West will not deal with, it is argued that China's largest stock of foreign investment on the continent is not with these types of regimes, but in relatively well-governed and stable South Africa. The Chinese are looking for investment opportunities in democratic countries such as Ghana, Namibia, and Mauritius, and at the same time, they are also joining American and European investors in many less well-governed countries.[28]

On the issue of strengthening democracy and governance, in reality, there is no genuine difference between the West and China. For instance, Western and Chinese banks have granted credit to Angola in 2004 despite reservation from Western governments. In the aid sector, the largest recipient of US aid in Africa is Egypt, where Mubarak, and for almost three decades, refused to allow free and fair elections.[29] On the issue of human right and democracy, it is observed that African leaders should uphold the principles of good governance and human rights as necessary pillars of development and the right thing to do and not because of the preaching of others. Therefore, the Chinese investment in Africa does not discharge governments of their responsibilities any more than its presence in the EU or USA should erode human rights there.[30]

On the allegation that Chinese aid is mainly used to win access to resources, it is argued that the Chinese are careful to spread their official aid across all the countries with whom they have diplomatic relations, including many without any resources, such as Senegal, Mauritius, Mali, Rwanda, Togo, and Benin. China provides aid to every country among the 49 countries with which it has diplomatic relations, including those with higher per capita income, such as South Africa. China's use of commodity-secured lines of credit parallels similar commercial instruments long in use by Japan, and also, by Western banks. None of these are regarded as official development assistance, but as ways to promote business.[31]

On the assertion that Beijing is sending millions of Chinese farmers to settle in Africa, leading to "land grab," there is no hard evidence or facts on the number of Chinese who have moved to Africa. The number is estimated to be in the range of one million, compared with 6.5 million or so white Europeans who are residents on the continent. However, what is clear is that, at present, most Chinese immigrants are coming to Africa not to be farmers, but traders looking to open shops or small businesses, rather than grow rice. There is no doubt that some Chinese companies are bringing over their own workers; however, the issue should not be over-exaggerated. The biggest responsibility will be on African negotiators and deal brokers to make sure that such issues are well covered in commercial terms when contracting agreements between parties.

Most of the negative media coverage on the China–Africa relationship rests on rumours, myths, or outdated understandings. Trade between the two regions is huge, but official development assistance from China is far smaller than that from the West. China is now a powerful force in Africa. The Chinese presence in the continent is strategic, planned, long-term, and still unfolding.

However, China's rise in Africa is not totally without some concern among those who care about development on the continent. However, these concerns have more to do with the standards of companies and banks from a country where capitalism is still relatively underdeveloped and where corporate social responsibility is elementary at best. The West can help by gaining a more realistic picture of China's engagement, avoiding sensationalism, and admitting their own shortcomings, and perhaps, exploring the notion that China's model of consistent non-intervention may be preferable, for many reasons, to a China that regularly intervenes in other countries' domestic affairs or uses military force to foster political change.[32]

China is engaged at every level of the continent's economic activities. Its annual foreign assistance is about US$1.5 billion. The official news service, Xinhua, has more than 20 bureaus in Africa. There are about a dozen Confucius Institutes and the number is growing rapidly. China is expanding its radio transmission to Africa in various languages. It is training a wide range of African officials and journalists in China, and in 2009, increased its annual scholarships for African students to 4000.[33]

China has been effective at cultivating close state-to-state ties at the highest levels. President Hu Jintao has made six trips—two as vice president and four as president—to Africa, visiting multiple countries. Premier Wen Jiabao and senior officials in the Chinese Communist Party also make regular visits to the continent. The Chinese foreign minister, beginning in 1991, made his first overseas visit, and does so every year to Africa—a fact not lost to African leaders.[34]

As the largest foreign investment and financing bank in China, the China Development Bank (CDB) has outstanding loans to Africa reaching US$2.4 billion by the end of 2009, covering areas such as infrastructure, transportation, electricity and water supply, telecommunications, as well as social welfare, including housing, health care, education, agriculture, and SMEs.[35] CBD is also granting lines of credit, syndicated loans, and project financing. The CDB is also implementing a US$1 billion worth of special loans designated for SMEs in Africa. These loans are based on the principle of "mutual benefits" and "minimal interest." The SMEs facility aims at improving corporate governance in African SMEs, raising their level of profitability as well as promoting their ability against risk. In this way, the CDB hopes to optimise the structure of the African economy, provide more employment opportunities, and achieve sustainable development for African countries. In the agricultural sector, the CDB has carried out an overall plan for agricultural cooperation with African countries, and it has promoted a number of agriculture projects.[36]

Based on the above, it is time to move beyond fruitless arguments and accept China's role in Africa. It is also time for China to enhance that role and dispel all types of criticism and practically demonstrate to the critics that its relation with Africa is based on mutual benefits. The reality is that China has already become an indisputably significant force in Africa's development, with substantially increased commitments and engagements in the past few years. Pragmatism argues for moving the discussion ahead to how China's involvement can reap the greatest benefit for both the Africans and the Chinese.[37]

Part of China's presence in Africa is to do with how the steady internationalisation of China's renminbi will affect Africa. Standard Bank asserted that the political and economic intent of China aligns neatly with Africa. It has been forecasted that we will see at least 40 %, or US$100 billion, of China's trade with Africa being made using the Chinese currency unit by 2015. This amounts to more than the total Sino–African trade in 2010. In addition, at least US$10 billion of Chinese investment into Africa will be denominated in renminbi over the same period. Among the main benefits for Africa of the internationalisation of the renminbi will be cheaper funding and lower transaction costs, all on a large scale. At the same time, from the Chinese side, renminbi internationalisation is really about adding efficiency and resilience to China's own trade and investment flows, and triggering further financial liberalisation. China aims at broadening its currency's geographical reach and the use of renminbi for investment purposes. Chinese firms will continue their efforts to internationalise the country's currency. But Africa, more than anywhere else, offers them a new opportunity to "go out in renminbi." Africa can help China reach critical mass with the internationalisation process, and African nations should use the alignment of China's policy trajectory to its advantage. Among the underlying reasons is that there are as many as one million Chinese people in Africa. Chinese firms will continue looking for opportunities to grow their businesses in Africa, opening renminbi accounts and using renminbi products while Chinese workers will want to send money home. More importantly, investment in Africa will find support through cheaper sources of funding and better protected capital (through hedging instruments). This will result in more favourable terms for African projects. The support for currency internationalisation by political elites also means that funding could be specifically drawn off to renminbi-financed projects. Internationalisation will lower transaction costs, enable better working capital, and improve risk management practices, which, along with various incentives, will support trade flows. In money markets, short-term renminbi credit facilities, deposit, and call accounts will be demanded. In global markets, requirements will include a host of trading products. In transactional products, Chinese corporates will need renminbi-denominated accounts, cash settlement transactions, and notes. In addition, remittance flows will need to be calibrated. More investment flows will also require on-the-ground expertise.[38] In short, the Chinese–African relation seems to thus far be satisfactory to China as well as to Africa. This warm relation contradicts the idea of marginalisation of Africa. To the contrary, it brings economic and political advantages to both parties. Increased aid without preconditions, debt cancellation, and flourishing trade are mutually beneficial to China and Africa.[39]

Addressing the issue in one of its editorials, *The Guardian* noted that many Africans do not see China as a new colonial power or one that is grapping Africa mineral. On the contrary, many Africans are grateful to China and its investments. The newspaper added that Western countries are not best placed to lecture Africa on what is beneficial to the continent.[40]

Pointing to the different nature of relations between Africa and China on one side, and Africa and the West on the other, it has been stressed that despite attempts by many Western analysts to characterise China's and India's relations with Africa as a type of imperialism or neo-colonialism, there are a number of features of China's and India's relations with Africa that distinguish them from the Western engagement. First and foremost,

China, India, and all African countries are still developing countries, with identical problems and ambitions. China and India are not associated with the structural adjustment policies that impoverished Africa over the past three decades. Besides, China and India earlier supported the African liberation movement in different ways and the two countries have no tradition or attempts of colonialising any part of Africa.[41]

## Africa–India Partnership

India's economic partnership with African countries has been vibrant, extending beyond trade and investment to technology transfers, knowledge sharing, and skills development. Africa's bilateral trade with India has flourished rapidly during the past two decades, growing steadily from US$5.5 billion in 2001 to around US$45 billion in 2010 and over US$50 billion in 2011.[42] The total trade volume between India and Africa has increased seven-fold. They target taking the two-way commerce to US$70 billion by the end 2015 on the back of increasing economic engagement between the two sides. Between 2000 and 2007, the Indian investment in Africa jumped by 837 %, and in 2009, Africa hosted about 33 % of total Indian foreign investment. India's investment in Africa is diversified and includes sectors such as petroleum, natural gas exploitation, telecommunication, traffic, IT, and so on. India has institutionalised its relationship with African countries by launching the India–Africa Forum in April 2008. Following that forum, India extended US$5.4 billion to Africa, worth as lines of credit for a period of five years. India also announced a duty-free trade preference scheme for 33 African countries, among the least-developed nations,[43] as part of India's duty-free tariff preferential scheme for 49 least developed countries (LDCs) in the world.

A new generation of Indian corporates are establishing their presence in Africa. Indian companies have a vast and long presence in the African continent. Bharti is the new giant to enter the African market through its acquisition of Zen Telecomm which was one of the largest telecom companies in Africa. It is one of the latest examples of the rapid strides India is taking towards developing interest in Africa. Indian companies are now doing business in more than 20 African countries. India has also taken care to distinguish its approach towards Africa by embracing the concept of empowerment of the continent, as opposed to mere profit-seeking. Bharti is following other Indian corporations—ranging from Tata Group to Dr. Reddy's Labs—that have invested close to US$6 billion in Africa over the past few years. Other companies involved in the continent are Videocon, Suzlon, Godrej, Mahindra and Mahindra, UB Group, Cipla, NIIT, Kirloskar, and Essar India. India is guided by the objectives of promoting partnership, rural economies, and going green in its business ties with Africa.

India's surging economic engagement with Africa, driven by the private sector, is aimed at spurring the development goals of African countries. The rationale is to develop a sustainable partnership. The first part is strategic, in the sense that Africa is a huge source of natural resources, and in many respects, the last unexplored frontier. The second part is that for Indian companies looking to grow, Africa represents a great opportunity. Indian companies have, over the years, developed business models with low-cost operations to work in an environment of low per capita earnings, and low spending power. Africa thus represents a natural opportunity for them to be able to expand. The Bharti–Zain deal is a good example of this opportunity. Bharti Airtel Ltd. now operates in 16 African countries, part of a dramatic expansion of Indian investment in Africa. The company has also signed a deal with China's Huawei Technologies Co. to help manage and modernise its network in Africa.[44]

This Indian move is backed by a strong economic growth at home. Both regions have exhibited resilience after the downturn caused by the global crisis. Indian and African economies have emerged stronger in the global economic arena post the global economic meltdown, primarily due to the similarities between the economic management and priorities of both nations. Like India, many African countries ran discretionary economic policies such as minimising debt burdens, controlling inflation, and strengthening fiscal deficits before the crisis and found themselves cushioned in the face of a severe downturn. Indian leaders often asserted that India does not want to follow trajectories of economic extraction and economic development at the expense of others. For India, African countries represent partners for sustainable development. India's participation in Africa is believed to follow a model where investments will create employment and skill development for Africans, and this will offer opportunities for Africa's value-added exports that go much beyond natural resources. The Action Plan talked about the creation of training programmes and the establishment of 19 institutions in Africa, paid for by the Indian government. Several educational institutions are already in place. These include the India Africa Institute of Foreign Trade (IAIFT) in Uganda, the India–Africa Institute of Information Technology (IAIIT) in Ghana, the India

Africa Diamond Institute in Botswana, and the India–Africa Institute of Education, Planning and Administration (IAIEPA) in Burundi, which are some of the flagship projects that are set up to further Africa's human resource development.[45] The action plan envisages India setting up a host of training institutes in Africa in areas of diamond polishing, IT information technology, vocational education, and pan-African stock exchange.

India has also enhanced its relations with African countries in the energy sector. Around 24 % of India's crude oil imports are sourced from Africa. Indian national oil companies such as the Oil and Natural Gas Corporation Videsh Limited (OVL) has invested in equity assets in African countries.[46]India's endeavour is to build a win-win partnership. Total trade between India and Sub-Saharan Africa has been growing at "a phenomenal rate" of more than 26 % per year.[47] Indian oil companies are venturing into Angola, Burkina Faso, Equatorial Guinea, Ghana, Guinea Bissau, and Senegal. There have been significant investments in other raw materials. Vedanta Resources invested about US$750 million in a Zambian copper mine project, while Arcelor Mittal is the other leading global steel company. India has also launched a US$1 billion iron ore mining project in Liberia, which is expected to create around 3500 direct jobs and another 15,000 to 20,000 indirect jobs.

The soaring trade volumes reflect a positive trade balance for Africa, as it exports more goods to India than it imports. India's imports from Africa grew from US$587.5 million to US$18.8 billion between 1990 and 2009, whilst its exports to the continent increased from US$436.8 million to US$13.2 billion during the same period.[48] In absolute terms, Africa's share of Indian FDI outflows increased from US$243 million in 2000 to US$2.4 billion in 2008. To meet the country's growing energy needs, India's Oil and National Gas Corporation acquired shares in oil exploration ventures in some African countries. India has also invested in hydrocarbon sector and in offshore drilling.

The African Development Bank (AfDB) Group and the Export-Import Bank of India (Exim Bank) signed a Memorandum of Understanding (MOU) in November 2009 for co-financing projects in Africa. In addition to providing lines of credit to African countries with a total credit value of US$3.4 billion, Exim Bank has been working closely with AfDB in providing advisory services and exchanging information on business and investment opportunities.[49] The government of India extends lines of credit (LOCs) through the Export-Import (EXIM) Bank of India to governments, banks, and financial institutions at concessional rates. EXIM is due to set up a representative office in Addis Ababa, Ethiopia, to promote trade and investment flows between India and the East African subregion. This will be its third office in Africa. EXIM has approved the largest single line of credit to Ethiopia (US$600 million) for the Tindaho Sugar Project. EXIM has 85 lines of credit, covering 47 countries in Africa, with a total value of US$2.76 billion.[50] EXIM Bank also signed in early 2012 a Memorandum of Understanding with Ecobank to promote and finance trade and investment flows between Africa and India. The agreement will see EXIM Bank co-operating with Ecobank to explore joint trade and investment opportunities in the future across Ecobank's unrivalled footprint of 32 countries in Middle Africa.[51]

In the agriculture sector, Indian investments are not only improving farm technologies and productivity in Africa, they are also promoting agro-business through technical assistance and skills transfers. This in turn will help improving the quality of infrastructure, increase access to microfinance, and scale up local entrepreneurship. In the area of health, in 2008–2009, Africa accounted for 14 % of India's US$8 billion pharmaceutical exports. Indian pharmaceutical companies such as Ranbaxy Laboratories Limited, have established a presence in many African countries with the aim of providing a wide range of quality and affordable generic drugs. In respect to ICT, India has helped to fund the development of various projects across Africa, such as its ambitious Pan-African e-Network Project, which was developed jointly by the Indian government and the African Union to promote online education and telemedicine programmes across the continent.[52]

## Brazil's Growing Relation with Africa

Brazil's trade with Africa increased more than six-fold from 2000 to 2008, from US$4.2 billion to US$25.9 billion. In 2009, this volume of trade decreased to US$17.1 billion due to the effects of the global crisis. However, 2010 was marked by an upward trend in trade between Brazil and Africa, to US$20.0 billion. In terms of the ranking of Africa's major trading partners, Brazil is in third place, behind China and India, but ahead of Russia. More than 80 % of Brazil's imports from the African continent are mineral products and oil and gas. It is worth noting that Africa's imports from Brazil are more diversified than its exports, and include agricultural products, vehicles, and parts. Brazil's plan to position itself as the world's leading producer and exporter of renewable energy has been a key commercial driver of its agricultural focus in Africa. Given the continent's large potential for agricultural production, the Brazilian government has pledged to assist African countries to exploit the production and export opportunities of agriculture and biofuels, through trade, technology, and skills transfer. A number of partnerships have been concluded with several African countries, such as Ghana, where EMBRAPA, the Brazilian Enterprise for Agricultural Research, opened an office in 2008, with an emphasis on helping the country to develop its ethanol industry. This was followed in November 2010 by the investment of US$300 million in a sugarcane plantation whereby the factory is expected to produce over 100,000 cubic metres of ethanol, which is set to become Ghana's fourth major export after cocoa, gold, and timber. EMBRAPA has also been spreading Brazilian know-how and technology across Africa in several projects, ranging from assisting Senegal in developing its rice sector, to helping Tanzania with its dairy industry.[53]

Brazilian investment in agriculture has increased considerably in a number of African countries. Agriculture has been a key contributor to the Brazilian. Brazil's prudent management and state investment in the sector has enabled the country to position itself as one of the world's top food exporters. Inspired by its success in agriculture and biofuels, Brazil has been assisting Africa in increasing its food and energy security as well as in bolstering its economic independence. Although Brazil's focus on Africa's agriculture is driven by its strategic and commercial motives to become a leader in renewable energy, it is helping the continent to leverage its potential and trigger technical innovation by providing financial and technical assistance.[54]

Former president Luiz Inacio Lula da Silva, who stepped down in January 2011, was very instrumental in strengthening this relation. He spent a good part of his eight years in power selling Brazil as Africa's partner and highlighting the ways in which Brazil is built. He noted that "Brazilian society was built on the work, the sweat and the blood of Africans." He was quoted saying that "Brazil would not be what it is today without the participation of millions of Africans who helped build our country."[55] Lula visited 25 African nations, doubled the number of Brazilian embassies in Africa, and boosted trade to US$26 billion in 2008 from US$3.1 billion in 2000.

In terms of financing, Brazilian firms looking for opportunities to invest in Africa can tap BNDES, Brazil's national development bank, for financing, while Banco do Brasil, Latin America's largest bank by assets and

Brazil's biggest state-run bank, announced expansion plans to exploit growing demand for loans and other products in Africa. Despite the fact that BNDES plays an important role, it is limited by the conditions that prohibit it from financing in more unstable markets.[56] This is considered to be one reason for the huge gap between China and Brazil's performance in Africa.

## Japan–Africa Partnership

While Africa's relations with the BRIC countries and some other emerging economies received wide coverage, Japan's relations with the continent have attracted little attention. Similarly, the EU–Africa Partnership Agreements or the U.S.–Africa Growth Opportunity Act have been widely publicised, while comparatively little is known about Japan's Tokyo International Conference on African Development (TICAD). Japan's involvement in Africa in the last two decades is generally framed through the Tokyo International Conference on African Development (TICAD) and the Official Development Assistance (ODA). TICAD was established in 1993 by the government of Japan and hosts it with other international organisations such as the United Nations Office of the Special Advisor on Africa (UN-OSAA), United Nations Development Programme (UNDP), the World Bank, and the African Union Commission (AUC). TICAD is more than a conference. It is a multilateral framework for Africa's development that helps push Africa's development challenges onto the world stage. TICAD's goal of fostering African development rests on two principles. These are: African "ownership" and international "partnership."

TICAD has successfully convened every five years since 1993:

- TICAD I, held in 1993, identified development aid as the driver of sustainable development programmes in Africa to promote stability and prosperity on the continent through development partners. Specifically, the Conference adopted the "Tokyo Declaration on African Development" whose aims were to pursue political and economic reforms; marshal the Asian development experiences for the benefit of Africa; increase private sector development; pursue regional cooperation and integration; and promote South–South cooperation.
- TICAD II, in 1998, was preoccupied with two development challenges in Africa: poverty reduction and the continent's full integration into the global economy.

- At TICAD III, there was support for the New Economic Partnership for African Development (NEPAD) which advocates continent-wide development, regional priorities, and African-led development efforts.
- TICAD IV theme was "Towards a Vibrant Africa" and the strengthening regional infrastructure such as roads and power, the use of ODA for private sector initiatives, and the prevention and eradication of diseases.[57]
- The theme for TICAD V held in Yokohama, Japan, June 1–3, 2013 was "Hand in Hand with a More Dynamic Africa." The conference aimed to keep Africa's current economic growth on a stable path and extend the benefits of this development to all sections of society. TICAD V discussions were based on the three interrelated themes of "Robust and Sustainable Economy," "Inclusive and Resilient Society," and "Peace and Stability."

Japan pledged 3.2 trillion yen (US$32 billion) to Africa TICAD V as the country seeks to catch up with China in pursuing resources, markets, and influence in the continent. Africa's economic growth is luring Japanese exporters, while the government wants to tap the natural gas and oil there. Japan is also trying to encourage investment by Japanese companies and support advances in health, education, and agriculture. Most of Japan's current purchases from Africa consist of metals and fuels, while Japan exports mostly vehicles and machinery. Japan is also seeking rare earth minerals. The conference renews focus on Africa as a business partner and not just an aid recipient.[58] As stressed by Japan International Cooperation Agency President, Akihiko Tanaka, "With Sub-Saharan Africa providing some of the fastest growing economies in the world, Japan is willing to collaborate with its African friends to foster inclusive and sustainable growth."[59]

Since the first Tokyo International Conference on African Development held 20 years ago, circumstances in Japan and Africa were vastly different than they are today and it is clear both sides have undergone drastic transformations. Although the government has achieved the pledges it made in the previous four TICAD meetings, including doubling development aid to Africa, laying out the foundation for a new relationship with the continent, much remains to be done. Africa's roles and responsibility are also changing, and with it, the concept of international cooperation for Africa. Moreover, whereas the first four TICAD meetings focused on assisting development, reducing debt, and expanding ODA, the theme of the fifth session was on how to strengthen economic partnership with Africa while respecting its ownership rights. It is about the need to boost trade and investment, in a bid to transform the relationship from an aid-led one to a business partnership.

While Eastern Asia and the United States remain central to Tokyo's diplomacy, Africa's importance will continue to grow.[60] At the same, "Japan understands the need to strengthen ties with African countries against the backdrop of growing interest from rivals such as China and South Korea."[61] The growth of the middle class in Africa shows the importance of the continent as a business partner in providing new markets for Japanese firms struggling with a contracting customer base at home. It is this context; the Japanese Prime Minister told a press conference at the end of the three-day TICAD V International Conference that "Africa will be a growth centre over the next couple of decades until the middle of this century... Now is the time for us to invest in Africa."[62] He was also quoted saying that "Japan will not simply bring natural resources from Africa to Japan. We want to realise industrialization in Africa that will generate employment and growth."[63]

Comparing China's relation with Africa and that of Japan, Japan's importance to Africa has slipped behind that of China, whose more aggressive approach has given it five times the trading volume and eight times the direct investment.[64]

## South Korea's Interest in Africa

South Korea is another country interested in Africa. There is a South Korean belief that better ties with African states could open a market for investment in infrastructure construction and might allow for greater exploitation of resources and the enlargement of export markets.[65] The Asian economic power has already reached agreement with different countries such South Africa, Democratic Republic of Congo, Ethiopia, Tanzania, Mauritania, Niger Kenya, Zimbabwe, and Madagascar for the implementation of some specific projects, ranging from copper and cobalt mines building to oil exploration, agriculture water infrastructure, solar energy, oil and gas opportunities, and uranium projects. The Korea Trade-Investment Promotion Agency (KOTRA) established the Korea Business Centres in Ethiopia, Ghana, and Cameroon in 2011, bringing the total of such centres to seven around the continent. These centres were established with the intention of easing Korean entry into African markets.[66]

South Korea is also involved in the continent through aid and investment. In November 2010, the President of South Korea's Rural Development Agency (RDA) signed a memorandum of understanding titled "The Korea-Africa Food and Agricultural Cooperation Initiative" (KAFACI), which emphasises capacity-building. KAFACI currently has 16 African countries members. Considering the success registered between the Korea's Rural Development Agency RDA and Kenya, success is likely to follow in these other African countries. During the 2010 KOAFEC (Korea-Africa Economic Cooperation) Ministerial Conference, South Korea announced that it intends to increase its aid to Africa to approximately US$1 billion. The country has also extended loan and financing facility in a number of projects in different African countries. It is believed that South Korea's rapid economic and social development, and especially, South Korea's IT and agricultural expertise, hold valuable promise for the continent's future.[67]

Africa's economic relationships with Korea are increasing rapidly and are drawing the attention of Korean policymakers and business houses. These relations extend beyond trade and investment and involve knowledge sharing and policy dialogue too. The volume of trade between Africa and Korea has increased rapidly, reaching US$13.9 billion in 2009, up from US$6.4 billion in 2000. In relative terms, Africa remains a marginal trade partner for Korea. Africa accounts for only 3.3 % of total Korean exports and 1 % of imports. Considering the potential of the African market, Korean investments still remain marginal in the continent.[68]

The competition among the different emerging economies towards investment in Africa is a positive sign as every player will try to distinguish itself from its competitors. Korea needs to demonstrate what is different about its engagement with Africa, based on the principles it espouses and to what extent it results in a win-win situation.

## Turkey–Africa Partnership

The Ottoman Empire had extensive relations with Africa over the centuries, with the territory of a number of current members of the African Union, including Algeria, Chad, Djibouti, Egypt, Eritrea, Ethiopia, Libya, Niger, Somalia, Sudan, and Tunisia falling, whether in whole or in part, under the suzerainty of the Sublime Porte at various historical moments till as late as 1912.[69]

During the wave of colonialism, the Ottoman State competed with the Portuguese in Eastern Africa and with Spain in North Africa for power and influence. In northern Sub-Saharan Africa, the Ottomans were part of the balance of power system, having friendship and alliance with the Kanem Bornu Empire that prevailed in northern Nigeria, Niger, and Chad. The Kanem Bornu Empire even signed a defence pact in 1575 with the Ottoman State during the time of Sultan Murad III, upon which, the sultan sent military equipment and trainers to the region.[70]

However, the new engagement of Turkey in the continent started with the new millennium when Turkey began to take a serious interest in Africa during the mid-2000s, placing Africa within its multidimensional and dynamic foreign policy doctrine to diversify economic and political ties.[71] This has been reflected in several initiatives. According to Sedat Laciner, director of the think-tank Usak in Ankara, member of Tusiad (the Turkish Industry and Business Association, "Turkey's failure to understand the importance of Africa during the cold war years and lack of friends there, damaged its economic and political interests."[72] Major developments in Africa Turkish relations can be summarised as follows:

1. Turkey designated 2005 "Year of Africa" and Prime Minister Recep Tayyip Erdogan travelled south of the Equator, when he visited South Africa and Ethiopia.
2. In a new initiative in 2007, Turkey hosted a summit of the world's least developed countries, of which 33 of them are in Africa, and undertook to allocate nearly US$20 million to development aid in Africa. The summit was attended by representatives from 50 African countries. This resulted in what is known as Istanbul Declaration on Africa–Turkey Partnership, which affirmed the need to consolidate and further expand Africa–Turkey partnership at all levels and in all fields and to establish a long-term and stable partnership based on equality and mutual benefit. Specifically, the declaration outlined priorities for cooperation on trade and investment, agriculture and water resources management, health, peace and security, infrastructure and energy, culture and education, media and communications, and environmental concerns.
3. The inauguration of the first Ankara University African Studies Research and Application Centre in December 2008 marked another advance, which aims at providing expertise needed to manage the fast-multiplying web of relationships Turks are establishing across

Africa. The Centre mandate was to train researchers specialising on the African continent, to establish a library and a documentation and archive unit which can serve as a point of reference, hold national and international meetings regarding issues relating to Africa, and to provide private or public institutions with consultation services. In his speech at the new institution's inauguration, former President Gül declared that, "Turkey does not see Africa only as the cradle of civilization but also as the centre of the future of humanity. In fact, Africa, with its virtue and wisdom that has been distilled to our day through centuries passed, its young and dynamic population and vast natural resources is above all a continent of opportunity for the countries and peoples of Africa."[73]

4. Istanbul had been also the venue for the first Turkey–Africa Cooperation Summit, which included bilateral meetings with 42 countries.
5. That autumn, Turkey secured a non-permanent seat on the United Nations Security Council, thanks to the support of 51 out of the 53 African countries.
6. In just a decade, Turkey's diplomatic and trade relations with Africa have been transformed, with Turkey's embassies in Africa having tripled.
7. Turkey won observer status at the African Union in 2005.
8. Turkey has participated in five peacekeeping missions in Africa.

On the economic front, the Turkey–Africa relationship has also been characterised by several positive developments:

1. Turkey is one of the non-African ("non-regional") members of the African Development Bank.
2. The country is eying entering into a free trade agreement with the East African Community by 2019.
3. Turkish Airlines, the world's eighth largest airline, flies to 14 African cities in 12 countries.
4. Turkish exports to Africa have jumped from US$1.5 billion in 2001 to over US$10 billion in 2010.
5. The value of trade between Turkey and Sub-Saharan Africa (primarily South Africa and Nigeria) is estimated to have reached nearly US$20 billion in 2009, around three times the figure for 2003. The leading sectors for Turkish investment are construction, manufacturing, and agriculture. The Turkish economy's growth requires

new markets and resources, making Africa's huge untapped resources and large market size a new centre of Turkish attention.[74]

6. While Turkey itself is classified as a developing country, its government provides scholarships for African students each year to study in Turkish universities and other institutions.[75] Scholarships have become an important part of Turkish aid to the region. Between 2003 and 2012, more than 5500 students from SSA countries were awarded scholarships at Turkish universities. There are about 13,000 African students studying in Turkey, with 1,000 new scholarships being made every year.[76]
7. Turkey established over 60 high-quality modern schools in 30 African countries.[77]
8. More than 400 Turkish small and medium enterprises have found a foothold in Africa.
9. Products made in Turkey (building materials, agrifood products, engineering products, machinery, textiles, ready-to-wear clothing, medical equipment, information technology, personal hygiene products, cleaning products, and jewellery) are 20–30 % cheaper than their European equivalents and enjoy a better reputation among African consumers than those made in China.[78]

Yet, the recent financial economic crisis was one of the reasons behind Turkey's interest in the continent. Small- and medium-sized Turkish enterprises have been seeking alternatives to their export markets. Africa presents a lot of opportunities for those seeking new investment options. During this period of crisis, many SMEs have begun to think of Africa as the only saviour, said Rızanur Meral, the president of the Confederation of Businessmen and Industrialists of Turkey, or TUSKON. The record decline in exports to the EU has been the biggest catalyst to search for new markets. Hundreds of Turkish businessmen entered the African market and many business contracts have been signed.[79]

Tamer Taşkın, chairman of the Turkish–African Business Council, which operates under the umbrella of the Foreign Economic Relations Board (DEİK), recently declared that for Turkey, Africa was not a temporary alternative market to Europe, but a permanent export destination,

"Things like safaris, droughts, hunger and poverty come to people's minds when Africa is mentioned. That is why no one from around the world goes there. This is an opportunity for us."[80]

The Turkish International Cooperation and Development Agency (TIKA) supports development projects in 37 countries from regional offices in Addis Ababa, Khartoum, and Dakar. TIKA tends to concentrate on long-term efforts, rather than crisis operations. Typical of a TIKA initiative is the Agricultural Development Program currently being implemented in more than ten countries.

On the security front, Turkey deploys military and police personnel in support of five UN peacekeeping missions in Africa. Since early 2009, the Turkish navy has deployed half a dozen frigates as part of the US-led Combined Task Force (CTF) 151, a multinational naval force carrying out anti-piracy operations off the coast of Somalia.[81]

Despite the growing interest of Turkey in Africa, in absolute terms, the quantitative impact of Turkey's increasing links to Africa has not yet begun to approach the volume of the Chinese or Indian investment in the continent, much less the extensive networks of the United States or the former colonial powers. Nonetheless, the phenomenon is significant, according to some observers for several reasons:

1. Turkey's experience as a medium-sized country that has both modernised politically and developed economically is one that resonates with many African countries, and as a matter of fact, is probably a more reasonable model for their emulation than China or India, both of which are unique in their global standing.
2. African states stand to benefit from Turkey's new interest in their continent insofar as the addition of yet another partner enables them to diversify their sources of foreign investments and partnerships so as to not become too dependent on the Western powers or BRIC countries.
3. Not only does Africa clearly provide a new market for the growing Turkish economy, at a time when Turkey's integration into the European Union is in doubt, the continent provides Ankara with a much-needed avenue to diversify its diplomatic portfolio.
4. It is clear from the above that for Turkey, developing strong economic and political ties with Africa is critical for expanding export markets and diversifying energy resources, as well as consolidating its image as an emerging global power with a human-centred and conciliatory approach.[82]

## Africa and GCC

Africa has had contact with Islam even before it reached Medina. The first *Hijra* by Muslims was to Africa, which was selected by the Prophet as a safe refuge to his followers to escape the atrocities of the pagans in Makkah. This was based on a very wise strategy that analysed the geopolitical environment in the region and after considering all possible alternatives. Africa has been selected for a fundamental reason as stated by the Prophet, "it has a king where no one can face injustice under his rule."[83] The *hadith* has great ramifications in terms of preparing grounds for Islamic finance in Africa. Africa was not selected because it is the most powerful nation on earth at that time so that Muslims will be protected, nor because it is so prosperous that the new refugees would not face hardship; rather, the continent was selected because of how it values justice, which is the backbone of civilisation. More interestingly, the Islamic traditions are clear that the king converted to Islam while his followers remained Christian. Here again, we are presented another great value for any civilisation—namely, the value of freedom. The King did not force his followers to follow suite and the people did not revolt against him because he selected another religion. Thus, civilisation is not about military might and luxurious lifestyles, as many historian and contemporary social scientists try to convey, but about values. The most important values that can be the basic foundations of any economic development are those of justice and freedom. Thus, any attempt to introduce Islamic finance in Africa shall be judged by these values. Translated into modern terminologies and systems, we can assert justice and freedom are the pillars of the concepts of good governance and democracy. For African governments to attract Islamic investments, they have to strengthen rules of law and good governance.

In term of trading relations between the Arab Gulf and Africa, they existed before Islam, but developed after the rise of Islam in the seventh century. During the period of the spread of Islam, camel caravans from different Muslim kingdoms of the continent were connecting the Gulf via North Africa and the Tran-Saharan routes bringing gold, among other products, to world markets. Coastal East Africa was, on the contrary, the trade hub that connected the Arab Gulf with the city states of Eastern Africa for trade in precious metals such as gold, ivory, and iron that were exported to world markets as far as China. This relation gained further prominence during the 1800s, when the empire of Oman shifted its capital to the island of Zanzibar. However, these trading contacts between the Arab Gulf and Africa almost discontinued during the colonial era, which witnessed major transformation in the direction and pattern of trade in favour of Western industrialised markets. The oil era that resulted in massive economic development in the Gulf also did not help in enhancing trade with Africa to a significant level.

Despite the fact that the two regions have many things in common, such as the fact that the majority of the population in both regions are Muslims, the neighbourhood and geographical position, the historical, economic, and cultural ties, or the fact that the majority of Arab are in Africa, economics ties have remained limited. However, things have started to change during the last two decades.[84]

The GCC's enormous financial liquidity, combined with growing competitiveness in industries have given the region a niche position in the world economy. Simultaneously, the African region, powered by its natural resources of precious metals and minerals, is fast emerging as an economic growth hotspot besides the growing speed in which the two regions complement each other that are reshaping their relations.[85] Africa is fast emerging as one of the shining stars in the global economic climate. The continent has become a new source of economic growth. This new paradigm that combines the strengths of GCC and Africa's potential can hardly be overstated. Both regions are witnessing an economic renaissance and bilateral economic relations that are based on the strengths of the two regions.[86]

Until recently, favourable oil market conditions and the fiscal stimulus provided by GCC governments to sustain the growth of non-oil activities have helped to overcome the most severe effects of the global crisis. Sub-Saharan Africa's resilience through the global financial crisis, on the contrary, is widely articulated as the result of sound economic policy implementation before and during the crisis.[87]

Between 1994 and 2004, if we take into exception Kenya and the Arab states in the continent, formal or substantial trade between the two regions was almost non-existent. However, higher economic growth momentum in the two regions resulted in increasing trade flows in the mid-2000s. This is primarily due to the changing structure of production in both regions, apart from trade in other commodities in which both regions have achieved comparative advantages.

Over the 2000–09 period, the trade direction strongly favoured the GCC. In nominal terms, GCC's exports to Africa grew nearly three-fold and its imports from Africa registered nearly four-fold growth. GCC–Africa two-way trade increased from US$2.8 billion in 1990 to US$6.8 billion in 2000, and further surged to US$25.7 billion in 2008. Due to the global economic downturn, it fell to US$18.1 billion in 2009. Bilateral trade has grown by 170 % from 2000 to 2009. GCC's exports to and imports from Africa have registered an annual average growth rate of 14.7 % and 27.5 %, respectively. Looking at the trade volume between the GCC and other regional economic blocs in Africa, trade is highly concentrated to two regional economic blocs in Africa—namely, the Common Market for Eastern and Southern Africa (COMESA) and Southern Africa Customs Union (SACU).[88]

Among GCC member states, the UAE, particularly Dubai, seems to be very active in fostering strong trade relations with African countries, and in particular, with the COMESA member states by encouraging trade between the two regions. This is evident from the hosting of the 4th COMESA Investment Forum by the Emirates. The Forum was held in Dubai during March 23–24, 2011 and attended by more than 1500 participants from over 80 different countries under the theme "Unlocking the Markets of the Future."

According to a report by Dubai Chamber of Commerce Industry, the volume of non-oil trade between Dubai and COMESA in 2009 was AED 26.6 billion (US$7.24 billion). Regarding investment, between January 2003 and January 2011, the COMESA region has recorded 115 Direct Foreign Investments (FDI) projects in 10 COMESA countries originating from the United Arab Emirates.[89]

The UAE trade with the COMESA increased significantly between 2002 and 2008. The volume of imports from the 19 member COMESA region to the UAE increased at a compounded annual growth rate of 36 %, while export and re-export from the UAE to COMESA registered an increase of 47 % and 19 %, respectively. The rates of return on investments in COMESA are considerably greater than in more matured markets and even other emerging markets.[90] These have averaged 29 % since the 1990s, opposed to just 10 % from the EU. For instance, the average GDP growth in the COMESA countries was 5.7 % in 2009, while in the same year for the Euro zone and MENA region, the growth was minus 4 % and 2.5 %, respectively. The rate of FDI growth in the COMESA states between 2004 and 2009 was close to 180 %, while it was close to 20 % in the EU, 125 % for ASEAN, 70 % for G20, and 50 % for G8.[91]

Approximately 80 % of the UAE's imports from Africa are primary products, such as food produce and beverages. During the first half of 2014, Dubai's total non-oil trade with Africa reached a value of around US$16.3 billion, according to Dubai Customs. Furthermore, over 500,000 African nationals currently reside in Dubai, over 800,000 African nationals visited Dubai in 2013 alone and it is estimated that, by 2020, tourism from Africa to Dubai will reach over 1.5 million visitors per year.[92]

At the concluded Africa-Global-Business-Forum 2014, Dubai Chamber's President and CEO noted that the active participation of leading UAE companies mirrors their intention to explore further investment opportunities in Africa. He added that, "Dubai holds in high value its relationships with the nations of Africa and …This gathering of heads of states, ministers, decision makers, and businessmen from Africa and the rest of the world is a unique opportunity to showcase the strong potential that the African continent holds for investors and investees alike. Our geographical proximity and cultural affinity position us well to bring this great opportunity to the world and to bring the world to Africa."[93]

Dubai is venturing into Africa mainly through one of its sovereign wealth funds, the Investment Corporation of Dubai (ICD). The fund planned investments include infrastructure, civil aviation, agriculture, telecoms, and financial sector. In the infrastructure sector, for instance, the ICD has recently concluded a US$300 million stake to buy a 1.4 % stake in Dangote Cement, the largest firm on Nigeria's stock market, which controls two-thirds of the cement market and has around US$23 billion in market value.

According to Frost & Sullivan Africa, the average cement consumption in most African regions is very low compared to international averages, and therefore, there is an opportunity to facilitate the industry future growth. The prospects of the industry growth is also supported by other factors such as population growth, urbanisation, and housing development. Dangote Cement planned to expand production capacity from about 35 million tons a year to more than 60 million tons a year by 2018 as it grows domestically and across 12 other African countries.

On the civil aviation front, Emirates Airlines, owned by the ICD, reached a ten-year agreement with the Angolan government to manage the national carrier, TAAG Linhas Aéreas De Angola, and a partnership with Nigeria's Arik Air. Currently, Emirates fleet investment in Africa is estimated at US$7 billion with operating costs of over US$2 billion. In the past five years, Emirates has carried over 1.6 million passengers and

40,000 tons of cargo between Africa and China, underscoring the vital trade relationship that the continent has with the East. By 2020, Emirates expects to provide an additional 8.5 million seats to its African capacity, to add at least 10 new routes in Africa by 2025.

In the agriculture industry, one of the main discussions between ICD and Dangote has been Dangote's spending plan of about US$3 billion to boost production of sugar and rice. Africa can be a good option to offset its limited domestic food production capacity, given its fertile soil and abundant water resources. ICD, on the contrary, projects to establish huge farms across Africa to provide agricultural products to the UAE economy.

The Telecoms area is another promising investment sector and Etisalat, also owned by ICD, has a presence in several African markets, including Sudan, Tanzania, Benin, Gabon, and Ivory Coast. In May 2013, it finalised the acquisition of a 53 % stake in Maroc Telecom, giving it access to Burkina Faso, Mauritania, and Mali. Etisalat also owns an 82 % stake in Atlantique Telecom, which operates under the Moov brand and is operational in Benin, the Central African Republic, Gabon, Burkina Faso, Niger, Ivory Coast, and Togo. Etisalat enjoyed a monopoly in the UAE's domestic market until a few years ago and has over 6.3 million registered subscribers in the UAE, out of its regional subscriber base of approximately 33 million—making it the second biggest telecom operator in the Middle East region. Etisalat is reported to be planning to inject another US$5.5 billion in African markets, US$4.1 billion of which in East Africa, and US$1.4 billion in West Africa.

On the financial arena, Dubai Islamic Bank is exploring opportunities in Kenya and surrounding countries in Africa, looking for acquisitions, joint ventures, or start-ups. Describing Africa as a "virgin territory for Islamic finance," DIB's chief executive, Adnan Chilwan, told Reuters that countries such as Kenya, where the financial regulator is preparing a ten-year capital markets development strategy that includes Islamic finance, are a viable investment hotspot for Islamic banking, including *ṣukūk* issues. Kenya will open the door for more branches across the region, including Tanzania and Uganda. Moreover, DIB could also have a major role in helping a rising number of African companies that are catching the eyes of major stock exchanges around the world. In this way, Dubai is encouraging African companies to open up offices in UAE to make use of its financial infrastructure, listing African companies on Dubai Financial Market (DFM)'s rebounding exchange.[94]

Another important initiative taken recently is the move by Qatar National Bank (QNB), which already has a presence in North Africa, acquiring a stake in Ecobank Transnational and considered to be "a well calculated move" by *the Economist Intelligence Unit*, adding that, "the growth of Islamic finance in Africa is another facilitator of GCC investment."

A recent report by *the Economist Intelligence Unit*, maintained that the Gulf's interest into Africa is broadening, by sector and geographical location and GCC countries are giving more attention to new and unfamiliar markets. The Gulf's geographical closeness to the continent and its modern airlines companies are helping to grow trade. Gulf investors are looking for both equity and direct investment opportunities in the continent.[95]

An earlier report pointed to growing trade between the two regions and the fact that the economic emergence of Sub-Saharan Africa presents massive opportunities for the GCC.[96] According to the report, trade has increased at an average of 11 % per year since 1980. That is more than double the rate of growth in trade between the GCC and the OECD, suggesting that Africa's share of total GCC exports and imports is likely to keep rising strongly. A good indicator of the rising importance of the continent is the variation in how multinationals are classifying the region.[97]

However, as pointed out by the Chief Executive Officer of Invest AD in his Forward to a report entitled *Into Africa Institutional Investor Intentions to 2016*, the emergence of a strong middle class in many African countries is fuelling demand for all sorts of products and services. Investors see the potential for high returns in such ventures. They will commit capital, which, in turn, creates jobs and helps lift incomes. Similar experiences have been successful in Asia and Latin America. It is now Africa's turn for an economic lift-off.[98]

The GCC could be attracted to Africa's abundant arable land, particularly as the Gulf States move towards implementing food security strategies in the wake of the 2008 global food crisis,[99] and as international food prices are expected to keep rising in the long term. According to a recent report by the World Bank, 56 million hectares of land were leased or sold to foreign investors in 2008 and 2009, 70 % of which was in Africa. Sovereign wealth funds, state-owned food companies, and private investors have shown increasing interest in securing long-term leases on land for use in export-oriented farming.[100] It is clear that although the volume of trade between Africa and the Gulf is still small, but one area that could increase, this volume is agriculture as Gulf countries have a sense of food shortage and Africa has the land; this provides major investment opportunities in the agriculture sector in Africa.[101] Given the limitation due to unfavourable climatic conditions, water shortage, limited availability of arable land in the region, and the fact that these countries need to import almost 90 % of their food requirements, the GCC governments are currently pursuing different strategies in order to secure their food supply.

1. Investing in agriculture in countries where there is surplus land and favourable climate, especially countries with which they share close economic and cultural ties and geographic proximity.
2. Encouraging the domestic food processing industry so that imports of processed food decrease. The aim is to source domestic and foreign raw materials from outside, and then, process them within the region.
3. Building strategic food reserves along the lines of energy reserves in the US and food stockpiles in India.[102]

Yet, it appears certain, according to *The Economist Intelligence Unit,* that the GCC will become more dependent on imported food. An important reason for this is water scarcity, which means that domestic agricultural production tends to be costly.[103] Saudi Arabia, for instance, has announced that it will phase out domestic wheat production by 2016 in order to save water. The report adds that across the GCC, aggregate spending on food imports is projected to more than double, from US$24 billion in 2008 to US$49 billion by 2020. Thus, as the GCC presses ahead with investments in agriculture overseas, it could potentially give a significant boost to agricultural production in poor countries. GCC states might also be able to supply these countries with cheap fertilisers at cost price. More importantly, the GCC would be competing with China and India for land in Africa in 2020.[104] Referring to the above situation, NCB Capital in Saudi Arabia noted that the Saudi government decided to reduce its direct wheat purchases from farmers by 12.5 % every year and shifting towards wheat imports by 2016. It will be unwise to waste 1,000 tone of water to produce a ton of wheat.

Taking into consideration this new reality, authorities in the GCC started to outsource agriculture, without forgetting to promote sustainable development of the local agriculture sector.[105] Saudi Arabia for instance, is encouraging companies to invest in Africa. One of these examples is the investment in Ethiopia by Saudi Star Agricultural Development, a food company owned by billionaire Mohammed al-Amoudi, which is planning to invest US$2.5 billion by 2020 to develop a rice-farming project on

10,000 ha of land on lease for 60 years. It also has plans to rent an additional 290,000 ha from the government.[106]

It is worth emphasising here that interest by GCC countries in agriculture in Africa should not be limited to food security only. It can also be a huge avenue of investment and revenues generation. The example of the Singaporean giant OLAM Company in the agriculture industry and its presence in more than 20 African countries is a good example to follow.

Africa possesses not only vast amounts of arable land for agriculture, but also precious minerals, including platinum, uranium, bauxite, iron, coal, copper, lead, and diamonds.[107] Any cooperation between the two regions in developing the mining industry will definitely be for their mutual benefit. Among the few GCC entrepreneur interested in Africa in general, and this sector in particular, is the UAE business tycoon Mohamed Alabbar, who is keen to tap opportunities in Africa and expects his natural resources exploration company to be worth up to US$20 billion within a decade. Besides his role as chairman of Emaar Properties, the UAE's largest developer, Alabbar also runs Africa Middle East Resources, which aims at unlocking the value of natural resources in Africa, the Middle East, Central Asia, and the Subcontinent. The Johannesburg-based company focuses on finding and securing natural resources for key mining and energy stakeholders, while emphasising on base metals, precious metals, and oil and gas. The company is seeking growth through natural expansion of projects across Africa as well as acquisitions.[108] He was quoted saying that:

> Africa is neglected. The size of Africa with one billion people, 300m middle income, fabulous opportunities, welcoming government but unfortunately we all like to do business in easy environment...so who are the guys who like the challenge...I am really excited by it [Africa].[109]

Commenting on Albbar's interest in Africa, *The Financial Times* reported the Dubai's tycoon is building a private business with the hope of placing the emirate at the centre of a commodities trading triangle linking resource-rich Africa with the emerging economies of Asia.[110]

The company currently has interests in Madagascar, Guinea, Congo, Niger, Angola, and Gabon. It is active in gold, bauxite, and iron ore in Guinea-Conakry and oil and gas concessions in Uganda. AMER is also in advanced discussions on uranium and hydrocarbon interests in Niger, gold and coal deposits in Madagascar, phosphate concessions in Mauritania, copper in the Democratic Republic of Congo, and oil and gas in Gabon.[111]

Many in Dubai, according to *The Financial Times*, regard Africa as the emirate's new frontier. With good communication links and numerous flights across the continent, Dubai has emerged as a secondary hub for Africans looking eastward, rather than the traditional centres of London and Paris.[112] This is clearly reflected on the use of Dubai as travel connection for many African. As has been pointed out by *The Economist*, "Dubai, is still the best hub for African travellers."[113]

Another area of possible cooperation between the two regions is the Information Communication Technology (ICT). One of the driving forces behind the long term growth of the ICT industry in the region is Africa's rapid population growth and steady increase in urbanisation, an ever-expanding work force, and a burgeoning middle class. This has resulted in the emergence of a middle class with discretionary income to spend on ICT products.[114] The private sector has been spearheading infrastructure investments in the region over the last two decades and the telecom sector has often been the most attractive sector for investment. The interest in Sub-Saharan Africa's telecom was not dampened by the economic downturn of 2009. Favourable prospects for the telecom sector are evidenced in the rapid growth in mobile subscription in 2009 that led to a renewed interest in the acquisition of the region's mobile assets. This is clearly evident from some of the following deals:

- Essar Group's acquisition of Warid Telecom assets in Uganda and Congo-Brazzaville in a deal valued at US$300 million.
- Vodafone's obtaining of a controlling stake in Vodacom (present in South Africa, DRC, Lesotho, Mozambique, and Tanzania).
- Tata Communications increasing its stake in South Africa's second national operator Neotel to 56 %.
- The South African company Telkom's obtaining of the final 25 % stake in Nigerian operator Multi-links Telecom (which provides fixed, mobile, data, long distance, and international telecom services).[115]

Between 1990 and 2008, more than 40 % of the infrastructure projects in the region with private sector participation has been in the telecom sector. In terms of the total amount the sector has received over the last two decades, US$62 billion out of a total of US$82 billion has been invested in the region's infrastructure. Given the fact that the GCC market is experiencing an overcrowding caused by too many licences, GCC regulators are starting to limit the availability of licences. Moreover, where licences are put up for sale, the premiums are exorbitant due to the large number of bidders. Africa, particularly Sub-Saharan Africa, presents the ideal market conditions for any possible expansion.[116]

However, while discussing opportunities in the telecom sector in Africa, one case that needs to be clarified is Zain's experience in Africa. The company polled out of Africa after a few years of presence in the continent. Some have explained Zain's exit as one of the consequence of the financial crisis. However, some observers maintain that until 2009, the general view was that GCC telecom companies would continue to target investments in Sub-Saharan Africa, with optimistic news coming out of the region. The global economic slowdown, however, has reduced the value of the assets of telecom companies across the world. Before the crisis, players such as Batelco, Wataniya, and Qtel were mulling over the idea of getting into Africa's market. Similarly, non-Gulf operators, such as Vodafone, Vivendi, Bharti Airtel, Essar, and Reliance Communications were all pushing for a Sub-Saharan African niche. Against this backdrop, the sale by the Zain Group to Bharti Airtel of the majority of its African operations raised concerns among the region's telecom professionals. However, contextualising Zain's sale is crucial for understanding the prospects that the Sub-Saharan African telecom market holds for other Gulf operators.

The official line of explanation from Zain was that the exit is executed to allow the company to focus on its highly cash generative operations in the Middle East and to substantially improve its balance sheet. However, many analysts pointed out that the sale raised many questions due to the following:

- The company has only been operating in Africa for four years.
- It had just completed a very expensive rebranding operation.
- The general view is that there was room for future growth and profitability owing to the region's large populations and low mobile penetration rates.
- Zain's exit from the region's telecom market owes itself to situations specific to the company and not a general condition of the region's telecom market.
- Perhaps the offer from Bharti Airtel of US$10.7 billion was so attractive and simply too sweet for the company's executives to turn down.[117]

Bharti Airtel's acquisition of Africa's operations of Zain for US$10.7 billion was the second-largest overseas acquisition by an Indian group. The largest was the US$12.2 billion acquisition of European steelmaker Corus by the Tata Group in 2007. This clearly shows that foreign companies are indeed investing a lot of money in Africa due to the huge potential gains.[118] The Sub-Saharan market fundamentals seem to be strong and its future prospects are very promising, given the socio-economic and demographic trends that are poised to sustain and reinforce the market's expansion in the region. Rapid population growth coupled with increased urbanisation, an ever-expanding workforce, and a burgeoning middle class with new sources of discretionary income will together form the foundation on which future growth in the region's telecommunications sector will be anchored.[119] The sector still has a lot of potential for growth. Although there has been remarkable growth in some segments of Sub-Saharan Africa's telecommunications market, the region still has a long way to go before attaining levels comparable to the rest of the world.[120] Credit Suisse, for instance, pointed out that although Africa remains the fastest-growing mobile telecom market in the world with enormous growth rate, the region still offers substantial opportunities for growth since only four out of every ten African have access to a mobile phone today. This translates into an "unconnected" market of around 600 million people.[121] One of the noticeable things across Africa these days is how many people have cell phones. For instance, a reported 71 % of adults in Nigeria own cell phones with 62 % in Botswana, and more than half the population in Ghana and Kenya, according to a 2011 Gallup poll.[122]

Asset management is another promising area. One of the old companies from the GCC having interest in Africa is the Accra-based Kingdom Zephyr Africa Management, created by New York investment firm Zephyr Management LP and Kingdom Holding Company, headed by HRH Prince Alwaleed Bin Abdulaziz of Saudi Arabia. Both Zephyr Management and Kingdom Holding have been investing in Africa for more than 15 years. Kingdom Zephyr now manages two funds. Its first fund, Pan-African Investment Partners I Fund (PAIP I), raised US$123 million. Now fully invested, PAIP I mainly focuses its investments in Africa's fast-growing financial services sector, banking, microfinance, and insurance. Nevertheless, it was also quick to spot excellent investment opportunities in real estate and telecoms—Celtel, for example, is one of the fund's early investments. PAIP I's geographical reach covers the entire continent. Kingdom Zephyr then launched PAIP II, making a first close of

US$325 million in 2008 and completing a final close of US$492 million by February 2010. This came in the face of the global economic downturn, demonstrating investors' confidence in emerging markets, particular in Africa.[123]

Long-term and visionary ideas are necessary for formulating a good relationship between the two regions, according to Hisham Al Shirawi, Chairman, Economic Zones World, in his address to the 4th COMESA Investment Forum. He added that with COMESA's total land mass covering 11 million sq. kms, a 29th world ranking in terms of gross domestic product (GDP) and 32nd ranking in terms of total trade, such business opportunities simply could not be ignored.[124]

For the above sectors and others to develop and expand, it should be supported by a vibrant banking and financial sector. In a recently concluded conference, the delegates noted that the flow of investments was limited largely due to the absence of GCC banks in Africa.[125] In order to fill this gap, the introduction of Islamic finance in Africa will benefit both regions. The GCC's asset management industry is estimated to be worth close to US$2 trillion[126] and just a fraction of this could make a real change in the economic development of the continent. It is time for investors from the GCC region not just to look to the West as the only destination for investment opportunities. It is time to give consideration to other markets with higher returns that have registered some of the strongest growth in the last decade. We have to look for markets that have been able to come out of the recent financial crisis before other regions could and are projected at the same time by international financial institutions to register some of the highest GDP growth in the next five years. Africa is a good example of these markets despite some risks such as lack of infrastructure, and sometimes, inadequate regulations, which are inherent to such markets and which could be improved only by genuine investors who can impose the necessary changes to the system.

Compared to other regions, the GCC trade with Africa still trails behind and trade links have, up until now, been limited. Thus, there is a need for extra effort by all parties to make a real change. Sovereign investors through their sovereign fund have the means and the wealth to make a huge difference in this fledgling market. It is time for the GCC countries to make strategic decision by investing in Africa. The opportunity is there and all that remains is to grasp it. It is also worth noting that the huge rewards now being harvested by China and other countries as a result of their focused efforts to invest and develop Africa are a testament to the vast potential in the continent. The GCC is ideally positioned to follow suit, if it can only get its game into gear.[127] As rightly pointed out Rassem Zok, CEO, Standard Bank Plc, MENA, "Africa is on the radar screen of a lot of the countries in the Middle East," and "Africa is regarded by many developed economies as one of the final remaining frontier markets with significant opportunities ... and the GCC countries are very aware of this."[128]

As rightly noted by Deloitte, Africa offers potential for great rewards; at the same time, there are also significant risks associated with an expansion strategy in Africa. The degree and nature of these risks vary significantly from one African country to another.[129]

Former chief economist at the Dubai International Financial Centre (DIFC) and member of the IMF's Regional Advisory Group for MENA, while commenting on the barriers to greater GCC investment in Africa, particularly high political risk compared to the high yield opportunities that Africa offers, Nasser H Saidi asked, "Why should the GCC countries invest in US Treasury bills at 0.5 % yield when next door you can have risk-adjusted returns on investments of 15–30 %?"[130]

The development of Islamic finance in Africa and its ability to attract investments from the GCC or elsewhere faces various challenges. Some of these challenges are global in nature, facing the industry in general while others are peculiar to its implementation in Africa. However, as pointed out by *The Economist Intelligence Unit*, "Strengthening regulation of Islamic finance could also catalyse infrastructure funding from the Gulf."[131]

## Notes

1. Zahid Torres –Rahman & Michel Lalor, *The New Africa Emerging Opportunities for Business and Africa*, May 2011, p. 2.
2. PricewaterhouseCoopers, "10 Minutes on Investing in Africa", pp. 1–2.
3. Mwagi S. Kimenyi & Zenia Lewis (2011). "THE BRICS and the new scramble for Africa" in *Foresight Africa: The Continent's Greatest Challenges and Opportunities for 2011*, pp. 19–21; Robin Wigglesworth, "Investors start a new scramble for Africa" *Financial Times*, February 7, 2013, www.ft.com, retrieved March 2013; Pádraig Carmody, *The New Scramble for Africa* Cambridge: Polity Press 2011; Mark Leftly, "The new scramble for Africa", *The Independent* Sunday, October 28, 2012, www.independent.co.uk retrieved January 2013; David Makwerere &

Ronald Chipaike, "China and the United States of America in Africa: A New Scramble or a New Cold War?", *International Journal of Humanities and Social Science* Vol. 2, No. 17; September 2012, pp. 311–319.

4. Monica Ioana Enescu, *Emerging powers: New economic partners for Africa?* p. 4.
5. Mwagi S. Kimenyi & Zenia Lewis, "The BRICS and the new scramble for Africa", in *Foresight Africa: The Continent's Greatest Challenges and Opportunities for 2011*, pp. 19–21.
6. Monica Ioana Enescu, *Emerging powers: New economic partners for Africa?* p. 1.
7. *Africa Quarterly*, "Emerging Powers: A time for new dreams", *Africa Quarterly*, Indian Journal of African Affairs, Volume 51, No. 3–4, August 2011–January 2012, p. 7.
8. Ibid.
9. Monica Ioana Enescu, *Emerging powers: New economic partners for Africa?* p. 1.
10. Barfour Osei & Alex Mutebi Mubiru, "Chinese Trade and Investment Activities in Africa", The African Development Bank Group", *Policy Brief*, Volume 1, Issue 4, 29 July, 2010, p. 2.
11. David H. Shinn, "The Rise of Non-Western Influence in Africa", pp. 14–16.
12. Ibid.
13. *The Guardian*, "A fresh chapter is opening in Africa's history after two centuries of injustice, a new continent is emerging", February 19, 2011, www.guardian.co.uk, retrieved January 2012.
14. Peter Wonacott, "U.S. Aims to Gain New Edge in Africa" *The Wall Street Journal*, June 11, 2011, www.online.wsj.com, retrieved January 2012.
15. Ibid.
16. *The Economist*, "The hopeful continent Africa rising", December 3, 2011.
17. *The Economist*, "Africa's impressive growth", Jan. 6th 2011.
18. David H. Shinn, "The Rise of Non-Western Influence in Africa", pp. 14–16.
19. Charles Roxburgh & Others, *Lion on the Move: The progress and Potential of African Economies*, p. 45.
20. Barfour Osei& Alex Mutebi Mubiru, "Chinese Trade and Investment Activities in Africa", The African Development Bank Group", *Policy Brief*, Volume1, Issue 4, 29 July, 2010, p. 1.
21. Shawn Ladd, "Emerging Africa Expected To See Rise in Investment", *IMF Survey Magazine: Countries & Regions*, January 12, 2011, www.imf.org, Retrieved June 2011.
22. *The Economist*, "Chinese in Africa: The Chinese are coming ...to Africa", April 22, 2011, www.economist.com, retrieved January 2012.

23. Simon Freemantle & Jeremy Stevens, *Africa Macro Insight and Strategy BRIC—Africa The Redback's Rise Opportunities to Africa*, Standard Bank 29 August 2011, www.standardbank.com, retrieved January 2012, p. 6.
24. *The Economist*, "Rumble in the jungle Why the Beijing Regime need to act to avert a Backlash against Chinese Investors in Poor Countries", April 20, 2011, www.economist.com, retrieved January 2012.
25. Barfour Osei& Alex Mutebi Mubiru, "Chinese Trade and Investment Activities in Africa", The African Development Bank Group", *Policy Brief*, Volume1, Issue 4, 29 July, 2010, p. 3.
26. Deborah Brautigam, "China in Africa: Seven Myths", ARI 23/20011, Elcano Royal Institute, Feb8, 2011, www.realinstitutoelcano.org, retrieved January 2012.
27. Ibid.
28. Ibid.
29. Ibid.
30. Paul Kagame, "Why Africa welcomes the Chinese", *The Guardian*, November 2, 2009, www.guardian.co.uk, retrieved January 2012.
31. Ibid.
32. Deborah Brautigam, "China in Africa: Seven Myths", ARI 23/20011, Elcano Royal Institute, Feb. 8, 2011, www.realinstitutoelcano.org, retrieved January 2012.
33. David H. Shinn, "The Rise of Non-Western Influence in Africa", pp. 14–16.
34. Ibid.
35. The 3rd COMESA Investment Forum Connecting Africa to the World 12–13 April, 2010, Sharm El Sheikh, Egypt, Conference Report, p. 20.
36. Ibid.
37. Steve Davis and Jonathan Woetzel, "Making the most of Chinese aid to Africa", *McKinsey Quarterly*, June 2010, www.mckinsey.com, retrieved June 2012.
38. Simon Freemantle & Jeremy Stevens, *Africa Macro Insight and Strategy BRIC—Africa The Redback's Rise Opportunities to Africa*, p. 1.
39. Denis M. Tull, "China's engagement in Africa: scope, significance and consequences, *Journal of Modern African Studies*, 44, 3, 2006, Cambridge, pp. 459–479.
40. *The Guardian*, "A fresh chapter is opening in Africa's history after two centuries of injustice, a new continent is emerging", February 19, 2011 www.guardian.co.uk, retrieved January 2012.
41. K Mathews, "Emerging Powers in Africa: An Overview", *Africa Quarterly*, Indian Journal of African Affairs, Volume 51, No. 3–4, August 2011–January 2012, p. 23.
42. Ibid.

43. Backgrounder: "India, Africa eye closer tie amid fast development of economic, trade flow", www.news.xinhuanet.com, May 19, 2011, retrieved June, 2011.
44. Peter Wonacott, "U.S. Aims to Gain New Edge in Africa", *The Wall Street Journal*, June 11, 2011, www.online.wsj.com, retrieved January 2012.
45. Manish Chand, "India to set up training institutes in Africa" *Africa Quarterly*, Indian Journal of African Affairs Volume 50, No. 4, Nov 2010–Jan 2011, p. 8.
46. M. Mahtab Alam Rizvi, *India's Economic Engagement of Africa: Partnering Africa*, January 2011, Institute for Defense Studies and Analyses http://www.idsa.in/event/indiapartneringafrica.
47. Indrajit Basu, "India Inc. woos Africa", *Asia Times*, 2010, www.atimes.com, retrieved June 2011.
48. Habiba Ben Barka & Kupukile Mlambo, *India Economic Engagement with Africa*, The African Development Bank Group, Africa Economic Brief, Volume 2, Issue 6, 11 May, 2011, www.afdb.org, retrieved December, 2012, p. 1.
49. Ibid, p. 5.
50. Ibid, p. 7.
51. Ecobank, "Ecobank Signs MoU with Export-Import Bank of India", www.ecobank.com, retrieved June 2012.
52. Habiba Ben Barka& Kupukile Mlambo, *India Economic Engagement with Africa*, p. 6.
53. Habiba Ben Barka& Kupukile Mlambo, *Brazil's Economic Engagement with Africa*, Africa Economic Brief, African Development Bank, Volume 2, Issue 5, 11 May, 2011, www.afdb.org, retrieved December, 2012, p. 4.
54. Ibid.
55. BBC, "Brazil's Lula pays tribute to Africa's historic role", July 4, 2010, www.bbc.co.uk, retrieved June 2011.
56. David Lewis, "Special Report: In Africa, can Brazil be the anti-China?" *Reuters*, Feb. 23, 2011, www.reuters.com, retrieved January 2012.
57. For more details See, Bertha Z. Osei-Hwedie & Kwaku Osei-Hwedie, "Japan's TICAD: Alternative Global Framework for Africa's Development? *Zambia Social Science Journal* Volume 1, number 2, November 2010, pp. 123–140.
58. Isabel Reynolds and Takashi Hirokawa, "Abe Offers $32 Billion to Africa as Japan Seeks Resources Access", Bloomberg, Jun 1, 2013, www.bloomberg.com, retrieved June 2013.
59. Akihiko Tanaka, "Developing Africa Growth built on principles", *The Time*, May 1, 2013, www.thetimes.co.uk retrieved May 2013.
60. Jun Hongo, "TICAD to redefine Japan aid to Africa", May 13, 2013, www.japantimes.com, retrieved May 2013

61. *The Strait Times*, Japan eyes business ties in Africa summit to boost trade and investment May 30, 2013, www.straitstimes.com, retrieved May 2013.
62. Anna Nagar, "Now is the time to invest in Africa: Japan Premier Shinzo Abe", www.economictimes.indiatimes.com, June 3, 2013, retrieved June 2013.
63. Ibid.
64. Ibid.
65. Casper Hendrik Claassen, "South Korea In Africa Understanding South Korea Interest in Africa", July 18, 2011 www.consultancyafrica.com, retrieved December 2011.
66. Ibid.
67. Casper Hendrik Claassen, "Korea Aid and Investment Fostering an Agriculture Revolution", May 16 2011, www.consultancyafrica.com, retrieved December 2011.
68. Gil Seong Kang, *The Korea- Africa Partnership: Beyond Trade and Investment*, Africa Economic Brief African Development Bank, vol. 2, issue 9, 2011, www.afdb.org, retrieved December, 2012, p. 1.
69. Mehemet O Zkan and Birol Akgu, "Turkey's opening to Africa" *Journal of Modern African Studies*, 48, 4 (2010), pp. 525–546; J. Peter Pham, "Turkey's Return to Africa", *World Defense Review*, May 27, 2010, www.worlddefensereview.com, retrieved June 2011.
70. Ibid.
71. The Journal of Turkish weekly, "Turkey Makes Inroads into Africa", *The Journal of Turkish weekly*, Tuesday, 20 December 2011, www.turkish-weekly.net, retrieved March 2012.
72. Alain Vickey, "Turkey Moves into Africa", Le Monde Diplomatique May 2011, www.mondediplo.com, retrieved June 2012.
73. J. Peter Pham, "Turkey's Return to Africa", *World Defense Review*, May 27, 2010, www.worlddefensereview.com, retrieved June 2011.
74. The Journal of Turkish Weekly, "Turkey Makes Inroads into Africa", *The Journal of Turkish Weekly*, Tuesday, 20 December 2011.
75. J. Peter Pham, "Turkey's Return to Africa", *World Defense Review*, May 27, 2010.
76. David Shinn, "Turkey's Engagement in Sub-Saharan Africa Shifting Alliances and Strategic Diversification", Research Paper Africa Programme, September 2015, www.chathamhouse.org, p. 14.
77. The Journal of Turkish Weekly, "Turkey Makes Inroads into Africa".
78. Alain Vickey, "Turkey Moves into Africa", *Le Monde Diplomatique*, May 2011.
79. Selma Simsek Bektas, "Africa as a Savior for Turkish Firms", Hurriyet, Istanbul, 4 March 2011.

80. "Turkish goods warmly welcomed in African markets", May 15, 2010, www.todayszaman.com, retrieved June 2012.
81. J. Peter Pham, "Turkey's Return to Africa", *World Defense Review*, May 27, 2010.
82. Mehemet O Zkan and Birol Akgu, "Turkey's opening to Africa" *Journal of Modern African Studies*, 48, 4 (2010), pp. 525–546.
83. See Ibn Hajar, Ahmad Ibn Ali, Fath Al Bari Sharh Sahih Al Bukhari, Hadith no 3659, Dar Al Rayyan Li al Turath, 1986.
84. Samir Pradhan, "GCC-Africa Trade: Trends, Prospects and Policy Imperatives" Gulf-Africa Investment Conference 2010: Fostering Economic Relations, 4–5 December 2010 Riyadh, Kingdom of Saudi Arabia, p. 35–43.
85. Ibid.
86. Abdulaziz Sager, "The GCC and Africa: Growing Economic Complementarities", paper presented at Gulf-Africa Investment Conference—2010"December 04–05, 2010, Riyadh, Saudi Arabia.
87. Samir Pradhan, "GCC-Africa Trade: Trends, Prospects and Policy Imperatives".
88. Ibid.
89. *Zawya*, "Economic and business partnerships enhanced as 4th COMESA Investment Forum ends", March 27, 2011, www.zawya.com, retrieved January 2012.
90. Conference Report on the 4th COMESA Investment Forum "Dubai to Africa Unlocking the Market of the Future", 23–24 March 2011, p. 6.
91. Atique Naqvi, "Africa Calling", *Trends*, May 2011, pp. 49–54.
92. Fabio Vanorio, "Sovereign Wealth Funds and Islamic Finance: How can Africa benefit?" *Business Islamica*, November 2014, www.businessislamica.com, pp. 27–28.
93. See, www.dubaichamber.com/-Africa-global-business-forum-2014.
94. Fabio Vanorio, "Sovereign Wealth Funds and Islamic Finance: How can Africa benefit?" *Business Islamica*, November 2014, www.businessislamica.com, pp. 27–28.
95. Iain Douglas and Louise Redvers, *GCC Trade and Investment Flows*, The Economist Intelligence Unit 2014, p. 4.
96. Ayesha Sabavala and Ali al-Saffar, *GCC Trade and Investment Flows: The Emerging-Market Surge*, p. 16.
97. Ibid.
98. James Watson & Others, *Into Africa Institutional investor intentions to 2016*, p. 2.
99. Ayesha Sabavala and Ali al-Saffar, *GCC Trade and Investment Flows: The Emerging-Market Surge*, p. 4.
100. Ibid, p. 19.

101. Ibid.
102. Alpen Capital, *GCC Food Industry*, June 28, 2011, www.alpencapital.com, retrieved June 2012, pp. 15. 16.
103. The Economist Intelligence Unit, *The GCC in 2020: Outlook for the Gulf and the Global Economy*, March 2009, www.eiu.com, retrieved January2011, p. 3.
104. Ibid, p. 16.
105. Jarmo T. Kotilaine, *GCC Agriculture*, NCB Capital, March 2010, p. 14.
106. arabiabusiness.com "Saudi Arabia keen on African farm investments" May 11, 2012.
107. Ayesha Sabavala and Ali al-Saffar, *GCC Trade and Investment Flows: The Emerging-Market Surge*, p. 19.
108. Andy Sambidge, "Alabbar says African venture could be worth $20bn"*Arabian Business*, 12 November 2011, www.arabianbusiness.com, retrieved January 2012.
109. Ibid.
110. Simeon Kerr, "Emaar founder eyes Africa's commodity riches", *The Financial Times*, May 4 2011.
111. Andy Sambidge, "Alabbar says African venture could be worth $20bn"*Arabian Business*, 12 November 2011www.arabianbusiness.com, retrieved January 2012.
112. Simeon Kerr, "Emaar founder eyes Africa's commodity riches", *The Financial Times*, May 4 2011, www.ft.com, retrieved June 2012.
113. *The Economist*, "Africa's hopeful economies The sun shines bright", Dec 3 2011.
114. Kenneth Ngwa Anye "Telecommunication Markets and Trends in Sub-Saharan Africa", p. 5.
115. Ibid, p. 7.
116. Ibid, p. 10.
117. Kenneth Ngwa Anye, "Telecommunication Markets and Trends in Sub-Saharan Africa", p. 11.
118. The 3rd COMESA Investment Forum Connecting Africa to the World 12–13 April, 2010, Sharm El Sheikh, Egypt, Conference Report, p. 21.
119. Kenneth Ngwa Anye, "Telecommunication Markets and Trends in Sub-Saharan Africa", p. 20.
120. Ibid.
121. Robert Ruthann, *Africa's Development Prospects Remain Intact*, p. 2.
122. David Smith and Lucy Lamble, "Africa's burgeoning middle class brings hope to a continent" *The Guardian*, December 25, 2011, www.guardian.co.uk, retrieved March 2012.
123. Stephen Williams, "The advantage of local knowledge", *African Banker*, 4th Quarter2010, pp. 34–39.

124. *Zawya*, Economic and business partnerships enhanced as 4th COMESA Investment Forum ends, March 27, 2011, www.zawya.com, retrieved January 2012.
125. Shahid Ali Khan, "Gulf-African Investment Conference concludes with series of recommendations", *Saudi Gazette*, December 6, 2010, www.saudigazette.com, retrieved June 2011.
126. Reuters and arabianbusiness, "Gulf investors look west for bigger returns", May 24, 2011, www.arabianbusiness.com, retrieved December 2011.
127. Lauren Mcaughtry, "Islamic trade finance in Africa: Ripe for the picking", *Islamic Finance News Supplement*, June 2013, p. 6.
128. Iain Douglas and Louise Redvers, *GCC Trade and Investment Flows*, The Economist Intelligence Unit 2014, p. 16.
129. Deloitte, *Investments into Africa Tackling Tax and Regulatory Challenges*, p. 1.
130. Iain Douglas and Louise Redvers, *GCC Trade and Investment Flows*, p. 17.
131. The Economist Intelligence Unit, *Risk and Reward: The Gulf Push into African Infrastructure*, commissioned by Dubai Chamber, 2014.

CHAPTER 8

# Islamic Finance in Africa: Challenges Ahead

The challenges facing the growth of Islamic finance in Africa are manifold. Some of these challenges are related to the sustainability of the present economic growth; thus, any investment—whether Islamic or otherwise—is attracted by economic realities on the ground. The second type of challenges is related to the outstanding issues in Islamic finance itself and that would continue to be present in the African context as well. The last category will be those peculiar problems that need to be addressed in the implementation of Islamic finance in the African environment. While addressing the issue of exceptional economic growth in Africa and the prospect of Islamic finance, we should keep in mind that one of the key challenges that might affect any attempt to attract Islamic finance investment to develop the continent's vast resources, its infrastructure, agriculture, and to meet the demands of a fast growing consumer sector, particularly their demands for inclusive financial services, is the issue of perception with its far-reaching implications.

## Perception and Investment

Many of the best opportunities exist where perceptions differ from reality. This is particularly true of Africa, where perceptions are dominated by dictatorships, diseases, famine, and economic stagnation. The reality is very different in much of the continent, where advancing democracy and improving development and strong economic growth are well entrenched.



M. Al Bashir M. Al Amine, *Islamic Finance and Africa's Economic Resurgence*, DOI 10.1007/978-3-319-28835-2_8

The figures speak for themselves. Since 2000, GDP growth for Africa has averaged around 5 % per annum. This is significantly higher than population growth, which means GDP per capita—and therefore, wealth—is increasing. This will enable the continent to build on previous performance, when it was one of the few parts of the world to post positive economic growth. One of the main reasons for this strong performance has been trade, particularly with new dynamic economies headed by the BRIC countries. Trade between Africa and these countries, increased by more than seven times, from US$22 billion to US$166 billion between 2000 and 2008, compared with a threefold increase in world trade from US$13 trillion to US$36 trillion. The BRIC countries are not hampered by outdated perceptions of Africa and see the continent for what it is as—a fantastic investment destination—especially when these four states are set to be among the largest economies in the world in the coming decades. This, in turn, provides a great opportunity for Africa.[1]

In order to sustain the current growth and attract foreign investment, African countries must vigorously market themselves as a good investment destination. This marketing would be most effective if carried out as the continent's agenda or at a regional level. Thus, African governments need to emphasise the concept of working with other countries in the region in order to create a critical mass. Perceptions need to change to reflect the reality on the ground and not just based on media manipulation and distorted coverage. Many around the world are still not aware of the positive strides Africa has taken. Governments in the region must plan for the long term in order to ensure that increased local benefits are realised from investment in these industries. Thus, economic trade zones can work in unison so that investors will find the critical mass they need.[2]

Addressing the marred narrative about Africa, Obiageli Katryn Ezekwesili, the Vice President of Africa Region at the World Bank noted that the trend of focusing on Africa's challenges and problems, rather than on its opportunities and successes, is one of the continent's most enduring stereotypes. He stressed that despite remarkable economic growth over the past decade and growing middle-class consumers, the narrative about Africa has remained one of poverty, disease, and conflict. This suggests that in order to change this narrative, what is required is not only sustained economic progress, but also, concerted efforts for telling Africa success.[3]

As Muhtar Kent, Coca-Cola CEO, rightly observed, enormous misperceptions about Africa still exist, particularly in the mainstream media, where the continent is still considered as a place of civil unrest, famine, and war. Often, the great achievements of African countries are not even cited.[4] For Muhtar Kent "Africa is the untold story, and could be the big story, of the next decade."[5]

In a similar note, Zephyr Management CEO and founder pointed to the unrelentingly negative role of the media on Africa. The reported stories are about starvation, dengue fever, and political fights and not about the successful African entrepreneurship.[6] Mr. York Zucchi is another entrepreneur who invested in the continent in healthcare, education, and IT and employs 1850 people across 26 countries on the continent, and was quoted by *the Wall Street Journal*, saying the perception attached to Africa is often outdated and detached from realities. Yet, this mismatch provides a very nice space for those who have appetite for risk to come into a relatively uncompetitive market.[7]

Such kinds of successes are not unique, according to the *Wall Street Journal*. Entrepreneurs are reaping huge returns from African markets, but they often have to build their businesses alone in the early stages. This is because capital tends to be concentrated in the small pool of large companies on the continent. The current structure of the industry also means that smaller investors find it hard to access these frontier markets.[8] However, a successful entrepreneur is in a position to transform these challenges into opportunities. Ibrahim Moo is of the opinion that "the perception of Africa is much worse than the reality. And whenever there is gap between perception and reality there's a fantastic business opportunity."[9] Similarly, Nick Price, who is the portfolio manager of Fidelity Funds Emerging Europe, Middle East & Africa (EMEA) Fund, stated that "to me Africa is a classic example of the gap between perception and reality which leads to investment opportunity."[10]

The issue of perception has been articulated by many observers, some of whom are already having business in Africa and are close to reality on the ground. Investors' perception is improving and positively changing gradually. They believe that Africa has become more attractive and the continent's prospect is positive.[11]According to Ernst & Young, a perception gap remains between those already doing business in Africa, who are believers in the emerging African growth story, and those who have not yet invested and continue to associate the continent with instability and corruption. While FDI projects continue to grow strongly, Africa still lags behind most other regions in capturing the imagination of many international investors. However, this does not change the view of the international advisory firm, which continues maintaining that, "we are even more confident that Africa time has arrived."

It is evident that there is a need to bridge this perception gap by telling Africa new stories of economic growth and opportunity, democratic progress, and human development. There is a need to change the stereotypes, demystify Africa, and to rewrite the news headlines with confidence and without shying away from the challenges that remain.[12] However, the perception of Africa as a place to do business and for companies to establish or develop business is improving year on year.[13]

Ernst & Young maintained that although Africa's attractiveness as an investment destination is continuing to improve, this has not been reflected in actual investment through foreign direct investment in Africa. It is reported that two-thirds of investors established in Africa have an investment strategy for growth on the continent. Only 10 % of investors with no presence have done likewise. Comparing the continent's attractiveness to that of other regions, the 2014 Ernst & Young survey shows that companies with a presence also perceive Africa to be relatively more attractive than Asia. In stark contrast, those with no business presence in Africa view the continent as the world's least attractive investment destination.[14] Thus, "investors not established in Africa generally base their thinking on ill-informed opinion, which is completely divorced from on-the-ground realities. There is no doubt that Africa is an inherently challenging place to do business, however, many companies pursuing long-term African strategies have generated excellent returns from their investments. In fact, empirical analysis reveals that return on investment from projects in Africa have consistently been among the highest, if not the highest, in the world since the 1990s."[15]

Looking at Africa as a high-risk destination by some potential foreign investors is often based on perceptions that are 20–30 years out of date, according to Ernst & Young. Moreover, many of these perceptions are simply erroneous, and therefore, it is important to dispel these myths. But it is also important to highlight the real challenges of doing business on the continent and some of the real stories of companies that are successfully seizing the African opportunity.[16] It is important to note here that when Ernst & Young's first attractiveness survey was carried out in 2011, Africa ranked 8 out of 10 world regions—with only Central America and the ex-Soviet states being less appealing to investors. In 2013, however, Africa moved into joint second position, alongside Asia. In addition, almost three out of four respondents believed that Africa would become a more appealing investment option over the coming years. This outstanding improvement in such a short space of time demonstrates the extent to which investor's perceptions of Africa are beginning to change.

Similar observations have been noted by the Singaporean OLAM company, which has presence in more than 20 African countries and has a 30-year presence on the African continent. The company had announced plans for December 2011 to invest about US$100 million in Nigeria alone.[17] According to the company, land acquisition costs in Africa are a fraction of what they are in Asia and labour costs, after adjusting for lower labour productivity, are still better in Africa. Thus, OLAM maintains that taking into consideration the lower wage, price inflation, regulatory arbitrage opportunities, lower competitive intensity, and higher perceived risk of execution in Africa, returns in Africa would probably be twice the returns from similar investments in Asia.[18]

What is positive is that things have started to change and the continent was able to gain increased attention, not just in the media, but also from large think-tanks, research institutes, blue-chip companies, and even from big global investors. For the first time, conservative institutional investors and pension funds are starting to explore the opportunities on the continent. *Islamic Finance News* noted that "As the world turns, so do peoples' perception, and these days Africa is seen as a diamond in the rough, with growing optimism surrounding its fiscal and political future."[19]

The media is an important factor in shaping this perception about Africa. It is not possible to comprehend the issue of perception without linking it to the media and its impact on investment in the continent. The issue has been overlooked for too long. Decisions about whether and where to invest in Africa need to be based on accurate information that distinguish a basket case from a bread basket. The media has a crucial role to play in this regard. The continent has suffered for a long time from distorted media reporting and it is believed that a more balanced reporting of business in Africa will definitely stimulate economic development on the continent.[20] Thus, a study entitled "Hiding the Real Africa" documented how easily Africa makes the evening newscasts and newspaper headlines in the West when a major famine, pandemic, or violent crisis breaks while successful economic news are unreported. The study reported how, for example, more than 245 articles on Africa published in 2010 by the 10 most-read US newspapers focused on poverty. Only five of them mentioned wealth and growth. Similar negative reporting is observed in major Western television reports on Africa between mid-2008 and mid-2009 by

Media Tenor. The economy did not even feature in the top 10 issues. This negative reporting is occurring despite the fact that 2008 was a strong year for sub-Saharan Africa, whose GDP grew 5 % to US$1.6 trillion, stimulated by improvements in many sectors, not just natural resources and at the time where US GDP growth dropped to zero.[21]

A study on the role of non-governmental organisations (NGOs) and the negative perception of Africa pointed out that NGOs prefer bad news. It is reported that between 1998 and 2002, the number of stories about famine in Africa tripled. One of the main reasons for the continued dominance of such negative stereotypes was the influence of Western-based NGOs. These organisations understandably tend to focus not on what has been accomplished, but on convincing people how much remains to be done. As a practical matter, they also need to attract funding. These pressures create incentives to present as gloomy a picture of Africa as possible in order to keep attention and money flowing, and to enlist journalists in disseminating that picture. For instance, in the mid-1970s, there were less than half a dozen NGOs in a particular country, but now, the same country will likely have 250. This explosive NGO growth means increasing competition for funds. This is directly translated into action, and therefore, when you are fundraising, you have to prove that there is a need. This is translated into children starving, mothers dying, and so on... Thus, if you are not negative enough, you will not get funding. According to the report, the competition is sometimes so fierce that many NGOs do not want to hear good news. Added to that, the media will resort to plagiarism to get people's attention. Moreover, we have also the role of celebrities, whereby the simplest sell is a celebrity visiting an aid project.[22]

It is also fair to acknowledge that in recent years, there has been a growth in African business reporting by international media corporations, according to a survey by Diageo. African-specific business websites have been launched, such as Reuters Africa and CNBC Africa. There has also been an increase in the number of African business and investment-focused magazines, including Africa Investor, IC Publications, specifically *African Banker*, launched in May 2007, and '*This Is Africa*,' a publication from *The Financial Times Business*, to name a few. At the same time, the number of African business-related articles published in newspapers such as the *Financial Times*, *The Economist*, and *The Banker* has increased too. This media trend of increased African business and investment coverage is a positive factor for the business climate in Africa, but more is still needed. Many things, including access to communication technologies and greater freedom of speech, have contributed to this. Impressive economic development has also played its part.

According to Diageo's study, the media's interest in covering African business is driven by three factors. First, African economies are developing quickly, registering a higher GDP growth than the global average, resulting in more stories to cover. Second, media legislation and regulatory environments are taking place, supported by better communication technologies, which is making it easier for journalists to operate. Third, the unprecedented investment flows over the past few years from China, India, and other emerging markets are sparking media interest. Moreover, global awareness of the returns available in Africa has grown significantly. Increased media reporting of business in Africa has attracted more investment from international and local investors, which in turn, has increased media business coverage. It is a virtuous cycle. However, investors stress that more can be done to change perceptions about the risks and opportunities. This is based on the fact that many people still do not understand African markets. Risks are overestimated and returns are underestimated.[23]

Diageo's study found that African business coverage had improved, especially in upmarket media such as *The Financial Times*, *The Economist*, and the *BBC World Service*. It was also noted that there remains a general bias within the mainstream media when it comes to reporting on African issues. Much of the concern of many investors whether in the West or the East about Africa is fuelled by media reports that can miss the bigger picture. Comparisons between Africa and other emerging countries are not made. When given the option to compare corruption in Africa to other regions, most people would perceive Africa to be more corrupt. However, the reality is that the level of corruption in many African courtiers is much better than many other emerging markets. The international media tends to lump Africa together without comparison or distinction.[24]

One of these misconceptions is stereotyping Africa as one homogenous nation. This has damaged the reputation of some successful countries. However, despite the different challenges, there is an improved flow of business-related information, which can influence investors' perceptions of risk on the continent. 68 % of Diageo's study sample noted that risks on the continent are reducing and no one stated that risks will increase over the near future while 62 % of the respondents cited that Africa had a better risk/return profile compared to other emerging markets.[25]

Without the media, investors cannot stay on top of trends and developments and this may affect their existing investments and reduce their ability to capitalise on opportunities for future investments. More institutional investors will be attracted to the continent as the media devote more coverage to stock exchanges that have been underreported. Awareness of frontier markets will grow stronger as media coverage of these countries increases. The risk profile of these countries and the companies operating there will also begin to change as it becomes easier to understand and calculate the risks and opportunities. The media can contribute greatly to reducing information asymmetries. Markets systematically overestimate the risk of investing in Africa—particularly compared to risks associated with investments in other parts of the world.[26]

One of the most difficult struggles being fought by those who wish to attract investment into Africa is to destroy the widely held belief that Africa is one big country. Africa, in reality, is a collection of widely diverse and exciting countries, with varying prospects and challenges.[27] One obvious example of this diversification is in the legal diversity of the continent. There are many different legal systems in place. The underlying influence in those systems is often linked to the country's colonial past and the degree of its influence. Thus, we see the influence of common law in East and some parts of West Africa's legislations. The civil law is very influential in Francophone Africa, with countries in the West Central and North Africa. Besides, we have the Lusophone Africa and Roman Dutch law in Southern Africa. These systems are then shaped with local customary or indigenous laws, and in a number of African countries, these laws have some bearing of Sharī'ah or Islamic law, and finally, often these legislations incorporate legal concepts from other international jurisdictions. It is also important to note here the availability of regional legal developments such as the harmonisation of business laws in the 16 countries in the OHADA region and the development of the East African economic community with its own legislative body.[28]

The good news is that things are changing positively, notwithstanding the fact that news screens still remain filled with images of famine, war, and civil insurrections. However, we should always remember that Africa is multifaceted and be able to realise that these difficulties mask a wider vibrancy in many countries in the continent. Although one of Africa's biggest challenges is to overcome the deeply entrenched perceptions, some striking shifts can be observed among investors, according to a recent report by the *Economist Intelligence Unit*. The key findings of the report are:[29]

1. Institutional investors see Africa as holding the greatest overall investment potential of all frontier markets globally. When asked to choose two regions out of five, two-thirds (66 %) of investors with an interest in frontier markets see African frontier markets holding the greatest opportunity. This puts the continent ahead of frontier Asian markets (selected by 44 %) and Latin American ones (29 %).
2. Many economic forecasters predict that the region's growth rate will outstrip all others in the coming 5 years.
3. Institutional investors plan to increase their asset allocation in African markets over the coming 5 years.
4. Investors are moving towards longer-term investment strategies for Africa, rather than more speculative, short-term bets with nearly two-thirds (64 %) of investors agreeing that market volatility, partly due to limited liquidity, now requires a longer-term investment approach.
5. Africa's emerging middle class is catching investors' eyes, ahead of commodities and natural resources. Four in ten investors (39 %), when asked to choose the top 3 out of 12 features, selected this as the most attractive aspect of investing in African frontier markets, ahead of high commodity prices (34 %) or high growth rates (35 %).
6. Investors now worry more about technical concerns than about macroeconomic and political risks, at least in key markets. Investors were asked to choose up to three main concerns out of a list of 15 challenges of investing in African frontier markets. Although bribery and corruption is still the headline worry for investors (selected by 41 %), this is immediately followed by concerns about weak institutions (40 %) and illiquidity in capital markets (36 %) in a clear reflection of the steady political and economic stability of many key markets in the continent over the past decade.[30] However, this does not deny the fact that overall, bribery and corruption remain investors' main worry, according to a survey *by Economist Intelligence Unit.*[31] Although it is widely recognised that improvements are being made on this front, it is also acknowledged that this is where Africa's perception problem is greatest. Yet, another survey puts corruption at the third place.[32] It important to emphasise here corruption is hardly unique to Africa. It is similarly rife in other emerging markets. At same time it should be noted that there's a perception gap. Regarding corruption, the reality is perhaps different and some frontier markets are sometimes less corrupt than some well-known

> developed markets. More interestingly, according to the above survey concerns about corruption are twice as high among investors with no current exposure to African markets compared to investors with current exposure (64 % compared to 33 %).[33]

Based on the above and in order to change decades, if not centuries, of negative perception and bad reporting, there is a need to rebrand the continent. Rebranding Africa is a necessity in order to improve the way in which Africa, its companies, and products are perceived both locally and internationally. By definition, a brand is a guarantee of quality and consistency, and this is what must be taken into consideration when trying to rebrand Africa. From a macro perspective, it is central to ensure consistency on continental, regional, and national level. African governments need to make rebranding Africa a priority, and in collaboration, they must set out a clear framework detailing how this will be achieved. This framework needs to be populated by positive and real stories. The process could be multidimensional by rebranding each country, enforcing regional integration, rebranding regional blocs, and then, rebranding the continent as a whole. In changing the perception of a country, a holistic approach needs to be adopted, combining visionary leadership, political will, an ethos of dignity and pride, and a reestablishment of national cultural values.[34]

Governments need to make branding Africa a priority not only externally, but also for its own population. As Africa's brain-drain is a real concern for the growth of the continent, ideologies need to change and national pride must be encouraged. The media can play a central role in disseminating the image of a rebranded continent. However, the primary goal of the media is to be honest about the issues facing Africa and should never lose its main function of monitoring governments and calling them to account. But African journalists need to tell their own stories to the world as currently most stories about Africa are told by foreign media. Being positive about Africa does not mean hiding bad news. Journalists should both expose ills and portray the good of the continent.[35]

The UN estimates that Africa requires a 7 % growth rate per annum in order to eliminate poverty, but not many African countries have been able to sustain this rate. African countries should be mindful that they are competing for investments with other regions worldwide, and hence, it is essential that they adopt and perform well on some of key metrics that investors look at when they decide whether to invest in a country. The first metric is the Transparency International Index. It is important that this metric is addressed whether a country is truly corrupt or is simply perceived to be so, as this index matters to investors and many rely on it. The next metric is the World Economic Forum Competitiveness Index. The third metric is credit rating, and despite some of its inherent imperfections, plays an important factor in attracting investors and fund. Another metric is The Ibrahim Index of African Governance, which is funded and led by an African institution. The final metric is a country's ranking in the World Bank's "Doing Business" report. It should be noted that accuracy and reliability of these metric and index should not be taken for guaranteed, but at the same time, disregarding them will also have negative consequences. The performance of Rwanda, despite its going through genocide 15 years ago, is now ranked as the most improved in the 2010 report globally. This is a jump of approximately 60 places. Thus, according the World Bank's Doing Business report 2010, for the first time since *Doing Business* started tracking reforms, a Sub-Saharan African economy, Rwanda, led the world in reforms.[36] The lesson to learn from Rwanda is that clear thinking and clear policies are needed in order to attract investors. At the same time, it is not enough for a country to take the right steps on its own, as a neighbouring country's mismanagement of their economy will affect the rest of the countries around it. There is, thus, a need for greater regional integration.[37] In its 2012 report, efforts made by African countries are well recognised by the World Bank Doing Business Report although a lot still needs to be done. These efforts include, among others, changing regulatory environment to make it easier for domestic firms to start up and operate.[38]

*Doing Business* 2015 highlighted that 39 of the 47 countries in Sub-Saharan Africa covered in the report implemented one or more regulatory reforms, making it easier to do business. Moreover, of the 230 business reforms documented worldwide, countries in Sub-Saharan Africa were responsible for the largest share. The report also highlighted the performance of the 10 most-improved countries worldwide, whereby five of these countries are in Sub-Saharan Africa.[39]

Towards implementing Islamic finance in Africa, the issue of perception and misconception is not limited to the case of Africa and its suitability for investment. There is also a need to dispel some of the misconceptions that Islamic finance is about the implementation of Sharī'ah or the alleged link between the industry and terrorism. In fact, many in the continent have not been exposed to the idea of Islamic finance and some are opposing the industry based on the unjustified fear of the unknown. This can be illustrated by a decision by The Reserve Bank of Malawi in 2011 that it will not approve the opening of any Islamic banks in the country because the banking act and constitution does not allow Sharī'ah law.

The main concerns for the rejection are also attributed to fears of Islamic banking being exploited to structure accounts concealing illegal activities or money laundering.[40] However, a paper titled "A Case for Islamic Banking in Malawi" argues that Islamic banking and finance run in accordance with the law of the land. It is argued that the introduction of Islamic finance could neither be seen to be at odds with the secular principles enshrined in the constitution, nor as a means to support or promote a particular religion. It is within the definition of the term "banking," as defined in the Banking Act. The definition has three essential features: acceptance of deposits from the public; the use of money so accepted for lending or investment, and; liberty to the depositor to withdraw the money.[41] The decision comes at the time when the absence of Islamic banking in the country's financial system is considered by some observers as causing Malawi to lose potential FDI from the Islamic world. Moreover, Islamic banking can also encourage the current Muslim businessmen to be involved in Islamic finance, thereby developing their business at a much faster rate.

With regard to terrorism, it should be clear to sceptics, as articulated by Zaid Ibrahim & Co., that Sharī'ah prohibits the use of violence against innocent victims and considers it a crime, and hence, categorically, condemns terrorism. This means that, as a matter of principle, an Islamic financial institution is strictly prohibited from assisting, those involved in terror-related activities.[42]

Post 9/11 has made anything anti-Islamic fashionable and profitable. International politics have seen prejudice and animosity against Islam escalating to new heights. Islamic finance has been unfairly brandished by certain quarters as a front for terrorism finance. While the complex and opaque nature of international finance may expose even Islamic financial institutions to unwarily become a tool for those with criminal intent. Despite all conspiracy theories and long-winded connections raised to link Islamic finance with terrorism, there is hardly evidence to justify such allegations. Various lawsuits and sanctions have been initiated against some financial institutions and key Islamic finance figures for alleged involvement with terror activities, but most have been struck out. Irrational phobia against Islam in general, and Islamic finance in particular, continues long after 9/11, with the US Treasury recently also getting entangled in a lawsuit when a Gulf war veteran challenged in court the validity of its action to bailout AIG during the global financial crisis, simply because AIG was involved in an Islamic insurance (Takāful) business.[43]

The reality is, Islamic financial institutions, just like other financial institutions in any jurisdictions, are subject to and bound by strict laws and regulations, including anti-terrorism and anti-money laundering laws. If there is any proof that any Islamic financial institutions are involved in or supporting terror activities, the due process of the law shall be allowed to take its course in order to ensure the respective culprits are brought to justice.[44] This conclusion has also been reached by the IMF noting that Islamic banks are just responding to the needs of Muslim customers; they are not religious institutions. Like conventional banks, they are profit-maximising entities. They act as intermediaries between savers and investors and offer custodial and other services practised by traditional banks.[45]

Besides the issue of perception, we have numerous other challenges that need to be addressed, as mentioned at the beginning of this chapter. Of paramount importance are those challenges facing Africa and the sustainability of its economic growth.

## African Economic Challenges

To capitalise on the many, albeit diverse opportunities that exist in Africa, it is necessary to first explore the challenges that face Africa, both from the people and the business perspectives. Yet, as is rightly stressed by the World Bank, "the key challenge for the continent is how to turn the ongoing recovery into strong, sustained, and shared growth that will lead to notable improvements in people's lives."[46] Similarly, it has been rightly concluded by *the Economist Intelligence Unit* that, "To a large extent, the growth story is now widely known; the new questions concern the pattern, quality and sustainability of that growth."[47] While for others, the question is not whether you should be doing business in Africa, but rather, how?[48] Among the many areas that require close attention from African leaders in order to sustain the current growth are the following:

1. Attracting FDI into diversified and higher value-added sectors remains the ongoing challenge for Africa's economies. The primary sector consistently remains the main focus of foreign investment. Africa predominantly exports primary products and imports manu-

factured products. This has an adverse effect and has led to large-scale commodity dependence. Importantly, the exporting of primary products such as mineral resources tends to concentrate the gains in the hands of a wealthy few and is not the suitable means of contributing towards poverty alleviation as unequal income distribution remains one of Africa's biggest challenges. This hampers the possibility of growth in consumer expenditure and related parts of the economy, such as retail and wholesale, smaller manufacturing industries, the housing market, and so on. Commodity dependence has another downside, given the fact that it does not lead to the development of productive capacity. Short-term gains are taken at the expense of long-term strategies, which should benefit all.[49]

2. Increasing trade with the rest of the world and intra-African trade through the diversification of trade, both in terms of structure and destination.[50] The World Bank recently stressed that regional integration is necessary to address the issues of the small economic size of many countries and the often arbitrarily drawn borders that pay little heed to the distribution of natural endowments. Such regional trade will allow Africa to achieve its potential in terms of regional trade. Regional trade integration has long been a strategic objective for Africa. However, the market remains highly fragmented. While there has been some success in terms of removing import duties within regional communities, a range of non-tariff and regulatory barriers still raise transaction costs and limit the movement of goods, services, people, and capital across borders. The end result is that Africa has integrated with the rest of the world faster than with itself.[51]

The key findings of the study are:

- The African market remains highly fragmented, preventing enormous opportunities for cross-border trade from being exploited, and in turn, generating new jobs.
- Effective regional integration is more than simply removing tariffs. It is about addressing the barriers that undermine the daily operations of ordinary producers and traders of both goods and services.
- The incidence of barriers to regional trade fall most heavily, and disproportionately, on the poor and on women, and is preventing

them from earning a living in activities where they have a comparative advantage—catering for smaller, local markets across the border.
- Action is required at both the supra-national and national levels. Regional communities can provide the framework for reform but responsibility for implementation lies with each member country.[52]

A related challenge is the lack of a coherent regional approach to managing and harnessing partnership agreements, which could improve the competitiveness of the countries within Africa and drive FDI. On the back of the need for combined and coherent strategies, it is crucial that there is a greater degree of cooperation between the private sector and the governments.[53]

3. Reducing inefficiencies related to poor transport infrastructure, including the maintenance of the existing infrastructure and the provision of new infrastructure. For instance, only 29.7 % of the African road network is paved. The continent's railway network is also very poor. These factors contribute to high transport costs on the continent, compared to the rest of world.[54] A major challenge confronting the development of African infrastructure is the lack of adequate financing. Recent estimates by the World Bank indicate that annual infrastructure investment requirement in Africa is about US$93 billion over the next decade, more than double the previous estimate by the Commission for Africa.[55] One measure towards addressing this problem is tying exploitation of natural resources to infrastructure development. Fortunately, thing are moving in the right direction in this area. By 2010, around one-quarter of natural resource contracts in Africa had been tied to an "infrastructure industrialisation component," up from 1 % in the 1990s, according to a report by McKinsey & Company.[56]
4. Another complicated challenge is the lack of bargaining power in multilateral negotiations. It is critical that Africa comes together as one bargaining power so as to promote an agenda that will harness the capabilities and resources of the African continent to the benefit of all Africans. It is a reality that each country has its unique political, humanitarian, and economic requirements; however, a minimum degree of cooperation is a must.[57]
5. Like other petroleum-rich countries, African countries relying on oil face acute challenges in maintaining political momentum for

reforms, resisting the temptation to overinvest (particularly in the resource sector), and maintaining political stability—in order to avoid the "oil curse" that has afflicted other oil exporters around the world.[58]

6. There is substantial evidence that reducing political instability and improving security within and among several regions through peaceful resolution of conflicts in Africa is a fundamental prerequisite for sustainable economic development and growth. Africa remains home to a number of significant conflicts. These conflicts impart considerable costs on the countries concerned as well as their neighbours. Furthermore, there are many fragile states, and the possibility of new conflicts is real. The causes of conflicts in Africa include ethnic distrust, religious discrimination and intolerance, corruption, injustice, and poor governance. External powers might intervene in the politics of the African countries where they wish to influence the governments considered to be geopolitically strategic or sensitive to their own interests. The ultimate resolution of conflicts in Africa requires political leadership that skilfully adopts formulas that suit the peculiar conditions of these African states. Africa will need creative leadership that sees beyond "winner takes all," and instead, designs accommodative arrangements to include representations of all tribes and religions. African conflicts may not be solved by focusing on the correctness of electoral procedures alone. It may be even more critical to ensure that the design of the constitution assures an acceptable representation of all groups in all the structures of government. The resolution of conflicts and the establishment of a harmonious coexistence among Africans require, as elsewhere, the irrevocable and certain assurance of economic and political justice for all.[59] Foreign intervention—in particular, military intervention—shall be opposed by all means. African leaders need to be stand strongly behind the notion of African solutions to African problems. Unfortunately, the recent crisis in Libya has exposed the hollowness of the AU being an African solution to Africa's problems, according to some observers.
7. Besides working to ensure political stability, African governments have a challenging task in clamping down on corruption in order to create an environment conducive for business. Rules and regulations have to be implemented and have to be consistent, predictable, transparent, and communicated effectively so that everyone knows

what needs to be done. Bureaucracy needs to be minimised. Corruption has to be curbed by enforcing punishment. Although these milestones are well known, it is also crucial to understand how to sustain and manage such reforms in the long term. Pointing out to the dear consequences of corruption on Africa, Global Financial Integrity, a Washington-based NGO, estimates that US$358 billion flowed out of Africa through corruption, trade mispricing, and other illicit activities between 2000 and 2008.[60] Estimating these figures for the period extending between 1970 and 2008, the study reveals that the 39-year period from 1970 through 2008 estimated that such flows have totalled US$854 billion across the period examined. Yet, this estimate is conservative, as it addresses only one form of trade mispricing. The study maintained that if we adjust the US$854 billion estimate and take into account some of the other components of illicit flows not covered, it is not unreasonable to estimate total illicit outflows from the continent across the 39 years at some US$1.8 trillion.[61]

Some observers consider the issue of corruption as one of three issues that investors take into consideration from a business perspective, before deciding to invest in a country. These are the sustainability of rules, the types of resources a government offers to the private sector, and the prevailing problem of corruption. However, as highlighted by *The Guardian*, although Africa has been affected by corruption, corruption is not African syndrome. Many Western oil companies have used slush funds to bribe officials in developing countries.[62]

Therefore, transparency and fairness in the way these extraction deals are conducted are vital. The amendment to the landmark Dodd-Frank finance reform bill is a welcomed initiative. The Cardin-Lugar amendment is an attempt to force real transparency in the extractive industries and in the exploitation of minerals. It makes it legally binding for all companies registered on the New York Stock Exchange to reveal the details of their extraction deals with African countries. In turn, this empowers civic societies with the information they need to hold their governments to account. Sudanese entrepreneur Mo Ibrahim, as reported by *The Guardian*, said that the Cardin-Lugar amendment is more important to Africa than the debt relief of the last decade. Thus, major economic giants benefiting from Africa resources are exhorted to call for similar initiatives.[63] Although different surveys have given corruption different degree as a barrier to investment, the overall conclusion is that it is one of the primary concerns, and therefore, needs to be addressed adequately.

African countries need to acquire credit ratings to attract more investors. However, the high cost that major credit rating agencies ask for and the lack of appreciation of the benefits of ratings are some of the reasons why some African countries are reluctant to pursue obtaining credit ratings. The financial discipline that a credit rating brings to the financial system, given the reluctance of many Africans to carry out some of the needed reform, is another reason. Seeking credit ratings would help unlocking funding from the international and domestic markets to finance their development needs.[64]

8. Another prerequisite for sustainable growth is providing good education for the people. There is little disagreement amongst development economists that investments in human capital—specifically, education and health—are crucial for social and economic development of nations. It is widely accepted that nations cannot raise the quality of life of their citizens without substantial and consistent investments in human capital. When education is lacking, then employment opportunities are not being created fast enough, leaving little optimism for graduates. The question concerning educational services is very much a chicken and egg situation. Does improving education result in improved economies, or do successful economies result in improvements in education?[65] Even though African countries have spent relatively large proportions of their national resources on education, the stock of human capital with higher education academic qualifications in Africa continues to be very low, by international standards. The areas of higher education undertaken by a majority of African students are not in fields such as science, engineering, technology, and business, as is the case in rapidly growing emerging economies of South Korea and China, but often, in social sciences and humanities. The result is a skill mismatch—university graduates remain unemployed, while African countries continue to face shortages of skilled labour.[66] For instance, while about 50 % or more of students in tertiary educational institutions in countries such as Korea, China, and Taiwan are enrolled in science, engineering, technology (SET) and business, only about 20 % of tertiary education students in Africa are enrolled in these subjects.[67] Education is a major challenge, so educating Africa's

young has to be one of the highest priorities for public policy across the continent.[68] Africa has to learn from the best practices of nations that have succeeded. Using Asia as an example, we have to see how investing in education, and more specifically, in science and technology, has facilitated development.

It is important to emphasise here that for several decades, African governments and donor institutions have placed great emphasis on primary and secondary education, but have neglected tertiary education as an added means to improve economic growth and mitigate poverty. For example, from 1985 to 1989, 17 % of the World Bank's worldwide education sector spending was on higher education. But from 1995 to 1999, the proportion allotted to higher education declined to just 7 %. Higher education in Africa has suffered from such reductions in spending. As a result enrolment rates for higher education in Sub-Saharan Africa, in particular, are by far the lowest in the world, based on the assumption that primary and secondary schooling are more important than tertiary education for poverty reduction.

However, several studies recently challenged the proposition that tertiary education has little role in promoting poverty alleviation. It has been upheld that higher education can produce both public and private benefits. The private benefits for individuals are well established, and include better employment prospects, higher salaries, and a greater ability to save and invest. These benefits may result in better health and improved quality of life. One possible channel through which higher education can enhance economic development is through technological catch-up, whereby tertiary education can help economies gain ground on more technologically advanced societies, as graduates are likely to be more aware of and better able to use new technologies.[69]

The neglect of tertiary education in Africa has impacted on other dimensions of human development. For example, to provide quality primary and secondary education, it is necessary that institutions of higher learning produce well-trained teachers and in sufficient quantities. Likewise, qualified nurses and medical personnel are required to provide basic healthcare. But these professionals are in short supply in Africa such that it is not possible to provide quality education and basic healthcare to most of the population. For Africa to achieve and sustain high rates of growth, it is necessary for major transformations in the structure of production as well as education in technological gap to take place and these require a large pool of labour force with tertiary education.

While primary school education is absolutely critical and establishes the necessary foundation for higher levels of education, evidence now shows that the neglect of higher education in Africa is costing the continent dearly in terms of economic growth. Primary and secondary educations are not sufficient to meet the challenges of the economies in a globalised world. For these reasons, higher education must be considered a pivotal issue in development.

Moreover, as the continent faces considerable levels of brain drain, investments in higher education will help to retain those students and encourage them to apply their talents domestically rather than abroad. Meanwhile, if higher education investment is not given the priority it deserves, African education systems are likely to witness increased levels of deterioration.[70]

9. Another problem facing the continent is that of Africa's brain-drain. The lack of patriotism and an apathy about political processes means that Africa's potential leaders are choosing not to stay in the continent. To counter this, the "push factor" needs to be reduced to retain talent. In particular, there is a need for changing the negative image of Africa within and outside the continent.[71]
10. On research and development, Africa needs to develop its own technology and value-added products. Currently, there is no financial institution in Africa that is willing to underwrite research and development since it is a long-term and high-risk venture.[72]
11. Regulations and procedures of international standards are prerequisites for any real move to attract investment into the continent. The IFC and the World Bank upheld that if the best of East African regulations and procedures were implemented across the board, the business regulatory environment in East Africa, as measured by the report, would be comparable to that in Japan. In the past 5 years, all East African Community economies have made it easier to do business. The average ranking for those countries is 117 out of 183 economies overall in *Doing Business* 2011. Kenya has some of the most business-friendly regulations for dealing with construction permits. Ugandan courts resolve insolvency relatively efficiently and Rwanda is among the easiest places to start a business. If each East African countries were to adopt the region's best practice for each *Doing Business* indicator, East Africa would rank 18, bringing the community closer to the global top performers.[73] Yet,

many African leaders are still dragging their feet, as is pointed out by Dambisa Moyo, a Zambian economist that "Although it takes just 3 days to register and open a business in Rwanda, for example, that compares with 213 for Guinea."[74] It is imperative that as part of the regulations and procedures, there is a need for an arbitration and dispute settlement framework of international standard to be in place to ensure a fair system and protection with low transaction costs.

The recent interest in Africa, whether by the emerging economies or with the developed one, is opening up opportunities for Africa to diversify its trading partners in new markets and to forge new mutually beneficial partnerships and comes with major challenges. This interest is not solely based on an altruistic goal to improve the economic well-being of Africans. Everyone is trying to maximise their own strategic economic and political interests, and therefore, African policymakers must also be strategic in dealing with all these new partners.[75] A particular issue that needs careful attention and management from African policymakers is natural resource exploitation contracts. There are real concerns over the lack of transparency in the signing of these contracts Therefore, African nations must invest in the contracting process and African policymakers must push for more transparency in the contracting process. Similarly, while such aid is helping Africa narrow the infrastructure gap, it is important that this aid not be used as a way to endow monopoly rights for the BRICs in the exploitation of Africa's natural resources or to hold African countries hostage to future contracts related to new projects and maintenance.[76] As rightly pointed out by *the Economist*, foreign investors should abide the Extractive Industries Transparency Initiative and African governments should insist on total openness in the deals they strike with foreign companies and governments.[77]

Despite the general improvement in business conditions achieved in the last decade, many African countries remain among the world's most challenging environments in which to do business.[78] As such, Africa needs to double its effort in making it easier to do business in the continent. A number of initiatives can be taken in that direction, such as making it easier to start businesses, cutting some taxes and truthfully collecting the ones they impose. Moreover, there is a need for land ownership reform to facilitate getting credit, and more importantly, politicians need to abide by democratic rules and power transfer.[79]

Besides the growing business relation and trade between Africa and the BRIC countries, it is very important that Western governments also open up to trade with the continent rather than just giving aid. For the USA, the America's African Growth and Opportunity Act is a good start, but it needs to be widened and copied by other nations.[80]

## Islamic Finance Challenges: Africa's Peculiarities

1. There is a need for supervisory authorities to ensure that the Islamic financial system is fully integrated with the rest of the financial system. The integration process does not only entail allowing Islamic institutions to operate, but also, providing a comprehensive legal and regulatory framework, as well as developing a supportive financial infrastructure. African countries could benefit from the experiences of other countries that have already made the necessary changes.
2. Understanding the different types of risks associated with Islamic finance with particular reference to local environment is another challenge. There is a need to design the appropriate risk mitigation and consumer protection frameworks.
3. The need for developing an institutional Islamic financial system of corporate governance that comprises dedicated management, committed board committee, and well-versed Sharī'ah supervisory committee, which are all consistent and in line with international corporate governance standards and practices. In this area, Islamic financial institutions are invited to work closely with the Islamic finance support institutions, such as the Islamic Financial Services Board (IFSB) and the Accounting and Auditing Organisation for Islamic Financial Institutions (AAOIFI).
4. The requirement for institutions that plan to offer Islamic products is to develop Sharī'ah-compliant products which are acceptable within the legal and regulatory framework of the country, starting, for instance, with Sharī'ah-compliant products having close economic outcome to that of conventional services such as *murābaḥah*, *istisnā*, *salam*, and *Ijārah*.
5. To review and assess the existing infrastructures such as deposit insurance schemes, government securities, inter-bank money market and the function of central banks as lender of last resort, to see whether they fit well with in the Islamic finance framework or require some necessary changes and amendments.

6. In case a country has opted for the existence of Islamic and conventional financial institutions working side by side—as it is expected to be the suitable choice at this stage in most African countries—there is a need to establish an appropriate legal, institutional, and regulatory framework that allows the two systems to interface and benefit from complementing and supplementing each other.[81]
7. Regulators in some African countries have concerns about the prudential returns and disclosure report formats. This is based on the fact that these formats were basically tailored for institutions that have the element of interest in their financial system. Therefore, regulators in these countries are obliged to be creative to tailor returns and disclosures formats that cater to the Islamic finance market.
8. There is a need to clear the misconception regarding Islamic banking, particularly in countries where Muslims are minorities or have some religious tension. Customers need to be informed that Islamic financial institutions are not religious institutions. They are profit-maximising intermediaries between savers and investors and offering other traditional banking services, but on Sharī'ah-compliant basis. The future of Islamic finance in Africa should not be confined to the Muslim community. Counties with Muslim minority can still benefit from this type of financing. Islamic banks could set up operations in those parts of Africa where the model of banking has proven to be attractive for ethical reasons.[82]
9. As elaborated earlier, the Banking Acts in many countries prohibit wholesale trading and restrict holding land and buildings while in a Sharī'ah-compliant financing, always there is an element of trading and owning of assets such as land and building. This challenge has been addressed in some countries through the mechanism of granting exemptions to Islamic financial institutions upon request. Here again, African countries can benefit from the experience of other countries in this regard.
10. Closely related to the above is the need to work towards a better mortgage legislation and documentation for the development of available financial system, whether it is Sharī'ah-compliant or conventional.
11. The conventional banking legal system in these countries requires all banks to pay interest on savings accounts as long as the minimum balance is maintained. This challenge has been addressed in

some countries by incorporating in the Banking Act the leeway for banks to give some form of return for Sharī'ah-compliant savings products.

12. Bankers and their legal advisers in the countries adopting Islamic finance would need to develop a thorough understanding of Islamic law to ensure that the financial products they offer meet full regulatory requirements and are Sharī'ah-compliant at the same time.
13. Sharī'ah advisors who will be advising the new institutions should be able to combine their in-depth knowledge of Islamic law with particular emphasis on the modern practice of Islamic finance principles, combined with a familiarity with conventional financial and economic concepts and the local legal requirements. Therefore, there is a need to develop the know-how to meet the required pool of experts in the field. Issuers of Islamic financial products, on their part, have a role to play in creating awareness, and in educating the public on the merits of Islamic finance. There is a need for a closer cooperation between local Sharī'ah scholars and the renowned Sharī'ah scholars worldwide, especially those associated with organisations such as the AAOIFI or the Islamic Fiqh Academy, for a smooth success of Islamic finance in these countries. This particular key governance concern was highlighted by The Bank of Zambia Governor, saying that "In this regard, there will be need to work with various interest groups in identifying such resources locally."[83]

Islamic finance in Africa also faces the challenge of tax. The tax issue is not limited to Africa. It is a general concern. Ignoring potential tax issues is not an option. A change in the tax statutes will almost certainly be necessary, and the tax authority needs to devise and publish policies in this issue in order to give certainty to financiers and customers alike. Without such a change, it is unlikely that Islamic finance will be able to flourish in these countries. An African government introducing Islamic finance will need to consider several issues in determining the nature of its tax regime, including whether it wishes for Islamic finance to be taxed in an identical way to non-Islamic finance, or wishes to legislate on a structure-by-structure basis or explicitly introduce Sharī'ah concepts into the statutes. While African governments need to be aware of the challenges and time involved in introducing an Islamic finance tax regime, the experiences of other countries that have already amended their legislation provide an invaluable precedent.[84] The South African government, for instance, has recently confirmed that it is in the process of introducing tax neutrality laws for *mudārabah* (trust financing), *murābaḥah* (cost-plus financing), and diminishing *mushārakah* (diminishing shared ownership) contracts. The proposed tax neutrality measures are just the start and the wider objective to introduce a comprehensive regulatory and legal framework to facilitate Islamic finance in the country, both for financial inclusion and market liberalisation and development reasons. The development of Islamic finance in South Africa is critical to the expansion of the National Treasury's strategy to position South Africa as a gateway into Africa. The treasury envisages South Africa as being a central hub for Islamic product development and ensuring the rollout of such products into African markets.[85] This ambition is also based on the country's ideal location for multinationals to base their regional operation for investments into Sub-Saharan Africa due to its world-class financial services, strong and clear financial regulatory architecture, and good infrastructure. The proposed amendments will remove various tax hurdles. The proposed amendments will also level the playing field in respect to certain Islamic financial products when undertaking savings and investments.[86] The proposed amendments seek to place *mudārabah*, *murābaḥah*, and diminishing *mushārakah* on an equal tax footing with conventional finance products.[87] There are also further proposed amendments relating to diminishing *mushārakah*, which is commonly used in Islamic home financing or mortgage products. The amendments propose the abolition of the double stamp duty (property transfer tax), which is implicit in the Islamic contract because it involves the transfer of title at the front and back end of the scheme. In the UK, for instance, HM Treasury has done away with the double tax stamp duty on the basis that the net economic effect of the diminishing *mushārakah* is similar to that of a conventional mortgage, albeit the Islamic scheme involves two transfer contracts, and as such, would be unfair to punish the Islamic contract with a double tax. Thus, the need for reform in the tax regime is a necessity in order to attract investment, whether in the form of Islamic finance or others.[88] The tax issue is not peculiar to Africa as it represents a challenging situation in many other jurisdictions. Referring to the issue, KPMG pointed out that Although there have been significant progress in the taxation of Islamic products, however, further reform is required to enable Islamic institutions to compete on a level playing field with non- Sharī'ah compliant institutions.[89]

The advisory firm articulated that one of the major challenges facing the industry internationally is that tax laws generally cater to conventional banking products while many Islamic products are structured to replicate the economic effects of conventional products. The legal form of these products is very different from conventional products. This may lead to differences in tax treatment that may potentially place Islamic banks and their customers at a disadvantage compared to banks with conventional products. The issue has also been highlighted by the World Bank noting that regulators need to provide a level playing field for Islamic transactions, such as financial sector regulation and tax code, as Islamic financing products have tax implications, which are not present in conventional deals.[90]

The main reason for the legal form of Islamic products being different from conventional products stems from the need for compliance with Sharī'ah, which is generally expressed in the prohibition on interest (*ribā*) and the principle that money, in itself, is not regarded as an asset that can generate a return by itself. Consequently, Islamic finance generally has to be asset-backed or asset-based, such as finance being provided, based on the need to purchase a tangible asset. Loans can only be interest-free. The sharing of risk between the contracting parties is encouraged.

Most African countries do not have specific tax legislation related to Islamic banking products. There is a need to place Islamic banking products on an equal footing with conventional one and legislations should be drafted to treat certain Islamic banking products on a similar basis as conventional products.[91] African countries could also benefit from the efforts of many countries around the world on how to accommodate Islamic finance into the local tax system. It is worth noting that Senegal *ṣukūk*, for instance, were exempted from any tax. This is not the result of any specific regulatory framework applicable to Islamic finance, but based on existing financial legislation applicable to investment vehicles. Thus, it is believed that other countries in WAEMU are likely to use the same framework should they plan to issue *ṣukūk*. This will be another encouragement factor for *ṣukūk* investors and would support cross-border financing.[92]

14. Dearth of skilled and experienced personnel in Islamic banking to regulate, supervise, or operate Islamic finance industry. This is a problem that will act against the speedy and smooth emergence of Islamic banks in many African countries. The current generation of bank personnel will have to acquire many new skills and learn new procedures necessary to effectively conduct Islamic banking. Even if a bank is not an Islamic bank, its management staff will still have

to be familiar with Islamic banking techniques to effectively operate alongside Islamic banks in the industry. This challenge will require a short-term solution through the training of existing staff, but also a long-term efficient programme through the formation of new graduates with thorough Islamic banking knowledge in close collaboration with local and international universities.

## General Challenges Facing the Islamic Finance Industry

In their quest to adopt and implement Islamic finance in their respective countries, African regulators and financial policymakers need to have a clear understanding of the challenges facing the global Islamic finance industry. Among the challenges facing the global Islamic finance industry are:

1. Lack of Sharī'ah-compliant liquidity management instruments. This is a problem that still exists even in countries having long experience in Islamic finance. African countries are required to benefit from the experience of others and build on it.
2. Standardisation is another challenge facing the Islamic finance industry. Referring to the issue, Ernest &Young points out that, "the overall lack of standardisation in Islamic finance means that individual instruments often need to be structured in a piecemeal fashion, which makes them more costly at the outset."[93] To address the standardisation challenges at a global level, it would be unthinkable for the industry to face it alone. As rightly observed by KPMG, multilateral institutions such as the International Monetary Fund, the World Bank, or the Basel Committee of the Bank of International Settlements should be involved so that the Islamic finance industry is not excluded from best practice and universal prudential and supervision standards.[94] At the same time, although concerns over the lack of standardisation may be justified to some extent in view of the relatively short life of the Islamic finance industry, the issue is sometimes blown out of proportion and over-exaggerated. The reality is that the majority of the products and services offered by Islamic financial institutions are already available around the world with

pretty much a standard approach of how things are done. To be fair to Islamic finance, it is wise to acknowledge that conventional banking practices are also not entirely standardised across the globe either. Variations and divergence still exist from one country to another[95]

3. The rapid growth of Islamic finance and its expansion through different jurisdictions has increased the urgency to improve exit rules in the event of default, insolvency, and the need for restructuring and reorganisation. There is also a need to establish reliable mechanisms for dealing with cases defaults, as well as transparent frameworks to address adverse outcomes, with special adaptations for risk sharing. Setting up these mechanisms requires the specification of parties' rights under Sharī'ah-compliant finance, especially in the case of cross-border transactions. More work is needed to ensure convergence between best insolvency practices on the conventional and Sharī'ah-compliant sides.[96]
4. The Islamic financial market is still characterised by local dimensions. In order to be competitive, there is a need to enhance the international aspect. As articulated by Hussain Al Qemzi, CEO of Noor Islamic Bank, "If we are to challenge the conventional banks' entrenched position in international financial deals, we must develop the capacity to structure multi-currency and cross-border transactions and to build scale. To do that we need to build deeper relationships between the key markets and between individual banks, so that we are better placed to compete on a global scale." He adds, "The time has come for us to stop focusing on our differences as reasons for not doing business. It is time to talk about how Islamic finance can contribute to long-term inclusive, equitable and sustainable economic growth not just in Muslim countries, but in every country across the globe."[97]

## Overcoming Challenges Through Cooperation with Multinational Partners

In their endeavour to promote Islamic finance in Africa, Islamic finance players can also strengthen their position by working closely with some of the multinational financial institutions already active in Africa and working in different development projects. More importantly, these institutions, based on past experiences, are open to any cooperation with Islamic financial institutions. They include the Islamic Development Bank, the World Bank, in particular, through its private sector arm, the International Finance Corporation (IFC), the International Monetary Fund (IMF), and the African Development Bank (AfDB). All these institutions are exposed to Islamic finance, with varying degree, as an option in their dealings with Muslim countries, and have already resulted in the launching of Islamic financing mechanisms to finance their activities.

Apart from the financial help in terms of investment and assistance, these development partners can also provide a range of assistance to help African governments, financial institutions, and markets participants to overcome some of the barriers and obstacles and expand financial services in a productive fashion. Support from development partners can take various forms, including, but not limited to, assisting governments to amend legislation or ineffective policies and regulations that needs to be updated, providing capacity building to regulatory institutions to implement those changes, and to oversee financial institutions, and directly assisting private institutions to improve their practice.[98] Apart from regulation and supervision, these multilateral agencies can provide advisory assistance to help banks establish stronger risk management systems and improve their corporate governance to ensure that the interests of all stakeholders are served.[99]

Pointing to the role of multilateral development institutions in Islamic finance, a managing director at the World Bank asserted that his institution, besides other multilateral development institutions, has longstanding programmes to support the Islamic finance industry and has already used Islamic instruments to finance their finance and development projects. It is believed that Islamic finance could help meeting the choice of many people, enhancing financial inclusion and contributing towards financial stability and development.[100]

## Cooperation with the Islamic Development Bank (IDB)

The Islamic Development Bank is the primary institution working towards the advancement of Islamic finance globally. It is also working very hard towards economic development and poverty eradication in its member states. Half of its member countries are in Africa. As such, many strongly believe that the IDB could be playing a leading role in the promotion and advancement of Islamic banking and finance in Africa. To fulfil the above objectives, the IDB has already launched several development programmes for Africa. The multilateral institution has financed 1321 projects in Sub-Saharan Africa totalling US$7.499 billion. It is worth noting that the IDB financed its first project after inception in Africa in 1976 with a US$7 million financing facility towards the Song-Loulou Hydroelectric power project in Cameroon.[101]

A number of ambitious and promising projects were mooted by the IDB. Most of these plans are already in the implementation stage. The following are some of these programmes:

1. The IDB launched a few years ago the Ouagadougou Declaration, signed in Burkino Faso during the IDB board of governors' annual meeting. The Ouagadougou Declaration is a US$2 billion programme directed towards investment in education, primary healthcare, technical assistance, and capacity building. The programme has, in fact, disbursed over US$2.38 billion until 2010 and has been rolled over.[102]
2. Another major programme by the IDB is the Special Programme for the Development of Africa (SPDA). It is expected that the SPDA would, over the 5-year period, generate a total financing volume of US$12 billion. The programme focuses on the following priority areas: (a) increase productivity of agriculture for food security; (b) assist countries to develop and manage water and sanitation projects; (c) support power generation and distribution capacities; (d) support construction and maintenance of transport infrastructure; (e) reinforce the education sector to prepare the youth for the workplace and inculcate ethical attitude and passion for achievement; and (f) fight major communicable diseases and contribute to the strengthening of the health system.[103] At a recent forum on the implementation of the SPDA held in Yaoundé, Cameroon, a mid-term report was presented. African Governors hailed the achievements made under the programme over the past 2 years. During this period, the IDB Group approved financing to the tune of US$1.8 billion for African member countries, which accounts for an implementation rate of 43 % of the total budget of the SDPA.[104]
3. Another programme by the IDB is the Program for Infrastructure in Africa (PIDA), which is specifically targeted to support regional infrastructure integration initiatives.

4. Beside the above programs, there is also the US$10 billion Islamic Solidarity Fund for Development (ISFD), which is an endowment fund to reduce poverty and which targets the Least Developed Countries (LCDs). The programme has so far disbursed US$2.6 billion. The Fund aims to: (a) reduce poverty, (b) build the productive capacities of the OIC member states, (c) reduce illiteracy, and (d) eradicate diseases and epidemics, particularly malaria, tuberculosis (TB) and AIDS. The ISFD was officially launched during the Thirty-second Meeting of the IDB Board of Governors, held during May 29–30, 2007 in Dakar, Senegal.[105]
5. Another program by the IDB is the US$1.5 billion Jeddah Declaration for Food Security, which once again targets LCDs, especially the 21 countries in Africa and is aimed at strengthening food supply by assisting small farmers in acquiring agricultural inputs.[106]
6. The ICD, in particular, has so far managed to mobilise significant resources through strategic partnerships designed to finance ambitious affordable housing projects in both Senegal and Mali. It is hoped that the IDB Group will envisage similar operations in other African countries, given the importance of housing when it comes to improving the living conditions of the people. Similarly, the IDB's initiative aimed at conducting feasibility studies on transport links between member countries. It was hoped that the initiative would materialise in projects such as the Dakar–Port Sudan railway and the Trans-Saharan highway linking North and West Africa.[107]
7. Furthermore, the bank is striving to forge constructive partnership with various donors in order to co-finance projects and other joint ventures in member countries. These include, for example, the signing of co-financing agreements with the International Fund for Agricultural Development (IFAD) and the Food and Agriculture Organisation (FAO) to finance agricultural development projects designed to assist member countries in Africa and Asia.[108]
8. In another move, the Islamic Corporation for the Development of the Private Sector, the private sector funding arm of the IDB Group, has launched a joint venture holding company with Turkey's Asya Participation Bank, called Tamweel Africa SA, whose main aim is to support Islamic financial institutions in Sub-Saharan Africa, especially by extending financing to SMEs. Tamweel Africa, which has a capital of US$50 million and is based in Dakar, Senegal, and which bought the shares of the three former Islamic banks in West Africa

> owned by Dar Al-Maal Al-Islamic (DMI), headed by Prince Muhammed Al-Faisal, started operations in January 2010. ICD holds 60 % of the equity and Asya Participation Bank owns 40 % of the equity, for which it paid US$15 million. It is also reported that Tamweel Africa owns 66 % of Islamic Bank of Niger; 77.5 % of Islamic Bank of Senegal; 100 % of Islamic Bank of Guinea; and 100 % of Islamic Bank of Mauritania. Asya Participation bank is providing the technical expertise, the management system, and the knowledge base for Tamweel Africa.[109]

Although the above efforts are important and diversified, IDB's efforts in developing the Islamic financial sector in Africa are limited and did not cater to the immense opportunities in the continent. Indeed, Tamweel Africa SA is a welcome initiative; however, in order to develop the Islamic financial industry in Africa, the IDB has the moral obligation to come up with some bold initiatives such as having a fund of US$500 million that can constitute part of the seeds capital of at least 30–40 banks in 30–40 African countries. It is not necessary that the full capitalisation of these banks comes from outside. Many wealthy individuals from different African countries can provide the needed capital. However, what is lacking is the expertise and moral and political support. The example of businessmen from Ethiopia who have contributed the full capital for the formation of ZamZam bank, in line with local regulations and which was unfortunately later prevented, is a good example. The IDB can also help in bringing other international players such as the World Bank, the IMF, the African Development Bank, and other development institutions to participate in such initiatives towards financial inclusion. The presence of such multilateral financial institutions is very important for diffusing some of the political, religious, and business concerns.

Another important observation on the IDB programmes is that despite the huge capital and effort deployed, these programmes are not given the needed publicity as the programmes based on Islamic principles. Thus, it is very possible that the IDB has already implemented many projects in specific countries, but nobody is aware that these projects have been implemented in a manner different from that of conventional institutions offering similar programmes. This lack of awareness is not limited to the general public, but even among the official authorities in these countries. It is hoped that future development projects by the IDB are supported by focus seminars on Islamic finance aimed at creating public awareness on the Islamic dimension of the development project financed. Alleviating poverty through development projects is a noble objective by itself, but implementing it through Islamic principles is an additional and equally important objective in its own right. On the contrary, the promotion of Islamic finance in African countries would not take its real shape unless the Islamic Corporation for the Development of the Private Sector has expanded its involvement through partnership with local entrepreneurs in establishing local financial institutions.

## World Bank Support

The World Bank Group's support for Islamic finance cuts across its institutions. Until recently, the Bank does not have a specialised unit, but individuals across the bank work in partnership with Islamic financial institutions on specific deals and issues as they arise for time to time. To build the bank's staff capacity on Islamic banking and finance, there have been a series of lectures on the topic held in the bank's Washington headquarters. Recently, the bank has established an Islamic Finance Working Group within the bank to facilitate knowledge sharing within the institution.

The bank's objectives for engagement in Islamic finance are primarily to have Islamic finance as an additional source of funding to supplement conventional finance to support economic development, poverty eradication, and expand financial inclusion. The bank's contribution is also be in the form of overall financial stability and issues related to regulatory and operational policies through Financial Sector Assessment Programs (FSAPs). The bank also builds partnerships with national authorities, international entities, and other stakeholders.[110] In order to achieve the above objectives, the bank focuses on five key pillars:

1. Capacity building, knowledge management, sharing and dissemination. Thus, the bank works with Central Banks in order to strengthen financial infrastructure and capacity to monitor financial sectors risk as Islamic finance grows. It will also help towards better understanding of risk management and governance issues of Islamic financial institutions towards timely identification of financial sector risks.
2. Advocacy to influence policy direction in market development and regulatory approaches by convening debate on Islamic finance, working towards cross-border harmonisation and regulation of Islamic finance product and services.

3. Diagnostic and analytical work in Islamic finance through the incorporation of Islamic finance in the benchmark tool for analysis of the financial sector in FSAP. At the national level, further diagnostic is needed in the development of national strategies towards access to finance, whether Islamic or conventional.
4. Technical assistance to support the development of a viable Islamic finance industry including banking, Islamic insurance or *Takāful*, and financial markets. The technical assistance can also be through the development of uniform prudential standards across countries and regions. These objectives can be achieved through close collaboration with standard setting bodies such as IFSB and AAOIFI and the Islamic Development Bank or by improving access to finance to satisfy the growing demand for Islamic instruments.
5. Islamic financing by the Bank and its affiliates such as the International Finance Corporation (IFC) and the Multilateral Investment Guarantee Agency (MIGA), whereby a number of projects have been financed so far.[111]

The World Bank Group recognises the potential of the Islamic finance industry. This is reflected in different forms. For instance, besides support to the IFSB–the international standard setter for the Islamic Finance industry–for its technical work and advocacy, the Bank group has been selectively supporting specific transactions with the objective of promoting innovative Sharī'ah-compliant financing vehicles and the development of regulatory systems and corporate governance to underpin their operations. **Within the Bank group, International Finance Corporation (IFC) was the first to facilitate the establishment of *Mudārabah* (engaged in leasing business) in Pakistan. The IFC has recently issued its first US$100 million *ṣukūk* in Dubai and Bahrain markets, the first partial credit guarantee that complies with Islamic finance principles, and invited Yemen's Saba Islamic Bank to join the IFC's global trade finance programme as an issuing bank. Overall, the IFC has signed a total of 18 IF deals. The Multilateral Investment Guarantee Agency (MIGA), which deals with providing investment guarantees against political risk, was tapped to provide political risk insurance for a critical project in Djibouti that was be**ing funded through an Islamic financing structure. The US$427 million guarantee announced in January 2008 supported investments into a new container terminal in Djibouti. The World Bank has also set up an Islamic development working group to promote Islamic finance. The bank will work with regulators and with other banks to promote the introduction of Sharī'ah-compliant financial services, in particular, examining ways on how to exploit IF to promote access to development, product development, and infrastructure financing.[112]

MIGA issued guarantees to DP World Djibouti FZCO (DPW), Standard Chartered Bank (SCB), Dubai Islamic Bank PJSC (DIB), and WestLB AG for their investments in Doraleh Container Terminal S.A.R.L. in Djibouti. The guarantees included US$5 million to cover DPW's equity investment into the project and US$422 million to cover funding provided by DIB, SCB, West LB, and other participating banks under an Islamic project finance facility. The coverage was for a period of 10 years against the risks of transfer restriction, war and civil disturbance, expropriation, and breach of contract. MIGA's gross exposure under the project was US$427 million. By supporting this project, MIGA were to help Djibouti meet the growing volume of trade and strengthen its position as the gateway to the African hinterland. Development and expansion of port infrastructure is also a pillar of the World Bank Group's Country Assistance Strategy for Djibouti.[113] The success in putting together this project opened the door for PRI to support future complex projects with Islamic financing.[114]

The participants at the 2008 Symposium on International Political Risk Management, hosted by MIGA and Georgetown University on December 4, 2008, recognised that the concept of Sharī'ah-compliant coverage was still representing uncharted territory. At the same time, it offers significant potential due to the limited number of traditional Islamic providers of PRI as very few providers of Islamic finance have investment insurance portfolios or the underwriting expertise and capacity to provide PRI. Although the Islamic finance projects are still a small portion of the overall volume of investments, they are growing. They present opportunities for underwriting new projects, entering new markets and providing support for investments into developing countries. The Islamic Corporation for the Insurance of Investments and Export Credit (ICIEC) provides such insurance, although representing only small percentage of its portfolio.[115]

Another Sharī'ah-compliant project backed by MIGA is the *murābaḥah* facility for Indonesia's Telecoms expansion. The World Bank arm provided US$450 million in investment guarantees to support the expansion of telecommunications services in Indonesia. MIGA's guarantees were backing a US$450 million *murābaḥah* financing facility underwritten by Deutsche Bank and Saudi British Bank (SABB). The MIGA-backed

Islamic finance facility is part of a larger US$1.2 billion financing package for the expansion of Indonesian telecom company PT Natrindo Telepon Seluler (NTS), known by the brand "Axis." Axis is a GSM and 3G cellular service provider offering wireless communication services in more than 400 cities across Indonesia.[116] Speaking on the occasion, Izumi Kobayashi, MIGA's Executive Vice President emphasised that his institution is committed to working with investors in providing political risk insurance for Islamic financial transactions with development objectives.[117]

Yet, such kinds of insurance are not without challenges. The range of challenges includes, among others bridging the cultural differences, introducing significant modification to policy terms and conditions, and seeking approval of the Sharī'ah board responsible for the endorsement of the project.[118]

This interest of MIGA on Islamic finance is simultaneously backed by the multilateral institution's strong presence and interest in Africa, which continues to be one of MIGA's strategic priorities, especially in the wake of the financial crisis. Since its inception, MIGA has issued nearly US$2.9 billion in guarantees for investments in Africa, supporting more than 130 projects in 30 countries. MIGA's support for projects in the continent also underscores the institution's commitment to the poorest countries as well as the agency's capacity to assist countries emerging from conflict and fragile states.

However, the bank is more active in Islamic finance through its finance arm the IFC. As stated by IFC Vice President for Finance & Treasurer, "Islam's traditional emphasis on social responsibility makes Islamic finance a natural match for IFC."[119] What is very interesting in the case of Islamic finance in Africa and the role of the IFC is the fact that the financing arm of the World Bank is very well involved in Africa through different initiatives, and at the same time, well involved in Islamic finance. IFC's strategy in Africa emphasises three key areas: improving the investment climate; enhancing support to micro, small, and medium enterprises; and developing new projects in priority sectors such as building infrastructure, advancing healthcare, developing agribusiness, and promoting the recovery of countries affected by conflict. During the fiscal year that ended in June 2010, IFC increased its investments in Sub-Saharan Africa to US$2.4 billion for its own account of US$1.8 billion a year earlier. It was the first time IFC's annual investments surpassed US$2.0 billion in the region. IFC mobilised an additional US$1.1 billion from other investors and approved 40 new advisory services projects.[120]

The IFC has been actively involved in supporting the development of African financial institutions and markets for several decades.[121] Since the 1980s, the IFC's support of emerging market development has included issuing local currency bonds. In 2007, IFC became the first international issuer in the West African regional stock exchange (BRVM) with its CFAF 22 billion (US$40 million) "kola bond" issue, earning an emerging markets' deal-of-the-year award. This was followed in 2009 in Central Africa with the "moabi bond" worth CFAF 20 billion (US$43 million). These issues have helped deepen these markets and should help in attracting further issues.[122]

The IFC's investment initiatives in Africa have also come up in the form of helping paving the way for an Initial Public Offering (IPO) on local equity markets. This may take the form of an IFC investment at the time of an IPO, whereby the IFC's involvement would help reassure other institutional and retail investors of the quality of the issue. For example, the IFC invested alongside the IPO for Onatel, the national telecommunications operator in Burkina Faso, and the first Burkina-based IPO on the regional Bourse. The IFC may also invest through equity in major companies with the objective of supporting a broad-based IPO at a later date, in which the IFC may then also participate by selling some of its shareholding and exiting such deals via different mechanisms such as public listings on local securities markets to help expand the depth and liquidity in those markets. IFC investment in a company can also help serving as a "stamp of approval" to help pave the way for a subsequent public offering.[123]

From the above, it is clear that the IFC and the World Bank are deeply involved in the development of the financial sector in African countries, and at the same time, have profound interest in Islamic finance, with its traditional emphasis on social responsibility making it a natural match for IFC. Some of the above initiatives by IFC can be undertaken in the future as a joint venture between the IFC and established Islamic financial institutions, particularly the IDB through its specialised arms in order to boost the image of Islamic finance in the continent and enhance their developmental objectives. In a parallel dimension, IFC formed an Islamic Finance Working Group that aims to develop a more strategic approach to Islamic finance activities. The efforts of the working group and the expansion of IFC field offices in the Middle East and North Africa region have contributed to a committed portfolio of over US$190 million in loans and equity in the region.[124] IFC has also responded to the increasing demand for Sharīʾah-compliant products in the Middle East and North

Africa (MENA) region and has engaged in Islamic finance transactions in Saudi Arabia and United Arab Emirates. In the mid-1990s, IFC first became involved in Islamic financing, as noted earlier, when it financed *mudārabah* entities engaged in leasing in Pakistan.

The ability to offer Islamic products in the MENA region has improved IFC's visibility as an innovative multilateral institution providing product offerings for different segments of the client base. It is expected that the demand for Sharī'ah-compliant products will increase in other regions, including East Asia, South Asia, Central Asia, and Africa. IFC is currently exploring these opportunities. In addition, IFC is working on developing documentation designed to be acceptable to Islamic banks.[125]

More positively, IFC has recently indicated its willingness to support Islamic banking in Nigeria. IFC believes that making Islamic finance products more available could help develop financial markets and promote economic growth, especially by increasing access to education, small business financing, and housing finance. The corporation has observed that Islamic finance represents an untapped source of capital and a new frontier of business opportunities that will help it meet the goals for increasing investment in the world's poorest countries. IFC's goal for Islamic banking in Nigeria is to innovatively channel the Muslim world's growing financial resources towards meeting development challenges in the country and the world at large.[126]

The first direct involvement by the IFC by Islamic finance in Sub-Saharan Africa was in early April 2013, when IFC announced the investment of US$5 million equity in Gulf African Bank by taking up a 15 % shareholding stake in the bank. The investment aims at expanding access to financial services in Africa, supporting corporate finance and lending to small and medium businesses and reaching a greater number of small businesses and women entrepreneurs, who are often excluded from banking services. It is IFC's first engagement with an Islamic finance institution in Sub-Saharan Africa. The Gulf African Bank is one of Kenya's only two Islamic banks. The bank will reportedly use IFC's financing to increase finance for retail and corporate customers, develop programmes for women entrepreneurs, and extend more services to SMEs. In addition to the equity investment, a further US$3 million trade line will be made available to Gulf African Bank under IFC's Global Trade Finance Program. The programme complements the capacity of banks to deliver trade financing by mitigating risk in new or challenging markets where trade lines may be constrained.[127]

The relationship between the Gulf African Bank and IFC has been extended further in 2014, with the Gulf African Bank becoming the newest member of IFC's Africa Micro, Small, and Medium Enterprise Finance Program, which works with banks in 18 African countries to increase lending to entrepreneurs. Through the Program, IFC will provide the Gulf African Bank with advisory services to help the bank offer a greater range of products to SMEs in Kenya, including many owned by women. IFC and the bank will work on improving customer relationship management, accessibility, and speed of service. Oumar Seydi, IFC Director for East and Southern Africa, noted that SMEs represent an untapped market opportunity in developing countries. IFC partnership with Gulf African Bank aims at increasing financial services to entrepreneurs, enabling them to grow and drive Kenya's economy forward. He added that "having invested in Gulf African Bank twice, IFC is confident that Islamic finance products will reach many businesses that would otherwise be excluded from banking.".[128]

## IMF Engagement

Regarding the International Monetary Fund's involvement in Islamic finance, it is worth noting that while IMF staff have conducted research in the area of Islamic finance as far back as the mid-1980s, the institution did not commence much work in this area until about 10 years ago. The start of this work, both technical assistance and surveillance, coincided with the Fund's recognition that it needed to be more aware of what was happening in the financial sector in the light of the crises that were hitting many emerging markets. Work on Islamic finance is guided by the same policy that guides all financial sector oversight. Unlike the World Bank, the Fund does not have a separate division that handles Islamic finance, but incorporates work in this field into the existing functional activities.

In terms of country-level engagement, the IMF is involved in assisting governments to set up appropriate regulatory frameworks for handling Islamic banks. Standard oversight mechanisms, such as required capital adequacy ratios, are hard to apply directly to Sharī'ah-compliant banks. The IMF indicates that its work in this area is fast expanding as more countries are interested in improving their surveillance of these banks as they grow in prevalence and size. The Fund has also worked at the global level to facilitate the development of standards. In 2002, it helped establish the Malaysia-based Islamic Financial Services Board (IFSB), which issues global prudential standards and guiding principles for the Islamic financial industry. The IFSB standards are designed to complement the standards issued by the Basel Committee of the Bank for International Settlements, which is also an IFSB member. The IMF also works with the Accounting and Auditing Organisation for Islamic Financial Institutions.[129]

Comparing the role of the World Bank in Islamic banking and finance and that of the IMF, it can be deduced that the World Bank has so far been more active in promoting Islamic finance than the IMF. Thus, while the IMF does not provide direct lending on the same scale as the World Bank, it can play a more proactive and influential role in developing the *ṣukūk* markets in the countries it assists financially, through both encouraging *ṣukūk* issuance, as it did in some limited cases, and much more, issuing its own Islamic financing. However, the IMF's current main contribution is limited to assisting governments in setting up regulatory frameworks for handling Islamic banks.[130] Thus, it is hoped that IMF would play a more active role in developing Islamic finance in Africa as part of its mandate in supporting and developing the financial sector of member countries and to improving the economies of member countries. The IMF has already assisted some developing countries in issuing *ṣukūk* and it could do the same in the African context. For instance, in February 2011, it assisted Yemen in its YER$500 million (US$2.33 million) debut *ṣukūk* programme. It has also previously assisted Iran and Sudan with consultation programmes for *ṣukūk* issuance, and in 2010, it worked with Pakistan to develop a Rs. 100 billion (US$1.16 billion) plan for a sovereign *ṣukūk* issuance to reduce government dependency on IMF loans. The IMF also has a technical agreement with the IDB to assist its member countries to formulate policies to raise financing, including raising funds using Sharī'ah-compliant instruments.[131]

In October 9, 2014, the Interdepartmental Working Group on Islamic Finance (IDWGIF) of the IMF held its first meeting with its External Advisory Group (EAG) in Washington, DC to discuss issues related to Islamic banking and the development of *ṣukūk* markets and its potential for financing infrastructure investment and for providing instruments to facilitate liquidity management and central banking operations. The discussions covered regulation and supervision, the scope for Islamic financial institutions to improve access to finance, including for SMEs, the implications of Basel III requirements for capital and liquidity on the industry, and the potential for enhancing Sharī'ah and corporate governance. It should be noted that the EAG includes in its membership the secretary general and CEO of Islamic finance" support institutions such as IFSB, AAOIFI, IIFM, CIBAFI, IILM, and the IDB, and was established by the IMF to help identify policy challenges facing the Islamic finance industry and facilitate coordination with those international institutions involved in establishing standards for the industry.[132]

## Cooperation with the African Development Bank

Another multilateral institution that Islamic financial institutions can cooperate with in their endeavour to promote Islamic finance in Africa is the African Development Bank (AfDB). The bank is already making good steps in that direction, although they seem to be far below the real potential and capabilities of the bank. This is clear from the bank signing an MoU with the Islamic Development Bank (IDB) to invest in joint projects common to both multilateral development banks (MDBs). Under the MoU, the two MDBs will commit to contribute US$500 million each in a US$1 billion cooperation, based on the AfDB's medium-term strategy and the IDB special programme for the development of Africa (SPDA). The deal's main focus is to assist in scaling up interventions in Africa in the fields of agriculture, infrastructure, water and sanitation, education, and healthcare. The objective of this co-financing MoU aims at fostering economic development and social progress in order to coordinate co-financing projects and promote economic development and technical cooperation in mutual member countries. This is aimed at reducing poverty levels in the African continent and uplifting the level of revenues.[133] Despite these initial steps, the African Development Bank is still lagging behind the World Bank, the IMF, and the Asian Development Bank in making use of Islamic finance in its development objectives. The latter is suitable in this comparison as it is a regional multilateral institution with some members already using Islamic finance.

The Asian Development Bank is highly involved in Islamic finance. This is in line with regional efforts to develop Islamic finance that have prepared an enabling environment for ADB to further spur the growth of Islamic finance. By enhancing regional financial integration and contributing to managing capital inflows into the region, these efforts should contribute to regional financial market stability. Moreover, experience in the Islamic finance industry shows that one of the biggest challenges facing its integration into the global financial system is how to harmonise standards needed to sustain its continued rapid growth. Based on this background, the Asian Development Bank (ADB), cognizant of the growing significance of Islamic finance among its developing member countries, joined the IFSB as an observer in 2003 and became an associate member in 2006. In 2004, ADB provided Technical assistance (TA) to the Islamic Financial Services Board (IFSB), which sets regulatory standards for Islamic financial institutions. The TA funded technical experts to work on a number of regulatory concerns that resulted in new transparency and market discipline standards, financial soundness indicators for Islamic institutions, and assessments of the potential for Islamic asset securitisation. ADB and IFSB agreed to continue this collaboration under a new TA, approved in March 2009, which aimed at following up on and expanding upon earlier initiatives. The new TA would address development of prudential and supervision standards for Islamic financial markets.

ADB's regional technical assistance for the Development of International Prudential Standards for Islamic Financial Services was co-financed by Islamic Development Bank (IDB) and provided support for the IFSB. In this context, ADB's Office of the General Counsel formed an internal working group on Islamic finance to better coordinate ADB activities in this area and develop a short background paper on Islamic finance, with recommendations to enhance ADB support. ADB's Office of Regional Economic Integration includes a section in Asian Bonds Online on Islamic finance, which provides information regarding Islamic finance market infrastructure, rules and regulations, as well as updates on Islamic finance activities and data in the region. In September 2008, ADB's Private Sector Operations Department signed with IDB a landmark co-financing agreement that would allow the two banks to work together on projects in common member countries. ADB and IDB will provide up to US$2 billion equivalent, respectively, over the next 3 years to finance projects in common member countries. TA for the Development of International Prudential Standards for Islamic Financial Services is another landmark project that resulted in IFSB adopting a new transparency and market discipline standard, new compilation guidelines for collecting Islamic finance statistics, identification and initial analysis of key issues and gaps in Islamic finance regulation and supervision, and recommendations for strengthening the legal and regulatory framework for Islamic asset securitisation as a basis for developing Islamic capital markets. This work also complements already ongoing efforts to design prudential standards for Islamic finance in the areas of capital adequacy, supervisory review, and risk management. It has also helped provide Basel II equivalent standards and guidelines for Islamic finance. It should be noted that the TA will be conducted in consultation and coordination with IFSB staff and members, including IDB, IMF, World Bank, and the Bank for International Settlements.

This TA aims to facilitate the implementation of standards, guidelines, and market development strategies. The key TA activities include to:

1. Help IFSB develop legal and liquidity infrastructure needed for Islamic finance's sound development and effective supervision. As part of efforts to develop liquidity infrastructure, specific aspects of the strategy for Islamic money and government securities markets will be worked out in detail, including guidance on qualitative and quantitative benchmarks for regulatory requirements and the supervisory assessment of liquidity risk management. To strengthen the legal infrastructure, certain key legal Sharī'ah issues in Islamic asset securitisation will be addressed.
2. Support IFSB in working out strategies for Islamic capital market development in coordination with IFSB's ongoing work on liquidity infrastructure. The work will include measures to strengthen sovereign *ṣukūk* issues in domestic markets, integrate *ṣukūk* issuance in the overall public debt and financing management framework, and develop active and well-regulated secondary markets for *ṣukūk*.
3. Assist IFSB in preparing a diagnostic study in the area of interface between positive laws and the Sharī'ah across all types of Sharī'ah-compliant asset securitisation contracts. This shall include a platform to engage legal jurists and Sharī'ah scholars to find solutions for complex legal and Sharī'ah issues through advanced sharing of jurisprudential thoughts and methodologies.
4. Help IFSB provide further education on IFSB standards and guidelines through case studies and workshops to facilitate the implementation of the standards.
5. Assist IFSB in continuing the efforts to compile prudential and structural Islamic finance indicators, based on the compilation guide already developed.[134]

To complement regional initiatives, ADB is also working directly with a number of financial sector regulators, such as in Indonesia and Pakistan, to develop an enabling legal and regulatory framework for Islamic finance. ADB has thus been involved in several initiatives that have assisted in opening the Asian market to Islamic financing sources. This project will be ADB's first involvement in parallel private sector efforts to develop the market.[135] The ADB is also involved in Islamic microfinance initiatives in some member countries such as Pakistan.

Arguing on the reasons behind establishing such a fund, the existing supply of infrastructure finance does not come close to meeting the scale of demand. There exist great wealth in many Middle Eastern countries, generated in large part from substantial oil revenues, which have greatly increased the fortunes of high net-worth individuals and sovereign wealth funds. The Council on Foreign Relations estimates that the sovereign wealth funds in the Gulf Cooperation Council countries held US$1.2 trillion in 2008. Despite the recent volatility, great wealth still resides in the region and investors are increasingly interested in channelling this capital into investment opportunities that comply with Sharī'ah law and values.

There is a need to unlock the capital. Yet, institutional investors in many Middle Eastern countries that might otherwise have appetites for investment risk in the Fund's target countries require Sharī'ah-compliant investment opportunities, and are thus precluded from investing in traditional PE funds that are not specifically structured to accommodate that requirement. Indeed, the number of PE funds set up to accommodate Sharī'ah-compliant investment is limited. Project sponsors across ADB's developing member countries are constrained by the general undersupply of risk capital in their regions (particularly given the recent reversals in capital flows), and are eager to tap into the large pools of wealth that exist in many countries throughout the Middle East, but are unable to access that money in the absence of suitably structured funds that can serve as intermediaries between investors and project sponsors. To help bridge this gap, ADB will collaborate with IDB to establish a Sharī'ah-compliant PE fund (the Islamic Infrastructure Fund, L.P., or the Fund) to invest in infrastructure projects across those member countries common to both institutions. By structuring the Fund to accommodate the needs of investors for Sharī'ah-compliant investment vehicles, the Fund will "unlock" for project sponsors in the target region a large pool of money-seeking investment opportunities. This will, in turn, channel more equity capital into infrastructure projects throughout the region, and will also allow project sponsors specifically seeking Islamic funding access to financing tools structured around their particular requirements.[136]

ADB will add value to the Fund in a number of ways. ADB's principal contribution comes in the form of sponsoring and establishing the

Fund from the outset. Without ADB's support, the Fund would not exist. Through its investment, ADB will demonstrate its confidence in the transaction, which may be an example to encourage further investment by other development institutions and institutional investors. ADB will assist in deal sourcing on an ongoing basis, and its seat on the Fund's investment committee will allow ADB to comment and vote on each transaction contemplated by the Fund.[137] One of the latest initiatives by the Asian Development Bank (ADB) is the Bank's consideration to launch a medium-term note (MTN) programme worth several billion dollars for Islamic bonds, or *ṣukūk*, to finance infrastructure in Asia. The use of such an instrument, it is believed, will allow access for tapping a wider wealth pool.[138]

The above is in line with a recent report by Standard and Poor's titled "Will Islamic Finance Play a Key Role in Funding Asia's Huge Infrastructure Task?" The report discusses Asia's need to look for alternatives financing avenues to finance its huge infrastructure needs. The report stresses, "it is particularly pertinent for Asia, which is struggling to keep up with the escalating infrastructure needs of the region's surging population amid solid economic growth. With the outlook for global lending markets still uncertain, part of the solution for Asia may lie in finding alternatives to conventional financing. Islamic finance is one such alternative."[139] Moreover, the report stresses that infrastructure projects are a logical fit for Islamic finance, which is governed by Sharī'ah principles and predicated on asset-backing and shared business risk. Indeed, "the asset-backing nature of Islamic financing may provide a better funding match for infrastructure projects than traditional lenders, such as banks. What is more, *ṣukūk* investors typically have an appetite for longer tenors than bank loans, and prefer stable and predictable cash flow—traits that are typically associated with infrastructure projects."[140]

If Asia, which is in a better position in terms of infrastructure, could look to Islamic finance as an alternative to meet its demand, the case is more relevant in Africa due to the huge demand for infrastructure in the continent and the fact that the continent is lagging behind in many aspects. Moreover, if the ADB is well involved in Islamic finance through initiatives in funding infrastructure, cooperating with the IFSB in drafting standards and joining it as a member or in supporting Islamic microfinance initiative in member countries, why does the African Development Bank not do the same? The bank can play an important role towards financial inclusion in the continent, providing technical advice and financing infrastructure projects using Islamic finance products. The Secretary General of the IILM, Rifat Abdel Karim, stressed that Islamic finance provides an opportunity for the AfDB of an additional alternative source of funding to finance development projects in its member countries. AfDB as AAA rating institution can make use of this high-quality credit rating by issuing ***sukūk*** to mobilise funds at a low cost from investors who, perhaps in the past, were not among those targeted by the bank to fund infrastructure projects.[141]

If everybody is interested in Islamic finance and taking concrete steps in that direction, particularly multilateral development institutions such as the Islamic Development Bank, the Asian Development Bank, the World Bank, and the African Development Bank, they need to double their efforts not only due to the great potentials of the industry, but also due to real demands for it in the continent.

## Notes

1. David McIlroy "Africa Rising" *Quantum Finance in Perspective*, Issue 12, July 2010, pp. 23–25.
2. Ernst & Young's *2011 Africa Attractiveness Survey, It is Time for Africa*, May 2011, pp. 10–11.
3. Punam Chuhan-Pole & Manka Angwafo (Editors), *Yes Africa Can: Success Stories from a Dynamic Continent*, The World Bank, 2011, p. ix.
4. Olaf Meier, "It is still possible to Gain Access To Attractive Investment Targets with Relatively Low Capital Input", in Ernst & Young's *2011 Africa Attractiveness Survey, It is Time for Africa*, May 2011, p. 18.
5. Ernst & Young's *2012 Africa Attractiveness Survey Building Bridges*, p. 3.
6. Tom Barry, "Uneven Playing field Blocks Investment", *African Banker*, 4th Quarter, 2011, p. 31.
7. Peter Guest, "Spelling Out Growth", *Wall Street Journal*, September 18, 2011, www.online.wsj.com retrieved January 2012.
8. Ibid.
9. Neanda Salvaterra, "Mobile Pioneer Sees Rich Promise in Africa".
10. Nick Price, "Africa Between Perception and Reality", Fidelity International, www.fidelity.com.sg, January 2011 retrieved June 2011.
11. Ernst & Young's *2011 Africa Attractiveness Survey, It is Time for Africa*, May 2011, p. 16.
12. Ernst & Young's *2012 Africa attractiveness Survey Building Bridges*, p. 3.
13. Ibid.
14. Ernst & Young, "Africa's Perception Gab Continues to Linger", EY's attractiveness survey Africa 2014, pp. 62–63.

15. See, Africa by Numbers 2013–2014 Assessing Risks and Opportunities in Africa" 2013, Ernst & Young www.ey.com, retrieved January 2014.
16. Ibid.
17. Charmian Kok, "Forget China, invest in Africa says Russia's Renaissance", *Reuters*, December 12, 2011, www.reuters.com, retrieved February 2012.
18. Olam's *Annual Report 2011,* p. 53.
19. *Islamic finance News*, Special Supplement, *Africa the Sleeping Giant*, August 2011, p. 1.
20. Diageo, *Africa Media and Investment*, Africa Business Reporting Award 2009, supported by Diageo www.diageoafricabusinessreportingawards.com, retrieved June 2010, p. 1.
21. Karen Rothmyer, *They Wanted Journalists to Say 'Wow' How NGOs Affect U.S. Media Coverage of Africa*, Discussion Paper Series, Joan Shorenstein Center on the Press, Politics and Public Policy, January 2011, www.hks.harvard.edu, retrieved June 2012, pp. 2–3.
22. Karen Rothmyer, "Hiding the Real Africa Why NGOs prefer bad news", *Columbia Journalism Review*, www.cjr.org, March/April 2011, retrieved March 2012.
23. Ibid, p. 17.
24. Ibid, p. 18.
25. Ibid, p. 19.
26. Ibid.
27. Xhanti Payi, "African Monetary Union risks perpetuating the myth Africa is one country", *The Financial Times*, September 28, 2011, www.ft.com, retrieved June 2012.
28. Ibid.
29. See, James Watson & Others, Into *Africa Institutional investor intentions to 2016*, p. 5.
30. Ibid.
31. Ibid.
32. Ernst & Young, *Ernst & Young's 2011 Africa Attractiveness Survey, It is Time for Africa*, p. 5.
33. James Watson & Others, *Into Africa Institutional investor intentions to 2016*, p. 12.
34. *The 3rd COMESA Investment Forum Connecting Africa to the World* April 12–13, 2010, Sharm El Sheikh. Egypt, Conference Report, p. 38.
35. Ibid, p. 9.
36. World Bank, *Doing Business Report 2010*, p. 2.
37. See, Dambisa Moyo in her Key note address to *The 3rd COMESA Investment Forum Connecting Africa to the World* April 12–13, 2010, Sharm El Sheikh, Egypt, Conference Report, pp. 15–16.

38. World Bank, *Doing Business Report 2012*, www.doingbusiness.org, retrieved February 2013, p. 1.
39. World Bank, *Doing Business Report 2015*, www.doingbusiness.org, retrieved February 2015.
40. *Islamic Finance Asia* May 2011.
41. Richard Chirambo, "Researchers Back Idea of Islamic Banks in Malawi" *The Daily Time*, Wednesday, 02 May 2012 www.bnltimes.com, retrieved June 2012.
42. ZaidIbrahim &Co, *Demystifying Islamic finance: Correcting Misconceptions Advancing Value Proposition*, p. 7
43. Ibid.
44. Ibid.
45. Patrick Imam and Kangni Kpodar, "Islamic Banking: How Has it Diffused?", p. 3.
46. The World Bank, *Africa Competiveness Report* 2011, p. xi.
47. James Watson & Others, *Into Africa Institutional investor intentions to 2016*, p. 20.
48. Ernst & Young's 2011 *Africa Attractiveness Survey*, *It is Time for Africa*, p. 32.
49. KPMG, *KPMG Survey of Current Economic and Business Conditions in Africa*, p. 5.
50. Ibid.
51. The World Bank, *De-Fragmenting Africa Deepening Regional Trade Integration in Goods and Services*, 2012, www.worldbank.org, retrieved January 2013, p. xv.
52. Ibid, pp. 71–72.
53. KPMG, *KPMG Survey of Current Economic and Business Conditions in Africa*, p. 5.
54. Ibid.
55. Ibid.
56. The Economist Intelligence Unit, *Risk and Reward: The Gulf Push into African Infrastructure*, commissioned by Dubai Chamber, 2014.
57. KPMG, *KPMG Survey of Current Economic and Business Conditions in Africa*, p. 5.
58. Acha Leke & others, "What's driving Africa's growth" *Mckinsey Quarterly*, Mckinsey Global Institute, June 2010, www.mckinsey.com
59. Ezra S. Suruma, "Conflict and prospects for Economic Growth", in *Foresight Africa The Continent's Greatest Challenges and Opportunities for 2011*, Africa Growth initiative, Brookings, January 2011, www.brookings.edu, retrieved June 2012, p. 7.
60. William Wallis, Andrew England and Katrina Manson, "Africa: Ripe for Appraisal", *Financial Times* May 18, 2011.

61. Global Financial Integrity, *Illicit Financial Flows from Africa: Hidden Resource for Development.* March 2010, www.gfintegrity.org, retrieved April 2011, p. 1.
62. *The Guardian*, "A fresh chapter is opening in Africa's history after two centuries of injustice, a new continent is emerging", February 19, 2011, www.guardian.co.uk, retrieved January 2012.
63. Ibid.
64. Aristide Ahouassou, "African Countries Credit Ratings: Key for Effective Resource Mobilization on International Capital Markets", AfDB, May 24, 2011 www.afdb.org. Retrieved December 2011.
65. *The 3rd COMESA Investment Forum Connecting Africa to the World* April 12–13, 2010, Sharm El Sheikh, Egypt, Conference Report, p. 15.
66. The World Bank, *Africa's Competitiveness Report 2011*, World Bank, www.siteresources.worldbank.org, retrieved June 2012, p. xiv.
67. Ibid.
68. Acha Leke, "What's driving Africa's growth", McKenzy Quarterly, June 2010.
69. David Bloom, David Canning, and Kevin Chan, *Higher Education and Economic Development in Africa*, World Bank 2006, www.worldbank.org, retrieved June 2012, p. i.
70. Olu Ajakaiye and Mwangi S. Kimenyi, "Higher Education and Economic Development in Africa: Introduction and Overview", *Journal of African Economies*, vol. 20, p. iii12.
71. *The 3rd COMESA Investment Forum Connecting Africa to the World* April 12–13, 2010, Sharm El Sheikh, Egypt, Conference Report, p. 31.
72. Ibid.
73. The World *Bank, Doing Business in the East African Community 2011*, p. 3 www.worldbank.org, retrieved January 2012; "East Africa could match Japan in ease of doing business" Thursday, August 25, 2011 www.cpifinancial.net
74. William Wallis, Andrew England and Katrina Manson, "Africa: Ripe for Appraisal", *Financial Times* May 18, 2011.
75. Mwagi S. Kimenyi & Zenia Lewis, "THE BRICS and the new scramble for tant Africa" in *Foresight Africa: The Continent's Greatest Challenges and Opportunities for 2011*, pp. 19–21.
76. Ibid.
77. *The Economist*, "The hopeful continent Africa rising", December 3, 2011.
78. Noel Gordon & Others, *At the Tipping Point: Financial Services in Africa comes of age How Financial Institutions can Capitalise on the Growth Opportunities in Africa*, Accenture, 2011, p. 7.
79. *The Economist*, "The hopeful continent Africa rising", December 3, 2011.
80. Ibid.

81. Jumah Reli, Deputy Governor Bank of Tanzania speech at a high Level Seminar on the Oversight of Islamic finance, Tanzania, Dares Salaam, July 15–17, 2009, www.eastafritac.org, p. 3, retrieved March 2010, p. 6.
82. Hafsa Kara, "The Gulf's Islamic banks are targeting Africa's opportunities", *The Banker*, January 31, 2011, www.thebanker.com, retrieved July 2012.
83. Michael Gondwe, "Talking Notes at the Launch of the Islamic Finance Guidelines", A Key Note Address by the Governor, Bank of Zambia, 30 December 2014.
84. Jeremy Cape, "Tax and Islamic Finance–The choices for governments in Africa", *The African Business Journal*, May 10, 2010, www.tabj.co.za, retrieved January 2012.
85. Mustak Parker, "Winds of change in S. African tax laws for Islamic finance products", *Arab News*, September 26, 2010. www.arabnews.com, retrieved June 2011.
86. Ibid.
87. Ibid.
88. Andrew Bing, "A longer-term Vision is Crucial", in *Ernst & Young's 2011 Africa Attractiveness Survey, It is Time for Africa*, p. 20.
89. KPMG, "Islamic Finance Credential", www.kpmg.com, May 2006, retrieved May 211, p. 3.
90. Douglas Pearce, *Financial Inclusion in the Middle East and North Africa: Analysis and Roadmap Recommendations*, p. 33.
91. Yasmeen Suliman, "Islamic banking in Africa and related tax issues" KPMG, www.kpmg.com, September 28, 2010, retrieved June 2011.
92. Samira Mensah & Others, *Regulations and Fiscal Incentives Could Speed Islamic Finance Development In Africa.*
93. Edwin Chew and others, "Islamic finance offers capital opportunities", *Capital Agenda Insights*, www.ey.com, February 2011, retrieved June 2012, p. 2.
94. KPMG, Growth and diversification in Islamic Finance, 2007, www.kpmg.com, retrieved June 2011, p. 19.
95. ZaidIbrahim &Co, *Demystifying Islamic finance: Correcting Misconceptions Advancing Value Proposition*, p. 11.
96. Mahmoud Mohieldin, "Realizing the Potential of Islamic Finance" *Economic Premise*, The World Bank, Issue 77, March 2012, p. 4.
97. Naznnem Halim, "Cross-Border Trade on the Rise" *Islamic Finance news*, IFN Supplement Middle East 2011, December 5, 2011, www.islamicfinancenews, retrieved April 2012.
98. Thierry Tanoh, "How Can Development Partners Support the Financial Sector in Africa?", Private Sector Development Private Magazine, ISSUE 5—MARCH 2010—AFRICA'S FINANCIAL MARKETS: A REAL DEVELOPMENT TOOL? www.proparco.fr, retrieved August 2011, p. 20.

99. Ibid.
100. Mahmoud Mohieldin, "Realizing the Potential of Islamic Finance", p. 1.
101. Mushtak Parker, "IDB joins hands with AfDB to boost development" *Arab News*, December 26, 2010.
102. Ibid.
103. Ekmeleddin Ihsanoglu, Keynote Address on *Enhancing Economic Cooperation Among Muslim Countries- The Role of OIC* H.E. Prof. Dr. Ekmeleddin Ihsanoglu Secretary General, Organization of Islamic Conference IIUM *Journal of Economics and Management*, The International Islamic University Malaysia, 17, no. 1 (2009): 13–30.
104. Mahamat Ali Hassan Statement on behalf of the African Group Delivered by the IDB Governor for the Republic of Chad 35th Annual meeting of the IDB Board of Governors Baku Azerbaijan June 23–24, 2010. Original Text French, www.isdb.org, retrieved January 2012, p. 3.
105. Ekmeleddin Ihsanoglu, Keynote Address on *Enhancing Economic Cooperation Among Muslim Countries- The Role of OIC.*
106. Mushtak Parker, "IDB joins hands with AfDB to boost development" *Arab News*, December 26, 2010, www.arabnews.com, retrieved June 2011.
107. Mahamat Ali Hassan Statement on behalf of the African Group Delivered by the IDB Governor for the Republic of Chad 35th Annual meeting of the IDB Board of Governors, Baku Azerbaijan, June 23–24, 2010. Original Text French, p. 5.
108. Ibid, p. 4.
109. Mushtak Parker, "IDB joins hands with AfDB to boost development" *Arab News*, December 26, 2010, www.arabnews.com, retrieved June 2011.
110. Alwaleed F. Alatabani, "Approach and Attitude Towards Islamic Banking and Finance: A Multilateral Perspective", paper presented at the International Conference on Islamic Banking and Finance in Africa, Midrand, South Africa April 14–15, 2010, slide 6.
111. Ibid, slides no. 10–12.
112. Shamshad Akhtar, Vice President Middle East and North Africa The World Bank, Key note address at the Islamic Finance Seminar Banca d'Italia Symposium on Islamic Finance in Roma: Developments in MENA region 11 November 2009, www.worldbank.org, retrieved June 2012.
113. See, The Multilateral Investment Guarantee Agency (MIGA), "Project Brief", www.miga.org, 2011, retrieved June 2012.
114. Kevin W. Lu, Gero Verheyen, and Srilal M. Perera (Editors), *Investing with Confidence Understanding Political Risk Management in the 21st Century*, The World Bank, Washington, DC, 2009, www.worldbank.org, retrieved June 2012, p. x.

115. Ibid, p. xv.
116. The Multilateral Investment Guarantee Agency (MIGA), Press Release, "MIGA Covers Murābaḥah Facility for Indonesia Telecoms Expansion" June 16,2011, www.miga.org, retrieved April 2012.
117. Ibid.
118. Kevin W. Lu, Gero Verheyen, and Srilal M. Perera (Editors), *Investing with Confidence Understanding Political Risk Management in the 21st Century*, p. 257.
119. International Finance Corporation (IFC), "Islamic Finance A new Frontier of Opportunity", www.ifc.org, retrieved June 2012.
120. International Finance Corporation (IFC), "IFC Promotes Increased Development with Record Year in Africa: Annual investments surpass $2 billion on the continent for the first time", August 31, 2010, www.ifc.org, retrieved June 2012.
121. Thierry Tanoh, "How Can Development Partners Support the Financial Sector in Africa?", pp. 20–22.
122. Ibid.
123. Thierry Tanoh, "How Can Development Partners Support the Financial Sector in Africa?", p. 22.
124. Reuters, "IFC IFC Debuts $100 Million Islamic Bond on Dubai", October 21, 2009, www.reuters.com, retrieved November 2011.
125. Khaleel Ahmed, "Islamic Finance", www.ifc.org
126. Uhomoibhi Toni Aburime and Felix Alio, "Islamic Banking: Theories, Practices and Insights For Nigeria" *International Review of Business Research Papers*, vol. 5, no. 1 January 2009, pp. 321–339.
127. International Finance Corporation (IFC) "IFC Makes First Islamic Finance Investment in Sub-Saharan Africa", March 28, 2013, www.ifc.org, retrieved April 2012.
128. "IFC Expands Partnership with Gulf African Bank to Support Islamic Finance and Entrepreneurs in Kenya", April 29, 2014, www.ifc.org, retrieved February 2015.
129. Bretton Woods Project, "The IFIs and Islamic finance", Bretton Woods update, Number 59, January –February 2008, p. 5, http://www.brettonwoodsproject.org, retrieved June 2012.
130. *Islamic Finance News*, "The IMF and Islamic finance: A roadmap for the future?", September 21, 2011, vol. 8, Issue 37, www.islamicfinancenews.com, retrieved January 2012.
131. Ibid.
132. IMF, "The IMF Launches Consultations with its External Advisory Group on Islamic Finance", Press Release No. 14/468, October 11, 2014, retrieved February 2015.

133. Mushtak Parker, "IDB joins hands with AfDB to boost development", *Arab News*, December 26, 2010, www.arabnews.com, retrieved June 2011.
134. The Asian Development Bank, *Development of Prudential and Supervision Standards for Islamic Financial Markets* Project Number: 42520 Regional Policy and Advisory Technical Assistance (R-PATA) March 2009 (Co-financed by the Islamic Financial Services Board), www.adb.org, retrieved June 2011, p. 4.
135. The Asian Development Bank (ADB), *Report and Recommendation of the President to the Board of Directors on the Proposed Equity Investment Islamic Infrastructure Fund, L.P.* Project Number: 42911 April 2009, www.adb.org, retrieved June 2011, p. 6.
136. Ibid, p. 4.
137. Ibid, p. 8.
138. Frederick Rischter, "ADB mulls multi-billion dollar Islamic MTN programme", www.arabianbusiness.com, Wednesday, May 5, 2010, retrieved April 2011.
139. Mustak Parker, "will Islamic finance play as key role in funding Asia S&P", *Arab News*, October 23, 2011, www.arabnews.com, retrieved June 2012.
140. Allan Redimerio & Andrew Palmer, *Will Islamic Finance Play a Key Role in Funding Asia's Huge Infrastructure Task?*, p. 2.
141. Rifaat Ahmed Abdel Karim, *Islamic Finance: An Alternative Funding Source for the African Development Bank?* in *Africa Capacity Development*, African Development Bank, vol. 3, Issue 3, December 2012, www.afdb.org, retrieved February 2013, pp. 6–7.

CHAPTER 9

# Conclusion

The bright prospect for Islamic finance in Africa is based on the combination of two successful experiments that are well acknowledged internationally. These are the exceptional growth of the Islamic finance industry over the last decades as one of the fastest growing segments of international finance, based on its distinguishing characteristics and principles, on the one hand, and the remarkable successes and unprecedented growth of many African economies in the last decade, on the other. The convergence of the two success stories is expected to create a powerful contributor towards financial inclusion, project financing, and economic development in the continent. Not only have the two stories been successful, but the widely projected future of both experiments is bright and promising.

The future prospect of Islamic finance and its possible contribution to global financial stability in general has been well articulated by many. It has been stressed that the growth and relevance of Islamic finance in the global financial markets cannot be overlooked, given the annual growth rate of the industry or its the assets growth. Islamic banks displayed stronger resilience during the global financial crisis due to their adherence to Sharī'ah principles. These principles include, among others, the principle of risk-sharing and ethical conduct in doing business. Moreover, credit is available primarily for the purchase of real goods and services. Islamic finance also restricts the sale of debt, short-selling, and excessive uncertainty. It also bans the sale of assets not owned. The above principles have generated interest in the international community and how to explore the

 
M. Al Bashir M. Al Amine, *Islamic Finance and Africa's Economic Resurgence*, DOI 10.1007/978-3-319-28835-2_9

potential of Islamic finance as a form of financial intermediation that can promote financial stability.[1]

Thus, calling for Islamic finance to be adopted in Africa is a call to benefit from an industry that has established itself in a very short period as a viable industry and one of the best performing by international standards.

With regard to Africa and its economic growth and development, "The global investment paradigm is shifting now from 'should one invest in Africa' to that of 'managing the risk of not being in Africa'.[2] In fact, it is upheld that "those who do not invest at this rare moment in the continent's history will miss out."[3] The continent is fast becoming known as a rising star, with untapped growth potential. While there is still a window of opportunity for first-movers to grab a share of this growing market, the question is how long this window will remain open. The new frontier for growth is attracting the interest of companies from across the world and those who are not planning and acting now will miss the boat—as so many did when it came to China and India.[4]

The impressive economic growth of the continent, its growing investment potential or its positive outlook in the short, medium, and long terms, as detailed in this study, are widely acknowledged by multilateral development intuitions, international banking and financial conglomerates, and various leading international advisory and consultancy firms. Moreover, it has been reported and analysed by leading economic and financial media giants. These achievement and bright outlook are established facts that waits to be seized by investors, including those involved in Islamic finance.

Positive strides have been made by the continent in the last decade, whether in terms of GDP growth, improved economic stability, increase in foreign direct investment, and access to capital flows. Moreover, the rising urbanism, the growing consumer class, the decreasing number of conflicts, and the strengthening of democracy and freedom across the continent are among the factors that help establish Africa as a prime investment destination. In addition, many governments have lowered inflation, trimmed their foreign debt, and shrunk their budget deficits. Furthermore, a number of policies have been adopted to energise markets by privatising state-owned enterprises, reducing trade barriers, cutting corporate taxes, and strengthening regulatory and legal systems. The continent has also registered positive figures in terms of falling poverty rate and child mortality rates, while primary education completion rates are rising faster in the continent than anywhere else. Mobile phone penetration is skyrocketing while the voice of civil society is increasingly loud and various groups are demanding more accountability for resource revenues.

Besides the above, Africa is under-explored and the true extent of the continent's mineral wealth is impossible to determine at present. There is growing evidence that Africa's oil and gas production may be on the verge of dramatic growth and the recent discoveries in a number of countries are clear evidence. Yet, there are still some sceptics about Africa's achievements and potentials. However, as stressed by Ernst & Young, Africa's rise is real. Although there are people who still consider it to be a moot point, the evidence of the continent's progress is undeniable. A critical mass of African economies have grown at high and sustained rates and phenomenally resisted the ongoing global economic crisis. The size of the African economy has more than tripled since 2000. Many countries are forecast to continue experiencing high growth rates while a number of economies are predicted to remain among the fastest growing in the world for the foreseeable future.[5]

Besides Africa's diversified natural recourses, which can be an attractive target for Islamic finance investors, there are also tremendous opportunities in agribusiness with the continent having 60 % of the world's uncultivated arable land. The infrastructure sector is another big opportunity for Islamic finance investors, given the continent's lower capacity in terms of infrastructure. Moreover, energy investment is a crucial component to meet Africa's energy requirements, while transportation in all its aspects remains an important infrastructure gap requiring urgent financing. The health sector is another lucrative investment destination due to the growing consumer sector and the improved political and economic conditions of the continent.

The financial sector, on the contrary, holds very promising investment opportunities. Real potentials are tangible in the banking system, insurance sector, private equity, capital markets, and microfinance. The presence, interest, and attraction of international banks and financial institutions in Africa is rapidly growing, whether through the expansion of existing business, the acquisition of local financial institutions, partnership with others, or through the establishment of new ventures. Islamic financial institutions are under a moral obligation to be part of this transformation. The banking sector in Africa, for instance, grew at 15 % in the last decade and it is expected to do the same for the next decade.

African stock markets have performed well, both in terms of absolute returns and on a risk-adjusted basis. Given the fact that Sharī'ah-compliant indices are offered by a number of reputable international index providers, developing Sharī'ah-compliant indices in the African market is just a matter of political desire. The recent developments in Nigeria and the set up in 2012 of the NSE Lotus Islamic Index of Sharī'ah-compliant companies are a good example. Moreover, there is a growing interest in African credit and a number of sovereign states have already tested the international market in the past few years with successful and oversubscribed Eurobond and *ṣukūk* issues. Therefore, using *ṣukūk* for fund raising is high in the agenda of a number of African countries. Given its significant funding and infrastructure needs by the continent, S&P believe that Africa could benefit significantly from the development of an Islamic finance industry, and particularly, the issuance of *ṣukūk*. Multibillion-dollar additional financing are needed over the next decade to address the widening fiscal deficits and large infrastructure gaps.[6]

Yet, if the use of *ṣukūk* has been one of the useful mechanisms in addressing the funding requirements for infrastructure in Asia, its usefulness and suitability for the Africa's funding needs is much more evident.

Private equity is another area of opportunity for Islamic financial institutions in the African financial services. A number of PE funds have been active on the continent for many years and have established strong track records in a number of different sectors. Islamic PE houses have an opportunity to expand the boundaries of this segment of Islamic finance, considered to be one of the closest sectors to the spirit of Sharī'ah, given its close connection to the real sector of the economy and its structural basis as a profit–loss sharing industry.

Although the insurance sector in most African countries is still in its infancy, the market opportunity for the *Takāful* industry, as detailed in this research, is too significant to ignore. Africa is the birthplace of *Takāful* as it was for the Islamic banking industry, and therefore, the industry should play a leading role in the continent's financial and economic development. There are many factors that support the success of *Takāful* in Africa, such as the rapid growth of the industry that is far outstripping its conventional counterpart, the young population of the continent, and the lower penetration of insurance in most African countries.

The prospects of the financial sector are reinforced by technology and its effect in financial inclusion in Africa, as discussed in this study. Mobile banking is a good example. The majority of Africa's population lack non-cash methods of payment and this has been holding back development for decades. However, Africa faces an uphill battle to cut the number of unbanked citizens, bearing in mind its strategic position as a key to driving economic development. It is encouraging that the momentum is building and innovation is revolutionising the banking sector.[7] New technologies and initiatives are encouraging banks in Africa to rethink how they do business. They are introducing new models along with novel approaches to business process—all aimed at increasing banking services' penetration, boosting liquidity, driving profits, and cutting costs. Technology has played an increasingly important role in Africa's growth story, enabling consumers to use mobile phones to pay bills, move cash, and buy basic everyday items.

Things are moving fast in the continent and it is possible that development and economic growth in Africa could beat all forecasts, given the fact that many of African resources are yet to be discovered and exploited. Modern technology is making it easier to accomplish in a year what could be realised few decades ago in a decade. As pointed out by *The Wall Street Journal*, in 2010, Ghana jumped into the middle-income bracket overnight, a decade earlier than projected and before it began to see the windfalls from its newly found offshore oil resources.[8]

Besides the traditional influence and interest of the former colonial powers on the continent, many emerging economies—especially the BRIC countries—are showing increasing interest in the continent. The appeal of the continent is also evident in the activities of countries such as Japan, South Korea, Turkey, Iran, Israel, and some Gulf Cooperation Council countries in what is described by some observers as "the new scramble for Africa."

All factors and indications show that Islamic finance in Africa has a bright future. As it stands, implementing Islamic finance, which is the fastest growing segment of international financial markets in a continent that is hosting some of the fastest growing economies in the world, with the highest returns worldwide, could possibly create one of the miracles of the twenty-first century.

"Africa presents a tremendous opportunity for Islamic finance and is probably the next logical or strategic decision for leading financial institutions".[9] Diverse investors are keen to explore the untapped fiscal potential of the resource-rich and second most populous continent in the world.[10] The continent has the right ingredients and Islamic finance offers the right products and it just dependent on the countries, institutions, regulators, and decision makers in question, whether or not they decide to develop the industry. "Africa has everything to gain and nothing to lose by developing its Islamic financial sector."[11] Investing in Africa is about the future, particularly "as potential sites for low-cost manufacturing and outsourcing."[12] This explains the massive interest in Africa across the board.[13]

The bases for the success of Islamic finance in Africa as outlined in this study are overwhelming and well established. It includes, among others, a huge market of a billion people, lower percentage of banking penetration, and the fact that existing Islamic financial experiment in the continent is far below its real potential. This is supported by the higher rate of return on foreign investment in the continent and the growing openness and acceptability of the Islamic financial system by many regulators and politicians. The Islamic finance industry would complement the existing conventional banking system and is by no means presenting itself as a substitute. It would help bringing millions of new customers to the banking system, creating new financial relationship with global dimension, and generating a new wave of competition on how to serve better the business community. As noted by one regulator, "sustainable prosperity in Africa may be achieved with the inclusion of Islamic finance."[14]

The development of Islamic finance in Africa is not without challenges. Some of these challenges are peculiar to the continent's economic growth and development, while others are related to the development of the Islamic finance industry. Achieving sustainable economic growth in Africa requires the continent to deal with a number of issues. These include, among others, changing the outdated perception of the continent's image, the effects of corruption, and the infrastructure gap, particularly inefficiencies related to poor transport, electricity, railways, and healthcare. The continent also needs to deal with issues such as designing new methods for alternative FDI, managing political risk, the lack of security through conflicts resolution, and facing the fundamental issue of lack of local skilled talent.

Besides the general challenges facing the continent, the development of Islamic finance in Africa needs to face some peculiar challenges related specifically to the banking and financial sector, such as legal issues, slow court proceedings, the absence of credit assessment information, and little protection for property rights. The African financial sector also needs to confront the logistical issues of providing banking services to rural populations and the need to educate clients about the benefits of handing over their wealth to banks for safe-keeping.

Above and beyond the challenges facing the banking and financial sector, promoters of Islamic finance in the continent also need to take into consideration the particular challenges facing the Islamic finance industry worldwide, such as the call for an for an appropriate legal, institutional, and regulatory framework for the industry, the lack of well-versed Sharī'ah scholars eligible to supervise and monitor the different activities of newly established Islamic financial institutions and able to clear the misconception regarding the industry, particularly in countries where Muslims are minorities or countries having some religious tension. It is also important to face the issue of how to integrate the Islamic financial system with the rest of the financial system or addressing issues of corporate governance. Among the issues of apprehension across the industry, we have also the issue of tax and how to create a level playing field, the lack of Sharī'ah-compliant liquidity management instruments, the lack of mass awareness of Islamic finance and its benefits, the standardisation and harmonisation of Islamic products and the urgent need to improve exit rules in the events of default, restructuring, and insolvency.

Among the possible mechanisms to overcome some of the above challenges and towards better implementation of Islamic finance in the continent, the present research emphasised the need to cooperate and work in partnership with multinational institution such as the Islamic Development Bank (IDB), the World Bank and its specialised arms such as the International Finance Corporation (IFC) or the Multilateral Investment Guarantee Agency (MIGA), the International Monetary Fund (IMF), and the African Development Bank (AfDB). Given their expertise and influence, all these institutions can play an important role towards financial inclusion and economic development through Islamic finance. By all means, these institutions have a great responsibility in helping towards financial inclusion in the continent.

The IDB, for instance, has a number of ambitious special developmental programmes for Africa. However, in order to develop the Islamic financial industry in Africa, the IDB has the moral obligation to come up with some bold initiatives that will lead towards the establishment of Islamic financial institutions in the continent. It is not necessary that the full capitalisation of these banks comes from outside. Many wealthy individuals from different African countries can provide the needed capital. However, what is lacking is the expertise and moral and political support. The IDB can also help in bringing other international players such as the World Bank, the IMF, the African Development Bank, and other development institutions to participate in such initiatives towards financial inclusion. The presence of such multilateral financial institutions is very important for diffusing some of the political, religious, and business concerns.

The World Bank, whether directly or through its specialised arms, such as the International Finance Corporation (IFC) or The Multilateral Investment Guarantee Agency (MIGA), is already active in Islamic finance activities in different forms around the world, including some Islamic projects in Africa. The IMF is also highly involved in Islamic finance, particularly in the form of assisting governments in setting up regulatory frameworks.

The AfDB, on the contrary, is making progress towards embracing Islamic finance although the move seems to be far below the real potential and capabilities of the bank. Given the fact that the AfDB is the only mandated African financial institution to serve the continent as a whole, and given its ability and experience, hundreds of millions around Africa will definitely be looking for more involvement by the bank towards financial inclusion and the adoption of Islamic finance in its funding and technical assistance projects. Moreover, if the ADB is highly involved in Islamic finance, the AfDB can at least do the same. The bank can also play an important role towards financial inclusion in the continent, by providing technical assistance and advice and financing infrastructure projects using *ṣukūk*, given its AAA rating.

## Notes

1. Vijay Tata, "Development of Effective Insolvency Regimes for Islamic Financial Institutions", Paper presented at the Fifth Islamic Financial Stability Forum Manama, Bahrain—29 March 2012 Forum Theme: Effective Crisis Management and Resolution Framework. www.ifsb.org, retrieved October 2012, p. 3.
2. Sugan Palanee, "Africa is the next big frontier for Indian companies", *Business today*, May 10, 2011,www.businesstoday.intoday.in, retrieved October 2011.
3. Chriatian Wessels and others, *Inside Africa*, *Think*: *act study*, p. 51.
4. Accenture *Africa The New Frontier for Growth*, p. 69.
5. *Ernst & Young's attractiveness surveys Africa 2013 Getting Down to Business*, www.ey.com, retrieved May 2013, p. 2.
6. Samira Mensah & Others, *Regulations and Fiscal Incentives Could Speed Islamic Finance Development In Africa*, Standard & Poor's August 6, 2015, www.standardandpoors.com
7. This is Africa, "The Future of African Banking", *This is Africa*.

8. Peter Guest "Spelling Out Growth" *Wall Street Journal*, September 2011.
9. *Gulf Daily News*, "Major Islamic banking forum planned in Africa", September 16, 2012.
10. Nazneen Halim, "The Sleeping Giant", p. 1.
11. Ibid.
12. William Wallis, Andrew England and Katrina Manson, "Africa: Ripe for Appraisal", *Financial Times* May 18, 2011.
13. Ibid.
14. Mohammed Iqbal Belath, "Role of Islamic finance in the development of Africa", p. 3.

# Bibliography


1. Rehman, A. (2009, March 16). *The relevance of Islamic finance principles to the global financial crisis* (pp. 1–14). Panel discussion on the evolution of the global financial crisis from the current crisis, Harvard Law School. Islamic Legal Studies Program Islamic Finance Project. www.ifp.law.harvard.edu. Retrieved June 2011.
2. AAOIFI (2010). (Accounting and Auditing Organisation for Islamic Financial Institutions). Sharī'ah Standards No. 17 Investment ṣukūk. Bahrain: AAOIFI.
3. Accenture. (2010). *Africa the New Frontier for growth* (pp. 1–75). www.accenture.com. Retrieved May 2011.
4. Leke, A., et al. (2010, June). What's driving Africa's growth. *Mckinsey Quarterly*. Mckinsey Global Institute. www.mckinsey.com. Retrieved Jan 2011.
5. Leke, A., et al. (2014, August). *Lions go global: Deepening Africa's ties to the United States*. McKinsey & Company. http://www.mckinsey.com. Retrieved Jan 2015.
6. Halawi, A. (2011, June). ṣukūk Mondiale. *Business Islamica Magazine*. www.businessislamica.com. Retrieved Dec 2011.
7. Africa Microfinance Action Forum. (2008, October). *Diagnostic to action: Microfinance in Africa* (p. 113). www.swwb.org. Retrieved June 2011.
8. Africa Progress Panel. (2011). *Africa progress report 2011 the transformative power of partnership*. www.africaprogresspanel.org. Retrieved Jan 2012.
9. African Development Bank. (2011, September). *Africa in 50 years time: The road towards inclusive growth*. African Development Bank Group, Tunis. www.afdb.org. Retrieved Dec 2011.




M. Al Bashir M. Al Amine, *Islamic Finance and Africa's Economic Resurgence*, DOI 10.1007/978-3-319-28835-2

10. Belouafi, A., & Chachi, A. (2014). Islamic finance in the United Kingdom: Factors behind its development and growth. *Islamic Economic Studies, 22*(1), 37–78.
11. Tanaka, A. (2013, May 1). Developing Africa growth built on principles. *The Time*. www.thetimes.co.uk. Retrieved May 2013.
12. Shahine, A., & El Baltaji, D. (2011, April 11). Egypt delays ṣukūk, Africa lures Muslim funds: Islamic finance. *Bloomberg Businessweek*. www.bx.businessweek.com. Retrieved Aug 2011.
13. Vickey, A. (2011, May). Turkey moves into Africa. *Le Monde Diplomatique*. www.mondediplo.com. Retrieved June 2012.
14. Al-Amine, M., & Al-Bashir, M. (2012). *Global sukūk and Islamic securitisation market financial engineering and product innovation*. Leiden/Boston: Brill.
15. Chaia, A., et al. (2009, October). *Half of the world is unbanked* (pp. 1–17). Financial Access Initiative. www.financialaccesss.org. Retrieved 20 May.
16. Russell, A., & MacNamara, W. (2007, October 25). ICBC pays $5.5bn for Standard Bank stake. *Financial Times*. www.ft.com. Retrieved June 2012.
17. Nyalusi, A. (2015, February 24). Can FDI benefit developing African economies?. *Yale Economic Review*. www.yaleeconomicreview.org. Retrieved May.
18. Van Duyn, A. (2009, December 9). The US hold its breath on bonds. The future of Islamic finance. *Financial Times Special Report*, pp. 1–6. www.ft.com. Retrieved June 2011.
19. Al-Khawarizmi Group. (2012, Décembre 28). *Les Ṣukūks Une nouvelle alternative de financement pour le Maroc*. www.al-khawarizmi-group.com. Retrieved 18 May 2013.
20. Redimerio, A., & Palmer, A. (2011, October 13). *Will Islamic finance play a key role in funding Asia's huge infrastructure task?* (pp. 1–9). Standard & Poor's. www.standardandpoors.com. Retrieved Dec 2011.
21. Alleyne, T. S. C. (2014). *Managing volatile capital flows: Experiences and lessons for Sub- Saharan African frontier markets*. International Monetary Fund. www.imf.org
22. Alpen Capital. (2011, June 28). *GCC food industry* (pp. 1–71). www.alpen-capital.com. Retrieved June 2012.
23. Gait, A. H., & Worthington, A. C. (2009). *Libyan business firm attitudes towards Islamic methods of finance* (pp. 1–15). Griffic Business School Discussion Paper. www.equella.rcs.griffith.edu.au. Retrieved January 2011.
24. Gait, A. H. (2009). The impact of demographic variables on Libya retail consumer attitudes towards Islamic methods of finance. *Islamic Economic Studies, 17*(1), 1–18.
25. Alatabani, A. F. (2010, April 14–15). *Approach and attitude towards Islamic banking and finance: A multilateral perspective*. Paper presented at the international conference on Islamic banking and finance in Africa, Midrand.

26. Ogbonna, A. (2008, August 25). IFC to support Islamic banking services in Nigeria. *Sun.*. www.sunnewsonline.com. Retrieved May 2011.
27. Bing, A. (2011, May). A longer-term vision is crucial. In *Ernst & Young's 2011 Africa attractiveness survey, it is time for Africa* (p. 20). www.ey.com
28. England, A. (2012, January 2). International banks ramp up presence in Africa. *Financial Times*. www.ft.com. Retrieved June 2012.
29. Macartney, A. (2011). *Africa: A golden opportunity. A spotlight on mining and metals transactions*. www.ey.com. Ernst & Young 2011.
30. Andrianaivo, M., & Yartey, C. A. (2009, August). *Understanding the growth of African financial markets* (pp. 1–40). IMF working paper International Monetary Fund. www.imf.org. Retrieved June 2011.
31. Sambidge, A. (2011, November 12). Alabbar says African venture could be worth $20bn. *Arabian Business*. www.arabianbusiness.com. Retrieved Jan 2012.
32. Boumediene, A., & Caby, J. (2009, December). The stability of Islamic banks during the subprime crisis. *Social Science Research Network*. www.ssrn.com. Retrieved June 2011.
33. Anna Nagar. (2013, June 3). *Now is the time to invest in Africa: Japan Premier Shinzo Abe*. www.economictimes.indiatimes.com. Retrieved June 2013.
34. Hassoune, A., & Satel, A. (2008, March). *Islamic finance explores new horizons in Africa* (pp. 1–18). Moody's Global Banking. www.moodya.com. Retrieved May 2010.
35. Hassoune, A. (2010, April 4). *Derivatives in Islamic finance: Examining the role of innovation in the industry*. Moody. www.moodya.com. Retrieved May 2011.
36. Guerrero, A. (2011). Investors fall for Africa's charms. *Global Finance, 25*(6), 8–9.
37. Arabiabusiness. (2012, May 11). *Saudi Arabia keen on African farm investments*. www.arabianbusiness.com. Retrieved June 2012.
38. Ahouassou, A. (2011, May 24). *African countries credit ratings: Key for effective resource mobilisation on International capital markets*. African Development Bank. www.afdb.org. Retrieved Dec 2011.
39. Ekpe, A. (2010, March). Motives for a multiple listing on African stock exchanges: The Ecobank experience. Private sector development. Africa's financial markets: A real development tool? *Proparco's Magazine*, Issue 5, pp. 14–16.
40. Nazim, A. (2011, July 11–13). *The default choice for Islamic countries*. Paper presented at the International Takāful Summit 2011 in London, Jumeirah Carlton Towers, London.
41. Naqvi, A. (2011, May). Africa calling. *Trends Magazine*, pp. 49–54.
42. Lagorce, A. (2010, June 28). African markets offer opportunities for the smart investor. *MarketWatch*. www.marketwatch.com. Retrieved June 2011.

43. Autumn St John. (2010, November). Islamic wealth management opportunities in Africa. *Global Islamic Finance*, pp. 32–36.
44. Sabavala, A., & Ali al-Saffar. (2011). *GCC trade and investment flows: The emerging-market surge* (pp. 1–36). The Economist Intelligence Unit. www.eiu.com. Retrieved May 2012.
45. El Yaakoubi, A. (2014, November 25). Moroccan parliament approves Islamic finance legislation. *Reuters*.
46. Tayyebi, A. (2008, August). *Islamic finance: An ethical alternative to conventional finance?* (pp. 1–6). Discussion paper, The Association of Chartered Certified Accountants. www.financialislam.com. Retrieved June 2011.
47. Backgrounder: India. (2011, May 19). *Africa eye closer tie amid fast development of economic, trade flow*. www.news.xinhuanet.com. Retrieved June 2011.
48. Bank Sarasin. (2011). Islamic equity indices mirror regional and expansion trends. In Bank Sarasin, *Islamic wealth management report 2011* (pp. 1–40). www.sarasin.ch. Retrieved June 2012.
49. Osei, B., & Mubiru, A. M. (2010). Chinese trade and investment activities in Africa. *The African Development Bank Group Policy Brief, 1*(4), 1–11. www.afdb.org. Retrieved June 2011.
50. Umar, B. A. (2011, January 5). Islamic finance in Nigeria: Issues and challenges. *The Guardian Nigeria*. www.ngrguardiannews.com. Retrieved June 2011.
51. BBC. (2010, July). *Brazil's Lula pays tribute to Africa's historic role*. www.bbc.co.uk. Retrieved June 2011.
52. Ndulu, B. (2014, October). Tanzania's mobile-fuelled banking revolution. *The Banker*, p. 197.
53. Vozcaino, B. (2014, October 1). Luxembourg's debut sukuk sees strong demand from government accounts. *Reuters*. www.reuters.com. Retrieved Jan 2015.
54. Osei-Hwedie, B. Z., & Osei-Hwedie, K. (2010). Japan's TICAD: Alternative global framework for Africa's development? *Zambia Social Science Journal, 1*(2), 123–140.
55. Bloomberg. (2014, November 25). *JPMorgan says Kenya may be part of future Africa expansion*. www.bloomberg.com. Retrieved Dec 2014.
56. Bloomberg Businessweek. (2010, October 28). Africa: Coke's last frontier. www.businessweek.com. Retrieved June 2011.
57. BMB Islamic. (2011). *Global Islamic Finance Report. GIFR 2011*. BMB publication.
58. Bonorchis, R., & Seria, N. (2011). The rise of Middle Africa. *Bloomberg Markets Magazine, 6*(6), 107–111.
59. Judith, B., & Hart, L. (2000). *Making microfinance work better in the Middle East and North Africa* (pp. 1–49). World Bank Institute and Private and

Financial Sector Development Group, Middle East and North Africa Region. Washington, DC: World Bank. www.worldbank.org. Retrieved June 2011.
60. Bretton Woods Project. (2008). The IFIs and Islamic finance. *Bretton Woods update,* Number 59, January–February. http://www.brettonwoodsproject.org. Retrieved June 2012.
61. Caplen, B. (2015, January 5). Top 100 banks in Africa ranking: Africa continues to outperform. *The Banker.*
62. Fundanga, C., Governor, & Bank of Zambia. (2008, October 20). Opening remark to the Islamic banking conference under the theme "building partnership for development". Taj Pamodzi Hotel Lusaka. *BIS Review*, 31, pp. 1–3.
63. Campbell, C. (2009). Private equity in Africa—Lessons learned. *Thunderbird Quarterly*, Issue 2. www.thunderbird.edu. Retrieved June 2011.
64. Claassen, C. H. (2011, July 18). *South Korea in Africa understanding South Korea interest in Africa*. www.consultancyafrica.com
65. Robertson, C., Mhango, Y., & Ndebele, N. (2011, July 19). Africa: The bottom billion becomes the fastest billion. *Renaissance Capital*, pp. 1–43.
66. Roxburgh, C., et al. (2010, June). *Lion on the move: The progress and potential of African economies* (pp. 1–70). McKinney Global Institute. www.mckinsey.com. Retrieved Jan 2011.
67. Francavilla, C. (2013, May 17). Morocco to enact ṣukūk law. *This is Africa*. www.thisisafricaonline.com. Retrieved 18 May 2013.
68. Wessels, C., et al. (2012, January). *Inside Africa, think: Act study* (pp. 1–56), Roland Berger. www.rolandberger.com. Retrieved Jan 2013.
69. Aid, C. (2007). *Enough is enough: The debt repudiation option* (pp. 1–33). www.jubileedebtcampaign.org.uk. Retrieved Mar 2011.
70. Esters, C. (2011, January). Sub-Saharan African sovereigns have withstood external shocks well, but volatile commodity prices remain a risk. In *Europe, Middle East and Africa Market Outlook 2011* (pp. 33–37). Standards &Poor's. www.standardandpoors.com. Retrieved June 2011.
71. Harress, C. (2013, September 26). Islamic banking revolution: Africa is seeing an explosion in banks looking to cash in on continent's growing Muslim population. *International Business Times*. www.ibtimes.com. Retrieved Jan 2015.
72. Walugembe, C. (2009). Islamic banking in Uganda. *Legal Notes, 6*(1), 6–7.
73. Citigroup Inc. (NYSE: C). (2014, August 5). *Citi to source $2.5 billion to "power Africa"*. www.citigroup.com. Retrieved Dec 2014.
74. Gillet, C. (2011, May 10). *Is Africa about to take off* (pp. 1–10). Société Générale Economic Study Department. http://www.societegenerale.com. Retrieved Jan 2012.
75. Booth, C., & Wright, M. (2014, January 3). The real risk about investing in Africa is missing the boat. *African Business Review*. www.africanbusinessreview.co. Retrieved Jan 2015.

76. Capital, C., & Emerging Markets Private Equity Association. (2011, April 25). Emerging Markets Private Equity Association Survey 2011; Private equity Africa, "Global LPs interest in Africa spikes". www.privateequityafrica.com. Retrieved June 2012.
77. Conference report on the 4th COMESA Investment Forum "Dubai to Africa unlocking the market of the future" (pp. 1–70). 23–24 Mar 2011.
78. CPI Financial. (2009, February 9). *Islamic finance grows in London, rides out worst of crunch*. www.cpifinancial.net
79. Nkontchou, C. (2010, March). Recent evolution of the African financial markets. Private sector development, Africa's financial markets: A real development tool? *Proparco's Magazine*, Issue 5, pp. 3–5.
80. El Baltaji, D. (2010, September 28). Nigeria plans ṣukūk debut targeting role as Sharī'ah hub: Islamic finance. *Bloomberg*. www.bloomberg.com. Retrieved Feb 2012.
81. Staib, D., & Bevere, L. (2011, May). *World insurance in 2010 premium back to growth capital increase* (pp. 25–26). Swiss Reinsurance Company Limited.
82. Berman, D. (2011). *Moody's upbeat on Africa*. www.theglobeandmail.com. Retrieved June 2012.
83. Bloom, D., Canning, D., & Chan, K. (2006). *Higher education and economic development in Africa*. World Bank. www.worldbank.org. Retrieved June 2012.
84. Dolan, D. (2011, March 7). Citi eyes three new Africa markets. *Reuters*. www.reuters.com. Retrieved June 2011.
85. Opiokello, D. G. (2010, May 7). The aftermath of the financial crisis and the way forward. Closing remarks by deputy governor of the Bank of Uganda at the 3rd annual bankers' dinner, Kampala. *BIS Review*, 65, pp. 1–6.
86. Shinn, D. H. (2010). The rise of non-Western influence in Africa. *Global Studies Review, 6*(3), 14–16. www.globality-gmu.net. Retrieved Jan 2012.
87. Hodgkinson, D. (2007, November 7). *Islamic finance: Global perspectives* (pp. 1–3). Speech at the Islamic Finance Intelligence Summit FT Islamic Finance Forum. Radisson Edwardian Mayfair Hotel, London.
88. Lewis, D. (2011, February 23). Special report: In Africa, can Brazil be the anti-China? *Reuters*. www.reuters.com. Retrieved Jan 2012.
89. McIlroy, D. (2010, July). Africa rising. *Quantum Finance in Perspective*, Issue 12, pp. 23–25.
90. Oakley, D. (2009, December 8). Dubai debacles overshadows growth. The future of Islamic finance. *Financial Times special report* (p. 4). www.ft.com. Retrieved Mar 2010.
91. Smith, D., & Lamble, L. (2011, December 25). Africa's burgeoning middle class brings hope to a continent. *The Guardian*. www.guardian.co.uk. Retrieved Mar 2012.
92. Dawabit Wa Ussus Taqdim al-Muntajat Al-Masrfiyya Al-Badilah Al-Mutwafiqah Wa Ahkam Al- Sharī'ah al-Islamiyyah Fi al-Masarif Al-Tiijariyyah Fi Libiya

93. Brautigam, D. (2011, February 8). China in Africa: Seven myths. ARI 23/20011, Elcano Royal Institute. www.realinstitutoelcano.org. Retrieved Jan 2012.
94. Brautigam, D. (2011, February 8). China in Africa: Seven myths. ARI 23/2011. Elcano Royal Institute. www.realinstitutoelcano.org. Retrieved Jan 2012.
95. Deloitte. (2010, March). *Investments into Africa tackling tax and regulatory challenges.* www.deloitte.com. Retrieved June 2011.
96. Deloitte. (2010). *Understanding Islamic finance.* www.deloitte.com. Retrieved Apr 2011.
97. Tull, D. M. (2006). China's engagement in Africa: Scope, significance and consequences. *Journal of Modern African Studies, 44*(3), 459–479. Cambridge.
98. Diageo. (2009). *Africa media and investment* (pp. 1–28). Africa Business Reporting Award 2009, supported by Diageo. www.diageoafricabusinessre-portingawards.com. Retrieved June 2010.
99. Layfield, D. (2013). Seeking the opportunity, managing the risk. In *Ernst & Young's attractiveness surveys Africa 2013 getting down to business.* www.ey.com. Retrieved May 2013.
100. O'Neil, D. (2011). Africa banking champion leaps forward. *Euromoney, 42*(509), 332–336.
101. O'Neil, D. (2011). Chad joins local-currency spree. *Euromonney Magazine, 42*(507), 51.
102. Kaberuka, D. (2010, June). Capturing Africa business opportunity. *McKinsey Quarterly.* www.mckinsey.com. Retrieved Aug 2011.
103. Ecobank Research. (2014, April). Zambia: Successful issuance of Eurobond despite macroeconomic challenges. *Middle Africa Briefing Note-Fixed Income.* www.ecobank.co
104. Ecobank. (2011, August 1–7). *Chad's first local-currency bond, arranged by Ecobank Capital, oversubscribed.* www.ecobank.com. Retrieved Jan 2012.
105. Economist Intelligence Unit. (2012). *Africa: Open for business: The potential, challenges and risks.* www.eiu.com. Retrieved Dec 2012.
106. Yue, E. (2008, May 11–12). Deputy chief executive of the Hong Kong Monetary Authority and executive board chairman of the Treasury Markets Association. Hong Kong's possible role in Islamic finance at the Hong Kong showcase on Islamic finance, Dubai/Amman. *Bank of International Settlements Review (BIS Review)*, 59. www.bis.org
107. Yue, E. (2008, November 25). *Islamic finance—Its potential to bring new economic growth to Hong Kong* (pp. 1–4). Keynote address by Mr Eddie Yue, deputy chief executive of the Hong Kong Monetary Authority, for the Hong Kong Islamic Finance Forum, Hong Kong SAR. www.bis.org
108. Miguel, E. (2011, November–December). Africa unleashed. *Foreign Affairs.* www.foreignaffairs.com. Retrieved Mar 2012.

109. Chew, E., et al. (2011, February). Islamic finance offers capital opportunities. *Capital Agenda Insights*. www.ey.com. Retrieved June 2012.
110. Ihsanoglu, E. (2009). Key note address in enhancing economic cooperation among Muslim countries. *The Role of OIC IIUM Journal of Economics and Management. The International Islamic University Malaysia, 17*(1), 13–30.
111. Moore, E., & Hale, T. (2014, June 25). *UK sukuk bond sale attracts £2bn in orders*. www.ft.com. Retrieved Dec 2014.
112. Moore, E., England, A., & Wigglesworth, R. (2014, September 17). South Africa joins sukuk bond rush. *Financial Time*. Retrieved Dec 2014.
113. Idris, E. A. (2009). Islamic finance in Sudan: An overview. *Emerging Market Africa*, Issue 3, pp. 19–20.
114. Pera, E. (2011, March). A review of the Islamic finance industry. In *Eye on Africa* (Vol. 3, pp. 16–18). Ernst & Young.
115. Tumusiime-Mutebile, E. (2010). *Banking issues in Uganda, BIS Review 130/2009, "The progress made on the introduction of Islamic banking in Uganda* (pp. 1–2)*"*. Speech by Prof. Emmanuel Tumusiime-Mutebile Governor, Bank of Uganda, on the occasion of Eid-El-Fitri celebrations at BoU Western Gardens, Kampala, 25 Sept 2009. BIS Review 119/2010.
116. Heinrich, E. (2012, August 16). The secret of Africa's banking boom: Mobility. *Time Magazine*. www.techland.time.com. Retrieved Dec 2012.
117. Ernst & Young. (2009). *Ernst & Young's Islamic funds & investment report 2009*. www.ey.com. Retrieved March 2011.
118. Ernst & Young. (2013). *Ernst & Young's attractiveness surveys Africa 2013 getting down to business* (pp. 1–72). www.ey.com. Retrieved May 2013.
119. Ernst & Young (EYGM 2014). FDI in Africa in 2013: A mixed picture. In *EY's attractiveness survey Africa 2014* (pp. 62–63). www.ey.com. Retrieved Jan 2015.
120. Ernst & Young. (2011, May 2011). *Ernst & Young's 2011 Africa attractiveness survey, it is time for Africa* (pp. 1–56). www.ey.com. Retrieved Dec 2011.
121. Ernst & Young. (2014). Africa's perception gab continues to linger. In *EY's attractiveness survey Africa 2014* (pp. 62–63). www.ey.com. Retrieved Jan 2015.
122. Prasad, E. (2010, September 7). Is Africa poised to steady growth? *The Economist*. www.economist.com. Retrieved June 2011.
123. Kapstein, E. B. (2009, July–August). Africa capitalist revolution. *Foreign Affairs, 88*(4). www.foreignaffairs.com. Retrieved June 2011.
124. Yoshida, E. (2009, October 9). The development of Islamic finance in Japan. *Islamic Finance News, 6*(40). www.islamicfinancenews.com. Retrieved June 2010.
125. Yoshida, E. (2009, August). "Country Presentation: JAPAN" IFN 2009 Asia Forum. Mandarin Oriental, Kuala Lumpur, pp. 3–5.
126. Euromonney. (2011). *The Scramble for Angola, 42*(503), 60.
127. Suruma, E. S. (2011, January). Conflict and prospects for economic growth. In *Foresight Africa the continent's greatest challenges and opportunities for*

*2011 Africa growth initiative* (pp. 6–7), Brookings. www.brookings.edu. Retrieved June 2012.

128. Vanorio, F. (2014, November). Sovereign wealth funds and Islamic finance: How can Africa benefit? *Business Islamica* (pp. 27–28). www.businessislamica.com
129. Sunmonu, F., & Associates, Barristers, & Solicitors. (2007). Islamic financial services in Nigeria. *Islamic Finance News Guide 2007*, pp. 90–92.
130. Rintoul, F. (2010, July 18). Vibrant Africa beckons investors. *Financial Times*. www.ft.com. Retrieved Aug 2011.
131. Kanimba, F. (2010, May 10). Opening remarks by the governor, National Bank of Rwanda at the meeting of East African Community (IEAC) Monetary Affairs Committee (MAC) Arusha Tanzania, pp. 1–4. www.eac.int
132. Allen, F., et al. (2011). African financial systems: A review. *Review of Development Finance, 1*(2), 79–113. April–June.
133. Rischter, F. (2010, May 5). *ADB mulls multi-billion dollar Islamic MTN programme*. www.arabianBusiness.com
134. Ng'wanakilala, F. (2014, October). *IMF urges caution in Africa's Eurobond borrowing spree*. www.reuters.com. Retrieved Jan 2015.
135. Mwamba, G. (2011, March 30). Healthy returns. *This is Africa*. www.thisisafricaonline.com. Retrieved Dec 2011.
136. Mwamba, G. (2011, March 30). Structuring local solutions. *This is Africa*. www.thisisafricaonline.com. Retrieved June 2011.
137. Bandyopadhyay, G. (2011). Banking the unbanked: Going mobile in Africa. Standard chartered Asia, Africa and Middle East. In *The guide to working capital management 2009/2010* (pp. 59–67).
138. Lambe, G. (2011, February 23). Investors start to differentiate between African markets. *The Banker*, p. 23.
139. Seidel, G., et al. (2009). *Islamic finance comes of age Joint opportunities for Western and Arabic financial institutions* (pp. 1–4). Arthur D. Little Financial Services Viewpoint. www.adlittle.se. Retrieved June 2010.
140. Ghana Islamic Microfinance. (2014, June 20). *Islamic Development Bank to honor Ghana Islamic microfinance*. www.businessghana.com
141. Gil Seong Kang. (2011). The Korea-Africa partnership: Beyond trade and investment. *Africa Economic Brief African Development Bank*, *2*(9), 1–8. www.afdb.org. Retrieved Dec 2012.
142. Global Financial Integrity. (2010, March). *Illicit financial flows from Africa: Hidden resource for development* (pp. 1–38). www.gfintegrity.org. Retrieved Apr 2011.
143. Emefiele, G. I. (2014, July). *Thoughts on building effective supervision in the era of cross- border banks in Africa*. Keynote speech by governor Central Bank of Nigeria on the occasion of the 17th regular meeting of the college of supervisors of the West African Monetary Zone (CSWAMZ), CBN International Training Institute. www.cenbank.org. Retrieved Nov 2014.

144. Rung, G., et al. (2011). *Islamic finance: Building 150 financial institutions by 2020* (pp. 1–16). Oliver Wyman Financial Services, Oliver Wyman. www.oliverwyman.com. Retrieved May 2011.
145. Gulf News. (2011, June 14). *Nigeria on track to be Africa's Islamic finance hub*. www.gulfnews.com. Retrieved June 2011.
146. Barka, H. B., & Mlambo, K. (2011). India economic engagement with Africa. *The African Development Bank Group, Africa Economic Brief, 2*(6), 1–8. www.afdb.org. Retrieved Dec 2012.
147. Kara, H. (2011, January 31). The Gulf's Islamic banks are targeting Africa's opportunities. *The Banker*. www.thebanker.com. Retrieved July 2012.
148. Yunis, H. (2006). Growth of private equity fund using Islamic finance. *Islamic Finance News Guide*, pp. 67–68.
149. Heng, S. K. (2008, May 13). Managing director of the monetary authority of Singapore, at the 5th annual Islamic financial services board summit, Amman. Monetary Authority of Singapore's initiative to develop Singapore dollar sovereign-rated sukūk. *BIS Review*, 63, pp. 1–5. www.bis.org
150. Heng, S. K. (2009, January 19). Singapore's commitment to the development of Islamic finance. Opening remarks at the Singapore sukūk signing ceremony, Singapore. *BIS Review*, 9, pp. 1–2. www.bis.org
151. De Grandis, H., & Pinshaw, G. (2010, June). Banking building on success. In *Africa's path to growth sector by sector*. McKinsey & Company. www.mckinseyquarterly.com. Retrieved Jan 2011.
152. HM Treasury and The Rt Hon George Osborne MP. (2014, June). *Government issues first Islamic bond*. www.gov.uk. Retrieved Dec 2014.
153. Hong Kong Monetary Authority. (2014, September 11). *HKSAR government's inaugural sukuk offering*. www.hkma.gov.hk
154. Douglas, I., & Redvers, L. (2014). *GCC trade and investment flows* (p. 4). The Economist Intelligence Unit. www.economistinsights.com. Retrieved Feb 2015.
155. ICICI Securities Limited (ICICI Securities). (2014, September 22). *Ajanta Pharmaceuticals (AJAPHA)*. www.ajantapharma.com. Retrieved Dec 2014.
156. IFC. (2010, August). *IFC promotes increased development with record year in Africa: Annual investments surpass $2 billion on the continent for the first time*. Press Release. http://www.ifc.org. Retrieved June 2012.
157. IFIS Islamic Finance Information Service. (2010). *Global Sukūk Market H2-2010 report* (pp. 1–19). www.securities.com. Retrieved June 2011.
158. IFSB The Islamic Financial Services Board. (2009, January). *Capital adequacy requirements for sukūk securitisations and real estate investment*, Standard 7. www.ifsb.org. Retrieved June 2011.
159. IFSB-IRTI-IDB. (2010). *Islamic finance: Global financial stability*. www.ifsb.org. Retrieved Apr 2011.
160. IMF (2011, April). *Regional economic outlook. Sub-Saharan Africa recovery and new risks*. www.imf.org. Retrieved Jan 2012.

161. IMF Survey Magazine. (2010, October 4). Islamic banks: More resilient to crisis? *IMF Survey Magazine: IMF Research*. www.imf.org. Retrieved June 2011.
162. Basu, I. (2010). India Inc woos Africa. *Asia Times*. www.atimes.com. Retrieved June 2011.
163. International Finance Corporation. (2014, April 29). *IFC expands partnership with Gulf African Bank to support Islamic finance and entrepreneurs in Kenya*. www.ifc.org. Retrieved Feb 2015.
164. International Finance Corporation (IFC). (2007). *The business of health in Africa partnering with the private sector to improve people's lives*. www.ifc.org. Retrieved Jan 2012.
165. International Fund for Agriculture Development (IFAD). (2014, November). *Islamic microfinance: Unlocking new potential to fight rural poverty*. www.ifad.org. Retrieved Jan 2015.
166. International Fund for Agriculture Development (IFDA). (2012, December). *Islamic microfinance: Unlocking new potential to fight rural poverty* (pp. 1–4). www.ifad.org
167. International Monetary Fund. (2014, October 11). *The IMF launches consultations with its external advisory group on Islamic finance*. Press Release No. 14/468. www.imf.org. Retrieved Feb 2015.
168. International Monetary Fund. (2015, March). *Islamic finance and the role of the IMF* www.imf.org. Retrieved Feb 2015.
169. International Monetary Fund. (2013, March 6). *Libya—2013 Article IV Consultation Concluding Statement Preliminary Conclusions of the IMF Mission*. www.imf.org. Retrieved May 2013.
170. Reynolds, I., & Hirokawa, T. (2013, June 1). Abe offers $32 billion to Africa as Japan seeks resources access. *Bloomberg*. www.bloomberg.com. Retrieved June 2013.
171. MacFarlane, I. (2009, March). French fancy. *Islamic Banking and Finance*, pp. 36–37.
172. Islamic Banking & Finance. (2008, June). Morocco's mixed welcome for Sharī'ah financing, special report. *Executive Magazine*, Issue 107. www.executive-magazine.com
173. Islamic Finance Asia. (2011, March). *A phoenix from the ashes? The future of Islamic finance in Egypt*, Special Report, pp. 9–11.
174. Islamic Finance news. (2012, April). *230% increase in net profit*, *9*(1). www.islamicfinancenews.com. Retrieved May 2012.
175. Islamic Finance News. (2012, April 19). *StanChart in African push*, *9*(16). www.islamicfinancenews.com. Retrieved Dec 2012.
176. Peter Pham, J. (2010, May 27). Turkey's return to Africa. *World Defense Review*. www.worlddefensereview.com. Retrieved June 2011.
177. Watson, J., et al. (2012, January). *Into Africa institutional investor intentions to 2016* (pp. 1–28). Invest AD written & Economist Intelligence Unit. www.investad.com. Retrieved Sept 2012.

178. Kotilaine, J. T. (2010, March). *GCC agriculture* (pp. 1–28). NCB Capital.
179. Woodruff, J., & Hill, R. (2007, March 5). *Demystifying corporate Ṣukūk.* Fitch Rating. www.fitchrating.com. Retrieved June 2010.
180. Choi, J. (2011). The next chapter for private equity in Sub-Saharan Africa. In *Can private equity boosts African development?* (pp. 2–5). Private Sector and Development No. 12/October. www.proparco.fr. Retrieved Jan 2012.
181. Moyo, J. (2009, April 30–31). *Mapping of current ongoing initiatives related to bond market development in African summary of regional studies*, African Development Bank, Tunis. www.afdb.org. Retrieved Jan 2011.
182. Cape, J. (2010, May 10). Tax and Islamic finance—The choices for governments in Africa. *The African Business Journal.* www.tabj.co.za. Retrieved Jan 2012.
183. Clift, J. (2010, March 4). Africa faces twin challenges after global crisis. *IMF Survey Magazine.* www.imf.org. Retrieved June 2011.
184. Guo, J. (2010, February 18). How Africa is becoming the new Asia. *Newsweek Magazine, 155*(09). www.newsweek.com. Retrieved Apr 2011.
185. O'Neill, J., & Stupnystka, A. (2010, October 14). *How exiting is Africa potential* (pp. 1–8). Goldman Sachs Asset Management Strategy Series.
186. Lee, J., et al. (2010, October). *Frontiers in finance supplement Islamic finance: The new agenda KPMG* (pp. 1–10). www.kpmg.com. Retrieved Jan 2011.
187. Kruger, J. (2011, March). Hidden opportunities. In *Eye on Africa* (Vol. 3, pp. 15–16). Ernst & Young. www.ey.com. Retrieved Dec 2011.
188. DiVanna, J., & King, J. (2014, November). Islamic finance unstoppable rise. *The Banker.* Special supplement, Top 500 Islamic Financial Institutions.
189. DiVanna, J., & Hancock, M. (2011, November). Islamic finance roars again. *The Banker,* Special Supplement. *Top 500 Islamic Financial Institutions* (pp. 1–8).
190. Martin, J. (2005). Islamic banking goes global. *The Middle East, 357,* 50–52.
191. van der Merwe, J. P. (2010, September 30). *Africa: Local banks capturing the market.* www.allafrica.com. Retrieved Jan 2011.
192. Solé, J. (2007). *Introducing Islamic banks into conventional banking systems* (pp. 1–2). IMF working paper. www.imf.org. Retrieved Jan 2011.
193. Berris, J. (2009, July 27). Luxembourg guns for LSE's sukūk prestige. *The Lawyer.* www.thelawyer.com
194. Mazera, J. (2008). Islamic banking in Kenya. *Legal Notes, 5*(2), 3–4.
195. Reli, J. (2009, July 15–17). Deputy governor Bank of Tanzania speech at a high level seminar on the oversight of Islamic finance Tanzania, Dares Salaam, pp. 1–6. www.eastafritac.org. Retrieved Mar 2010.
196. Hongo, J. (2013, May 13). *TICAD to redefine Japan aid to Africa.* www.japantimes.co. Retrieved May 2013.
197. Hassan, K., & Kayed, R. N. (2009). The global financial crisis, risk management and social justice in Islamic finance. *ISRA International Journal of Islamic Finance, 1*(1), 33–58.

198. Saigal, K. (2014, September 23). Kenyan corporates to raid Eurobond market. *Euromoney*. http://www.euromoney.com. Retrieved Jan 2015.
199. Rothmer, K. (2011, March–April). Hiding the real Africa: Why NGOs prefer bad news. *Columbia Journalism Review*, www.cjr.org. Retrieved Mar 2012.
200. Rothmyer, K. (2011, January). *They wanted journalists to say 'wow' how NGOs affect U.S. media coverage of Africa* (pp. 1–35). Discussion paper series. Joan Shorenstein Centre on the Press. Politics and Public Policy. www.hks.harvard.edu. Retrieved June 2012.
201. Karim, N., Tarazi, M., & Reille, X. (2008, August). *Islamic microfinance: An emerging market niche* (pp. 1–16). Focus Note 49. Washington, DC: The Consultative Group to Assist the Poor (CGAP). www.cgap.org. Retrieved Jan 2011.
202. Anye, K. A. (2010, December 4–5). Telecommunication markets and trends in Sub-Saharan Africa. *Gulf-Africa investment conference 2010: Fostering economic relations* (pp. 1–23). Riyadh.
203. Lu, K. W., Verheyen, G., & Perera, S. M. (Eds.). (2009). *Investing with confidence understanding political risk management in the 21st century*. Washington, DC: The World Bank. www.worldbank.org. Retrieved June 2012.
204. Patel, K. (2012, January 24). Africa: No longer a leap of faith. *Financial Times*. www.ft.com. Retrieved June 2012.
205. KPMG. (2006, May). *Islamic finance credential*. www.kpmg.com. Retrieved May 2011.
206. KPMG. (2007). *Growth and diversification in Islamic finance* (pp. 1–22). www.kpmg.com. Retrieved June 2011.
207. KPMG. (2010, December). *KPMG survey of current economic and business conditions in Africa* (pp. 1–20). www.kpmg.com. Retrieved Mar 2011.
208. KPMG. (2009, March). *Development of an Islamic bond market in Hong Kong what are the tax implications?* (pp. 1–12). www.kpmg.com. Retrieved Jan 2011.
209. KPMG. (2011). Africa a continent whose time has come. *New Frontiers*, Issue 30, pp. 1–40. www.kpmg.com. Retrieved Mar 2012.
210. Thomas, K. (2010, June 30). Egypt Islamic finance sector faces uphill struggle. *Khalij Times*. www.khaleejtimes.com. Retrieved Mar 2011.
211. Mbacke, L. (2012, February 16). Senegal: Human capital a main concern. *Islamic Finance News Guide 2012*. www.islamicfinancenews.com. Retrieved Apr 2012.
212. Kiang, L. H. (2011). Opening address by the Minister for Trade and Industry and deputy chairman, Monetary Authority of Singapore at the 2nd world Islamic banking conference: Asia Summit 2011, 8 June 2011 at Pan Pacific Hotel Singapore. www.mondovisione.com. Retrieved Jan 2012.

213. Are, L., et al. (2010). *The African challengers: Global competitors emerges from the overlooked continent* (pp. 1–12). The Boston Consulting Group. www.bcg.com. Retrieved June 2011.
214. Bam, L. (2011, April 14). *Africa poised for growth.* www.deloittesa.wordpress.com. Retrieved Mar 2012.
215. Kabir Hassan, M., & Kayed, R. N. (2009). The global financial crisis, risk management and social justice in Islamic finance. *ISRA International Journal of Islamic Finance, 1*(1), 33–58.
216. Hassan, M. A. (2010, June 23–24). *Statement on behalf of the African group delivered by the IDB governor for the Republic of Chad 35th annual meeting of the IDB Board of Governors Baku Azerbaijan.* Original text french. www.isdb.org. Retrieved Jan 2012.
217. Hasan, M., & Dridi, J. (2010, September). *The effects of the global crisis on Islamic and conventional banks: A comparative study* (pp. 1–47). IMF working paper. www.imf.org. Retrieved June 2011.
218. Mohieldin, M. (2012, March). Realising the potential of Islamic finance. *Economic Premise.* The World Bank, Issue 77, pp. 1–7.
219. Rizvi, M. A. (2011, January). India's economic engagement of Africa: Partnering Africa. Institute for Defense Studies and Analyses. http://www.idsa.in/event/indiapartneringafrica
220. Making Finance Work for Africa (MFW4A) Conference. (2011, June 29–30). *Zipping finance and farming in Africa—Harnessing the continent's potential* (pp. 1–30). Kampala. www.mfw4a.org. Retrieved June 2012.
221. Quigley, M. (2011, January 7). Irish firm should see Africa's growth as an opportunity. *The Irish Times.* www.irishtimes.com. Retrieved June 2012.
222. Chand, M. (2011). India to set up training institutes in Africa. *Africa Quarterly Indian Journal of African Affairs, 50*(4), 8. November–January.
223. Pani, M. (2014, October 20). *Strong growth in Sub-Saharan Africa, but pockets of difficulty.* IMF African Department, www.imf.org. Retrieved Jan 2015.
224. Ashcroft, M. O. (2008). Microfinance in Africa: The challenges realities and success. *Micro Banking Bulletin, 17,* 5–11. www.themix.org. Retrieved Mar 2012.
225. Vasseux, M. (2009). *The next chapter in Islamic finance higher rewards but higher risks report* (pp. 1–37). Oliver Wyman. www.oliverwyman.com. Retrieved Jan 2011.
226. Curtin, M. (2010, October 6). Catching Africa's investment bug is proving contagious. *The Wall Street Journal.* www.online.wsj.com. Retrieved June 2011.
227. Hill, M. (2014, April 8). Zambia says $1 billion Eurobond was oversubscribed. *Bloomberg.* www.bloomberg.com. Retrieved Jan 2015.
228. Lahcen, M. (2007, March 23). Morocco permits commercial banks to market Islamic banking products. *Magharebia.* www.magharebia.com. Retrieved June 2011.

229. Pinkovskiy, M., & Sala-i-Martin, X. (2014, August). *Africa is on time*. Federal Reserve Bank of New York Staff Reports, Staff Report No. 686, www.newyorkfed.org. Retrieved Feb 2015.
230. Khamis, M., et al. (2010). *Impact of the global financial crisis on the Gulf Cooperation Council countries and challenges ahead* (pp. 1–81). International Monetary Fund, The Middle East and Central Asia Department, Washington, DC. www.imf.org. Retrieved June 2011.
231. El Zoghbi, M., & Tarazi, M. (2013, March). *Trends in sharia-compliant financial inclusion* (pp. 1–11). Consultative Group to Assist the Poor (CGAP), No. 84. www.cgap.org
232. Zkan, M. O., & Akgu, B. (2010). Turkey's opening to Africa. *Journal of Modern African Studies, 48*(4), 525–546.
233. Hancock, M. (2012, September). After the Arab Spring …capital markets. *The Banker*, pp. 128–129.
234. Gondwe, M. (2014, December 30). *Talking notes at the launch of the Islamic finance guidelines*. A key note address by the governor, Bank of Zambia. www.boz.zm. Retrieved Feb 2015.
235. Wat, M. (2015, January 5). Eurobonds ride high in Africa. *The Banker*. www.thebanker.com. Retrieved Jan 2015.
236. Gallgher, M. (2009, May). From niche to mainstream. *Islamic Banking and Finance*.
237. Mashayekhi, M., & Fernandes, D. (2007). *Trade and development aspects of insurance services and regulatory frameworks*. New York/Geneva: The United Nations. www.unctad.org. Retrieved Jan 2011.
238. Laldin, M. A. (2008, July). The generation game. *Islamic Business and Finance,* Issue 32, pp. 8–10.
239. Damak, M., & Volland, E. (2010, February 1). Islamic finance is likely to advance in 2010 on firm growth and widening geographic reach. In *Islamic Finance Outlook 2010*. Standard & Poor's.
240. Damak, M. (2010, September 27). *Ṣukūk: An African opportunity yet to be explored*. Interview with Les Afriques. www.lesafriques.com. Retrieved Jan 2011.
241. Damak, M. (2010). Afrique : le pont de la finance islamique. Les Afriques. Fevrier 22. www.lesafriques.com. Retrieved Jan 2011.
242. Damak, M. (2014, February). Islamic finance could make inroads into North Africa. In *Standard & Poor's Islamic Finance Outlook 2015*. www.standardandpoors.com. Retrieved Mar 2015.
243. Mead, M. F. (2010). *Islamic banking in Djibouti challenges and opportunities*. Project paper submitted for the fulfillment of the requirement of Master in Business Administration, Open University, Malaysia, Bahrain.
244. Olad, M. M. (2011, December 12). Islamic banking: Banking the unbanked. *The Reporter*.

245. Belath, M. I. (2012, September 6). Second deputy governor of the Bank of Mauritius, at the opening ceremony of the seminar on the "role of Islamic finance in the development of Africa". Balaclava. BIS central bankers' speeches. www.bis.org. Retrieved Dec 2012.
246. Enescu, M. I. (2011, September). *Emerging powers: New economic partners for Africa?* (pp. 1–9). Credit Agricole Aperiodic, No. 14. www.economic-research.credit-agricole.com
247. Monitor Company Group. (2010, December 4–5). Africa from the bottom up: Cities, economic growth and prosperity in Sub-Saharan Africa. *Gulf-Africa investment conference 2010: Fostering economic relations* (pp. 56–61). Riyadh.
248. Multilateral Investment Guarantee Agency. (2011, June 16). *MIGA covers murābaḥah facility for Indonesia telecoms expansion*. www.miga.org. Retrieved Apr 2012.
249. Multilateral Investment Guarantee Agency (MIGA). (2011). *Project brief.* www.miga.org. Retrieved June 2012.
250. Iqbal, M., & Khan, T. (Eds.). (2005). *Financial engineering and Islamic contracts.* Palgrave Macmillan UK.
251. Parker, M. (2009, December 28). Australia is opening up to Islamic finance. *Arab News.* www.arabnews.com. Retrieved June 2011.
252. Parker, M. (2009, April 6). France introduces tax neutrality laws. *Arab News.* www.arabnews.com. Retrieved June 2010.
253. Parker, M. (2010, May 29). Ex-IFSB chief sheds light on Islamic finance issues. *Arab News.* www.arabnews.com. Retrieved June 2011.
254. Parker, M. (2010, December 26). IDB joins hands with AfDB to boost development. *Arab News.* www.arabnews.com. Retrieved June 2011.
255. Parker, M. (2010, September 26). Winds of change in S. African tax laws for Islamic finance products. *Arab News.* www.arabnews.com. Retrieved June 2011.
256. Parker, M. (2010, May 16). World Bank declares Islamic finance a priority area. *Arab News.* www.arabnews.com. Retrieved June 2011.
257. Parker, M. (2011, September 18). Takāful market set to grow in S. Africa and beyond. *Arab News.* www.arabnews.com. Retrieved Dec 2011.
258. Parker, M. (2011, March 28). Kenya's ṣukūk ambitions must be tempered with reality. *Arab News.* www.arabnews.com. Retrieved June 2011.
259. Parker, M. (2011, October 23). Will Islamic finance play as key role in funding Asia S&P. *Arab News.* www.arabnews.com. Retrieved June 2012.
260. Parker, M. (2010, February 22). Asya Bank makes mark in cards. *Arab News.* www.arabnews.com. Retrieved June 2011.
261. Kimenyi, M. S., & Lewis, Z. (2011). THE BRICS and the new scramble for Africa. In *Foresight Africa: The continent's greatest challenges and opportunities for 2011* (pp. 19–21). The Brookings Institution. www.brookings.edu. Retrieved June 2012.

262. Kimeny, M. S. (2014, February 18). *Oil and gas boom in East Africa: Avoiding the curse*. www.brookings.edu. Retrieved Jan 2015.
263. Kimenyi, M. S. (2011). Africa's 2011 election. In *Foresight Africa: The continent's greatest challenges and opportunities for 2011* (pp. 3–5). The Brookings Institution. www.brookings.edu. Retrieved June 2012.
264. Chibiliti, M. (2008). Islamic trade financing: Challenges in Zambia. *Legal Notes, 5*(2), 7–8.
265. Nagashi. (2010, September 28). East Africa catching up with Islamic finance. *Arab News*. www.arabnews.com. Retrieved June 2011.
266. Rassool, N. (2011, July). Mauritius—An emerging centre for Islamic finance. *New Horizon*. www.newhorizon-islamicbanking.com. Retrieved Apr 2012.
267. Keita, N. (2010, January–February). *Sub-Saharan Africa: A challenging new frontier*. Credit Agricole Bimonthly No. 139. www.etudes-economiques.credit-agricole.com. Retrieved May 2011.
268. Saidi, N. (2009, November 7). *Islamic finance is coming of age: IFC lists sukūk in the DIFC*. Zawya. www.zawya.com. Retrieved June 2011.
269. National Treasury of South Africa. (2014, September 17). South Africa concludes debut sukuk bond. www.treasury.gov.za. Retrieved Jan 2015.
270. Halim, N. (2011, July 29). Banking on microfinance. *Islamic Finance News Supplement-IFN Supplement Africa*. www.islamicfinancenews.com. Retrieved Dec 2011.
271. Halim, N. (2011, July 29). The sleeping giant. *Islamic Finance News Supplement-IFN Supplement Africa*. www.islamicfinancenews.com. Retrieved Dec 2011.
272. Halim, N. (2011, December 5). Cross-border trade on the rise. *Islamic Finance News*. IFN Supplement Middle East. www.islamicfinancenews. Retrieved Apr 2012.
273. Salvaterra, N. (2011, April 18). Mobile pioneer sees rich promise in Africa. *The Wall Street Journal*. www.online.wsj.com. Retrieved Jan 2012.
274. Ford, N. (2012, November 12). The rise and rise of Islamic finance. *African Banker*. www.africanbusinessmagazine.com. Retrieved Jan 2013.
275. Okonjo-Iweala, N. (2010, June 2010). Fulfilling the promise of Sub-Saharan Africa. *McKinsey Quarterly*. www.mckinsey.com. Retrieved June 2011.
276. Page, N., et al. (2008). *Into Africa: Investment prospects in the Sub-Saharan banking sector*. PricewaterhouseCoopers. www.pwc.com. Retrieved Dec 2010.
277. Price, N. (2011, January). *Africa between perception and reality*. Fidelity International. www.fidelity.com.sg. Retrieved June 2011.
278. Hardi, N., & Volland, E. (2009, December 4). Islamic banking has reached critical mass in the Gulf after sustained growth, and expansion is to continue. In *Islamic Finance Outlook 2010* (pp. 20–21). Standard & Poor's.
279. Dudley, N. (2011, June). "Bond ambition" Angola's bright light. *The Banker Supplement*.

280. Ndung'u, N. (2014, February 25). *Essential groundwork for competing effectively in the Islamic banking environment.* Remarks by governor of the Central Bank of Kenya, at the launch of the regional certificate in participatory/Islamic banking, Kenya School of Monetary Studies, Nairobi. www.bis.org. Retrieved Dec 2014.
281. Ndung'u, N. (2011, March 28). *Islamic finance—a paradigm shift in Africa* (pp. 1–2). Remarks by Prof Njuguna Ndung'u, Governor of the Central Bank of Kenya, at the 3rd Gulf African Bank annual East & Central Africa Islamic finance conference, Nairobi. BIS central bankers' speeches. www.bis.org. Retrieved Dec 2011.
282. Ndung'u, N. (2011, October 13). Governor of the Central Bank of Kenya, at the 5th joint CMA/CBK/RBA/IRA board members retreat on collaboration among domestic financial sector regulators, Mombasa. Financial stability and financial inclusion, BIS central bankers' speeches (pp. 1–3). www.bis.org. Retrieved Jan 2012.
283. Ndung'u, N. (2010, May 3–4). *Islamic finance—The African experience* (pp. 1–2). Remarks by Prof Njuguna Ndung'u, Governor of the Central Bank of Kenya, at the 2nd Gulf African Bank annual East & Central Africa Islamic conference, Nairobi. *BIS Review*, 69. www.bis.org. Retrieved Jan 2012.
284. Gordon, N., et al. (2011). *At the tipping point: Financial services in Africa comes of age how financial institutions can capitalise on the growth opportunities in Africa* (pp. 1–32). Accenture. www.accenture.com. Retrieved Dec 2012.
285. Bourihane, N. (2010, November 6). La Finance Islamique se Répand en Algérie. *Le Temps d' Algerie*. www.letempsdz.com. Retrieved June 2011.
286. Ocean Equities Limited. (2011, March 9). Factbox: Changing Africa. *Weekly Review*. www.oceanequities.co.uk. Retrieved June 2011.
287. Meier, O. (2011, February). It is still possible to gain access to attractive investment targets with relatively low capital input. In *Ernst & Young's 2011 Africa attractiveness survey, it is time for Africa* (p. 18). www.ey.com. Retrieved June 2012.
288. Ajakaiye, O., & Kimenyi, M. S. (2011). Higher education and economic development in Africa: Introduction and overview. *Journal of African Economies, 20*, iii3–iii13. AERC Supplement 3.
289. Barbarinde, O. (2009). Renaissance Africa. *Thunderbird Quarterly*, Issue 2.
290. Omamuli, O. (2011, June 8). *Improving credit dynamics among sovereigns in Sub-Saharan Africa, despite challenges.* Moody's, Global Credit Research. www.moodys.com. Retrieved June 2012.
291. Oxford Analytica. (2010, September 3). Islamic finance moves toward common standards. *Forbes*. www.forbes.com. Retrieved Jan 2012.
292. Saghana, P. (2010, September 12). Africa Re Group launches Africa Retakaful. *Vanguard Online edition*. www.vanguardngr.com. Retrieved Jan 2012.

293. Habib, P. A. (2010, November 21). *Islamic finance capturing the African opportunity—North Africa opportunity and challenges*. Paper presented at the world Islamic banking conference Bahrain.

294. Imam, P., & Kpodar, K. (2010, August). *Islamic banking: How has it spread?* International Monetary Fund. www.imf.org. Retrieved Jan 2012.

295. Imam, P., & Kpodar, K. (2010, August). Islamic banking: How has it diffused?. International Monetary Fund. www.imf.org. Retrieved June 2011.

296. Kagenda, P. (2010, June 21). Islamic banking will bring minor change. *The Independent*. www.independent.co.ug, Retrieved July 2010.

297. Collier, P. (2010, June). The case for investing in Africa. *McKinsey Quarterly*. www.mckinsey.com. Retrieved Jan 2011.

298. Collier, P. (2010). *The plundered planet: Why we must—and how we can—manage nature for global prosperity*. New York: Oxford University Press.

299. Collier, P. (2011, December). Building an African infrastructure. *Finance & Development*, *48*(4), 18–21. International Monetary Fund (IMF). www.imf.org. Retrieved Jan 2012.

300. Collier, P., & Warnholz, J.- L. (2009, February). Now's the time to invest in Africa. *Harvard Business Review*.

301. Kagame, P. (2009, November 2). Why Africa welcomes the Chinese. *The Guardian*. www.guardian.co.uk. Retrieved Jan 2012.

302. Wallace, P. (2011, July). Ghana vows to avoid oil curse. *The Banker Supplement*, Ghana's Rising Star.

303. Wallace, P. (2012, January). Africa's banks on the brink of the big time. *The Banker*, p. 114.

304. Wallace, P. (2011, August). Banks on the climb. *The Banker*, pp. 16–18.

305. Wallace, P. (2012, April). Casablanca looks to dispel African divide. *The Banker*, p. 100.

306. Wallence, P. (2011, October). Into Africa. *The Banker Special Report New FX Boundaries*, pp. 12–13.

307. Pruvost, P.- H. (2011, March 1). *Global standards to give breadth and depth to the global ṣukūk market*. Standard &Poor's.

308. Perqin. (2010, October). *The private equity market in Africa* (pp. 1–4). Perqin Special Report. www.preqin.com. Retrieved June 2011.

309. Guest, P. (2011, September 18). Spelling out growth. *The Wall Street Journal*.

310. Wise, P. (2011, May). A colonial lifeline? *The Banker*.

311. Wonacott, P. (2011, June 11). U.S. aims to gain new edge in Africa. *The Wall Street Journal*. www.online.wsj.com. Retrieved Jan 2012.

312. Wonacott, P. (2011, May 2). A new class of consumers grows in Africa. *The Wall Street Journal*.

313. Alexender, P., & Hingel, G. (2011, November). The big Islamic finance opportunities Islamic banking. *The Banker, Special Supplement, Top 500 Islamic Financial Institutions*, pp. 9–10.

314. Becker, P., & van Zyl, M. (2011). *The dynamic African consumer market: Exploring growth opportunities in Sub-Saharan Africa* (pp. 1–44). Accenture. www.accenture.com. Retrieved Jan 2012.
315. PricewaterhouseCoopers. (2008). *Takaful: Growth opportunities in a dynamic Islamic market* (pp. 1–20). www.pwc.com. Retrieved Jan 2011.
316. PricewaterhouseCoopers. (2011). *The Africa business agenda*. www.pwc.com. Retrieved Dec 2012.
317. PricewaterhouseCoopers. (2011, September). *10 minutes on investing in Africa* (pp. 1–5). www.pwc.com
318. Private Equity Africa. (2011, April 8). *Giant at the gate*. www.privateequity-africa.com. Retrieved June 2012.
319. Ho, P., & Staib, D. (2008, October). *Insurance in the emerging market: Overview and prospects for Islamic insurance* (pp. 1–52). Swiss Reinsurance Company Limited. www.swissre.com. Retrieved Dec 2011.
320. Public-Private Infrastructure Advisory Facility (PPIAF) (2010). *Bond financing in Africa—The next big thing?* www.ppiaf.org. Retrieved Jan 2012.
321. Chuhan-Pole, P., & Angwafo, M. (Eds.). (2011). *Yes Africa can: Success stories from a dynamic continent*. The World Bank. www.worldbank.org. Retrieved June 2011.
322. Chuhan-Pole, P., et al. (2012, February). *Africa pulse*. World Bank. www.worldbank.org. Retrieved Jan 2012.
323. PWC. (2011, July). *Pwc announces ambitious growth strategy for Africa*. Press Release, www.pwc.com.
324. Baker, R., et al. (2014, May). Hiding in plain sight trade misinvoicing and the impact of revenue loss in Ghana, Kenya, Mozambique, Tanzania, and Uganda: 2002–2011. *Global Financial Integrity*. www.gfintegrity.org. Retrieved Feb 2015.
325. Klarmann, R. (2007). Islamic finance in Egypt. *Islamic Finance News Guide 2007*, pp. 92–93.
326. Kim, R., & Kapstein, E. B. (2014). *Banking on Africa Standard Chartered social and economic impact*. Standard Chartered. www.sc.com. Retrieved Jan 2015.
327. Reuter. (2011, June 22). *Chad bond likely to draw domestic interest: Analyst*. http://www.reuters.com. Retrieved Jan 2012.
328. Reuters. (2014, September 16). Goldman Sachs gets strong demand for landmark sukuk issue. *Reuters*.
329. Reuters. (2010, January 15). *HSBC seeks big growth, sukūk pickup in 2010*. http://www.reuters.com. Retrieved June 2011.
330. Reuters. (2011, May 23). *Bank Asya says plans acquisitions in Mali and Benin*. http://www.reuters.com. Retrieved Mar 2012.
331. Reuters. (2011, July 20). *Chad raises $232 million in bond issue–bank*. http://www.reuters.com. Retrieved Jan 2012.

332. Reuters. (2011, December 2.). *Forget China, invest in Africa says Russia renaissance*. http://www.reuters.com. Retrieved Feb 2012.
333. Reuters. (2011, July 4). *Nigeria's Stanbic wins approval for Islamic banking*. http://www.reuters.com. Retrieved Dec 2011.
334. Reuters. (2015, February 22). Cameroon's Afriland First Bank launches Islamic window. *Reuters*. www.reuters.com
335. Reuters. (2009, October 21). *IFC debuts $100 million Islamic bond on Dubai*. www.reuters.com. Retrieved Nov 2011.
336. Reuters. (2010, November 8). *Egypt aims for ṣukūk rules in Q1 2011—Regulator*. http://www.reuters.com. Retrieved Jan 2011.
337. De Oliveria, R. S. (2014, April 16). Avoiding Africa's oil curse what East Africa can learn from past booms. *Foreign Affairs*. www.foreignaffairs.com. Retrieved Jan 2015.
338. Bernstein, R. (2007, July 23). *Africa: The final frontier, Merrill Lynch- investment strategy* (pp. 1–36).www.ml.com. Retrieved Jan 2011.
339. Bernstein, R. (2007, July 23). *Africa: The final frontier, Merrill Lynch investment strategy*.
340. Chirambo, R. (2012, May 2). Researchers back idea of Islamic banks in Malawi. *The Daily Time*.
341. Taylor, R. (2011). *Growing in Africa: Capturing the opportunity for global consumer product business* (pp. 1–20). Ernst & Young. www.ey.com. Retrieved Jan 2012.
342. Karim, R. A. A. (2012, December). Islamic finance: An alternative funding source for the African Development Bank? In *Africa capacity development*. African Development Bank, *3*(3), 1–8. www.afdb.org. Retrieved Feb 2013.
343. Ringo & Associates. (2008, July). Islamic banking in Tanzania. *Legal Notes*, *5*(2).
344. Ruthann, R. (2011, January 11). *Africa's development prospects remain intac*, Equity Research, Credit Suisse. www.credit-suisse.com. Retrieved Feb 2012.
345. Amlot, R. (2015, February 17). *Coming to Africa*. www.cpifinancial.net. Retrieved Feb 2015.
346. Wigglesworth, R. (2009, May 6). Credit crunch may test industry beliefs. *Financial Times Special Report*, p. 1.
347. McKean, R., & Bennett, A. (2011, September). Structural differences. *The African handbook*, pp. 23–26.
348. Wilson, R., et al. (2011, October). *Islamic banking and finance in North Africa: Past development and future potential* (pp. 1–51). African Development Bank. www.afdb.org. Retrieved June 2012.
349. Bheenick, R. (2009, May 5). Putting Mauritius on the world's Islamic finance map. Address by the governor of the Bank of Mauritius, at the official launching of HSBC Amanah Islamic banking Mauritius. Les Guibies, Pailles, pp. 1–5. *BIS Review*, 55

350. Bheenick, R. (2009, May 19). Islamic finance and its development in Mauritius. Address by the governor of the Central Bank of Mauritius at the opening seminar on Islamic capital markets". Port Louis, pp. 1–5. *BIS Review*, 62.
351. Sullivan, R. (2011, November 6). Potentials of Africa growth outlook. *The Financial Times*. www.ft.com. Retrieved June 2012.
352. Sarrar, S., & Alexander, C. (2013, May 15). Libya Bank lending paralyzed amid interest ban: Islamic finance. *Bloomberg*. www.bloomberg.com. Retrieved May 2013.
353. Pradhan, S. (2010, December 4–5). GCC-Africa trade: Trends, prospects and policy imperatives. *Gulf-Africa investment conference 2010: Fostering economic relations*. Riyadh.
354. Mensah, S. (2014, February 4). After a mixed 2013, the global sukuk market looks promising in 2014. In *Standard & Poor's Islamic Finance Outlook 2015*. www.standardandpoors.com. Retrieved Mar 2015.
355. Sjolin, S. (2014, December 24). *You aren't investing in Africa—And you're missing out*. www.marketwatch.com. Retrieved Feb 2015.
356. Saudi Gazette. (2008, May 8). *CMA approves Jadwa Africa freestyle fund*. www.saudigazette.com. Retrieved June 2011.
357. Schaffnit-Chatterjee. (2013, July). *Sub-Saharan Africa: A bright spot in spite of key challenges*. Deutsche Bank Research. Current Issues/Emerging Markets. www.dbresearchech.com. Retrieved Dec 2014.
358. Bektas, S. S. (2011, March 4). Africa as a savior for Turkish firms. *Hurriyet*, Istanbul. www.hurriyet.com. Retrieved Dec 2011.
359. Pasha, S. (2011, November). Senegal eye first ṣukūk as Africa look to Islamic finance. *Reuters*. www.reuters.com. Retrieved Jan 2012.
360. Ali Khan, S. (2010, December 6). *Gulf-African investment conference concludes with series of recommendations*. Saudi Gazette. www.saudigazette.com. Retrieved June 2011.
361. Akhtar, S. (2009, November 11). Vice President Middle East and North Africa The World Bank, key note address at the Islamic finance seminar Banca d'Italia symposium on Islamic finance in Roma: Developments in MENA region. www.worldbank.org. Retrieved June 2012.
362. Ladd, S. (2011, January 12). Emerging Africa expected to see rise in investment. *IMF Survey Magazine: Countries & Regions*. www.imf.org. Retrieved Jan 2011.
363. Jacobs, S. (2014, July 1). Morocco inches towards Islamic finance. *The Banker*.
364. Verma, S. (2011, July 3). Africa's decade-long banking bull run in pictures. *The Financial Times*. www.ft.com. Retrieved Dec 2011.
365. Kerr, S. (2011, May 4). Emaar founder eyes Africa's commodity riches. *The Financial Times*. www.ft.com. Retrieved June 2012.

366. Freemantle, S., & Stevens, J. (2011, September 12). *Africa macro insight and strategy five trends powering Africa's enduring allure. Trend 1 A larger, younger, and more affluent population* (pp. 1–16). www.standardbank.com. Retrieved Jan 2012.
367. Freemantle, S., & Stevens, J. (2011, August 29). *Africa macro insight and strategy BRIC—Africa the redback's rise opportunities to Africa* (pp. 1–11). Standard Bank. www.standardbank.com. Retrieved Jan 2012.
368. Freemantle, S. (2011, 15 December). *Africa macro insight and strategy African election map 2011/2012* (pp. 1–8). Standard Bank. www.standardbank.com. Retrieved Feb 2012.
369. Freemantle, S. (2011, September 21). *Africa macro insight, five trends powering Africa's enduring allure, Trend 2 Africa transformational urban swell* (pp. 1–10). Standard Bank. www.standardbank.com. Retrieved Feb 2012.
370. Freemantle, S. (2011, October 10). *Africa macro insight, the five trends powering Africa's enduring allure, Trend 5 Africa deepening financial sector* (pp. 1–15). www.standardbank.com. Retrieved Feb 2012.
371. Freemantle, S. (2011, October 6). *Africa macro insight, the five trends powering Africa's enduring allure. Trend 4 Africa dormant resources potential* (pp. 1–15). Standard Bank. www.standardbank.com. Retrieved Jan 2012.
372. Willson, S. (2010, March 4). Private sector gains ground in Africa. *IMF Survey Magazine*. www.imf.org. Retrieved June 2011.
373. Jaffer, S. (2011, December–January). Growth opportunities for Takāful in Europe. *The European Financial Review*. www.europeanfinancialreview.com. Retrieved June 2011.
374. Standard Chartered Bank. (2014, March 19). *Kenya is our first African market to offer Islamic banking*. www.sc.com. Retrieved Jan 2015.
375. Wagstyl, S. (2011, October 4). Unilever: Mr Africa, I presume? *Financial Times*. www.ft.com. Retrieved Aug 2012.
376. Williams, S. (2010). The advantage of local knowledge. *African Banker*, 4th Quarter, pp. 34–39.
377. Davis, S., & Woetzel, J. (2010, June). Making the most of Chinese aid to Africa. *McKinsey Quarterly*. www.mckinsey.com. Retrieved June 2012.
378. Roy, S. (2011). Afren oils wheels of African bond markets. *Euromoney, 42*(503), 49–51.
379. Roy, S. (2011). Angola's elite looks to clean up in Portugal. *Euromoney, 42*(503), 55–61.
380. Roy, S. (2014, April 7). *Zambia launches US$ 1 billion 10 year Eurobond at yield of 8.625%*. www.reuters.com. Retrieved Jan 2015.
381. Palanee, S. (2011, May 10). Africa is the next big frontier for Indian companies. *Business Today*. www.businesstoday.intoday.in. Retrieved Oct 2011.
382. Summit Business Review. (2010, August 28). *Islamic banking: No ribā here?* www.sbreview.net. Retrieved June 2011.

383. The 3rd COMESA investment forum connecting Africa to the world. 12–13 Apr 2010. Sharm El Sheikh, Conference Report, pp. 1–21.
384. The Asian Development Bank. (2009, March). *Development of prudential and supervision standards for Islamic financial markets.* Project Number: 42520, Regional Policy and Advisory Technical Assistance (R-PATA). http://www.adb.org. Retrieved June 2011.
385. The Australian Trade Commission (Austrade). (2010, January). *Islamic finance*, pp. 1–40. www.austrade.gov.au. Retrieved Mar 2011.
386. The Banker. (2011, June). *African returns make it the place to be*, p. 6.
387. The Banker. (2011, June). *Africa offers huge returns on investment for foreign institutions.* www.thebanker.com. Retrieved June 2012.
388. The Citizen. (2014, September 20). Tanzania poised to be East Africa's Islamic banking hub. *The Citizen.* www.thecitizen.co.tz. Retrieved Jan 2015.
389. The Economist. (2008, May 8). Turning towards Mecca: Islamic banks join in the race for Africa, *387*(8579). www.economist.com. Retrieved June 2011.
390. The Economist. (2010, September 16). Africa's Banking boom, scrambled in Africa "Chinese and Western banks are flocking to Africa but finding a strategy that works isn't easy". www.economist.com. Retrieved Jan 2011.
391. The Economist. (2011, January 6). *Africa's impressive growth.* www.economist.com. Retrieved Dec 2011.
392. The Economist. (2011, January 7). *Democracy in Africa: Democratization and its discontents.* www.economist.com. Retrieved Dec 2011.
393. The Economist. (2011, December 3). *The hopeful continent Africa rising.*
394. The Economist. (2011, January 6). *The lions kings.* www.economist.com. Retrieved June 2011.
395. The Economist. (2011, April 20). *Why the Beijing regime need to act to avert a backlash against Chinese investors in poor countries.* www.economist.com. Retrieved Jan 2012.
396. The Economist. (2012, May 17). *African child mortality the best story in development.* www.economist.com. Retrieved Dec 2012.
397. The Economist Intelligence Unit. (2011, August). *Banking in Sub Saharah Africa to 2020 promising frontiers.* www.eiu.com. Retrieved Jan 2012.
398. The Economist Intelligence Unit. (2014). Risk and reward: The Gulf push into African infrastructure, commissioned by Dubai Chamber. www.economistinsights.com. Retrieved Jan 2015.
399. The Economist Intelligence Unit. (2009, March). *The GCC in 2020: Outlook for the Gulf and the global economy* (pp. 1–24). www.eiu.com. Retrieved Jan 2011.
400. The Economist. (2010, November 22). *South of the Sahara: Boom times, at least in part.* www.economist.com. Retrieved June 2011.
401. The Economist. (2011, April 22). *Chinese in Africa: The Chinese are coming …to Africa.* www.economist.com. Retrieved Jan 2012.

402. The Economist. (2011, April 20). *Rumble in the jungle—Why the Beijing regime need to act to avert a backlash against Chinese investors in poor countries.* www.economist.com. Retrieved Jan 2012.
403. The Guardian. (2011, February 19). *A fresh chapter is opening in Africa's history after two centuries of injustice, a new continent is emerging.* www.guardian.co.uk. Retrieved Jan 2012.
404. The Islamic Globe. (2011, September 14). Gabon court Islamic finance. *The Islamic Globe*, Issue 31. www.theislamicglobe.com. Retrieved May 2012.
405. The Islamic Globe. (2011, September 14). If not now, when. *The Islamic Globe*, Issue 31. www.theislamicglobe.com. Retrieved Sept 2011.
406. The Islamic Globe. (2011, October 5). *KCB rolls out retail account in Tanzania*, Issue 34. www.theislamicglobe.com. Retrieved Oct 2011.
407. The Islamic Globe. (2011, December). *Tanzania's first Islamic bank takes off.* www.theislamicglobe.com. Retrieved Dec 2011.
408. The Islamic Globe. (2011, September 21). *UAP looks to Takaful*, Issue 32. www.theislamicglobe.com. Retrieved Sept 2011.
409. The Islamic Globe. (2011, December 21). *Zanzibar's People's Bank opens Islamic window.* www.theislamicglobe.com. Retrieved Dec 2011.
410. The Islamic Globe. (2011, October, 26). *Kenya's CMA in ṣukūk call*, Issue 37. www.theislamicglobe.com. Retrieved Oct 2011.
411. The Islamic Globe. (2012, January 18). E. Africa's largest bank opens Islamic window. www.theislamicglobe.com. Retrieved Jan 2012.
412. The Islamic Globe. (2011, May 4). *Kenya Re moves into pan-Africa reTakaful.* www.theislamicglobe.com. Retrieved May 2011.
413. The Islamic Globe. (2012, January 12). *Kenya freeze Takaful.* www.theislamicglobe.com. Retrieved Jan 2012.
414. Turkey makes inroads into Africa" December 21, 2011 www.hizmetmovement.blogspot.com
415. The Strait Times. (2013, May 30). *Japan eyes business ties in Africa summit to boost trade and investment.* www.straitstimes.com. Retrieved May 2013.
416. The World Bank. (2011). *Africa's competitiveness report 2011.* World Bank. www.siteresources.worldbank.org. Retrieved June 2012.
417. World Bank, *Africa's future and the World Bank's support to it: Africa regional strategy*, 2011, Washington World Bank www.worldbank.org. Retrieved June 2012.
418. The World Bank. (2011). *Sub-Saharan Africa. Global economic prospects: Regional annex.* Washington, DC. www.worldbank.org. Retrieved Jan 2012.
419. The World Bank. (2012). *De-fragmenting Africa: Deepening regional trade integration in goods and services.* www.worldbank.org. Retrieved Jan 2013.
420. Tanoh, T. (2010, March 5). How can development partners support the financial sector in Africa? *Private Sector Development Private Magazine*, pp. 20–22. Africa's financial markets: A real development tool? www.proparco.fr. Retrieved Aug 2011.

421. The future of African banking. *This is Africa*. www.thisisafricaonline.com. Retrieved Jan 2012.
422. Molloy, T. (2009, November 5). Islamic banking system provides a unique opportunity in tough time. *Irish Independent*. www.independent.ie/business/irish. Retrieved Dec 2010.
423. Reuters, T., & Zawya. (2014). *Morocco Islamic finance 2014: Unlocking the kingdom's potential.* www.zawya.com. Retrieved Jan 2015.
424. Beck, T., et al. (2011, September). *Financing Africa through the crisis and beyond.* The African Development Bank, the German Federal Ministry for Economic Cooperation and Development and the World Bank. www.afdb.org. Retrieved Apr 2012.
425. Beck, T., Demirgüç-Kunt, A., & Merrouche, O. (2010, October). *Islamic vs. conventional banking business model, efficiency and stability* (pp. 1–44). The World Bank Development Research Group Finance and Private Sector Development Team. www.worldbank.org. Retrieved Jan 2011.
426. Motsoeneng, T. (2011, March 8). Shoddy infrastructure biggest obstacle for Africa. *Reuters*. www.reuters.com. Retrieved Jan 2012.
427. Times. (2008, March 28). Mauritania gets its first exclusive Islamic bank. *Times*.
428. Barry, T. (2011). Uneven playing field blocks investment. *African Banker*, 4th Quarter, p. 31.
429. Sulaiman, T. (2014, October 15). African local bonds—An untapped opportunity? *Financial Times*. www.ft.com. Retrieved Jan 2015.
430. Tripoli Post. (2008, June 7). Islamic finance moves slowly into North Africa. www.tripolipost.com. Retrieved June 2011.
431. Aburime, U. T., & Alio, F. (2009). Islamic banking: Theories, practices and insights for Nigeria. *International Review of Business Research Papers, 5*(1), 321–339.
432. Chapra, U. (2007). The case against interest: Is it compelling? *Thunderbird International Business Review, 49*(2), 161–186. March–April.
433. Chapra, U. (2008). *The global financial crisis: Can Islamic finance help minimising the severity and frequency of such crisis in the future?* (pp. 1–26). A paper prepared for presentation at the forum on the global financial crisis to be held at the Islamic Development Bank on 25 October.
434. United Nations. (2004, October 30). Economic development in Africa: Debt sustainability—oasis or mirage?. *South Bulletin* 90/91, 520–524.
435. United Nations Children's Fund (UNICEF). (2014, September). *Committing to child survival: A promise renewed progress report 2014.* www.files.unicef.org. Retrieved Jan 2015.
436. United Nations Economic Commission for Africa. (2011). *Economic report on Africa 2011.* www.uneca.org. Retrieved Jan 2012.
437. Vijay Tata. (2012, March 29). *Development of effective insolvency regimes for Islamic financial institutions* (pp. 1–10). Paper presented at the fifth Islamic

financial stability forum, Manama. Forum theme: Effective crisis management and resolution framework. www.ifsb.org. Retrieved Oct 2012.
438. Foster, V., & Briceño-Garmendia, C. (Eds.). (2010). *Africa's infrastructure: A time for transformation*. The World Bank. www.worldbank.org. Retrieved June 2011.
439. Emmanuel, V., & Damak, M. (2007, April). *Chief drivers behind Islamic finance's global expansion*. Commentary Report Standard and Poor's.
440. Crisp, W. (2013, May 29). *Libya's banks struggle to escape Gaddafi shadow*. www.euromoney.com. Retrieved May 2013.
441. Buiter, W., & Rahbari, E. (2011, February 21). *Global economics view global growth generators: Moving beyond 'emerging markets' and 'BRIC'* (pp. 1–9). Citigroup Global Market. www.cepr.org. Retrieved May 2011.
442. Wallis, W. (2011, June 14). Helios sets record for African private equity. *Financial Times*. www.ft.com. Retrieved Dec 2011.
443. Wallis, W. (2011, May 18). Andrew England and Katrina Manson. "Africa: Ripe for appraisal". *Financial Time*. www.ft.com. Retrieved Aug 2011.
444. World Bank. (2014, October). *Africa's pulse: Decades of sustained growth is transforming Africa's economies*. www.worldbank.org. Retrieved Dec 2014.
445. World Bank. (2015). *Doing business report 2015*. www.doingbusiness.org. Retrieved Feb 2015.
446. Sala-i- Martin, X., & Pinkovskiy, M. (2010). *African poverty is falling…much faster than you think!* (p. 1–38). Working paper no. 15775, Issued in February 2010. www.columbia.edu. Retrieved June 2011.
447. Suliman, Y. (2010, September 28). *Islamic banking in Africa and related tax issues*. KPMG www.kpmg.com. Retrieved June 2011.
448. Aseffa, Y. (2007). Insurance services liberalisation and capacity-building: The case of Africa. In *Trade and development aspects of insurance services and regulatory frameworks*. New York/Geneva: The United Nations. www.unctad.org. Retrieved June 2010.
449. Mersch, Y. (2009, November 17). Islamic finance—Partnerships opportunities between Luxembourg and the Arab countries. Speech by Yves Mersch, Governor of the Central Bank of Luxembourg, at the 5th economic forum Belgium-Luxembourg-Arab Countries, Brussels, pp. 1–4. *BIS Review*, 149.
450. Torres-Rahman, Z., & Lalor, M. (2011, May). *The new Africa: Emerging opportunities for business and Africa* (pp. 1–30). Business Action for Africa www.businessactionforafrica.org. Retrieved Dec 2011.
451. Zaid Ibrahim &Co. (2010, June). *Demystifying Islamic finance: Correcting misconceptions advancing value proposition* (pp. 1–44). www.zaidibrahim.com. Retrieved Jan 2011.
452. Mohd, Z. A. (2008, June). Takāful concepts and practice. *The African Reinsurer*, *022*, 5–12.
453. Zawya. (2008, May 6). *CMA approves Jadwa Africa equity freestyle fund*. www.zawya.com. Retrieved Jan 2011.

454. Zawya. (2011, March 27). *Economic and business partnerships enhanced as 4th COMESA investment forum ends*. www.zawya.com. Retrieved Jan 2012.
455. Zawya. (2010, July 14). *Senegal—Bahrain Islamic finance forum*. www.zawya.com. Retrieved June 2011.
456. Aziz, Z. A. (2006, January). *Towards positioning the Islamic finance as an integrated component of the international financial system* (pp. 1–4). Opening speech at the 5th annual Islamic finance summit, London.
457. Aziz, Z. A. (2007, October 18). Speech by the governor of the Central Bank of Malaysia, at the Islamic finance conference "Islamic finance in Southeast Asia: Local practices, global impact" (pp. 1–5). Georgetown University, Washington, DC. *BIS Review*, 121. www.bis.org
458. Aziz, Z. A. (2008, February 23). Islamic finance–Constant evolution and emerging opportunities. Speech by the governor of the Central Bank of Malaysia, at the Nikkei Islamic finance symposium 2008: "Islamic finance: Constant evolution and emerging opportunities" (pp. 1–6), Tokyo. *Bank for International Settlements Review (BIS Review)*, 23. www.bis.org
459. Aziz, Z. A. (2008, October 6). Governor's keynote address at state street Islamic finance congress 2008, Boston USA—"Islamic finance: A global growth opportunity amidst a challenging environment" (pp. 1–5). Boston. *Bank of International Settlements Review (BIS Review)*, 121. www.bis.org
460. Aziz, Z. A. (2010, May). Thoughts and visions on Islamic finance. Welcoming remarks by Dr Zeti Akhtar Aziz, Governor of the Central Bank of Malaysia, at the Malaysia showcase dinner, Manama, pp. 1–2. *Bank for International Settlement Review*, 60. www.bis.org
461. Aziz, Z. A. (2011, November 15). The new Islamic finance landscape. At the Islamic financial intelligence summit (IFIS) 2011, Kuala Lumpur, pp. 1–4. BIS central bankers' speeches. www.bis.org
462. Azizi, Z. A. (2011, May 4). Governor's speech at the 7th Islamic financial services board summit—Global financial architecture: Challenges for Islamic finance, Manama.
463. Brixiova, Z., et al. (2011, April). Closing Africa's infrastructure gap: Innovative financing and risks. *Africa economic brief. African Development Bank*, *2*(1), 1–7. www.afdb.org. Retrieved Jan 2012.

# Index



 
M. Al Bashir M. Al Amine, *Islamic Finance and Africa's Economic Resurgence*, DOI 10.1007/978-3-319-28835-2

## R



## S



## T

FSC
www.fsc.org
MIX
Papier | Fördert gute Waldnutzung
FSC® C083411

Kolibri 360 GmbH
Ferdinand-Jühlke-Straße 7
99095 Erfurt, Deutschland
produktsicherheit@kolibri360.de